Web Caching and Content Delivery

Proceedings of the Sixth International Web Content Caching and Distribution Workshop

Boston University, Boston, Massachusetts, USA
June 20–22, 2001

Web Caching and Content Delivery

Proceedings of the Sixth International Web Content Caching and Distribution Workshop

Boston University, Boston, Massachusetts, USA
June 20–22, 2001

Edited by

Azer Bestavros
Department of Computer Science, Boston University, Boston, MA, USA

and

Michael Rabinovich
AT&T, Florham Park, NJ, USA

2001
ELSEVIER
Amsterdam – London – New York – Oxford – Paris – Shannon – Tokyo

ELSEVIER SCIENCE B.V.
Sara Burgerhartstraat 25
P.O. Box 211, 1000 AE Amsterdam, The Netherlands

First edition 2001

Library of Congress Cataloging-in-Publication Data
A catalog record from the Library of Congress has been applied for.

ISBN: 0-444-50950-X

∞ The paper used in this publication meets the requirements of ANSI/NISO Z39.48-1992 (Permanence of Paper).
Printed in The Netherlands.

A Message from the Workshop Chairs

Dear Participant,

Welcome to the 6th International Web Caching and Content Delivery Workshop. This workshop series has established itself as a premier gathering of researchers and practitioners in the area of Web scalability. This year, we received a record 61 submissions, of which 21 were chosen to be presented as full-length papers and 4 as project synopses. We wish to thank the authors of selected submissions as well as those whose papers could not be accommodated in the program. In addition to technical papers, the workshop program includes three panels covering some of the hottest and/or most controversial topics in this field. We are grateful to the distinguished panelists for sharing their thoughts. These proceedings contain the full-length papers, synopses, and the descriptions of panels that were presented at the workshop (one of the accepted papers was not presented).

While the workshop has grown and matured over the years, it retains its character as an informal meeting that encourages spontaneous exchange of ideas. Another tradition of this workshop series, reinforced again this year, is the high degree of interaction between industry and academia.

This year's workshop is being held on the campus of Boston University, in the heart of Boston. Many people worked hard to make this workshop a success. We would like to thank them all. In particular, we would like to thank members of the program committee, who helped create a very strong program, and the steering committee, who were always there whenever we needed an advice or encouragement. We also thank all external reviewers for helping us deal with the unexpectedly high number of submissions. The generous financial support from our industrial sponsors allowed us to keep registration fees low, especially for students. This year, our sponsors included CISCO Systems, Infolibria Inc., Measurement Factory Inc., and Volera Inc. Our sincere thanks go to them. Finally, we would like to acknowledge the Computer Science Department at Boston University for its support as the workshop's host.

The Internet and the Web continue to grow. It is exciting to witness and contribute to this phenomenon. We hope you will find your participation in this workshop an enjoyable and fruitful experience.

Azer Bestavros and Michael Rabinovich

Co-Chairs
6th International Web Caching
and Content Delivery Workshop

Credits

Workshop Chairs

Azer Bestavros (CS Dept., Boston University)
Michael Rabinovich (AT&T Research)

Publication Chair

Valentino Cavalli, Terena

Steering Committee

Pei Cao, Cisco
Valentino Cavalli, Terena
Peter Danzig, University of Southern California
John Martin, Network Appliance
Wojtek Sylwestrzak, Warsaw University
Duane Wessels, NLANR

Program Committee

Virgilio Almeida (Federal University of Minas Gerais, Brazil)
John Byers (CS Dept., Boston University)
Jeff Chase (CS Dept., Duke University)
Mark Crovella (Network Appliance & CS Dept., Boston University)
Mike Dahlin (University of Texas, Austin)
Arun Iyengar (IBM T.J. Watson Research Center)
Balachander Krishnamurthy (AT&T Research)
Steve McCanne (FastForward Networks)
Jeff Mogul (Compaq Western Research Lab)
Keith Ross (Eurécom Institute)
Gary Tomlinson (Entera Inc.)
Craig Wills (CS Dept., Worcester Polytechnic Institute)

External Reviewers

Khalil Amiri
Martin Arlitt
Adam Bradley
Jim Challenger
Fred Douglis
Ron Doyle
Robert Filepp
Shudong Jin
Jussi Kangasharju
Terence Kelly
Richard King
Wagner Meira
Kobus Van Der Merwe
Cristina Murta
Stanislav Rost
Oliver Spatscheck
Sara Sprenkle
Jia Wang

Session chairs

Duane Wessels, Measurement Factory
Jeff Chase, Duke University
Mike Dahlin, University of Texas
Gary Tomlinson, Cacheflow
Valentino Cavalli, TERENA
Mark Crovella, Boston University
Craig Wills, Worcester Polytechnic Institute
Abdelsalam Heddaya, Infolibria

List of Contributors

Arup Acharya	*Internet Infrastructure and Computing Utilities, IBM T.J. Watson Research Center, Hawthorne, NY 10532, USA*
Virgílio Almeida	*Department of Computer Science, Universidade Federal de Minas Gerais, Belo Horizonte, MG 31270, Brazil*
Lisa Amini	*IBM T.J. Watson Research Center, Hawthorn, NY 10532, USA*
Oscar Ardaiz	*Computer Architecture Department, Polytechnic University Catalonia, Barcelona, Spain*
Martin Arlitt	*Hewlett-Packard Laboratories*
André Beck	*Bell Laboratories/Lucent Technologies, 101 Crawfords Corner Rd., Holmdel, NJ 07733, USA*
Micah Beck	*University of Tennessee and Lokomo Systems*
Azer Bestavros	*Department of Computer Science, Boston University, Boston, MA, USA*
Alexandros Biliris	*AT&T, Florham Park, NJ, USA*
Jack Brassil	*Hewlett-Packard Laboratories, USA*
John Buford	*Verizon Communications, 40 Sylvan Road, Waltham, MA 02451, USA*
John Byers	*Department of Computer Science, Boston University, Boston, MA, USA*
Brad Cain	*Cereva*
Pei Cao	*Cisco Systems*
Jeffrey S. Chase	*Department of Computer Science, Duke University, Durham, NC, USA*
E.G. Coffman Jr.	*Department of Electrical Engineering, Columbia University, New York, NY 10027, USA*
Chuck Cranor	*AT&T, Florham Park, NJ, USA*
Mike Dahlin	*Department of Computer Sciences, University of Texas at Austin, Austin, TX, USA*
Brian D. Davison	*Department of Computer Science, Rutgers, The State University of New Jersey, 110 Frelinghuysen Road, Piscataway, NJ 08854, USA*
Mark Day	*Cisco Systems*
Fred Douglis	*AT&T, Florham Park, NJ, USA*

Ronald P. Doyle	*IBM, Research Triangle Park, NC, USA*
Deborah Estrin	*Information Sciences Institute and UCLA, 4676 Admiralty Way, Suite 1001, Marina del Rey, CA 90292-6695, USA*
Dave Farber	*Digital Island*
Zongming Fei	*Laboratory for Advanced Networking, Department of Computer Science, University of Kentucky, 773 Anderson Hall, Lexington, KY 40506, USA*
Rodrigo Fonseca	*Department of Computer Science, Universidade Federal de Minas Gerais, Belo Horizonte, MG 31270, Brazil*
Avi Freedman	*Akamai Technologies*
Vincent W. Freeh	*Department of Computer Science and Engineering, University of Notre Dame, South Bend, USA*
Felix Freitag	*Computer Architecture Department, Polytechnic University Catalonia, Barcelona, Spain*
Pascal Frossard	*IBM T.J. Watson Research Center, Hawthorn, NY 10532, USA*
Syam Gadde	*Department of Computer Science, Duke University, Durham, NC, USA*
Ramesh Govindan	*USC/Information Sciences Institute, 4676 Admiralty Way, Suite 1001, Marina del Rey, CA 90292-6695, USA*
Markus Hofmann	*Bell Laboratories/Lucent Technologies, 101 Crawfords Corner Rd., Holmdel, NJ 07733, USA*
Amy S. Hughes	*USC/Information Sciences Institute, 4676 Admiralty Way, Suite 1001, Marina del Rey, CA 90292-6695, USA*
Predrag Jelenković	*Department of Electrical Engineering, Columbia University, New York, NY 10027, USA*
Jussi Kangasharju	*Institut Eurécom, Sophia Antipolis, France*
Terence Kelly	*Electrical Engineering and Computer Science, University of Michigan, Ann Arbor, MI 48109, USA*
Ravindranath Kokku	*Department of Computer Sciences, University of Texas at Austin, Austin, TX, USA*
Mimika Koletsou	*Department of Computer Science and Engineering, University of California, San Diego, 9500 Gilman Dr., MS 0114, La Jolla, CA 92093-0114, USA*
Serge A. Krashakov	*Landau Institute for Theoretical Physics, 142432 Chernogolovka, Russia*
Johnson Lee	*Verizon Communications, 40 Sylvan Road, Waltham, MA 02451, USA*
Sung-Ju Lee	*Hewlett-Packard Laboratories, 1501 Page Mill Road, Palo Alto, CA 94304-1126, USA*
Meng Li	*Verizon Communications, 40 Sylvan Road, Waltham, MA 02451, USA*

Richard Liston	*College of Computing, Georgia Institute of Technology, 801 Atlantic Drive, Atlanta, GA 30332-0280, USA*
Wei-Ying Ma	*Microsoft Research China, China*
Wagner Meira Jr.	*Department of Computer Science, Universidade Federal de Minas Gerais, Belo Horizonte, MG 31270, Brazil*
Daniel Menascé	*Department of Computer Science, George Mason University, Fairfax, VA 22030, USA*
William Miniscalco	*Verizon Communications, 40 Sylvan Road, Waltham, MA 02451, USA*
Jeffrey Mogul	*Compaq Western Research Lab*
Petar Momčilović	*Department of Electrical Engineering, Columbia University, New York, NY 10027, USA*
Leandro Navarro	*Computer Architecture Department, Polytechnic University Catalonia, Barcelona, Spain*
Mark Nottingham	*Akamai Technologies*
Vsevolod V. Panteleenko	*Department of Computer Science and Engineering, University of Notre Dame, South Bend, USA*
Flávia Peligrinelli	*Department of Computer Science, Universidade Federal de Minas Gerais, Belo Horizonte, MG 31270, Brazil*
Michael Rabinovich	*AT&T, Florham Park, NJ, USA*
Pavlin Radoslavov	*USC/Information Sciences Institute, 4676 Admiralty Way, Suite 1001, Marina del Rey, CA 90292-6695, USA*
Rudolf Riedi	*Department of Electrical and Computer Engineering, Rice University, Houston, TX 77251, USA*
James Roberts	*France Télécom R&D, Issy-les-Moulineaux, France*
Keith W. Ross	*Institut Eurécom, Sophia Antipolis, France*
Stanislav Rost	*MIT Laboratory for Computer Science, Cambridge, MA, USA*
Alex Rousskov	*The Measurement Factory*
Phil Rzewski	*Inktomi*
Anees Shaikh	*Internet Infrastructure and Computing Utilities, IBM T.J. Watson Research Center, Hawthorne, NY 10532, USA*
W. David Shambroom	*Verizon Communications, 40 Sylvan Road, Waltham, MA 02451, USA*
Sadia Sharif	*Department of Computer Sciences, University of Texas at Austin, Austin, TX, USA*
Lev N. Shchur	*Landau Institute for Theoretical Physics, 142432 Chernogolovka, Russia*
Bo Shen	*Hewlett-Packard Laboratories, 1501 Page Mill Road, Palo Alto, CA 94304-1126, USA*
Sandeep Sibal	*AT&T, Florham Park, NJ, USA*

Oliver Spatscheck — *AT&T, Florham Park, NJ, USA*

Walter Sturm — *AT&T, Florham Park, NJ, USA*

Renu Tewari — *Internet Infrastructure and Computing Utilities, IBM T.J. Watson Research Center, Hawthorne, NY 10532, USA*

Joseph D. Touch — *USC/Information Sciences Institute, 4676 Admiralty Way, Suite 1001, Marina del Rey, CA 90292-6695, USA*

Amin M. Vahdat — *Department of Computer Science, Duke University, Durham, NC, USA*

Arun Venkataramani — *Department of Computer Sciences, University of Texas at Austin, Austin, TX, USA*

Chitra Venkatramani — *IBM T.J. Watson Research Center, Hawthorn, NY 10532, USA*

Dinesh Verma — *Internet Infrastructure and Computing Utilities, IBM T.J. Watson Research Center, Hawthorne, NY 10532, USA*

Olivier Verscheure — *IBM T.J. Watson Research Center, Hawthorn, NY 10532, USA*

Geoffrey M. Voelker — *Department of Computer Science and Engineering, University of California, San Diego, 9500 Gilman Dr., MS 0114, La Jolla, CA 92093-0114, USA*

Carey Williamson — *University of Saskatchewan*

Praveen Yalagandula — *Department of Computer Sciences, University of Texas at Austin, Austin, TX, USA*

Ellen Zegura — *College of Computing, Georgia Institute of Technology, 801 Atlantic Drive, Atlanta, GA 30332-0280, USA*

Contents

A Message from the Workshop Chairs v
Credits vi
List of Contributors vii

Content Delivery Networks I

The Trickle-Down Effect: Web Caching and Server Request Distribution
Ronald P. Doyle, Jeffrey S. Chase, Syam Gadde, Amin M. Vahdat 1

CDN Brokering
Alexandros Biliris, Chuck Cranor, Fred Douglis, Michael Rabinovich, Sandeep Sibal, Oliver Spatscheck, Walter Sturm 19

Synopsis – Optimising Web Services with Intermediaries
Mark Nottingham 35

Content Delivery Networks II

Object Replication Strategies in Content Distribution Networks
Jussi Kangasharju, James Roberts, Keith W. Ross 39

Topology-Informed Internet Replica Placement
Pavlin Radoslavov, Ramesh Govindan, Deborah Estrin 55

A Novel Approach to Managing Consistency in Content Distribution Networks
Zongming Fei 71

Panel 1 – Resolved: Publish No More Papers on Web Cache Replacement Policies
Moderator: *Jeffrey Mogul;* Panelists: *Martin Arlitt, Pei Cao, Alex Rousskov, Carey Williamson* 87

Edge and Browser Services

Content Services Network: The Architecture and Protocols
Wei-Ying Ma, Bo Shen, Jack Brassil 89

Enabling the Internet to Deliver Content-Oriented Services
André Beck, Markus Hofmann 109

Synopsis – Multicast Injection for Application Network Deployment
Oscar Ardaiz, Felix Freitag, Leandro Navarro 125

Synopsis – Expanding the Scope of Prefetching through Inter-Application Cooperation
Amy S. Hughes, Joseph D. Touch 129

Architectures

Instantaneous Offloading of Transient Web Server Load
Vsevolod V. Panteleenko, Vincent W. Freeh 131

The Cyclone Server Architecture: Streamlining Delivery of Popular Content
Stanislav Rost, John Byers, Azer Bestavros 147

Synopsis – MPLS-based Request Routing
Arup Acharya, Anees Shaikh, Renu Tewari, Dinesh Verma 165

Panel 2 – Content Distribution Internetworking: Vital or Valueless?
Moderator: *Mark Day;* Panelists: *Lisa Amini, Brad Cain, Fred Douglass, Dave Farber, Avi Freedman, Phil Rzewski* 169

Prefetching

Provably Efficient Stream Merging
E.G. Coffman, Jr., Predrag Jelenković, Petar Momčilović 171

The Potential Costs and Benefits of Long-Term Prefetching for Content Distribution
Arun Venkataramani, Praveen Yalagandula, Ravindranath Kokku, Sadia Sharif, Mike Dahlin 185

Assertion: Prefetching With GET is Not Good
Brian D. Davison 203

Panel 3 – Rule-Based Active Edge Services
Moderator: *Micah Beck,* Panelists: *Markus Hofmann, Wei-Ying Ma, Mark Nottingham* 217

Workload Characterization

Thin-Client Web Access Patterns: Measurements from a Cache-Busting Proxy
Terence Kelly 219

Analysis of Web Workloads Using the Bootstrap Methodology
Johnson Lee, William Miniscalco, Meng Li, W. David Shambroom, John Buford . . 235

Analyzing Web Robots and their Impact on Caching
Virgílio Almeida, Daniel Menascé, Rudolf Riedi, Flávia Peligrinelli, Rodrigo Fonseca, Wagner Meira Jr. 249

Performance Measurement

Using a Proxy to Measure Client-Side Web Performance
Richard Liston, Ellen Zegura 267

The Medusa Proxy: A Tool for Exploring User-Perceived Web Performance
Mimika Koletsou, Geoffrey M. Voelker 281

Comparative Measurements of Internet Traffic Using Cache-Triangle
Serge A. Krashakov, Lev N. Shchur 295

Streaming Media Delivery

An Interactive Video Delivery and Caching System Using Video Summarization
Sung-Ju Lee, Wei-Ying Ma, Bo Shen 309

Joint Server Scheduling and Proxy Caching for Video Delivery
Olivier Verscheure, Chitra Venkatramani, Pascal Frossard, Lisa Amini 327

Author Index 345

Keyword Index 347

Web Caching and Content Delivery
A. Bestavros and M. Rabinovich (Editors)

The Trickle-Down Effect: Web Caching and Server Request Distribution *

Ronald P. Doyle [a,1], Jeffrey S. Chase [b,2], Syam Gadde [b,3], Amin M. Vahdat [b,4]

[a] *IBM, Research Triangle Park, NC, USA*
[b] *Department of Computer Science, Duke University, Durham, NC, USA*

Abstract

Web proxies and Content Delivery Networks (CDNs) are widely used to accelerate Web content delivery and to conserve Internet bandwidth. These caching agents are highly effective for static content, which is an important component of all Web-based services.

This paper explores the effect of ubiquitous Web caching on the request patterns seen by other components of an end-to-end content delivery architecture, including Web server clusters and interior caches. In particular, object popularity distributions in the Web tend to be Zipf-like, but caches disproportionately absorb requests for the most popular objects, changing the reference properties of the filtered request stream in fundamental ways. We call this the *trickle-down effect*.

This paper uses trace-driven simulation and synthetic traffic patterns to illustrate the trickle-down effect and to investigate its impact on other components of a content delivery architecture, focusing on the implications for request distribution strategies in server clusters.

Keywords: Zipf; Web proxy cache; URL hashing; Load balancing; Request distribution

1. Introduction

As traffic on the Internet continues to grow, proxy caches and Content Delivery Networks (CDNs) are increasingly used to make Web service more efficient. These caching agents serve requests from content replication points closer to the clients, reducing origin server load, consumed network bandwidth, and client response latency.

Several factors contribute to increasing use of Web caching. A few years ago, Web caches were used only by clients who explicitly configured their Web browsers to use

* This work is supported by the U.S. National Science Foundation through grants CCR-00-82912 and EIA-9972879. Gadde is supported by a U.S. Department of Education GAANN fellowship. Vahdat is supported by NSF CAREER award CCR-9984328.
[1] R. Doyle is also a PhD student in the Computer Science Department at Duke University. E-mail: rdoyle@us.ibm.com
[2] E-mail: chase@cs.duke.edu
[3] E-mail: gadde@cs.duke.edu
[4] E-mail: vahdat@cs.duke.edu

proxies. Today, access ISPs commonly reduce their bandwidth costs by automatically redirecting outgoing Web request traffic through interception proxies. At the same time, hosting providers often deploy surrogate caches to filter incoming request traffic for data center customers. Many Web sites also contract with third-party CDNs to serve their request traffic from caching sites at various points in the network.

Ubiquitous caching has the potential to reshape the Web traffic patterns observed by the other components of a content delivery system, including Web server sites and interior caches that receive requests 'downstream' from forward caches. Upstream caches filter the request stream and shift the downstream loads from popular static objects to less popular objects and dynamic (uncacheable) content. We refer to this as the *trickle-down effect*. It is important to understand this effect because assumptions about traffic patterns drive many of the local design choices in Web delivery architectures.

This paper explores the effects of Web caches on the properties of the request traffic behind them. We use trace-driven simulation and synthetic traffic patterns to illustrate the trickle-down effect and to investigate its implications for downstream components of an end-to-end content delivery architecture. We focus on Web requests that follow a Zipf-like object popularity distribution [18], which many studies have shown to closely model Web request traffic [5,8,11,17]. We then illustrate the importance of this effect by examining its impact on load distribution strategies and content cache effectiveness for downstream servers. The contribution of this paper is to demonstrate and quantify the key implications of the trickle-down effect on downstream servers at a given server request load:

- Forward caching disproportionately absorbs requests for the most popular objects. The miss stream consists of evenly distributed references to moderately popular objects and recently updated or expired objects, together with the heavy tail of the popularity distribution.
- By absorbing much of the locality in the request stream, upstream caches reduce the effectiveness of downstream content caches (e.g., server memory), increasing pressure on server storage systems. This phenomenon is well-known in the file system context [13].
- The reduced locality in the miss stream tends to increase the importance of content-aware request distribution (such as *URL hashing*) for effective caching in downstream server clusters.
- At the same time, forward caching suppresses the primary source of load imbalances in Web server clusters, reducing the need for dynamic load balancing when content-aware request distribution is used.

Our results emphasize the need to consider how deployment of caches and CDNs affects other functional components of the Internet infrastructure. More generally, in evaluating solutions and policies for managing Web content it is important to consider their role as components of a complete end-to-end content delivery architecture.

This paper is organized as follows. Section 2 discusses the relevance of our work to end-to-end content delivery, and outlines our experimental methodology. Section 3 presents analytical and experimental results illustrating the trickle-down effect, and examines its implications for server request distribution, load balancing, and cache management. Section 4 considers the question of how the trickle-down effect manifests in today's Web. Section 5 summarizes our conclusions.

2. Background

Fig. 1 depicts the key components involved in delivering content from a large Web site to a community of clients. The request stream originates at clients on the left-hand side, and filters through one or more caches; requests not absorbed by the caches pass through to the origin servers on the right-hand side. Caches filtering the request stream may include client browser caches, demand-side proxy caches acting on behalf of a community of clients or an access ISP, and supply-side surrogate caches (also called reverse proxies) acting on behalf of the Web site's hosting provider or a third-party CDN service. A variety of mechanisms route the request stream through caches: clients may be configured to use a cache, or the system may redirect requests by interposing on DNS domain name translation or by intercepting the request at the IP level. In addition, each cache may control the routing of its miss stream to the other components.

The last two years have seen an explosion of growth in Web caching and content delivery infrastructure. Key developments include CDN service offerings from Akamai, Digital Island, and others, increasing use of surrogate caching among hosting providers such as Exodus, and aggregation of content consumers into large ISPs employing transparent interception proxies based on L7 switch hardware from Cisco/Arrowpoint, Nortel/Alteon, Foundry, and others. Each of these development has fed the growth in demand for Web caching systems from vendors including Inktomi, Network Appliance, and CacheFlow.

One goal of this paper is to explore the effect of upstream caching on the effectiveness of downstream request distribution policies, e.g., at the origin site. The right-hand side of Fig. 1 depicts a typical origin site for a large-scale Web service. Many of today's Web sites are hosted on server farms, where a group of servers are clustered together to act as a unified server to external clients. Any given request could be handled by any of several servers, improving scalability and fault-tolerance. The switching infrastructure connecting the servers to the hosting network includes one or more redirecting server switches to route incoming request traffic to the servers. We refer to these switches as *request distributors* because they select the server to handle each incoming request. The server selection policy plays a key role in managing cluster resources to maximize throughput and meet quality-of-service goals.

Commercial server switches use a variety of server selection policies to distribute requests to maximize throughput and minimize response latency. *Server load balancing* policies (SLB) monitor server status and direct requests to lightly loaded servers. SLB switches are often called L4 switches because they make server selection decisions at connection setup time, and examine only the transport (layer 4) headers of the incoming

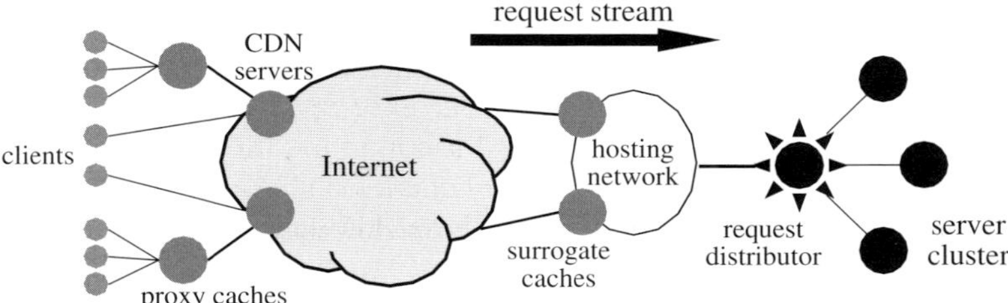

Fig. 1. End-to-end architecture for Web content delivery.

packet stream. *Content-aware* server selection policies prefer servers that can handle a given request most efficiently, for example, a server likely to have the requested data in cache. *URL hashing* (URLHASH) is a content-based policy that applies a simple deterministic hash function on the request URL to select a server. URL hashing is sometimes called an L7 policy because the switch must parse HTTP (layer 7) headers to extract the URL.

2.1. Zipf-like request traffic

Observations of Web request patterns drive the design choices and policies for all of these components of a Web delivery architecture. In particular, a number of studies indicate that requests to static Web objects follow a Zipf-like popularity distribution [5,8, 11,17]. The probability p_i of a request to the ith most popular document is proportional to $1/i^{\alpha}$, for some parameter α. A large number of requests target the most popular sites and the most popular objects, but the distribution has a long, heavy tail of less popular objects with poor reference locality. Higher α values increase the concentration of requests on the most popular objects.

One implication of the Web's Zipf-like behavior is that caching is highly effective for the most popular static (cacheable) objects, assuming that popularity dominates rate of change [17]. Unfortunately, caching is less effective on the heavy tail, which comprises a significant fraction of requests. This is why Web cache effectiveness typically improves only logarithmically with size, measured either by capacity or by user population.

Zipf-like behavior also has implications for request distribution strategies in server clusters. For example, it creates a tension between the competing goals of load balancing and locality. On the one hand, content-aware policies such as URLHASH effectively take advantage of the locality present in the request stream by preferring the same server for repeat requests, maximizing server memory hits for popular objects. However, URLHASH is vulnerable to load imbalances because the most popular objects receive the largest number of requests, and a single server handles all requests for any given object. SLB policies balance load, but they tend to scatter requests for each object across the servers, reducing server memory hits for moderately popular objects.

Recent research [2,3,15] has studied this tradeoff in depth, and developed *Locality Aware Request Distribution* (LARD) and related policies to balance these competing goals, combining the benefits of each approach. The LARD approach is commercialized by Zeus technology [1]. Other commercial request distributors use less sophisticated strategies. Server switches from Foundry, Nortel/Alteon and Cisco/Arrowpoint can assign multiple servers to each URLHASH bucket, and select from the target set using load information. The IBM Websphere Edge Server includes intelligent load balancing software for routing requests among servers based on content, server load, connection statistics, and customizable monitors. This product also contains a Web proxy cache.

2.2. Goals and methodology

This paper examines the impact of caching on downstream request traffic patterns, using the simulation pipeline depicted in Fig. 2. We limit our experiments to static, cacheable content, and we do not consider the effect of object rate of change or expiration. We use a simple Web cache simulator [9] to filter representative request traces through

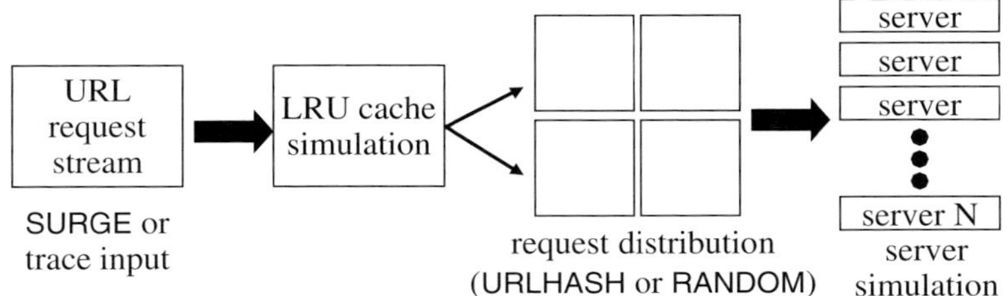

Fig. 2. Simulation pipeline for study of caching and request distribution.

caches of various sizes. Our model assumes a simple LRU replacement policy with no cache cooperation among the front-end cache and the servers. Our results are conservative in that we use small cache capacities relative to the aggregate content size. In these experiments we assume that a single cache filters requests from all clients; this assumption is reasonable for CDNs and proxies serving 20,000 or more users [17], but it exaggerates the trickle-down effect from proxies serving small populations.

We use simulations to explore the properties of the cache miss stream and their effects on downstream components, focusing on the effectiveness of server content caching and server request distribution policies. We study two server selection policies: URLHASH and RANDOM. These policies are sufficient to quantify the impact of the trickle-down effect on the performance potential of a range of policies for server request distribution. We substitute RANDOM for SLB because it is easier to simulate, and its locality properties are no worse than SLB.

Table 1 shows some characteristics of the server traces and synthetic request streams used in the study. The server traces are from IBM Corporation's main Web server (www.ibm.com). Because these traces are collected at the entry point(s) of a large, popular Web server, they capture the characteristics of request streams likely to be seen at the kind of server clusters we target in this study. The first trace contains 15.5M requests over a period of 3.5 days in June 1998, showing a best-fit Zipf α value of 0.764. We select this trace partly to facilitate direct comparison with the LARD study, which uses the same trace. The second IBM trace was collected on February 5-11, 2001. As shown in Table 1 the IBM traces deviate somewhat from expected Zipf-like behavior, e.g., they contain a small number of popular objects that account for an unusually large percentage of references.

We also use the SURGE Web server load generator [4] to synthesize Zipf-like request traces using α values between 0.6 and 0.9, to allow experimentation with a range of values

Table 1. Trace characteristics

Trace	Objects	Footprint	References	References from top 1% of objects	References from top 5% of objects
1998 IBM	38527	1 GB	15.5M	77%	94%
2001 IBM	52763	1.6 GB	43M	93%	97%
Zipf Alpha 0.9	40000	900 MB	4.2M	42%	57%
Zipf Alpha 0.8	20000	440 MB	7.5M	27%	42%
Zipf Alpha 0.7	20000	440 MB	16M	17%	30%

observed in previous traffic studies. The synthetic traces were generated with default SURGE settings for temporal locality and object size distributions.

3. Experimental results

This section presents experimental results in four subsections. Section 3.1 illustrates the traffic properties of the 'trickle-down' cache miss stream. Sections 3.2 and 3.3 examine the impact of these properties on load balancing and cache locality respectively.

3.1. Properties of the miss stream

Fig. 3 illustrates object reference frequency by rank before and after caching, on a log–log scale. As expected for Zipf-like distributions, the original traces roughly follow a straight line; the straight line breaks down for less popular objects because the traces are of bounded size. The figure shows that even a small forward cache 'skims the cream' off the request stream, absorbing requests for the most popular objects. The effect is to 'flatten' the distribution so that the most popular objects in the miss stream receive roughly the same number of requests. In fact, there are 1035 references to the most popular object in the $\alpha = 0.6$ miss stream from a 32MB cache, while the object with rank 1000 is referenced 816 times. The effect is even more pronounced in the lower graph from the 1998 IBM trace, which has a heavier concentration on the most popular objects in the original trace. Larger forward caches extend the flattening effect, but are qualitatively similar.

To illustrate the disproportionate effect of caches on popular objects, Fig. 4 shows per-object hit rates for popular objects in the same input traces, as a function of popularity rank. This graph shows that cache effectiveness falls off rapidly with object popularity. The effect is more pronounced in the IBM trace; its most popular objects miss in the cache even less often than for the $\alpha = 0.6$ trace, explaining the smaller number of references to these objects in the miss stream in Fig. 3.

The intuition behind the trickle-down effect is as follows. Suppose that requests to each object are evenly distributed in the input trace, and that it takes R requests of the trace to fill a cache of k distinct objects. The expected value of R is a function of the input distributions and the cache size, but we leave aside the question of how to compute it. (R is on the order of 10^5 for the 1998 IBM trace with a 32MB cache.) The probability that none of the R requests references the object with popularity rank i is $(1 - p_i)^R$; this gives the probability that a reference to object i misses in the cache after any R references. Thus the probability of a reference to object i in the miss stream is $q_i = p_i(1 - p_i)^R$; this gives the probability that any given element of an infinite request stream is a reference to object i and that the reference misses in the cache.

Fig. 5 shows a scaled plot of $q_i = p_i(1 - p_i)^R$ for a Zipf $\alpha = 0.7$ and $R = 10^4$. The graph shows that it is the moderately popular objects that are most likely to appear in the miss stream; these become the most popular objects in the filtered distributions of Fig. 3. This is because the probability of a forward cache miss $(1 - p_i)^R$ is vanishingly small for popular objects, thus few requests to popular objects pass through the cache. While this probability approaches unity for unpopular objects, requests for unpopular objects are rare to begin with. For comparison, Fig. 5 also shows the number of references to each object

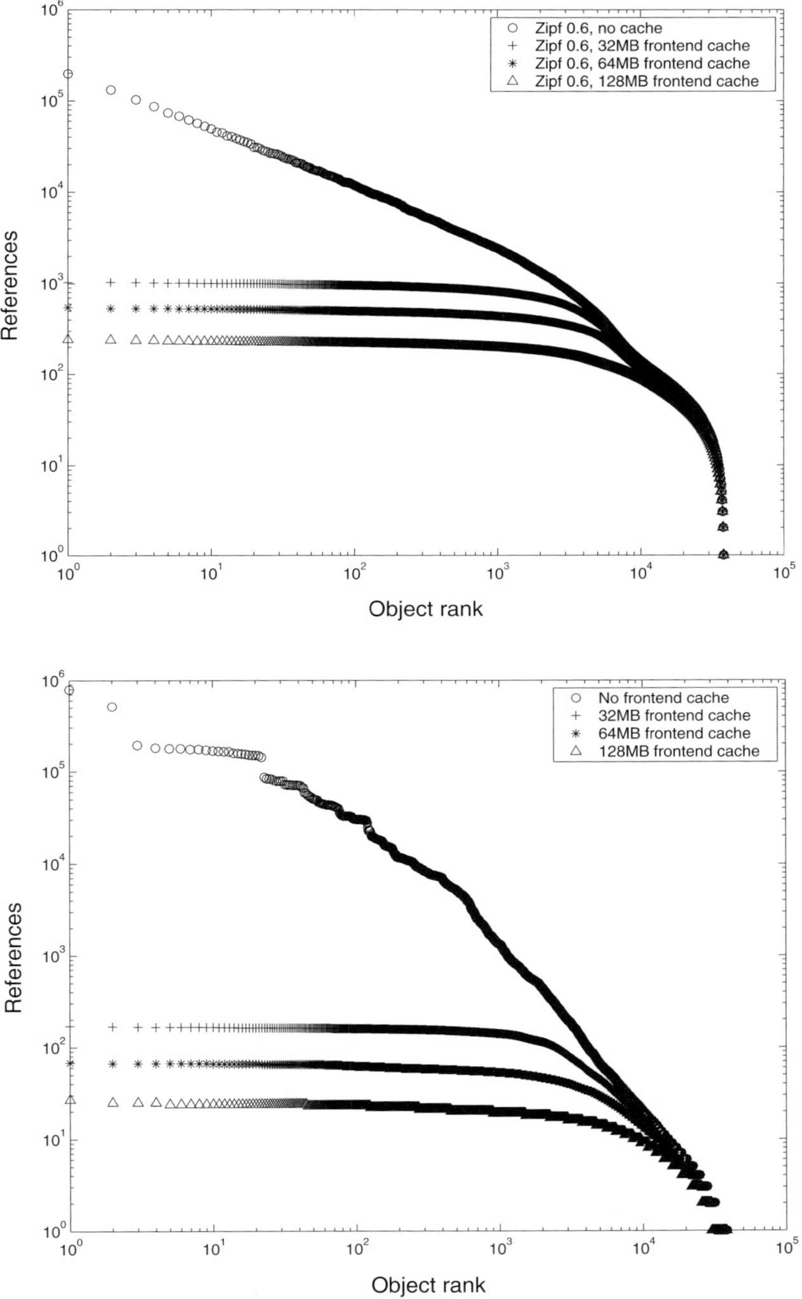

Fig. 3. Number of references to each object by rank (log–log), before and after caching. The upper graph is from a synthetic trace with $\alpha = 0.6$; the lower graph is from the 1998 IBM trace.

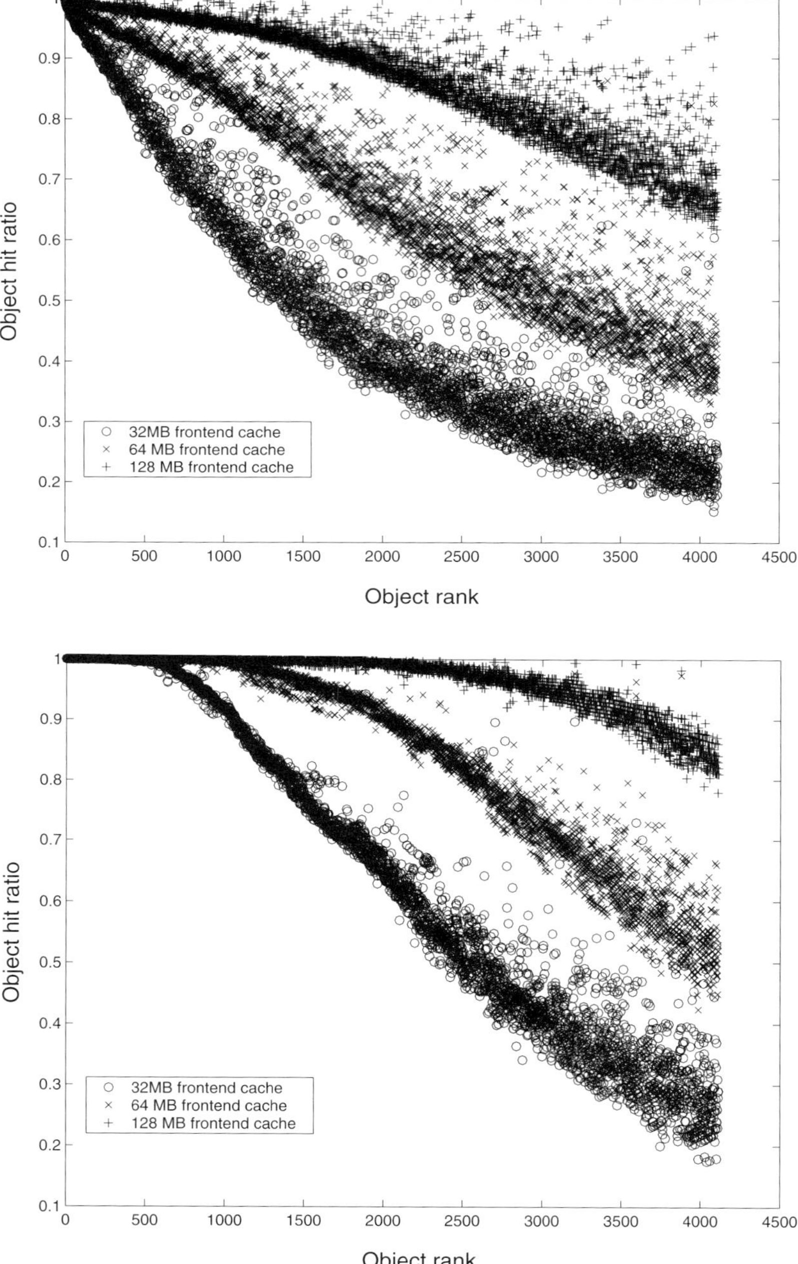

Fig. 4. Object hit rate in front-end caches, by object rank in the input trace. The upper graph is from a synthetic trace with $\alpha = 0.6$; the lower graph is from the 1998 IBM trace.

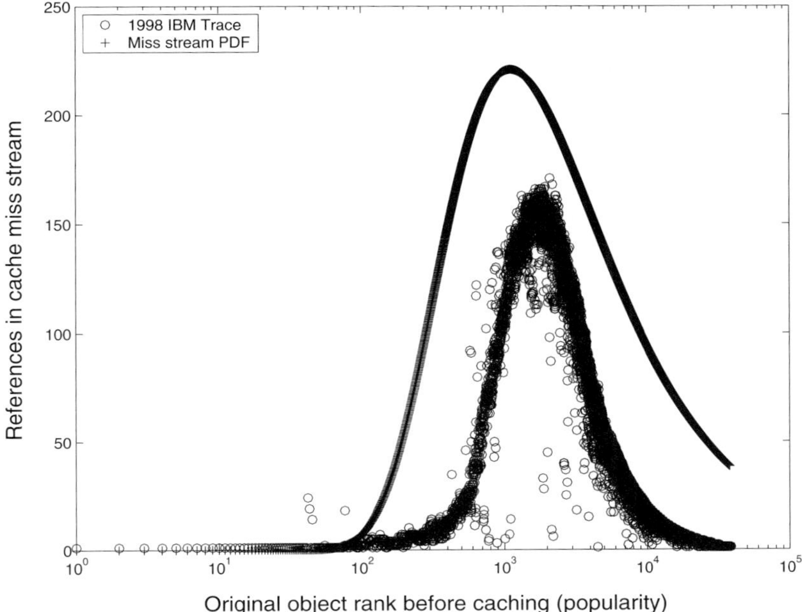

Fig. 5. Number of references to each object in the 32MB cache miss stream, ordered by rank in the 1998 IBM trace. The superimposed curve is a scaled plot of $q_i = p_i(1 - p_i)^R$ for a Zipf $\alpha = 0.7$ and $R = 10^4$.

after passing the 1998 IBM trace through a 32MB cache, as a function of object rank in the original input trace. This curve confirms our intuition.

3.2. Load balancing

These effects of forward caching on the reference distributions in the miss stream have important implications for downstream components. To illustrate, we now consider the impact on server request distribution policies. One implication is that the trickle-down effect suppresses the load skew caused by popular objects in Zipf-like request streams. This means that simple content-aware request routing policies such as URLHASH become less vulnerable to load imbalances than they have been in the past.

We used a simple server simulator to quantify this effect. The simulator assigns a fixed CPU cost for each connection (we assumed a single request per connection) and for each block transferred. A server cache miss also imposes a per-block CPU transfer cost from disk. Table 2 gives the simulation parameters for these costs, which are identical to those used in the LARD study [15].

Table 2. CPU cost parameters for simulation

Operation	CPU time in μs
Connection setup	145
Net transmit (512 bytes)	40
Disk transfer (4K bytes)	410

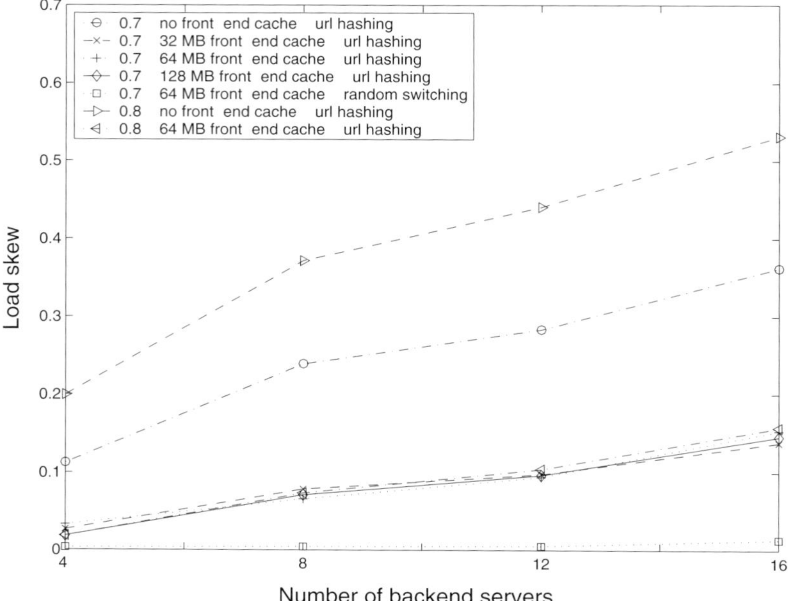

Fig. 6. Server load skew (synthetic traces with $\alpha = 0.7$ and $\alpha = 0.8$).

The simulation results compare load distributions from URLHASH and RANDOM request distribution of filtered traces across varying numbers of servers. The results exaggerate load imbalances relative to the LARD study in the following respect. We assume that all client requests are available at the start of the experiment, to eliminate server wait time between requests; this 'squeezes out' all idle time of underutilized servers to the end of the run. We then quantify load skew as the average percentage CPU time difference between the slowest server and all other servers:

$$\sum_{i}^{N}(T_{\text{slow}} - \text{Time}_i)/(N * T_{\text{slow}})$$

where T_{slow} is the CPU time for the slowest of the N servers. This conservative load skew metric gives the average idle time percentage of servers left underutilized due to load imbalances. A lower load skew figure indicates a more balanced load across the servers. This simulation assumes adequate I/O system bandwidth, and considers only the CPU cost to manage the I/O.

Fig. 6 shows the load skew results for RANDOM and URLHASH on the cache miss streams, as a function of the server cluster size N. These experiments use a server memory size of 32MB, as in the LARD study. RANDOM balances the load as expected. With no caching, the load skew for URLHASH on the $\alpha = 0.7$ Zipf trace with 8 servers is almost 25% and jumps to over 35% when using 16 servers, confirming the LARD result that load imbalances under URLHASH can significantly reduce cluster throughput, and that load imbalances grow with cluster size. The imbalance is worse for the $\alpha = 0.8$, which concentrates references to popular objects even more. However, these load imbalances are less severe after filtering the request streams through forward caches; for example, a small

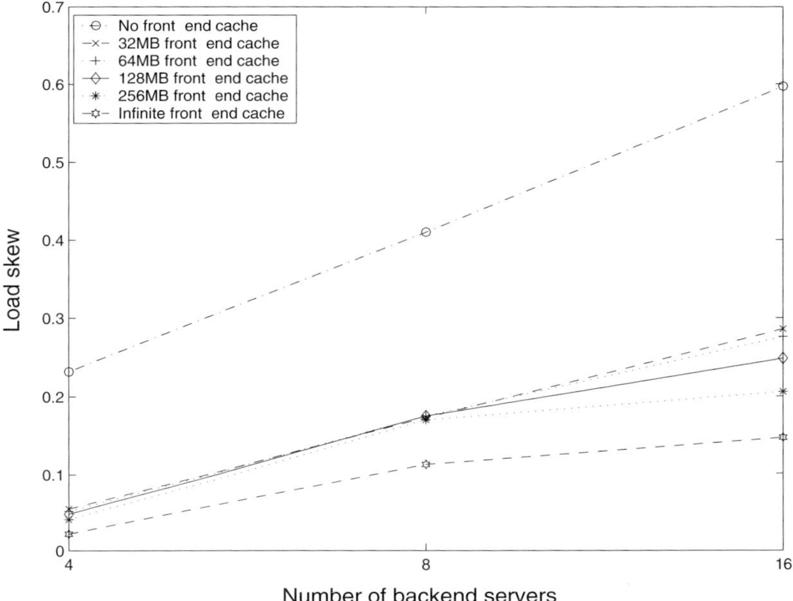

Fig. 7. Server load skew (2001 IBM trace).

cache drops the load skew to roughly 7% with 8 servers, independent of the α or the front-end cache size.

This effect is also visible with the IBM server traces, although a small number of very large objects introduce some skew (see below). For example, Fig. 7 shows the load skew results for URLHASH on the 2001 IBM trace with the nine largest objects removed (all over 8MB). While forward caching is less effective at eliminating load imbalances than for the synthetic traces, the 8 server load imbalance is never more than 20% with a forward cache of 64 MB or larger. To further validate our simulation, we ran the 2001 IBM trace against a cluster of 8 machines running FreeBSD and Apache Web Servers, gathering load information from the cluster while using URLHASH to distribute the requests among the cluster machines. The results of this experiment are qualitatively similar to Fig. 7, but the load skews are significantly lower for larger clusters and larger front-end cache sizes. One difference is that the test platforms have larger server memories (512 MB) than the simulated systems.

We ran additional experiments to investigate the impact of large objects on our results. We determined that much of the remaining load imbalance occurs because the caches in our simulations are ineffective at removing load skew due to variations in object size. In particular, large objects do not live in a small cache long enough to yield hits. For example, the objects in the IBM traces range in size up to 61 MB. Some of the largest objects are moderately popular, but their size makes them effectively uncacheable in our experiments.

To illustrate, Fig. 8 shows the distribution of *bytes transferred* (*size* $*$ *requests*) for objects in the 1998 IBM trace after filtering through caches of 32MB, 64MB, and 128MB. This metric approximates the amount of server work to serve requests for each object.

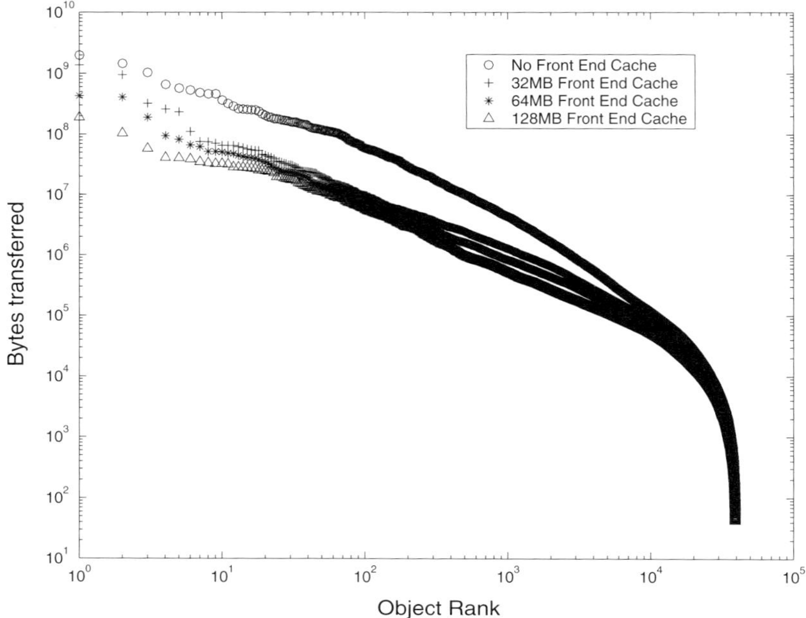

Fig. 8. Request distribution by size ∗ references (1998 IBM trace).

The graph shows that although the caches suppress popularity skew, they do not eliminate the skew in bytes transferred from the server for each object. In practice, effectiveness of forward caching is typically limited by population rather than size, and size-related imbalances may be resolved at the origin sites by segregating continuous media files and other large objects.

These results indicate that explicit load balancing for content-aware request distribution in Web server clusters is less important in the presence of upstream caching. That is, a simple URLHASH strategy at the back end is unlikely to develop significant load imbalances when forward caching is effective.

3.3. Effects on server locality

A key advantage of content-aware request distribution is that it maximizes server cache effectiveness. However, the heavy-tailed nature of Web popularity distributions implies a low marginal benefit from multiple levels of caching [10]. Thus, the trickle-down effect reduces the ability of a server cluster to serve requests from memory for a given server request rate, independent of the request distribution policy. Thus servers tend to be increasingly I/O-bound in the presence of upstream caching, although there may be significant locality remaining in requests from caches to reload recently modified or expired objects.

Fig. 9 illustrates this effect for ideal 256 MB and 512 MB aggregate server caches, as a function of front-end cache size. For the 1998 IBM trace, a 256 MB back-end cache is sufficient to serve more than 99% of references in the original trace from server memory. Even a 32 MB front-end cache absorbs 95% of the references in this trace, as predicted by

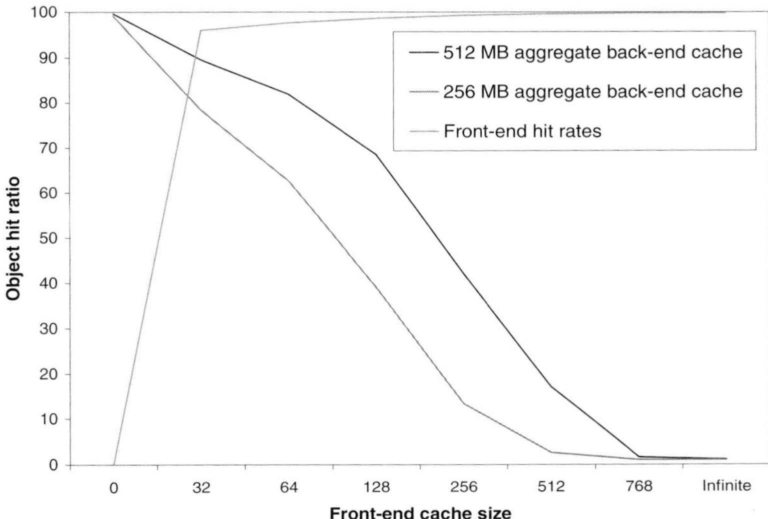

Fig. 9. Cache hit rates for front-end and back-end caches of varying sizes in the 1998 IBM Trace.

the data in Table 1. With a 32 MB front-end cache the server caches still yield hit ratios above 80% for the miss stream. As the front-end cache grows, the back-end caches are left with just the tail of the original distribution, so back-end hit rates drop. When front-end and back-end caches can each store 25% of the content, the back-end hit rate is only 15%.

This shows that the potential of content-aware request distribution to reduce server I/O load is diminished in the presence of upstream caching. Simulations with URLHASH show that back-end cache hit ratios closely follow Fig. 9, independent of the number of servers and their memory sizes. That is, URLHASH delivers an equivalent back-end hit ratio to an ideal unified cache of the same aggregate size for the traces we tested. For example, with a 128 MB front-end cache and 8 servers with 32 MB of memory each, URLHASH delivers the ideal back-end hit ratio of 41%.

Even so, upstream caching *increases* the marginal benefit from content-aware request distribution in many cases. Fig. 10 shows the effectiveness of RANDOM request distribution to quantify the server cache hits that are sacrificed by a locality-blind policy such as SLB. The graph gives hit ratios in a 256 MB aggregate back-end cache for the 1998 IBM trace filtered through front-end caches of varying sizes. The lines show cache hit ratios as a function of the number of servers in the cluster; larger clusters exacerbate redundant caching as described in Section 2, reducing overall cache effectiveness. With no front-end cache, RANDOM yields back-end hit ratios above 90% for this trace even with 16 servers. With a front-end cache absorbing requests for the most popular objects, RANDOM never delivers a back-end hit ratio above 38%, while Fig. 9 shows that a content-aware policy such as URLHASH could deliver hit ratios as high as 80% with a 32 MB front-end.

As the size of the front-end cache grows and the locality present in the miss stream drops, RANDOM becomes progressively less sensitive to the number of servers, and the performance gap between RANDOM and the ideal back-end narrows. Yet URLHASH significantly outperforms RANDOM on the filtered request streams across a range of configurations. Table 3 gives results from the 2001 IBM trace and a synthetic Zipf-like

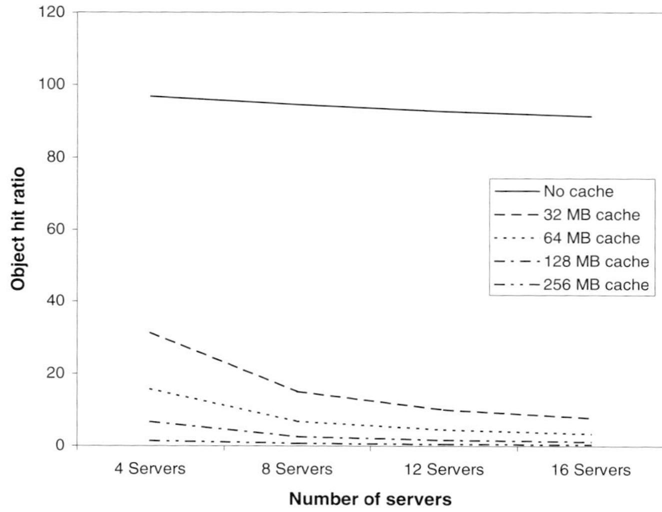

Fig. 10. Server cache hit rates (256 MB aggregate) with RANDOM request distribution as a function of cluster size, for various front-end cache sizes (1998 IBM trace).

Table 3. Server cache hit rates for a 16-server cluster with various traces and front-end cache sizes, 256MB and 512MB aggregate server cache

Trace	0 Front-End Cache		64MB Front-End Cache		128MB Front-End Cache	
	URL	Random	URL	Random	URL	Random
256MB Aggregate Server Cache						
1998 IBM	99%	92%	65%	3.5%	34%	1.6%
2001 IBM	98%	94%	46%	3.6%	28	1.6%
Zipf α 0.9	81%	43.7%	45%	3.0%	28%	1.6%
512MB Aggregate Server Cache						
1998 IBM	99.4%	94.4%	85%	7.5%	74%	3.3%
2001 IBM	99%	95.3%	70%	7.8%	55%	4.2%
Zipf α 0.9	93%	50%	76%	6.5%	65%	4.1%

trace with similar locality but more typical request concentrations for the most popular objects. In each case, even RANDOM delivers reasonable or competitive hit ratios for the original trace, but is not effective on the filtered traces. In contrast, URLHASH is effective at extracting the remaining locality from the filtered traces, yielding close-to-ideal hit ratios.

4. Is the trickle-down effect visible today?

The simulation data presented in earlier sections clearly show the potential impact of widespread caching on popularity distributions. Can we see preliminary evidence of such a trend in current Web traces, and if not, why not?

A first step is to isolate the effects of other non-caching related trends, such as observed changes in Zipf distributions. Padmanabhan and Qiu [14] show that Zipf α values for the MSNBC site during 1998 and 1999 were higher than in previous proxy and server traces. They note that these traces were taken at a time when CDNs and surrogate caches were not employed at this site, and observe that α values for Web traffic are increasing, i.e., a relatively small number of documents are becoming more popular. This increases the potential benefit from caching and replication. The study also notes that caching and CDNs will reduce the load on the servers. Our results explore how this caching might affect the properties of the request 'trickle' reaching the MSNBC server after CDNs or surrogates are deployed.

We looked for evidence of upstream proxy caches in the client request stream of the 2001 IBM trace. The IBM site uses the Network Dispatcher component of the Websphere Edge Server to balance load across servers, but, like the MSNBC site, IBM does not yet use surrogate caches or a CDN for this site. A few dozen clients generate more than 10,000 requests per day. While these are likely to be caches, there are no very large caches: no client generates more than 1% of requests. The top three clients account for 2% of the requests. This confirms that the potential of proxy caching in the Web is not yet fully realized, and that existing demand-side caches do not yet serve large enough user communities to have a significant impact on the request stream for sites that do not use CDNs. One factor may be that the IBM site is accessed primarily by businesses rather than consumers.

We also examine one day of May 2001 traces from the top-level NLANR caches [16], which cooperate to act as a unified root proxy cache. Intuition suggests that the popularity distributions for the incoming NLANR cache request stream would be flat for the most popular objects, because the request stream itself originates from caches in lower levels of the hierarchy. However, the effect is not visible in Fig. 11, which shows reference frequency distributions for 'cacheable' URLs in the request stream (upper line) and the root cache miss stream (lower line). We consider a URL 'cacheable' if it yields at least a 10% object hit ratio in the NLANR root cache. Even with this restriction, neither request stream shows the flattening characteristic of the trickle-down effect to the degree expected.

Further analysis reveals that the NLANR root cache effectiveness is highly variable, even for popular objects that appear to be cacheable. The fuzzy cloud below the upper line in Fig. 11 is a plot of object request frequency in the miss stream, ordered by object rank in the original trace. This shows an unexpectedly low correlation between object popularity and cache effectiveness, even for 'cacheable' objects (compare to Fig. 4).

The NLANR traces do not contain enough HTTP header information to determine why any given request was not served from the cache. One possibility is that expiration headers in responses caused the caches to discard many objects that would have yielded hits. Another possibility is that cookies or other headers rendered the responses uncacheable for other reasons. The cache software in this system used a complex procedure for identifying cacheable responses.

In summary, there is little empirical evidence to indicate that Web caches significantly impact the request traffic of recent server studies, even in popular Web sites such as IBM and MSNBC. However, this paper shows that Web caches will reshape the request stream, to the degree that they are effective at all. A range of factors compromise the effectiveness of Web caching today, including incomplete deployment of CDNs, small

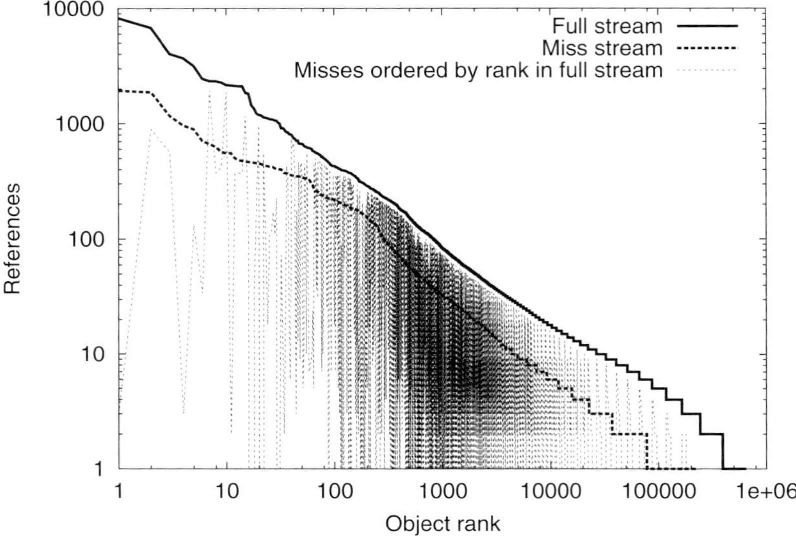

Fig. 11. Popularity distributions for the full trace and the miss stream from NLANR caches on May 30, 2001, plotted logarithmically on both axes. We ignore objects whose requests hit in the NLANR caches less than 10% of the time.

population sizes on demand-side caches, and confusion about what content is cacheable during the transition to HTTP 1.1.

5. Conclusions

This paper shows that key assumptions about Web server request traffic may lead us astray as proxy caches and Content Delivery Networks (CDNs) become increasingly ubiquitous and effective. To be sure, perfect caching would absorb *all/* static object requests, leaving origin sites to handle dynamic content and propagate object updates to the caching networks. But even imperfect caches can absorb the majority of requests to the most popular objects, shifting downstream traffic loads toward the heavy tail of Zipf-like Web request distributions. This 'trickle-down effect' impacts the design of downstream components.

Our results illustrate the importance of considering the impact of caching on other components of an end-to-end content delivery architecture. This paper explores key implications of the trickle-down effect for request distribution alternatives in back-end server clusters. The trickle-down effect suppresses the primary source of load imbalances in Web server farms, reducing the potential benefit from sophisticated load balancing strategies for static content. It also absorbs much of the locality in the request stream, reducing the benefit from downstream content caches (e.g., server memory). In the limit, upstream caches weaken the differences between request distribution strategies downstream. The various strategies are motivated largely by the locality and load skew inherent in the 'head' of Zipf-like request distributions, and behave similarly on the heavy tail. Even so, the partial reduction in locality from moderately effective forward caches makes content-aware request distribution (e.g., URL hashing) even more important in downstream server clusters to benefit from the locality that remains; content-blind policies such as server load balancing (SLB) severely compromise server cache effectiveness, even with small front-end caches.

This study focuses on static content. Dynamic Web requests are traditionally not cacheable. However, with techniques such as dynamic caching [12] and fragment caching [6,7] it is possible to cache part of the result of dynamic requests (which may apply to many different requests), gaining some benefit from locality. These effects must also be considered when studying the impacts of increased dynamic content in Web requests.

Acknowledgments

We would like to thank Erich Nahum of IBM Research for providing us the 1998 IBM Web server traces used in the LARD study. We would also like to thank Alister Lewis-Bowen and Andrew Frank-Loron for their help in obtaining the 2001 IBM server logs.

References

[1] Improving Web Server Performance with Zeus Load Balancer. http://www.zeus.co.uk/products/lb1/.

[2] M. Aron, P. Druschel, and W. Zwaenepoel. Efficient support for P-HTTP in cluster-based Web servers. In *Proceedings of USENIX '99 Technical Conference*, 1999.

[3] Mohit Aron, Darren Sanders, Peter Druschel, and Willy Zwaenepoel. Scalable content-aware request distribution in cluster-based network servers. In *Proceedings of the USENIX 2000 Technical Conference*, 2000.

[4] Paul Barford and Mark E. Crovella. Generating representative Web workloads for network and server performance evaluation. In *Proceedings of Performance '98/ACM SIGMETRICS '98*, pages 151–160, June 1998.

[5] Lee Breslau, Pei Cao, Li Fan, Graham Phillips, and Scott Shenker. Web caching and Zipf-like distributions: Evidence and implications. In *Proceedings of IEEE Infocom '99*, March 1999.

[6] J. Challenger, A. Iyengar, and P. Dantzig. A scalable system for consistently caching dynamic data. In *Proceedings of IEEE Infocom 1999 Conference*, March 1999.

[7] J. Challenger, A. Iyengar, K. Witting, C. Ferstat, and P. Reed. A publishing system for efficiently creating dynamic web content. In *Proceedings of the IEEE Infocom 2000 Conference*, March 2000.

[8] Carlos Cunha, Azer Bestavros, and Mark Crovella. Characteristics of WWW client-based traces. Technical Report 1995-010, 1, 1995.

[9] Syam Gadde. The Proxycizer Web proxy tool suite. http://www.cs.duke.edu/ari/Proxycizer/.

[10] Syam Gadde, Jeffrey S. Chase, and Michael Rabinovich. Web caching and content distribution: A view from the interior. *Computer Networks and ISDN Systems (Selected Papers from the Fifth International WWW Caching and Content Delivery Workshop)*, 24(2): 222–231, February 2001.

[11] Steve Glassman. A Caching Relay for the World Wide Web. In *First International World Wide Web Conference*, 1994.

[12] A. Iyengar and J. Challenger. Improving web server performance by caching dynamic data. In *Proc. USENIX Symp. on Internet Technologies and Systems*, December 1997.

[13] D. Muntz and P. Honeyman. Multi-level caching in distributed file systems, or your cache ain't nuthin' but trash. In *Proceedings of the Winter USENIX Technical Conference*, January 1992.

[14] V. Padmanabhan and L. Qiu. The content and access dynamics of a busy web site: Findings and implications. In *Proc. of SIGCOMM, Stockholm, Sweden, Aug. 28–Sept. 1*, 2000.

[15] Vivek S. Pai, Mohit Aron, Gaurav Banga, Michael Svendsen, Peter Druschel, Willy Zwaenopoel, and Erich Nahum. Locality-aware request distribution in cluster-based network servers. In *Proceedings*

of the Eighth International Conference on Architectural Support for Programming Languages and Operating Systems, October 1998.

[16] Duane Wessels, Traice Monk, K. Claffy, and Hans-Werner Braun. A distributed testbed for national information provisioning. http://ircache.nlanr.net/Cache/.

[17] Alec Wolman, Geo Voelker, Nitin Sharma, Neal Cardwell, Anna Karlin, and Henry Levy. On the scale and performance of cooperative Web proxy caching. In *Proceedings of the 17th ACM Symposium on Operating Systems Principles*, December 1999.

[18] G. Zipf. *Human Behavior and the Principle of Least Effort*. Addison Wesley, 1949.

Web Caching and Content Delivery
A. Bestavros and M. Rabinovich (Editors)

CDN Brokering

Alexandros Biliris, Chuck Cranor, Fred Douglis, Michael Rabinovich, Sandeep Sibal, Oliver Spatscheck, Walter Sturm

AT&T, Florham Park, NJ, USA*

Abstract

Content distribution networks (CDNs) increase the capacity of individual Web sites and attempt to deliver content from caches that are located 'closer' to end-users than the origin servers that provide the content. *CDN brokering* provides CDNs a way to interoperate by allowing one CDN to intelligently redirect clients dynamically to other CDNs. This paper describes the goals, architecture, and performance of a CDN brokerage system. Our system has been deployed on the Internet on a provisional basis, and our architectural ideas have helped advance the evolution of Internet standards for interoperating CDNs.

Keywords: Content distribution network; Web caching; Web performance; Domain name system

1. Introduction

As the scale and use of the Internet increase, Web content providers find it increasingly difficult to serve all users wishing to access their content with an appropriately low response time, especially in the face of unexpectedly high loads (often called 'flash crowd'). Content distribution networks (CDNs) have become a popular approach to address this problem; they typically deploy multiple caches throughout the Internet, allowing them to offload the management of these caches from individual content providers. This offers economies of scale and greater abilities to respond to high loads. CDNs also try to decrease latency for individual clients by satisfying client requests from nearby caches.

Despite these advantages, CDNs have their own limitations. It is extremely capital-intensive and operationally complex for CDNs to achieve the scale necessary to be present at the edge of every network or region of the world. Even where they have cache space close to a particular network, demand may outstrip capacity from time to time or failures may occur. Clearly the ability for multiple CDNs to interoperate can offer additional flexibility by letting one CDN direct clients to a different CDN in order to improve scale, fault tolerance and performance. This is sometimes referred to as 'Content Distribution Internetworking' (CDI), the subject of efforts within the IETF.

* Contact address: icds-broker@research.att.com

We define **CDN Brokering** as the ability of one CDN to redirect clients dynamically among two or more CDNs. While over the past few months the Content Alliance has put forth several documents [2,7–9,13] describing in general terms how one might let CDNs interoperate, this paper describes an architecture and implementation of a specific realization of this idea, which has been operational since July, 2000. We call our DNS-based system the *Intelligent Domain Name Server* (IDNS). IDNS responds to DNS requests intelligently based on a dynamic, load-sensitive configuration rather than using static information.

The rest of this paper is organized as follows. Section 2 discusses background and motivation. Section 3 describes CDN brokering in general terms and Section 4 addresses our specific software architecture. Section 5 discusses the performance of our system. Section 6 covers related work, and Section 7 concludes.

1.1. Terminology

Content provider companies that sign up for a CDN service are known as *customers* and Web clients (users or client proxies) that access customers' content are called *clients*.

Clients typically look up DNS information via name servers in their own network that act on behalf of a collection of computers; these client-side name servers are called *Client DNS servers*.

2. Background and motivation

Not all CDNs are created equal or have the same goals. Some are small, regional services that target a particular segment of the Internet, for instance a country of moderate size. Others have a large presence within a particular network, but are limited to the reach of that network unless they have extensive BGP peering relationships [14] or other connectivity that provide high bandwidth to many other networks. Still other CDNs are worldwide and attempt to encompass a large fraction of the Internet. However, deploying a CDN in many edge locations and managing those servers is an enormous commitment in capital and labor.

In fact, a CDN of any scale might find it financially advantageous to have an arrangement that allows it to wholesale capacity to other CDNs. Similarly, the ability to *buy* capacity at wholesale from another CDN in those rare cases when one's own CDN is overloaded or (partly) unavailable would provide extra insurance. Finally, a CDN that wishes to expand its presence might resell capacity from other CDNs on an ongoing basis, rather than under exceptional circumstances.

CDN brokering involves a mechanism that allows the broker to dynamically decide on the fraction of requests to be served from its own CDN, and to split the remaining requests among other partner CDNs, again according to some dynamically decided percentage.

3. Brokering components

In this section we describe in general terms how CDN brokering is accomplished. A brokering system needs a mechanism to select which CDN is the best to serve a particular request (Section 3.1), a way to direct clients to that CDN (Section 3.2), a way for a partner CDN to map requests back to an origin server to obtain content (Section 3.3), and an accounting mechanism to bill for traffic when appropriate (Section 3.4).

3.1. Selection

Selecting to which CDN a client should be directed requires two things. First, it requires a mechanism to identify where a request came from. Second, it requires information about suitable locations to which the client can be directed at any given instant. Generally speaking, the biggest decision in this regard is whether to serve the request within the brokering CDN or to redirect to another CDN. We discuss CDN selection in detail in Section 4 in the context of our architecture.

3.2. Redirection

Fig. 1 depicts a redirection mechanism for a brokering CDN, which we refer to as *B*. The diagram also shows two other 'partnering' CDNs, *G* and *H*. The edge servers are shown as rectangles and the DNS servers are shown as small ovals. Each of the CDNs has its own DNS server(s) that it uses to direct clients to its own servers. Of particular importance are the brokering DNS servers that allow *B* to redirect clients not just to one of its own servers, but to any other partnering CDN as well. This is accomplished through another layer of indirection as explained below.

An underlying assumption is that the redirection mechanism is using DNS and that *B* is authoritative for the hostnames its customers are having it serve, either directly or via a CNAME redirection. (There are other possible methods for what the Content Alliance refers to as 'request-routing' [2]; we compare our approach to some of them in Section 6

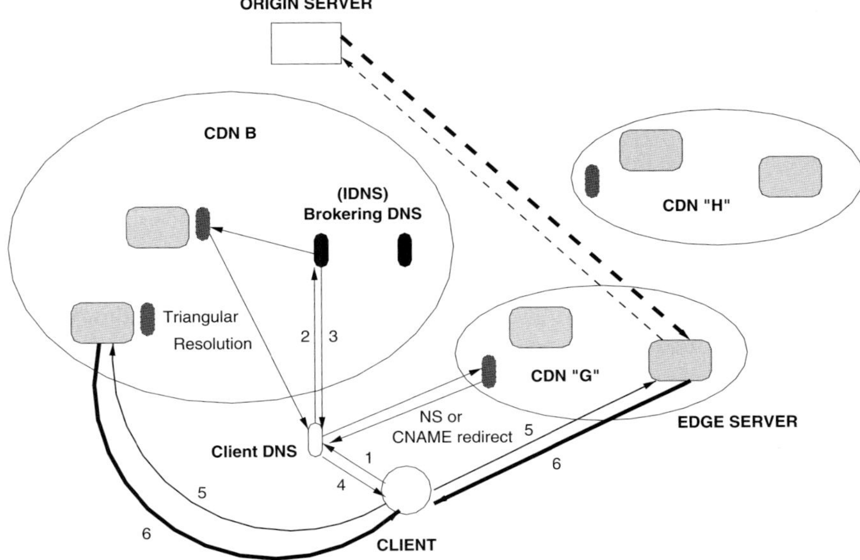

Fig. 1. High level schematic of the IDNS redirection mechanism.

below.) DNS systems use time-to-live (TTL) values to control the granularity of host assignments, and the selection of an appropriate TTL is important to balance the overhead of brokering against the impact of sending the clients of a particular client-side DNS server to one cache or CDN.

Assume that a customer has signed up for service with *B*, and a client requests content provided by this customer. The sequence of steps for a client to retrieve that content is as follows:

(1) The client attempts to resolve the domain name in the URL of the content piece hosted by *B* by sending a lookup request to the local Client DNS, unless the client has an unexpired response already cached.
(2) The Client DNS eventually contacts one of the brokering DNS servers (BDS) that is authoritative for that domain.
(3) The BDS then selects one of the following possibilities depending on the control policy that it supports:

Serve externally: A DNS-based brokering mechanism forwards the request to another CDN via DNS CNAME or NS response. The client DNS server resolves this response further to retrieve an A record. This approach is described further in Section 3.3.1.

Serve internally: If the BDS selects *B*'s own CDN, it has several options depending on whether it can assign a specific (virtual) cache directly:

- Return an A record that contains the IP address of a server within its own CDN. This is the most efficient option, but it requires the closest cooperation between the BDS and the rest of the brokering CDN, *B*.
- Perform a triangular resolution; i.e., forward the DNS query to a DNS resolver for *B*'s CDN, and let that DNS server respond directly to the client DNS server.
- Redirect the client DNS server explicitly to *B*'s internal DNS server, using the same techniques as for external CDNs.

(4) The Client DNS forwards the IP address (DNS A record) of the selected edge server to the client.
(5) The client sends the request for the content to the selected edge server.
(6) The edge server satisfies the client request either by serving it from its cache or from the origin server.

3.3. Naming

The previous subsection described how a client is directed to a server that will provide the requested content. Here we discuss how that server is selected within the partner network and how it knows what content to provide. These two issues are related, as they determine the naming conventions that different CDNs can use to internetwork.

3.3.1. DNS mapping

In Section 3.2, we described a choice in which *B* redirects a client DNS server to *G* using CNAME or NS, but did not describe what hostnames would be used or what *G* would do once it receives a request. For NS redirection, *G* is made authoritative for the lowest level of the domain name; since it sees the original hostname for the customer, it knows exactly which host's content is being requested. For CNAME redirection, however, the client DNS server is given a new DNS name in *G*'s domain. If *G* treats all servers equivalently, it needs no special information at the time of the DNS query: it will resolve to a cache, and use the HOST header of the HTTP request to identify the content. But if *G* serves content for this customer only from some of its caches, it must identify the customer at the time of the DNS lookup, and *B* and G must agree on the format of that name.

We use *semantic mapping* to exchange that information. *B* transforms hostnames automatically when redirecting, for instance:

```
a.example.com -> a.example.com.B.G.com
```

In this case, the presence of CDN *B* in the domain name in *G*'s DNS namespace implies that *B* has redirected the request to *G*. Although this semantic mapping does not prevent the encoding of individual object IDs in the DNS name we do not encourage such an encoding. Such an encoding would increase the number of DNS names used and consequently the load on the DNS system.

3.3.2. Obtaining content

A second problem is allowing *G* to serve the requested content.

To go to the origin server, *G*'s cache must be able to find the IP address for a host serving the content of `a.example.com`. Typically, CDNs statically configure caches to have a 'back door' from which to obtain content on a miss in order to avoid loops that would redirect queries for the original hostname back into the CDN itself. They might identify hosts by a specific IP address (bypassing DNS) or a hostname that does not resolve via the CDN. This static configuration must be done for each brokered site.

3.4. Accounting

Currently, CDNs charge their customers based on usage. They are responsible for collecting usage information and for making that information available to the customers when they issue bills. CDNs may bill each other explicitly for usage, or perform other forms of settlement, but regardless there must be a mechanism to exchange that information. Both the Content Alliance and the Content Bridge organizations have efforts underway to standardize this exchange [3,13], and we expect to adopt those methods once they are standardized.

4. IDNS architecture

Fig. 2 shows the high-level IDNS architecture. IDNS consists of two main elements: a DNS element and a control element. The first contains the DNS engine process which receives and answers DNS queries from the network. The control element maintains configuration information, receives live feedback and updates the tables used by the DNS engine to resolve requests. Communication between the two elements is done using a TCP socket based DNS/control interface.

IDNS's control element is the heart of the IDNS system. It consists of a control component and a set of agents. The agents are used to configure, manage, and obtain load feedback information from remote systems. The control component contains a load balancing algorithm that takes input from the agents and produces a set of tables (or a

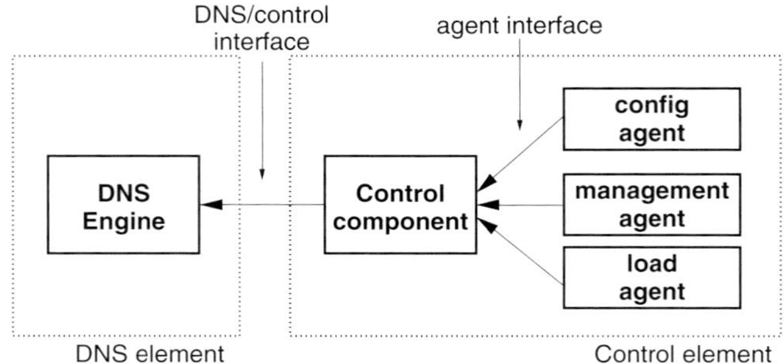

Fig. 2. Architectural overview of IDNS.

set of changes to the current tables) that are suitable for download into the DNS engine. These tables should contain the best distribution of CDN resolutions for a set of client regions, based on a given policy, that can be computed efficiently.

IDNS' configuration tables map client DNS server IP addresses to *regions* [11] and are used to select between CDNs serving a client's region by assigning a set of probability distributions. A region consists of a name and a set of IP prefixes associated with that region. Regions can be defined in many ways. For example, IP addresses can be grouped by IP-backbone connectivity or by country. Currently we use Krishnamurthy and Wang's [11] approach to clustering clients into regions. The control component passes the region definitions to the DNS element using a control update message. The DNS engine then uses an IP address longest prefix match subsystem to map a DNS server address to a region.

In the remainder of this section we examine the IDNS architecture in more detail.

4.1. DNS element

The DNS engine is a special-purpose DNS server, and was designed to be small and robust. Since it is a stand-alone process, other components of the IDNS system can fail and/or be restarted while the DNS engine will continue to resolve client DNS requests without interruption using its current configuration. The DNS element supports atomic updates to its database, and it continues to respond to DNS requests even when a database update is in progress. These features are achieved by taking advantage of the copy-on-write memory semantics provided by the UNIX kernel's virtual memory system.

4.1.1. DNS engine operations

At startup, the DNS engine initializes its tables, creates two sockets, and then enters its main loop. One socket is used to receive UDP DNS requests. The other is used for TCP DNS/control interface requests. These requests are processed one-at-a-time in the order they are received (requests received while an update is in progress are queued in the socket listen queue until they can be serviced). The TCP control connection has an inactivity timeout to prevent hung control processes from blocking access to the server.

The DNS element provides transactional update semantics to the control element. We use two processes, communicating via a pipe and sharing physical memory in a copy-on-write fashion, to ensure that exactly one process (with either the original or modified control tables) serves requests.

4.1.2. Table management

Internally, the DNS element stores its configuration in three types of data structures.

Region table: The region table, defined above, clusters all IP addresses into a set of regions. The DNS engine allows the fast matching of a given IP address into the region with the longest prefix match. A default region is used to handle IP addresses that cannot be mapped to any other region.

Distribution tables: There are multiple distribution tables, each being representative of a particular set of CDNs used to offer a particular service. Each of those distribution tables contains one entry per region, specifying what type of resolution should be used and to which CDN a DNS request should be resolved with which probability.

Customer table: The customer table associates customers defined by their DNS name with a particular distribution table. The reason for this level of indirection is that a distribution table is determined by the CDNs involved and that the same set of CDNs is likely to be used by multiple customers, though not every customer will use every CDN.

4.1.3. DNS engine lookup

To resolve a DNS request, the DNS engine first finds the client DNS server's region by searching the region table using longest prefix matching. It then maps the request to a distribution table using the requested DNS name and the customer table. Next, it determines a particular set of probabilities by using the region as an index in the distribution table. Using those probabilities, one of the CDNs in the selected entry of the distribution table is used to resolve the request. Therefore, the overall lookup overhead consists only of one longest prefix match, one hash table lookup, one array element lookup, and one simplified random number generation.

4.2. Control element

In this section we describe the control element data structures, load balancing, and control agents.

4.2.1. Control data structures

The control element's three main data structures used to describe brokering configuration are regions, customers and CDNs. The region data structure, as described in section 4.1.2, is used to cluster IP addresses into a more manageable set of regions. Customer entries consist of a brokered domain name, an origin domain name, and a set of CDNs that the customer may use. CDN entries consist of a name, capacity and current usage (expressed as bandwidth), the quality with which a CDN covers a given region, and a redirection method. Each region is assigned a coverage value indicating how well the region is covered by that CDN and this information is used for load balancing as described in the next section. The redirection method must be one of 'address' 'NS' or 'CNAME.'

Generally speaking, the control element configuration described by these data structures is dynamically adjusted by the control component using input from the control agents (see Section 4.2.3).

4.2.2. Load balancing

The main purpose of the control component is to asynchronously recalculate and update the tables used by the DNS engine according to current loads and a given policy.

The load balancing algorithm has to determine the mapping of `<region,set of CDNs>` to a probability distribution. This means that a client in the specified region will be redirected to a particular CDN with the given probability if the client requested the Web site of a customer which uses a particular set of CDNs. To provide protection against flash crowds while generally directing clients to nearby caches, the probability distribution has to be chosen carefully – considering how well a CDN covers a particular region and how much capacity is available.

Given the number of variables, the lack of predictability of client demand, and the possibility of stale and incomplete feedback, the design of a robust and scalable control algorithm is a non-trivial task. Currently, our algorithm takes the following steps when considering where to send clients from a given region:

(1) Eliminate all CDNs that are overloaded
(2) From the remaining CDNs, keep those that serve this region best as determined by their coverage values
(3) For the CDNs identified in step 2, distribute the load among them based on any available information on current capacity.

While we do not claim that this algorithm is optimal it is unclear how much improvement would be obtained from more sophistication unless the load feedback mechanism (described next) is able to provide more precise and immediate load information than is currently available. Finding such an optimal algorithm is outside the scope of this paper.

4.2.3. Agents

As shown in Fig. 2 the Control component receives input from the following three agents:

Configuration Agent: initializes the Control component with the appropriate configuration.

Management Agent: has a Web-based GUI interface that allows run-time editing of various aspects of the control component.

Load Agent: provides load information retrieved from participating CDNs. We use a structured feedback protocol, over a secure channel, to report load-related information to the load agent. Load reports include request rates and bandwidth consumption, as well as available capacity, both aggregated and on a per-region basis.

5. Performance

The costs and benefits of CDN brokering in general, and our IDNS implementation in particular, can be grouped into three categories. The first category is the performance of the brokering DNS server. The performance of a single DNS server directly influences the number of DNS servers required to support a particular site and, therefore, the capital cost of the deployment. The second category is the delay imposed by the additional level of redirection necessary to support brokering. This additional delay is the major potential cost of CDN brokering in terms of overall latency as perceived by a client. The third category consists of the potential benefits of CDN brokering: increased capacity, reduced cost, higher fault tolerance and better performance. Since we were not able to test the first three benefits in our live network, we will concentrate on a case study of the possible performance benefits.

5.1. IDNS performance

Since there is no established benchmark for evaluating the performance of DNS servers we will focus on the rate of DNS requests the server can answer successfully to measure its performance. This rate determines how many IDNS servers are required to support a given client population.

5.1.1. Test setup

To measure DNS request rates, we connected an IDNS server running FreeBSD 5.0 on a Dell PowerEdge 2450 Server with one 730MHz Pentium III processor and 1GB of RAM to a set of five DNS client simulators via gigabit Ethernet. To determine the best performance with an idle control component and an idle set of agents, we measured the maximum number of requests the server can sustain while supporting a configuration of five CDNs, 50 customers, and 250 regions.

In addition to performance without update load, we repeated the experiment while generating one load agent, capacity agent, or management agent update per second on the control component. Note that in this test we did not allow updates to the DNS engine to be aggregated (this would have reduced the load). The generated management updates randomly changed the number of CDNs, customers, and regions in the range from 1–10 CDNs, 1–100 customers, and 1–500 regions. This experiment represents the behavior of an extremely busy IDNS server. Note that IDNS scales to a real 'user community' by deploying a number of servers in proportion to the customer load.

We also examined the worst-case behavior of the IDNS server by using a control component that generates updates as fast as possible. In this test, the number of CDNs, customers, and regions used is in the same ranges as above.

5.1.2. Results

Fig. 3 shows the rate of successful DNS requests as a function of time. Both the experiment with no control updates and with one update per second show little variance and can sustain 8700 and 6800 requests per second respectively. Not surprisingly, the maximum control load experiment shows high variance, but the average rate is still on the order of 2000 requests per second.

Overall, the rate of 6800 requests per second in a realistic setting is fast enough to support multiple brokered sites. At that rate if a DNS timeout of five minutes is used by IDNS, an IDNS server can handle 2,040,000 client DNS servers (more than currently exist in the Internet). Since RFC1034 [12] requires two DNS servers for any site on the Internet, a realistic setup could serve up to 4,080,000 client DNS servers. The load on an individual IDNS server is even further reduced by the fact that some major browser implement in-memory DNS caching with essentially no timeouts.

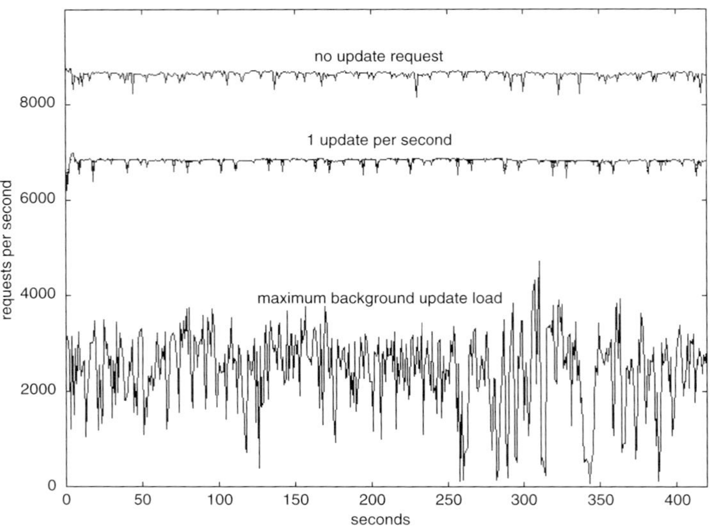

Fig. 3. IDNS performance.

5.2. Redirection overhead

Our second set of measurements help determine the overhead of additional DNS lookups imposed by the extra level of redirection necessary to support brokering. To evaluate this overhead we used six test Web sites and measured their performance from the view of almost 25,000 client DNS servers. (This list of client DNS servers was acquired using packet traces.)

5.2.1. Test setup

The test setup consists of six test sites and a measurement machine. On the measurement machine we used the `dig` DNS tool to issue requests to a list of 24,712 DNS servers. The six test sites fall into the following three categories:

Regular Site: One test site is a regular Web site included as a base case. The DNS server for this site directly returns an A record of a single Web server.

CDN Sites: Four of the test sites each use their own real-life CDNs to serve their content. These sites are used to show the typical DNS delay across four regular CDNs. Each of these sites use a CNAME record to redirect the DNS resolution of a client DNS server to their CDN. The CDNs then resolve the CNAME in accordance to their DNS-based redirection mechanism. Our results are averaged across the four CDNs measured.

Brokered Site: The final test site is brokered using IDNS. On this site, a client DNS server first requests the resolution from the authoritative DNS server of the site which redirects the client DNS server to the IDNS server using a CNAME. The IDNS server in turn redirects the client DNS server to one of four CDNs chosen randomly from the four CDNs measured above. Thus, the average of the four CDN sites is directly comparable to the results returned by the brokered site.

To measure the DNS delay of resolving the six test sites, we request a recursive resolution of the test site domain name twice in short succession from each client DNS server on our list. The first request triggers a resolution of the domain name using the remote DNS server as client DNS server. The second request is fulfilled from the cache on the remote DNS server and is used to calculate the delay from our measurement machine to the remote DNS server being probed. Thus, the delay imposed by the DNS resolution as seen by the remote DNS server is the difference between the first and second measurements.

We performed this experiment in two settings:

Cold Client DNS: In the cold client DNS experiment, we waited for more than two days between each run of the experiment to ensure that it was unlikely that the remote DNS server had any parts of the DNS records required to fulfill the resolution cached. A delay of two days is necessary because the root and top-level name servers specify a two-day TTL on the top-level DNS records.

'Lukewarm' Client DNS: In the 'lukewarm' client DNS experiment we performed each experiment twice, first to prime the caches of the client DNS servers, then 70 minutes later to measure the 'lukewarm' performance. A delay of 70 minutes times out the CNAME and A records; however, it most likely retains the supporting DNS records in the cache of the client DNS server.

The first experiment represents the behavior for a first hit to a site from a DNS server. The second experiment represents a subsequent request to the site and is therefore more representative of what a real user would perceive on a busy site.

5.2.2. Results

Table 1 and Table 2 summarize the results of the DNS delay measurements.

The first column indicates the percentage of DNS resolutions for which `dig` returned a valid result. `Dig` may not succeed if too many of the DNS datagrams required to recursively resolve the DNS name are dropped by the network. Another source of unsuccessful requests occurs when the request sent from the measurement machine to the remote DNS server is dropped. It is not surprising that the more complex resolution of a DNS name pointing to a CDN has a higher chance of a unsuccessful resolution.

Table 1. DNS delay with cold client DNS server cache

Measurement	Success rate	Average delay	Standard deviation
Regular site	99.3%	260 ms	36 ms
CDN average	96.0%	842 ms	22 ms
Brokered site	92.7%	993 ms	81 ms

Table 2. DNS delay with lukewarm client DNS server cache. The deviation was measured over ten runs

Measurement	Success rate	Average delay	Standard deviation
Regular site	99.8%	218 ms	29 ms
CDN average	97.3%	756 ms	83 ms
Brokered site	93.3%	843 ms	103 ms

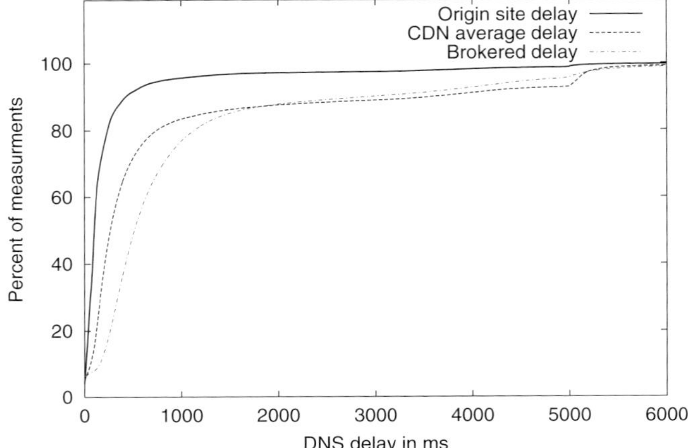

Fig. 4. DNS delay with cold DNS cache.

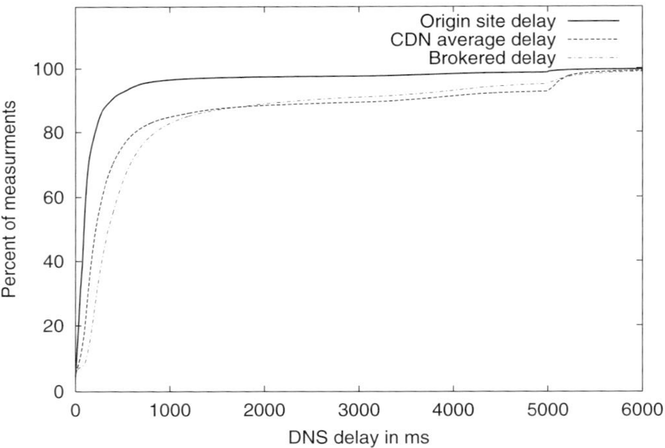

Fig. 5. DNS delay with lukewarm DNS cache.

Overall, the delay added by brokering on cold client DNS servers is on the order of 150 ms. In the more realistic case of lukewarm client DNS servers, the delay added (about 87 ms) is substantially smaller. It is interesting to observe that the gap between the CDN accelerated Web site and the origin site on a cold client DNS server is the order of 582 ms and in the case of lukewarm client DNS servers, the overhead imposed by CDNs is on the order of 538 ms.

Fig. 4 and Fig. 5 show the cumulative delay distribution of the cold and hot client DNS server experiment. In both figures the delay distributions for the CDNs and the brokered site show a bend at the five second mark. This represents a DNS timeout triggered by the loss of one or more DNS datagrams. Comparing the delay distributions, the higher average delay of the CDN and brokered sites seem to originate from the larger number of such DNS timeouts and the associated resolution time of more than five seconds.

5.3. Overall performance

In addition to the potential benefits of increased CDN capacity, reduced cost and better fault tolerance, brokering may also offers the opportunity to improve the performance of a Web site. To illustrate this point we performed a case study on two real CDNs: *G* and *H*. We refer to these CDNs anonymously because our purpose is to demonstrate the merits of brokering rather than to comprehensively evaluate specific CDNs (as in [10]). Note that neither CDN is owned by AT&T.

5.3.1. Test setup

First we establish the performance of *G* and *H* in different locations. To do this we downloaded two Web pages hosted by the CDNs from eleven different locations. The Web site used for *G* has a size of 39179 bytes and the Web site of *H* contains a total of 43944 bytes. Both pages consisted of one main HTML object containing thirteen embedded images. The test browser in each location first downloaded the HTML page and then downloaded the embedded images using four parallel connections. The experiment was performed at the same time for each CDN and repeated ten times.

Fig. 6 shows the results of the experiment. For each CDN, two values are reported. The values reported in Fig. 6a are the initial delay until the first byte is received, not including the DNS lookup delay. The values reported in Fig. 6b are the throughput on the application level in KBytes per second. The results show that neither *G* nor *H* performed better than the other in all eleven locations. In fact, in terms of throughput, *G* performed better in five locations whereas *H* performed better in six locations. The data shows that CDN brokering can be used to leverage the strength of both CDNs. Under the assumption that IDNS redirects each client to the better performing CDN, the average initial delay would decrease to 0.30 seconds and the average throughput would increase to 82,122 bytes per second. Compared to the 50,342 and 52,432 bytes per second each individual CDN can achieve, this is a substantial improvement.

As our case study shows, using two real CDNs measured from eleven locations, CDN brokering may not only provide benefits in terms of overload protection, cost and fault tolerance, but it also can provide performance benefits. However, it should be noted that the case study represents a limited measurement, and different CDNs and/or client sites will undoubtedly provide different results. Over time we expect to support many more types of customers using a variety of partner networks, as we further refine our algorithms and architecture.

6. Related work

Our content brokering proposal involves the symbiotic cooperation of multiple autonomous CDNs. Two recently announced efforts also aim at cooperation between autonomous content-delivering platforms. Content Bridge [6] is a standardization effort by an alliance of companies. Its goal is to allow cooperation between reverse proxy platforms (such as CDNs) and forward proxy platforms, so that CDNs ensure freshness of the their content cached by forward proxies, while forward proxies provide the CDNs with hit statistics of CDNs' content in return. The *content bridge* is a middleware layer between CDNs and forward proxies that facilitates this type of cooperation. In contrast, CDN

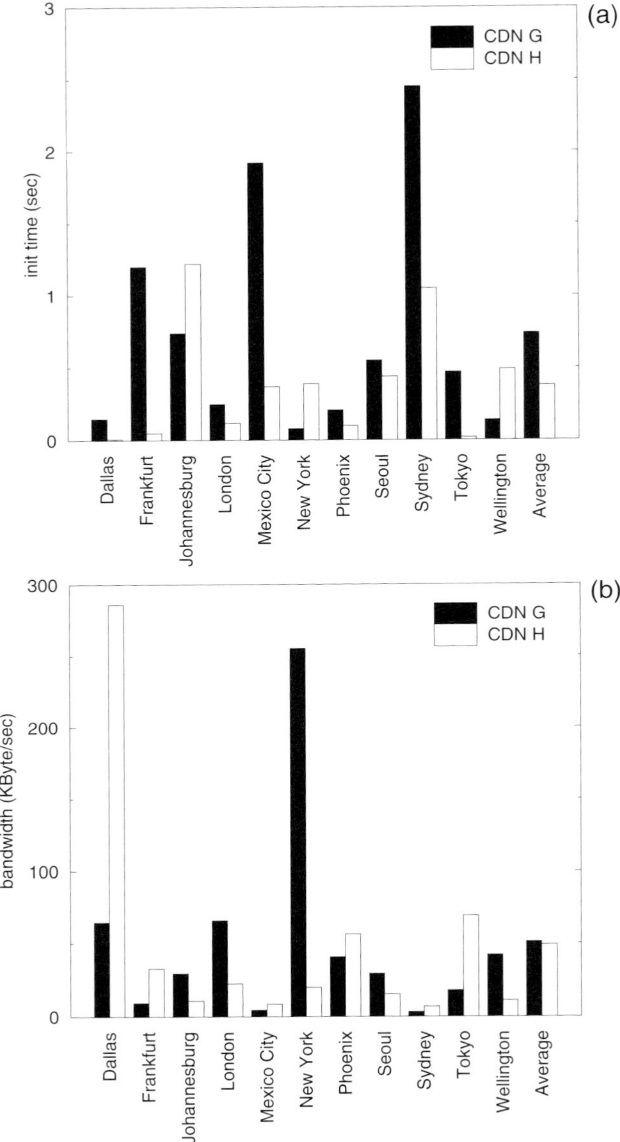

Fig. 6. Measurements for each CDN in each location.

brokering enables cooperation between CDNs with the ultimate goal of improving access to their content. Thus, the two proposals are orthogonal and complimentary.

The Content Alliance [5] is a standardization effort, organized initially by Cisco, whose goal is to develop standards for inter-CDN cooperation of the kind exemplified by our CDN brokering system. We are actively participating in this effort, which incorporates many of our ideas.

DNS-based load balancing has been widely used for load distribution among Web servers or caches; various products in this area include Alteon's GSLB [1] and Cisco's Distributed Director [4]. These companies disclose few details about their load balancing algorithms. Unlike these DNS-based implementations, CDN brokering uses DNS to load balance among entire CDNs.

Finally, Shaikh and Tewari [15] consider the problem of measuring the network proximity of client DNS servers with HTTP clients. This issue obviously has direct relevance to CDNs, which crucially rely on the assumption that the origins of a DNS query are indicative of the origins of the corresponding HTTP request. Our implementation of CDN brokering relies on this assumption as well, since it is also DNS-based. If this assumption is definitively shown to not hold, it will provide extra motivation for brokering using alternate mechanisms.

7. Conclusion

Content distribution internetworking is a new area, and the techniques and issues involved are actively being explored by ourselves and others. Here we have attempted to motivate the need for CDI: rather than one service trying to be omnipresent, which is demanding in both capital and manpower, a CDN can leverage agreements with other networks to provide good performance at an appropriately low cost. CDN brokering is a form of CDI that uses DNS outsourcing to permit a specialized DNS server to select a CDN at the time of hostname resolution.

IDNS, our patent-pending system for CDN brokering, is the first working example of this functionality of which we are aware. We have measured the scalability of the IDNS DNS server and the overhead of adding an extra level of indirection through the brokerage. We are currently supporting a limited number of AT&T customers using IDNS.

Acknowledgments

We would like to thank Kobus van der Merwe and Zhen Xiao for reading earlier drafts of the paper and giving us valuable comments. We would also like to thank the anonymous reviewers, who provided valuable feedback.

References

[1] Alteon Web Systems, Inc. Enhancing web user experience with global server load balancing White paper. http://www.alteonwebsystems.com/products/white_papers/GSLB/index.shtml.

[2] A. Barbir, B. Cain, F. Douglis, M. Green, M. Hofmann, R. Nair, D. Potter, and O. Spatscheck. *Known CDN Request-Routing Mechanisms*, Feb. 2001. Work in Progress, draft-cain-cdnp-known-request-routing-01.txt.

[3] B. Cain, P. Rzewski, and N. Robertson. *Cross-Network Accounting for HTTP*, Nov. 2000. Work in Progress, draft-rzewski-cnacct-00.txt.

[4] Cisco Systems, Inc. DistributedDirector. White paper. http://www.cisco.com/warp/public/734/distdir/dd_wp.htm.

[5] Content Alliance. http://www.content-peering.org.

[6] Content Bridge. http://www.content-bridge.com.

[7] M. Day, B. Cain, and G. Tomlinson. *A Model for CDN Peering*, Nov. 2000. Work in Progress, draft-day-cdnp-model-04.txt.

[8] M. Day and D. Gilletti. *Content Distribution Network Peering Scenarios*, Nov. 2000. Work in Progress, draft-day-cdnp-scenarios-02.txt.

[9] M. Green, B. Cain, G. Tomlinson, and S. Thomas. *CDN Peering Architectural Overview*, Nov. 2000. Work in Progress, draft-green-cdnp-gen-arch-02.txt.

[10] K.L. Johnson, J.F. Carr, M.S. Day, and M.F. Kaashoek. The measured performance of content distribution networks. In *Proceedings of the 5th International Web Caching and Content Delivery Workshop*, May 2000.

[11] B. Krishnamurthy and J. Wang. On network-aware clustering of Web clients. In *Proceedings of ACM SIGCOMM 2000*, pages 97–110, Aug. 2000.

[12] P.V. Mockapetris. RFC 1034: Domain names - concepts and facilities, Nov. 1987.

[13] R. Nair, D. Gilletti, and J. Scharber. *CDN Peering Authentication, Authorization, and Accounting Requirements*, Nov. 2000. Work in Progress, draft-gilletti-cdnp-aaa-reqs-00.txt.

[14] Y. Rekhter and T. Li. RFC 1771: A Border Gateway Protocol 4 (BGP-4), Mar. 1995.

[15] A. Shaikh and R. Tewari. On the effectiveness of DNS-based server selection. IBM Research Report RC 21785, IBM Thomas J. Watson Research Center, 2000.

Web Caching and Content Delivery
A. Bestavros and M. Rabinovich (Editors)

Synopsis

Optimising Web Services with Intermediaries

Mark Nottingham [1]

Akamai Technologies

Abstract

Intermediaries are often used to scale the Web infrastructure, offering improved performance, availability and scalability of services. This brief explores the possibilities of scaling Web services (services exposed by XML messaging solutions like SOAP and XML protocol) through optimisation in intermediaries, and proposes further work which leverages XML protocol's features to help scale them and improve performance.

1. Introduction

As the Web has grown, there has been an increasing need to address issues such as the scalability (the ability to handle growth in load efficiently), performance (as measured by the end users' perceived latency) and availability of Web sites. Intermediary solutions to these problems have been used for some time; first as caching proxies, and later in Content Delivery Networks, which use surrogates (intermediaries which act on behalf of the server, rather than the client) dispersed widely over the network to provide service.

HTTP intermediaries rely on certain aspects of requests and responses flowing through them to offer these benefits. For example, caching works because requests can be easily identified (through the Request-URI and a few headers), and the responses associated with them can be reused according to the HTTP's cache coherence rules.

While Web services use lower-layer intermediaries (such as HTTP proxies and surrogates or SMTP relays) for transit, those devices' optimisation mechanisms aren't aware of the semantics of a Web services message, and therefore can't fully exploit them.

For example, while it's possible to describe cacheability for a Web service's underlying HTTP response (e.g., with a Cache-Control or Expires header), this is only a basic means of providing hints about the message. In the best case, an HTTP cache would be indexed on the entire request as a string, meaning that a trivial change in the request's XML would cause it to be indexed as a separate entity.

This means that, by default, only the simplest Web services can leverage intermediaries for optimisation in very limited ways.

To allow intermediaries to more fully optimise Web services, such optimisation need

[1] E-mail: mnot@akamai.com

to be standardized, just as cacheability information for lower-layer HTTP entities is standardized in the HTTP. This will allow intermediaries to optimise a broad range of Web services without service-specific code being executed.

This paper outlines potential use cases for Web service intermediary optimisation, proposes a framework for optimisation, and identifies potential optimisation techniques.

2. Optimisation use cases

Although tentative, these use cases help illustrate the potential of optimising Web service intermediaries.

3. StockQuote service

By caching response elements containing rapidly-changing financial data for a period, a Stock Quote service could offer enhanced end-user perceived performance whilst reducing load on centralized servers. Furthermore, slowly-changing data in the same response could be given separate, longer-term cacheability, with different criteria for invalidation from the cache.

4. News service

An XML-based news 'channel' service can take advantage of a regular publication schedule to cache article summaries with an absolute time until validation (with the possibility of using partial content updates). Additionally, because some servers may provide many such services, channel requests and responses may be aggregated into a single message interchange for efficiency.

5. Distributed authentication service

A centralized Web site user authentication service can exploit geographic locality in client behaviour by allowing a distributed group of caches to keep authentication state, rendered as XML, at the 'edge' of the network. If the user changes their password, the request for change can act as a trigger for invalidating the cached entry.

6. File store service

An 'Internet hard drive' service, where users write to and read from a service as if it were a network-available disk, could be distributed to a number of 'edge' servers to improve end-user perceived latency by exploiting locality in their access patterns. This could be achieved through a combination of store-and-forward into a cache (i.e., write caching), reading from the cache, and invalidation events to stimulate synchronisation with a centralized server.

7. Order queue service

With store-and-forward techniques, service intermediaries can provide higher availability for a service than a centralized server alone, whilst offering the potential to manage load on the central server by aggregating messages to it.

8. Voting, poll and auction services

'Interactive' services can take advantage of 'best-guess' information in cache whilst updating critical information through message triggers and element invalidations.

9. Further work

This brief attemps to motivate research regarding optimising mechanisms in service intermediaries. Hopefully, this will generate interest in standardization of such techniques, development of a framework for their use, and integration into Web service toolkits and products.

Web Caching and Content Delivery
A. Bestavros and M. Rabinovich (Editors)

Object Replication Strategies in Content Distribution Networks

Jussi Kangasharju [a,1], James Roberts [b], Keith W. Ross [a]

[a] *Institut Eurécom, Sophia Antipolis, France*
[b] *France Télécom R&D, Issy-les-Moulineaux, France*

Abstract

Recently the Internet has witnessed the emergence of content distribution networks (CDNs). In this paper we study the problem of optimally replicating objects in CDN servers. In our model, each Internet Autonomous System (AS) is a node with finite storage capacity for replicating objects. The optimization problem is to replicate objects so that when clients fetch objects from the nearest CDN server with the requested object, the average number of ASs traversed is minimized. We formulate this problem as a combinatorial optimization problem. We show that this optimization problem is NP complete. We develop four natural heuristics and compare them numerically using real Internet topology data. We find that the best results are obtained with heuristics that have all the CDN servers cooperating in making the replication decisions. We also develop a model for studying the benefits of cooperation between nodes, which provides insight into peer-to-peer content distribution.

Keywords: Optimal replication strategies; Content distribution networks; Peer-to-peer networks; Cooperation

1. Introduction

Recently the Internet has witnessed the emergence of content distribution networks (CDNs). CDNs are targeted for speeding up the delivery of normal Web content and reduce the load on the origin servers and the network. CDNs, such as Akamai [1] or Digital Island [4], distribute content by placing it on content servers which are located near the users. A content provider can sign up for the service and have its content placed on the content servers. The content is replicated either on-demand when users request it, or it can be replicated beforehand, by pushing the content on the content servers.

In this paper we study the problem of optimally replicating objects in CDN servers. We consider each AS as a node in a graph with one CDN server with finite storage capacity for replicating objects. The optimization problem is to replicate objects so that the average number of ASs traversed is minimized when clients fetch objects from the nearest CDN server containing the requested object. We formulate this problem as

[1] E-mail: kangasha@eurecom.fr

a combinatorial optimization problem and show that this optimization problem is NP complete. We develop four natural heuristics and compare them numerically using real Internet topology data. Our results show that the best results are obtained with heuristics that have all the CDN servers cooperating in making the replication decisions. We also develop a model for studying the benefits of cooperation between nodes in a peer-to-peer networking context.

This paper is organized as follows. Section 2 presents the network topologies we used. In Section 3 we develop our cost model. Section 4 presents the replication heuristics we have developed and Section 5 presents our evaluation methods and results. Section 6 presents peer-to-peer content distribution and develops and evaluates a model for cooperation in peer-to-peer networks. Section 7 discusses related work. Finally, Section 8 concludes the paper and presents directions for future work.

2. Network model

Our network model is based on the actual Internet AS topology. To construct the topology, we will use data provided by NLANR [12]. This data represents summaries of Internet routing data collected in the Route Views Project [15] from 1997 to beginning of 2000. These summaries provide information about which ASs are connected to each other. From these summaries we constructed a graph where the nodes are the ASs and the edges are the inter-AS connections. We then calculated the shortest paths between all the node pairs, and used this data to form a distance matrix for the network.

As discussed in [5], this method is slightly inaccurate because we cannot infer that all the connections are valid. For example, consider a small ISP that buys connectivity from two bigger ISPs. For each of the providers, our graph will show an edge between the small ISP and the provider, but in reality the small ISP would not route traffic from one of its providers to another. This is not likely to be a problem, though, since in most cases the two providers in this case either have a direct link between them or are able to connect via a common provider.

A CDN tries to put its content servers as close to users as possible. By placing the clients and the content servers (storage nodes in our network) in the same nodes, we can simulate the ideal redirection where all clients are always redirected to the closest server (the redirection in this case is static). By studying different replication strategies we can determine which strategies a CDN should use when deciding which objects to replicate. Because a CDN has complete knowledge of its network, we can use strategies which require global information or cooperation.

2.1. Network topologies

We downloaded several different files from NLANR [12], each describing the AS topology on a different day. Table 1 shows the different topologies we used, the number of ASs in each one, the number of leaf ASs, the average length of the shortest path between any two nodes, and the average distance of the shortest path between any two leaf nodes.

From topologies in Table 1 and other topologies we downloaded (not shown), we see that the average distance between nodes tends to increase as the number of nodes in the network increases. It is also important to note that these topologies *do not* contain all of

Table 1. AS topologies

Date	Number of nodes	Number of leaf nodes	Average distance	Average leaf distance
97/12/21	3184	1423	3.76	4.34
99/01/11	549	136	3.40	4.18
99/12/08	767	222	3.03	3.38
99/12/11	1477	502	3.45	4.10

the ASs in the Internet, but only a subset of them. Therefore, the full Internet AS topology would likely have a higher average distance than any of the topologies we used.

3. Cost model

We consider a network where the nodes are the autonomous systems (ASs). For simplicity, we assume that one AS is the same as one ISP. We have I ASs in the network. AS i, $i \in 1, 2, \ldots, I$, has S_i bytes of storage capacity and has clients that request objects at aggregate rate λ_i.

We have J objects. Object j has a size of b_j, $j \in \{1, 2, \ldots, J\}$ and a request probability p_j which is the probability that a client will request this object. We assume that client request patterns are homogeneous, i.e., the p_j's are the same for all ASs. But this model can be extended to include other request patterns by using p_{ij}, which would be the request probability for object j from AS i.

We have the following variables:

$$x_{ij} = \begin{cases} 1 & \text{if object } j \text{ is stored at AS } i, \\ 0 & \text{otherwise.} \end{cases}$$

The storage is constrained by the space available at AS i, that is

$$\sum_{j=1}^{J} b_j x_{ij} \leq S_i \qquad i = 1, \ldots, I$$

The goal is to choose the x_{ij}'s so that a given performance metric is minimized. In this paper our goal is to minimize the average number of inter-AS hops that a request must traverse. This reflects the download time of an object to some degree and can thus be used as an indicator of the user perceived latency.

We denote the matrix of all x_{ij}'s by $\mathbf{x}$. Furthermore, we assume that each object j is initially placed on an origin server; we denote by O_j the AS that contains this origin server. We assume that all of the objects are always available in their origin servers, regardless of the placement $\mathbf{x}$. We denote the placement of objects to origin servers as $\mathbf{x}_o$. Note that this origin server placement does not count against the storage capacity S_{O_j}.

The average number of hops that a request must traverse from AS i is

$$C_i(\mathbf{x}) = \sum_{j=1}^{J} p_j d_{ij}(\mathbf{x}) \tag{1}$$

where $d_{ij}(\mathbf{x})$ is the shortest distance to a copy of object j from AS i under the placement

$\mathbf{x}$. This nearest copy is either in the origin AS O_j, or in another AS where the object has been replicated. We assume that the client is always redirected to the nearest copy. In this paper we do not consider the mechanisms used to redirect clients, but instead assume that such a mechanism is in place.

Let $\Lambda = \sum_i \lambda_i$ be the total request rate of all ASs. The average number of hops from all ASs is then

$$C(\mathbf{x}) = \frac{1}{\Lambda}\sum_{i=1}^{I}\lambda_i C_i(\mathbf{x}) = \frac{1}{\Lambda}\sum_{i=1}^{I}\sum_{j=1}^{J}\lambda_i p_j d_{ij}(\mathbf{x}) = \sum_{i=1}^{I}\sum_{j=1}^{J} s_{ij} d_{ij}(\mathbf{x}) \tag{2}$$

where $s_{ij} = \lambda_i p_j/\Lambda$. The placement $\mathbf{x}$ is subject to

$$\sum_{j=1}^{J} b_j x_{ij} \le S_i \qquad i = 1, \ldots, I$$

This cost function represents the long term average cost. For a large number of objects and ASs, it is not feasible to solve this problem optimally; in fact, as we show in the next section, this problem is NP-complete.

3.1. Proving NP-completeness

In order to prove that our optimization problem is NP-complete, we first formulate the problem as a decision problem. Given a target number of hops T, we ask is there a placement $\mathbf{x}$ such that

$$\sum_{i=1}^{I}\sum_{j=1}^{J} s_{ij} d_{ij}(\mathbf{x}) \le T$$

subject to

$$\sum_{j=1}^{J} b_j x_{ij} \le S_i \qquad i = 1, \ldots, I$$

We prove the NP-completeness of this problem by showing that it belongs in NP and then we reduce the knapsack problem to a special case of our problem. This proves the NP-completeness.

The problem is easily seen to be in NP. Given a placement $\mathbf{x}$ and number of hops T, we can verify in polynomial time whether the placement results in an average cost of less than T hops.

Next, we consider the special case where $S_1 = S$, $S_i = 0$, $i = 2, \ldots, I$, $\lambda_i = \lambda$, $i = 1, \ldots, I$, $p_j = p$, $j = 1, \ldots, J$, i.e., we have only one AS on which to place objects, all ASs have the same request rate, and all objects are equally popular.

Recall that each object j is always available at the origin AS O_j. The cost of getting object j for a client in AS i is $d_{ij}(\mathbf{x}_o)$. Because all clients always go to the nearest copy, placing copies on the only available AS can only decrease the cost for any client, i.e., $d_{ij}(\mathbf{x}) \le d_{ij}(\mathbf{x}_o)$ for all i and j. We define the utility of placing object j on AS i as $u(j) = \sum_i [d_{ij}(\mathbf{x}_o) - d_{ij}(\mathbf{x})]$, i.e., the decrease in number of hops we would obtain if we placed object j in the AS.

Given target decrease in number of hops T' we now ask if there is a set of objects J' such that

$$\sum_{j \in J'} b_j \leq S \quad \text{and} \quad \sum_{j \in J'} u(j) \geq T'$$

This problem is identical to the well-known NP-complete knapsack problem [6]. Given that our placement problem belongs in NP and that the knapsack problem reduces to it, we know that our placement problem is NP-complete.

4. Replication heuristics

Because our optimization problem is NP-complete, finding the optimal solution is not feasible. Therefore we have designed several heuristics that use the available information in different ways in order to get the best results.

In our simulations we use the following heuristics.

(1) **Random.** Assigns objects to storage nodes randomly subject to the storage constraints. We pick one object with uniform probability and one node with uniform probability, and we store the object in that node. If the node already stores that object, we pick a new object and a new node. As a result, an object can be assigned to several nodes, but a node will have at maximum one copy of an object.

(2) **Popularity.** Each node stores the most popular objects among its clients. The node sorts the objects in decreasing order of popularity and stores as many objects in this order as the storage constraint allows. The node can estimate the popularities by observing the requests it receives form its clients. This heuristic does not require the node to get any information from outside of the node. Note that in our case, the object popularities p_j are the same across all nodes, hence all the nodes will store the objects in the same order but subject to different storage constraints.

(3) **Greedy-Single.** Each node i calculates $C_{ij}=p_j d_{ij}(\mathbf{x}_o)$ for each object j. This represents the contribution of an individual object to (1) under the initial placement. The node then sorts the objects in decreasing order of C_{ij} and stores as many objects in this order as the storage constraint allows. The popularities are obtained as in the <it>Popularity</it> heuristics, but the CDN also needs information about the network topology in order to estimate the d_{ij}'s. Note that the C_{ij}'s are calculated only once under the placement $\mathbf{x}_o$ and are not adjusted when objects are stored. This means that every node stores objects independently of all the other nodes and no cooperation between nodes is required.

(4) **Greedy-Global.** The CDN first calculates $C_{ij} = \lambda_i p_j d_{ij}(\mathbf{x}_o)$ for all nodes i and objects j. Then the CDN picks the node-object-pair which has the highest C_{ij} and stores that object in that node. This results in a new placement $\mathbf{x}_1$. Then the CDN re-calculates the costs C_{ij} under the new placement and pick the node-object-pair that has the highest cost. We store that object in that node and obtain a new placement $\mathbf{x}_2$. We iterate this until all the storage nodes have been filled.

We do not consider any variants of these base heuristics, such as using popularity divided by object size, but evaluate only the performance of the base heuristics. Different variants of these heuristics have been studied in the context of Web caching (see [8] and references therein) and any such improvements could be used directly to enhance the performance of our heuristics.

5. Evaluation of heuristics

We evaluated the performances of our heuristics using the topologies from Section 2.1. We ran each heuristic on each topology using different parameters for object popularity and storage capacity in the nodes.

We assigned the popularities to the objects from a Zipf-like distribution where we varied the parameter from 0.6 to 1.0. Values between 0.6 and 0.8 have been typically observed in Web proxy traffic [2]. Much higher values, up to 1.4, have also been discovered in the context of popular Web servers [13]. Object sizes were randomly drawn from a uniform distribution. The storage capacity at each node was fixed to some percentage of the total size of the set of objects. We varied this percentage in the course of the experiments. All the client nodes had the same request rate λ.

We placed all the content servers at the leafs of the network, i.e., for all non-leaf ASs we set $S_i = 0$. Even though this assignment of storage capacity is artificial, it allows us to study the performances of our heuristics better. By placing all the storage capacity and objects at the edges, the average number of hops needed to obtain an object is higher than with a more realistic assignment. This makes it more important to replicate the right objects and lets us see more clearly the differences between our heuristics.

The baseline for our experiments was the initial placement $\mathbf{x}_o$ which we obtained by randomly assigning objects to storage nodes. We compared the performance of each of the heuristics to this baseline and report the relative performance obtained with each heuristic. Because the memory requirements for the experiments grow with the product IJ, we were not able to run all experiments for all the topologies.

Fig. 1 shows the results from experiments with 1000 objects. We only show results for two topologies, but we observed that the results for the remaining two were similar to the two shown here. On the x-axis we plot the amount of storage at a node as percentage of the total size of the objects. On the y-axis we plot the performance relative to the baseline. In each graph, we plot different curves for different heuristics and different values of the Zipf-parameter (0.6, and 1.0). Note that we only plot the *Random* heuristic with Zipf-parameter 1.0. The performance of the *Random* heuristic was similar for the other Zipf-values. The curves of the other heuristics for Zipf-values between 0.6 and 1.0 was between the curves plotted.

From Fig. 1 we can see that *Greedy-Global* is the best performing heuristic. The second best is *Greedy-Single*, followed closely by *Popularity*. *Random* heuristic is consistently the worst and does not achieve substantial reductions in number of hops, even for large storage capacities. As we mentioned, the performance of *Random* did not change much with different Zipf-parameter values.

As Fig. 1 shows, the gains increase logarithmically with increased storage capacity. The main determining factor is the Zipf-parameter value. The larger this value is, the smaller is the number of objects generating a large amount of requests. Thus, it is easy to significantly reduce the cost if only a small number of objects is very popular. To reduce the number of hops by 50%, we need only a small amount of storage for parameter 1.0 and up to 25% of total data set for parameter value 0.6.

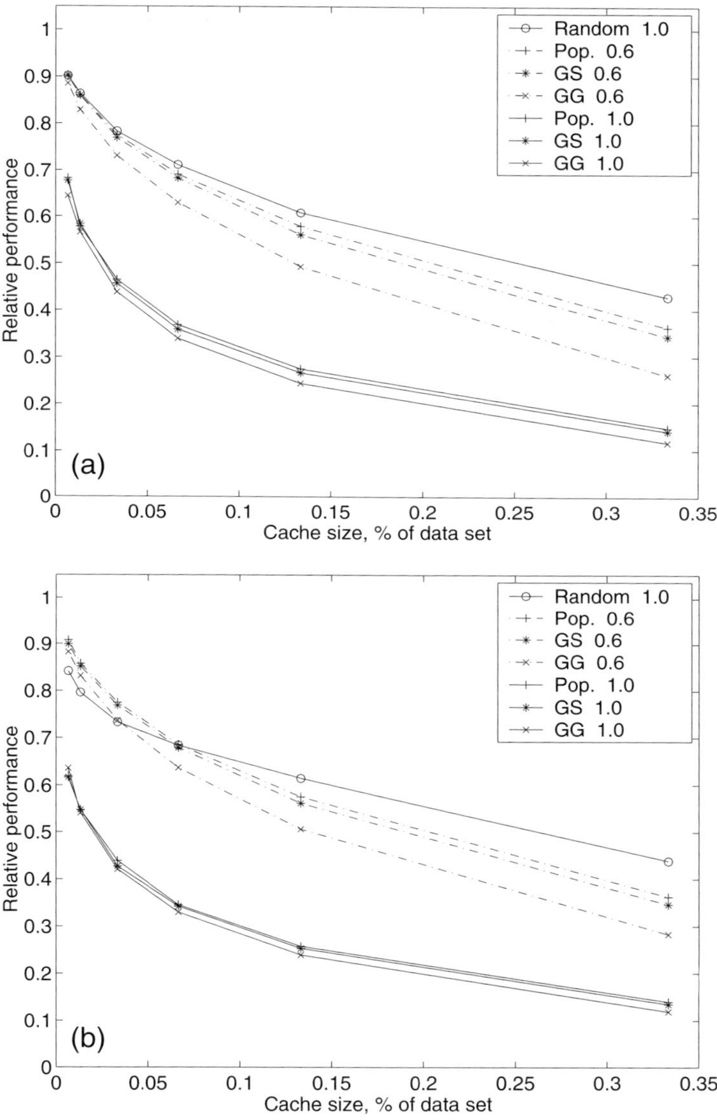

Fig. 1. Experiments with 1,000 objects. (a) 99/01/11; (b) 99/12/08.

In Fig. 2 we plot the results from experiments with 10,000 objects. Due to memory limitations, we were not able to run *Greedy-Global* for all the topologies, therefore it is not shown on the plots.

The results are very similar to the results from the previous experiment. *Random* is still the worst in terms of performance, but the difference between *Popularity* and *Greedy-Single* has decreased. This is because as the number of objects grows, the individual object popularities will get smaller. Therefore, the contribution of an individual object's retrieval cost to the global cost (2) will get proportionally smaller. Hence, the

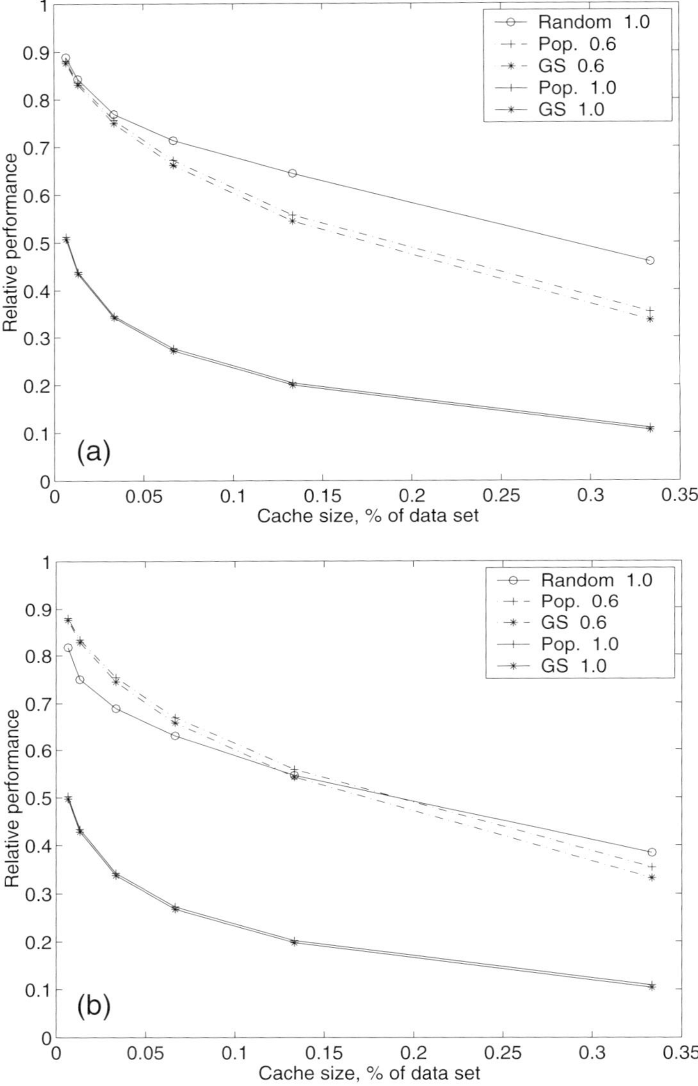

Fig. 2. Experiments with 10,000 objects. (a) 99/12/08; (b) 99/12/11

popularity of the object becomes more important in determining the cost. The product of popularity and distance used by *Greedy-Single* is still a slightly better indicator, but the difference is minimal.

From our results we can conclude that the best performance is obtained when the object replication is coordinated by a single source, in our case, this would be the CDN. The difference in performance between *Greedy-Global* and the other two heuristics is quite significant, especially for small Zipf-parameter values. In Fig. 1 we can see that the largest improvements in performance are up to 24%. This result shows that a *CDN should use a coordinated replication strategy* and not let the CDN servers act on their own.

6. Peer-to-peer content distribution

We now introduce a new form of content distribution, namely peer-to-peer content distribution. Peer-to-peer networks have recently emerged as a new form of content distribution and are mainly used to share individual files between users. In peer-to-peer networks, such as Napster [11], or Gnutella [7], individual users decide to share files with others. With the help of a directory service, users can determine where different files can be downloaded from. While this new model does not directly compete with the traditional Web browsing model, it is establishing itself as a means for distributing larger files, such as applications or music, between users. Because peer-to-peer networks are made up of individual users, we cannot use strategies which require global information and coordination of nodes as with CDNs. Instead we must restrict ourselves to strategies that need only locally available information; one example of such strategy is the *Popularity* heuristic.

As before, we assume that one AS in our network corresponds to one ISP. We can view the storage capacity in an AS as the aggregation of the peer-to-peer storage offered by the users in that AS. In a similar vein, $x_{ij} = 1$ means that at least one user in AS i has a copy of object j. We assume that the cost of retrieving objects from other users in the same AS is negligible; this is consistent with our definition of retrieval cost in Section 3. In this section we will investigate the benefits of cooperation between the users in different ASs. Our goal is to see if the users in a peer-to-peer network could gain anything from cooperating with other nearby users.

We will now develop a cooperation model for peer-to-peer content distribution under the popularity heuristic. For simplicity and ease of notation, we shall assume throughout this section that all objects have the same size, i.e., $b_j = b$ for $j = 1, \ldots, J$.

Consider two ASs, A and B. Denote the shortest path between them by D_{AB}. Let K be the number of objects that each AS can store. We do not assume anything about the relationship between the two ASs, except that the distance between them is D_{AB}. In particular, we do not assume that one is the access provider of the other one. We assume that $\lambda_A = \lambda_B$.

If both ASs act independently, they would both cache the K most popular objects and the average number of hops for requests from A and B would be

$$\frac{\lambda_A}{\lambda_A + \lambda_B} \sum_{j=K+1}^{J} p_j d_{Aj} + \frac{\lambda_A}{\lambda_A + \lambda_B} \sum_{j=K+1}^{J} p_j d_{Bj} = \frac{1}{2} \sum_{j=K+1}^{J} p_j d_{Aj} + \frac{1}{2} \sum_{j=K+1}^{J} p_j d_{Bj} \quad (3)$$

We now consider the case where the two ASs cooperate and do not necessarily both store the same objects. We assume that both of them store a copy of the L most popular objects ($L \leq K$), and that in addition A stores objects $(L+1), \ldots, K$, and B stores objects $(K+1), \ldots, (2K-L)$. Because the request rates are identical, it does not matter how the objects $(L+1), \ldots, (2K-L)$ are shared between A and B. Note that because of the same reason, we only need to consider replicating objects in A and B and not in the intermediate nodes.

The average number of hops for requests from A and B under this scheme is

$$\frac{1}{2}\sum_{j=K+1}^{2K-L} p_j D_{AB} + \frac{1}{2}\sum_{j=2K-L+1}^{J} p_j d_{Aj} + \frac{1}{2}\sum_{j=L+1}^{K} p_j D_{AB} + \frac{1}{2}\sum_{j=2K-L+1}^{J} p_j d_{Bj}$$
$$= \frac{1}{2}\sum_{j=L+1}^{2K-L} p_j D_{AB} + \frac{1}{2}\sum_{j=2K-L+1}^{J} (p_j d_{Aj} + p_j d_{Bj}) \tag{4}$$

The difference between (3) and (4) is

$$\frac{1}{2}\sum_{j=K+1}^{2K-L} (p_j d_{Aj} + p_j d_{Bj}) - \frac{1}{2}\sum_{j=L+1}^{2K-L} p_j D_{AB} \tag{5}$$

If (5) is greater than zero, then it is better for A and B to cooperate. By assuming $d_{Aj} = d_{Bj} = d_{\text{avg}}$, we can calculate the value of d_{avg} where cooperation becomes the preferred strategy. The equation becomes

$$\frac{1}{2}\sum_{j=K+1}^{2K-L} (p_j d_{\text{avg}} + p_j d_{\text{avg}}) - \frac{1}{2}\sum_{j=L+1}^{2K-L} p_j D_{AB} > 0 \tag{6}$$

Solving for d_{avg}, we get

$$d_{\text{avg}} > \frac{D_{AB}}{2} \frac{\sum_{j=L+1}^{2K-L} p_j}{\sum_{j=K+1}^{2K-L} p_j} \tag{7}$$

If (7) holds, then it is better for A and B to cooperate. Because d_{avg} is likely to be reasonably stable over long intervals and because p_j's are known to both parties, A and B can use (7) as a quick test to see whether they could gain anything by cooperating. For the test, A and B either need to specify the value of L or verify equation (7) over several values of L.

In the following, we will consider two values for D_{AB}, namely 1 and 2. If D_{AB} is equal to 1, then A and B are neighbors. We plotted (5) for several Zipf-parameter values, average distances d_{avg}, and values of K, and in all cases, cooperation is almost always superior to a non-cooperating strategy. In some instances, however, the difference between the two is small.

In Fig. 3 we show typical plots of (5). In these plots, we have 1,000 objects available and both nodes have capacity to store 50 objects, or 5% of the data set. We show two plots for two different values of the Zipf-distribution parameter. On the x-axis we plot the value of L, i.e., the number of objects stored at both A and B, and on the y-axis we show the value of (5), that is, the difference between individual and cooperative strategies in hops. If the difference is positive, then cooperation is better.

As we can see from the plots in Fig. 3, there are always some values of L for which cooperation gives better results, but in some cases the gains are small. We can see that as d_{avg} gets smaller, the gains become smaller. This is no surprise since a small d_{avg} means that the requested objects are typically already very close and cooperation would not help much. We also see that as d_{avg} increases, the potential gains increase significantly.

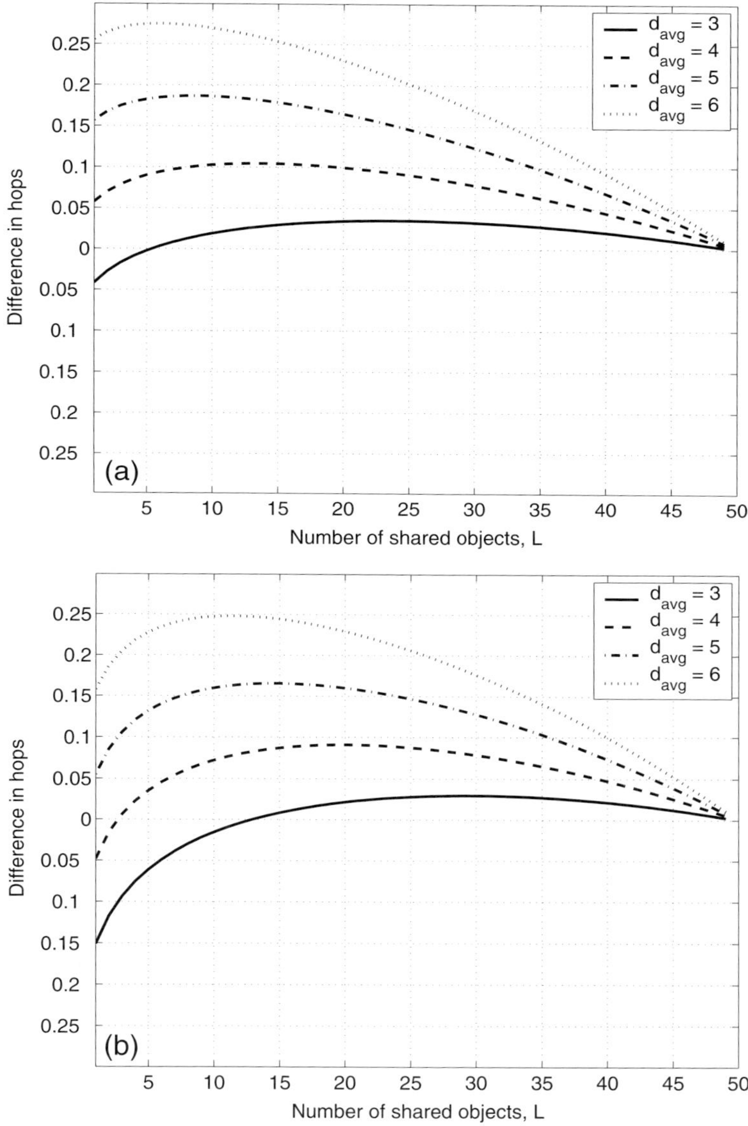

Fig. 3. Gain from cooperation for $K = 50$, 1000 objects. (a) Zipf 0.6; (b) Zipf 0.8.

Even though a gain of 0.2 hops may not seem much, it is important to note that the difference between *Popularity* heuristic and *Greedy-Single* was typically less than 0.05 hops. The difference between *Popularity* and *Greedy-Global* was 0.1–0.15 hops. Therefore, two cooperating nodes using the *Popularity* heuristic would obtain significantly better performance than they could hope to obtain by acting independently. We can conclude that *cooperation is much more efficient at reducing the cost* than changing a heuristic from a popularity based heuristic into a greedy one.

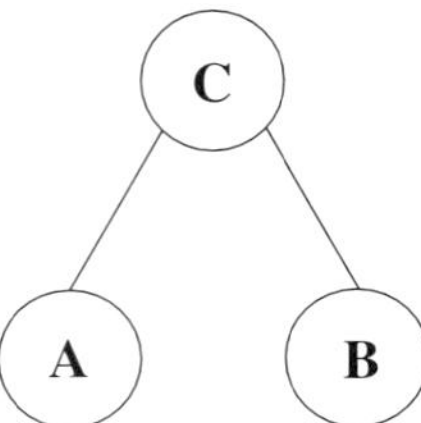

Fig. 4. 3-way cooperation.

If D_{AB} is equal to 2, then A and B are separated by one AS. One example of this case is shown in Fig. 4 where we have three nodes, one parent and two children. In this case, the cooperation would happen between the children. Fig. 5 shows the graphs for this case.

Comparing Fig. 3 and 5 we can see that the gains get smaller as D_{AB} increases. When D_{AB} increases even further, cooperation will no longer be beneficial to A and B. This is to be expected, since in the network topologies we used, the average distance between leaf nodes was around 4 and therefore the distance between A and B would be roughly the same as the distance to the origin server.

We also investigated cases where there are a very large number of objects in the network. In these cases, the general form of the gains matches those in Fig. 3 and 5, but the actual gain is slightly lower. This is because the storage nodes can only hold a very small fraction of the objects, and even two nodes co-operating cannot hold enough objects to reduce the average number of hops significantly. However, even in these cases, cooperation yielded a smaller average number of hops than not cooperating. For example, with 1 million objects and K equal to 2000, the maximum gain was around 0.2 hops as opposed to 0.27 with 1000 objects and $K = 50$ (for $d_{\text{avg}} = 6$).

7. Related work

Related work on replicating content has mostly concentrated on the problem of placing the replica servers for *one origin server*. In this paper we consider a more global case where we have content from several origin servers and we decide which objects to replicate on the replica servers.

In both [10] and [3], the authors consider the problem of placing replicas for one origin server on a tree topology. While the real Internet topology is not a tree, this simpler approach allows the authors to develop optimal algorithms. The tree-approach may not generalize, because it would require that the trees for different origin servers overlap at the replica sites which cannot be guaranteed without a manual selection of the replica sites. Also, in [10], the algorithm is of a high computational complexity $O(N^3M^2)$.

In [14] the authors present their algorithms for placing server replicas in a CDN. They assume that the replicas are complete replicas and they do not study replicating individual objects; in our work we make replication decisions on a per-object granularity. They formulate the problem as the NP-complete K-median problem, develop heuristics and evaluate their performance. They only consider placing replicas for a single origin server; our heuristics replicate objects from all the origin servers. All of their heuristics require information about the network topology as well as client request loads. Also,

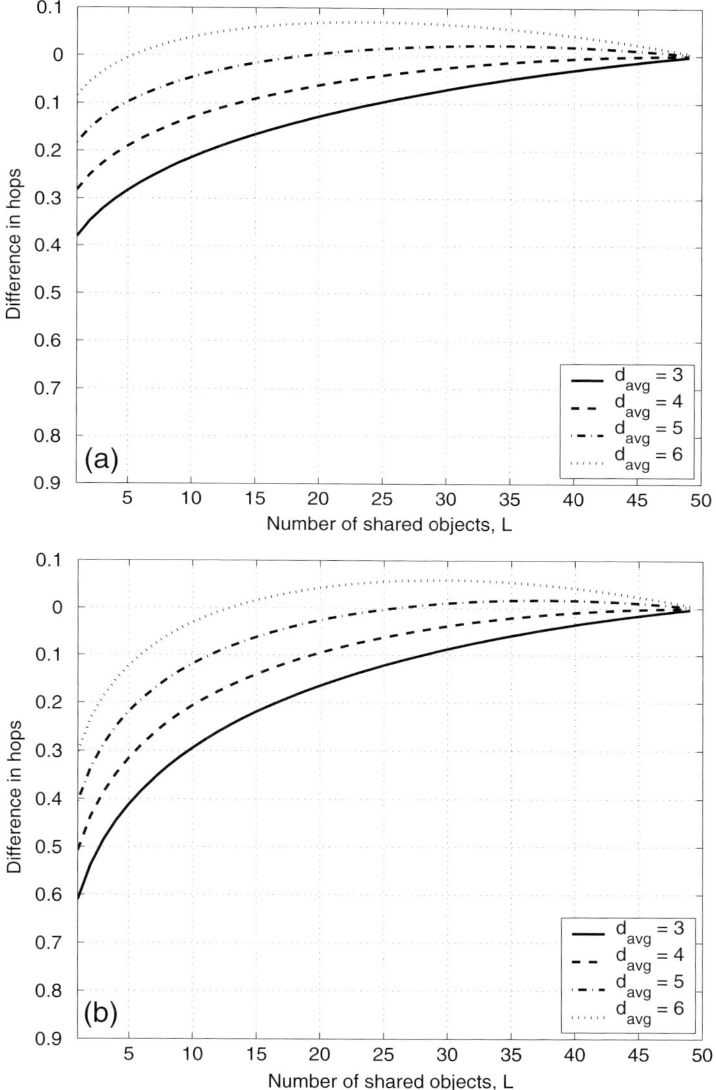

Fig. 5. Gain from cooperation for $D_{AB} = 2$, $K = 50$, 1000 objects. (a) Zipf 0.6; (b) Zipf 0.8.

in their work, all the replicas act independently and they do not study any cooperating schemes.

In [9] the authors consider the placement of intercepting proxies inside the network to reduce the download time. They present optimal solutions for simple topologies, such as line and ring, and consider the case of placing proxies for a single server in a tree topology. Relying on intercepting proxies requires that routing is stable during the lifetime of the connection.

8. Conclusion

In this paper we have studied the problem of optimally replicating objects in CDN servers. We treat each AS as a node with finite capacity for storing objects. Our optimization problem is to replicate objects so that when clients fetch objects from the nearest CDN server, the average number of ASs traversed is minimized. We have formulated this problem as a combinatorial optimization problem and have shown it to be NP complete.

We have developed four natural heuristics and compared them numerically using real Internet topology data. Our results show that the best performing heuristic is *Greedy-Global* which has all the CDN servers cooperating. The difference in performance between *Greedy-Global* and the simpler heuristics was up to 24%.

We have also studied peer-to-peer content distribution and developed a model for studying the benefits of cooperation between nodes. Our evaluation of the cooperation model shows that nodes using simple heuristics and intelligent cooperation can get significant performance gains.

The field of content distribution and peer-to-peer networks has significant potential for future research. Our future work will look more closely into inter-node cooperation and investigate the optimization problem more closely in order to establish lower bounds on the achievable performance. We also plan to extend our cost model to include other important factors, such as network traffic or server load.

Acknowledgments

The routing data summaries used in constructing the network topologies were provided by National Science Foundation Cooperative Agreement No. ANI-9807479, and the National Laboratory for Applied Network Research. We would also like to thank Anat Bremler-Barr of Tel Aviv University for the discussions about the topology models.

References

[1] Akamai. http://www.akamai.com

[2] L. Breslau, P. Cao, L. Fan, G. Phillips, and S. Shenker. Web caching and Zipf-like distributions: Evidence and implications. In *Proceedings of IEEE Infocom*, New York, NY, March 21–25, 1999.

[3] I. Cidon, S. Kutten, and R. Soffer. Optimal allocation of electronic content. In *Proceedings of IEEE Infocom*, Anchorage, AK, April 22–26, 2001.

[4] Digital Island Inc. http://www.digisle.net

[5] L. Gao. On inferring autonomous system relationships in the internet. In *Proceedings of IEEE Global Internet*, San Francisco, CA, November 28–30, 2000.

[6] M.R. Garey and D.S. Johnson. *Computers and Intractability: A Guide to the Theory of NP-Completeness*. Freeman, 1979.

[7] Gnutella web site. http://www.gnutella.co.uk/

[8] S. Jin and A. Bestavros. GreedyDual* web caching algorithm: Exploiting the two sources of temporal locality in web request streams. In *Proceedings of 5th Web Caching and Content Distribution Workshop*, Lisbon, Portugal, May 22–24, 2000.

[9] P. Krishnan, D. Raz, and Y. Shavitt. The cache location problem. *IEEE/ACM Transactions on Networking*, 8(5): 568–582, October 2000.

[10] B. Li, M.J. Golin, G.F. Italiano, and X. Deng. On the optimal placement of web proxies in the internet. In *Proceedings of IEEE Infocom*, New York, NY, March 21–25, 1999.

[11] Napster. http://www.napster.com
[12] NLANR measurement and operations analysis team. http://moat.nlanr.net
[13] V.N. Padmanabhan and L. Qiu. The content and access dynamics of a busy web site: Findings and implications. In *Proceedings of ACM SIGCOMM*, Stockholm, Sweden, August 28 – September 1, 2000.
[14] L. Qiu, V.N. Padmanabhan, and G.M. Voelker. On the placement of web server replicas. In *Proceedings of IEEE Infocom*, Anchorage, AK, April 22–26, 2001.
[15] Route views project homepage. http://www.antc.uoregon.edu/route-views/

Web Caching and Content Delivery
A. Bestavros and M. Rabinovich (Editors)

Topology-Informed Internet Replica Placement *

Pavlin Radoslavov [a,1], Ramesh Govindan [a,2], Deborah Estrin [b,3]

[a] *USC/Information Sciences Institute, 4676 Admiralty Way, Suite 1001, Marina del Rey, CA 90292-6695, USA*

[b] *Information Sciences Institute and UCLA, 4676 Admiralty Way, Suite 1001, Marina del Rey, CA 90292-6695, USA*

Abstract

Recently, several studies have looked into the problem of replicated server placement on the Internet. Some of those studies have demonstrated that there exists a replica placement algorithm that can perform within a factor of 1.1–1.5 of the optimal solution. However, this particular greedy algorithm requires detailed knowledge about network topology, and knowledge about expected client locations on the topology. One of these previous studies has also looked at topology-informed replica placement. They consider placing replicas at highly connected nodes in the Autonomous System level graph. In this paper we extend their work by investigating the performance of topology-informed placement on Internet router-level topology. In our evaluation, we consider approximated policy-based paths, and examine the sensitivity of our results to different client placements. We find that topology-informed replica placement methods can achieve average client latencies which are within a factor of 1.1–1.2 of the greedy algorithm, but only if the placement method is designed carefully.

Keywords: Content distribution network; Replica placement algorithms; Router fanout

---

1. Introduction

Content Distribution Networks (CDNs) [2,10,6] replicate Web content in an effort to reduce client access latency. This kind of replication can also reduce network overhead. However, the efficacy of content distribution can crucially depend on the placement of these replicas, and on the relative location of the client population.

In the past, there have been several studies that have addressed the problem of replica placement on the network and its impact on network performance [12,18,11,13]. A number of replica placement methods have been proposed and studied. Two of the

---

* This work was supported by the Defense Advanced Research Projects Agency under grant F30602-00-2-055. Any opinions, findings, and conclusions or recommendations expressed in this material are those of the authors and do not necessarily reflect the views of the Defense Advanced Research Projects Agency.

[1] E-mail: pavlin@catarina.usc.edu

[2] E-mail: govindan@isi.edu

[3] E-mail: estrin@isi.edu

studies [18,11] have considered a greedy placement strategy [4] which, compared to the computationally expensive optimal solution, performs remarkably well in practice (within a factor of 1.1–1.5), and is relatively insensitive to imperfect input data. Unfortunately, this greedy placement requires knowledge about the client locations in the network, and all pairwise inter-node distances, which information in many cases may not be available.

One of the previous studies [11] considers also topology-informed replica placement, where nodes are selected as replicas in decreasing order of their node degree [5]. Their results suggest that this method can perform almost as good as the greedy placement. However, due to lack of more detailed network topology, this particular study uses only Autonomous Systems (AS) topologies (real-world and generated) where each node represents a single AS, and a node link corresponds to AS-level BGP peering.

In this paper we extend their evaluation of fanout-based replica placement in several ways. First, instead of using a coarse-grained AS topology derived from BGP AS paths information [16], we have in our possession an approximate router-level Internet topology [8] which we use to obtain more detailed and accurate results. Second, instead of shortest-path routing, we generate router-level paths using approximate models of inter-AS routing policy [20]. With their technique, each router from the router-level topology is mapped to the AS it belongs to (based on that router IP address), and then AS-level shortest-path routing is combined with router-level shortest-path towards the next-hop AS. Finally, we look into results sensitivity by considering various client placement models, and some other topologies.

Our main findings are:

- In most cases the router-level fanout placement is almost as good as the greedy placement (within a factor of 1.1–1.2).
- A fanout-based replica placement method needs to be carefully designed to be efficient. For example, if we select first a well-connected AS and then we select a router within that AS, we must be very careful which particular router is selected.

Our conclusions do not depend on client locations. Only if the number of clients is very small, then there is a significant performance difference between the fanout-based replica placement and the greedy placement. The results are true also for random graphs, generated and real-world AS topologies, but do not apply for overlay topologies such as Mbone [14]. At the end of the paper we present a possible explanation when and why those results may hold.

The rest of the paper is organized as follows. In Section 2 we discuss some of the previous work. In Section 3 we describe the particular replica and client placement models we consider in this paper. Section 4 contains the performance evaluation results. Conclusions and future work are in Section 5.

2. Related work

A number of papers have addressed the problem of Web server replica or cache placement impact on performance. Note that some of the recently published papers are

[4] The particular greedy placement is also very similar to the one in [12].

[5] For the rest of the paper we will use interchangeably the terms *node degree* and *node fanout* to represent the number of links connecting a node with its neighbors. Also, we will use the term *well-connected node* to indicate a node that has a large fanout.

independent studies, but have notable similarity in problem formulation and final results. The replica or cache placement problem can be modeled after the *center placement problem*, a well-known problem in graph theory, and in particular two of its variations: *the facility location problem*, or *the minimum K-median problem* [5]. A number of approximate solutions have been proposed in the past [23], but they are either very computationally expensive, or are difficult to apply in practice.

Krishnan et al. [12] study the problem of placing transparent en-route network caches (TERCs), and in particular how various placement methods can be used to reduce the network traffic or the average access latency. Unlike our work where we assume the replicas can be placed anywhere in the network, their work allows the caches to be only on the path between a client and the server.

Qiu et al. [18] consider the problem of placement strategies for Web server replicas within the context of CDNs that offer Web server hosting services. They propose several placement algorithms, including a simple greedy placement which we use in this paper, and which is very similar to the greedy algorithm in [12]. They find that this greedy algorithm performs very well in practice (typically within a factor of 1.1–1.5 of the optimal solution). Further, its performance is relatively insensitive to imperfect input data such as client locations and network topology information. However, this study does not consider node-fanout based placement.

The study by Jamin et al. [11] is similar to [18]. Their work examines the impact of the number of replicas on the performance of various replica placement methods. Their main finding is that, regardless of the placement method, increasing the number of replicas is effective in reducing client download time only for a very small number of replicas. They also discuss an AS-level fanout-based placement, in which replicas are placed within ASs in decreasing order of node degree on the AS topology. The results suggest that the AS-level fanout-based placement can perform almost as well as the greedy placement. Our study is centered around this finding, and we try to verify it through more detailed simulations by using router-level Internet topology, instead of only AS-level topology, and by exploring in more details the impact of various replica and client placement methods.

3. Replica and client placement models

In this section we describe the replica placement models we are interested at, and are evaluated later in Section 4. We use each of those models to place a number of replicas on the topology, so we could eventually reduce the client access latency and the overall network overhead (compared to a single-server solution). We also describe the client placement models that we use to select a number of nodes as clients. Those models are used in Section 4.3.2 to perform the client-impact sensitivity evaluation. Before presenting the replica and client placement models, we describe the client-replica assignment we assume.

3.1. Client-replica assignment

In this paper we assume that each client selects the closest (in number of hops) replica. Indeed, it is possible to consider a more sophisticated scheme where a client selects in real-time the replica that offers the lowest latency, but for simplicity we ignore such schemes. The second assumption we make is that we do not limit the number of a clients that can be assigned to a replica. Both assumptions are similar to those in some of the previous work ([18,12,11]). One of the arguments to support the latter assumption is that typically it is much easier to increase the capacity of a particular replica (e.g. by creating a cluster of replicas at the same location), than deploying a new replica at different location for the sake of reducing other replicas' load. The latter assumption does not impact our conclusions even in the presence of flash crowds, because, as we demonstrate later in the paper, our results are robust to variations in client locations and client population size.

3.2. Replica placement models

In this paper we consider the following replica placement methods. The first method has been proposed in some of the previous work (see Section 2). In our study we use it as a base for comparison.

- **Greedy placement.** The greedy placement we choose is same as the greedy algorithm described in [18] and [11]. The basic idea is to choose the replicas one-by-one, a subject to a greedy selection: at each step we evaluate all nodes in the topology and choose the one that, if we place a replica there, the resulting network overhead will be minimized. The process is repeated until all replicas have been chosen. The input to this method is all pairwise inter-node distances, and the client placement locations.
- **Max-router fanout placement.** Given a network topology and the fanout of each node, we choose the replicas one-by-one in decreasing order of their node degree until all replicas have been chosen. The intuition behind this method is that the nodes with large fanout are eventually the closest (on average) to all other nodes, and therefore they are a better choice for replica location.
- **Max-as/max-router fanout placement.** This method assumes that each node/router has been assigned to some AS, and that all ASs have been connected into an AS-level topology. If R is the number of replicas to select, first we select the R ASs that have the largest fanout (on the AS-level topology). Then, within each selected AS, we choose the router that has the largest router-level fanout. Similar to the *max-router fanout* placement, the intuition is that the selected nodes will be closer to the rest of the nodes.
- **Max-as/min-router fanout placement.** This method is similar to the *max-AS/max-router fanout* placement, except that instead of selecting the router with largest fanout within each of the chosen ASs, we select the router with the smallest fanout. This placement may not make sense for practical purposes, but we need to consider it to evaluate the sensitivity of network performance to replica placement within an AS. Note that for the rest of the paper, when we use the term *fanout-based placement*, we do not include the *max-AS/min-router* fanout placement, unless stated otherwise.
- **Random placement.** In this method the replicas are chosen at random with uniform probability among all nodes in the topology. We consider it as an 'upper-bound' placement method in a sense that an efficient replica placement method should always be better than the random placement.

Unlike the previous work described in Section 2, we do not consider some of the existing optimal solutions that have been proven to be always within a small factor of the most optimal solution. As we mentioned earlier in Section 2, the greedy placement has been shown to perform very well in practice, within a factor of 1.1–1.5 of the computationally intensive optimal solutions. Therefore it is a reasonable choice for our needs and we can use it as a base of comparison.

3.3. Client placement models

To investigate the sensitivity of replica placement performance to client locations, we look into several client placement models. Our goal is not to explore all possible client placements, but to consider the extreme cases, along with the random case, because the extreme cases can give us the boundary of expected performance.

The first model we look into is the *random client placement*, where the client nodes are selected at random with uniform probability.

We also look into the extreme client placement as defined in [17], namely *extreme affinity* and *extreme disaffinity*. The extreme affinity model places the clients as close as possible to each other; the extreme disaffinity model places the clients as far as possible from each other. The particular algorithm we use to place a number of clients on a graph according to the affinity/disaffinity model is described in [24]. Below is a brief summary of that algorithm. The first client is selected at random among all nodes. Then, we assign to each node n_i that is not selected yet the probability $p_i = \alpha / w_i^{\beta}$, where w_i is the closest distance between node n_i and a node that is already selected as a client, α is calculated such that $\sum_{n_i} p_i = 1$, and β is the parameter that defines the degree of affinity or disaffinity. After a node is chosen to be a client, the probabilities of the remaining nodes are recomputed and the process is repeated until the desired number of clients is selected. Similar to [24], in our experiments we use $\beta = 15$ and $\beta = -15$ for extreme affinity and disaffinity respectively.

To verify our results with real-world data, we use Web server access logs to create the population of clients. In particular, we collect the unique IP addresses of all clients that have accessed the same Web server within some period of time. Then, we run a traceroute to each of the client addresses. Finally, we intersect each of the traceroute paths with the Internet map to find the last-hop router toward a Web client that is on that map. The set of all last-hop routers is our *Web clients set* that can be used to represent the population of the real-world Web clients.

4. Performance evaluation

In this section we present the main results from our evaluation. In particular, we use numerical simulations to compute the relative network performance. As part of our evaluation we look into the impact of various factors on performance: replica and client placement, client number, network topology. First we describe the metric space, and then we present the results when we vary each of the input factors we consider.

4.1. Metric space

The two particular metrics we are interested at are *average client latency* and *overall network overhead*. For simplicity, we assume that the latency between two nodes is proportional to the number of link-hops between them. A similar assumption has been used in a previous work [18]. Indeed, [9] shows that router-level hops correlate well with observed latency. That work points out that the number of ASs in the path to a destination has a higher correlation to latency. However, that study is several years old and Internet has evolved since then. Further, a more recent study has measured 50–70% correlation between network hop and round-trip time [15], and its authors claim that the router-level number of hops is more meaningful as a latency metric [6]. Finally, due to lack of information, we assume that the bandwidth capacity of all links is same. Obviously, those assumptions are not perfect, but without detailed network measurements this is the best we can do. Hence, the average client latency across all clients c can be computed as:

$$AveClientLatency = \frac{\sum_{clients(c)} Dist(c, Replica(c))}{NumberOfClients}$$

where $Replica(c)$ is the replica node for client c, and $Dist(c, Replica(c))$ is the distance between them in number of hops.

For similar reasons as above, we also assume that the overall network overhead is proportional to the number of link-hops used to disseminate the data from the replicas to all clients. At the same time, we ignore the network overhead to distribute the data from its original location to each of the replicas, because this overhead may be a small fraction of the network overhead to distribute the data from the replicas to a large number of clients. Hence, the overall network overhead for all clients can be computed using the following formula:

$$NetworkOverhead = \sum_{clients(c)} Dist(c, Replica(c))$$

In our evaluation, we are not interested in the absolute client latency or absolute network overhead metrics. Instead, we are interested in the *relative client latency* or *relative network overhead* of each replica placement method versus the greedy placement. Based on our assumptions, we have $AveClientLatency = \frac{NetworkOverhead}{NumberOfClients}$, therefore it is easy to see that when we perform *relative* comparison between two replica placement methods using the same set of clients, then the relative average client latency will be the same as the relative network overhead. Therefore, for the rest of the paper we use a single metric we call *efficiency ratio* to compute the relative performance between two replica placement methods. We always use the greedy placement as a base for comparison, hence the efficiency ratio of method M_i can be computed as:

$$EffRatio(M_i) = \frac{NetworkOverhead(M_i)}{NetworkOverhead(Greedy)}$$

4.2. Simulation setup

For most of our simulations (except for those described in Section 4.3.4 where we look at the topology impact factor), we use a real-world router-level topology. The topology information was collected by using a large number of traceroute requests sent over the Internet [8,22]. The resulting topology had 102639 nodes and 142303 links. Then we recursively removed all nodes that have a fanout of one to obtain a topology we call *Internet core*. The reason that we truncate the original topology is to remove the long,

[6] We also show, in Section 4.3.4, that if we consider latency defined in terms of AS-level hops, our findings hold even stronger.

Table 1. Metrics of used topologies

Topology	Nodes	Links	Diameter	Average distance	Average fanout
Internet core	27646	67310	26	8.3	4.9
Random graph	19596	40094	16	7.2	4.1
Power-law graph	10091	23253	9	3.2	4.6
AS	4830	9077	11	3.7	3.8
Mbone	4179	8549	26	10.1	4.1

'skinny' branches that do not represent well the network connectivity at the edges, but are an artifact from the particular methodology used to obtain the topology information.

To obtain more realistic results, instead of using shortest-path routing, we use AS-level hierarchical routing as described in [20]. With their technique, first each router from the router-level topology is mapped to the AS it belongs to, based on that router IP address and the AS-level topology [4] at the time the router-level topology data was collected. After that, the AS-level shortest-path routing is computed. Finally, to compute the router-level path between two nodes, the AS-level path is followed and within each AS the router-level shortest path is used to reach the closest node that belongs to the next-hop AS.

Within each set of simulations we fix the number of clients and vary the number of replicas, or vice-versa. The number of replicas varies between 1 and 50; the client population size varies as a fraction of the number of all nodes between 0.005 and 0.2. The replica and the client placement methods, as described in Section 3, are the other input to the simulations. In all simulations we use 100 different sets of algorithmically chosen clients (except for the Web-derived clients when we have 3 sets), and we average the results among all trials. The results we show are for the 95% confidence interval (note that in most cases this interval is very small and can be seen as a single dot)[7]. To create the set of Web-derived clients, we use the access logs of a busy Web server for three consecutive days, and we apply the technique described in Section 3.3 to compute the nodes on the router-level topology that represent the Web clients. The number of unique client addresses for each of the three days is 37401, 40833, 43558 respectively. Those clients, after the intersection of the traceroute paths with the router-level topology, are represented by 4015, 4158 and 4264 unique nodes on the Internet-core map (approximately 15% of all nodes).

We tried also some generated topologies, and some other real-world maps (see Section 4.3.4). Table 1 summarizes some of the metrics of all topologies.

4.3. Network efficiency results

First we present the results for different replica placement methods, which are of most interest to us. Then we look at how the client placement may have impact on performance. Finally, we look into other factors such as client number and network topology.

[7] We looked also into the min–max interval, and it was almost unnoticeable for the *max-router fanout* and *max-AS/max-router* placement methods.

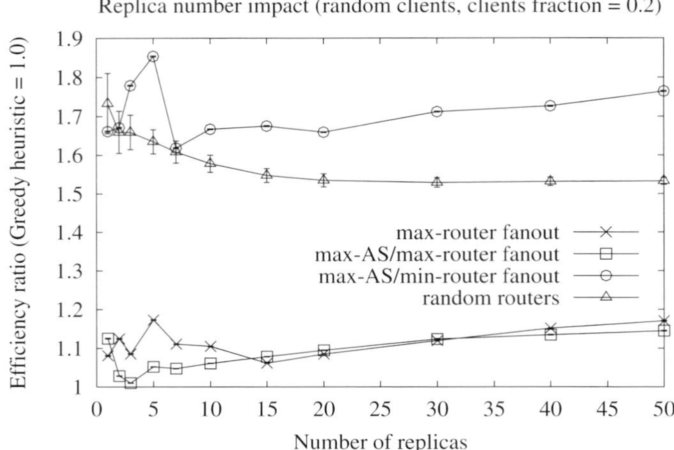

Fig. 1. Internet core: replica placement impact (random clients).

4.3.1. Replica placement impact

To evaluate the replica placement impact, we assume a fixed number of randomly placed clients (20% of all nodes), and the number of replicas varies between 1 and 50. Then we compute the relative network efficiency for different replica placement methods (as described in Section 3.2), by using the greedy algorithm results as the base for comparison (1.0).

The results from this simulation are on Fig. 1. The first observation we can make is that both *max-router fanout* and *max-AS/max-router fanout* placement methods perform very well, within a factor of 1.1–1.2 of the greedy placement, regardless of the number of replicas. This result is our first confirmation that the fanout-based placement methods perform well even on Internet router-level topology. On the other hand, the *max-AS/min-router fanout* placement performs even worse than random replica placement. This, to some extent, is a surprising result, because we expected that the AS fanout is the major factor that has impact on performance. Clearly, placement is very sensitive to the actual selection of routers within ASs – selecting the highest fanout AS alone for placing a replica is not sufficient.

4.3.2. Client placement impact

To evaluate the client placement impact on the results, first we consider the extreme cases of *affinity* and *disaffinity*. The particular model we use was described already in Section 3.3. Fig. 2 and Fig. 3 show the results for extreme affinity and extreme disaffinity respectively (the rest of the setup is same as in the case of random client placement in Section 4.3.1). Here again we can see that the *max-router* and *max-AS/max-router* fanout-based placement methods perform remarkably well within a factor of 1.1–1.2 of the greedy placement.

The results with the *Web clients* are on Fig. 4. Similar to the extreme affinity and extreme disaffinity client placement, with Web clients the fanout-based placement methods perform equally well.

It is interesting to note that, unlike the greedy placement, the fanout-based replica

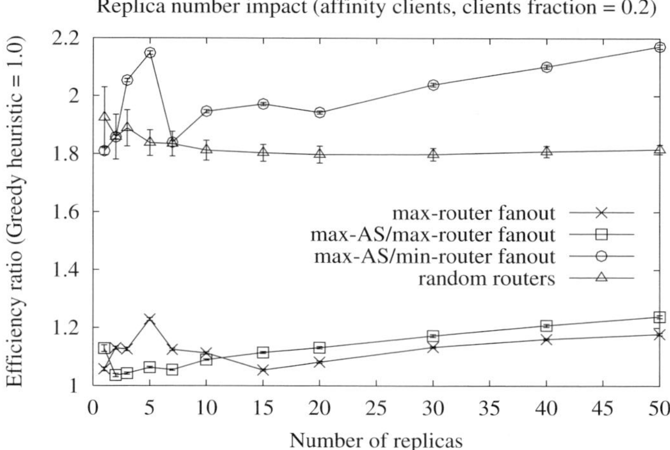

Fig. 2. Internet core: replica placement impact (extreme affinity clients).

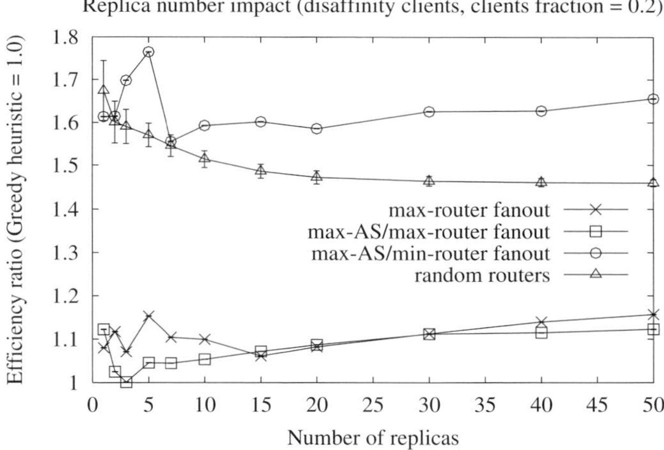

Fig. 3. Internet core: replica placement impact (extreme disaffinity clients).

placement methods do not take client locations into account, yet they can perform very well over a wide range of client placements (including realistic placements).

4.3.3. Client number impact

The next question we want to answer is how the client population size impacts the performance. In this set of simulations we fix the number of replicas to 50, and then we vary the fraction of nodes that are clients in the range 0.005–0.2. Figs. 5, 6 and 7 show the results for various client placement: random, extreme affinity and extreme disaffinity respectively.

We observe that when the number of clients is small, the fanout-based placement methods do not perform very well. This is especially true for extreme affinity client placement.

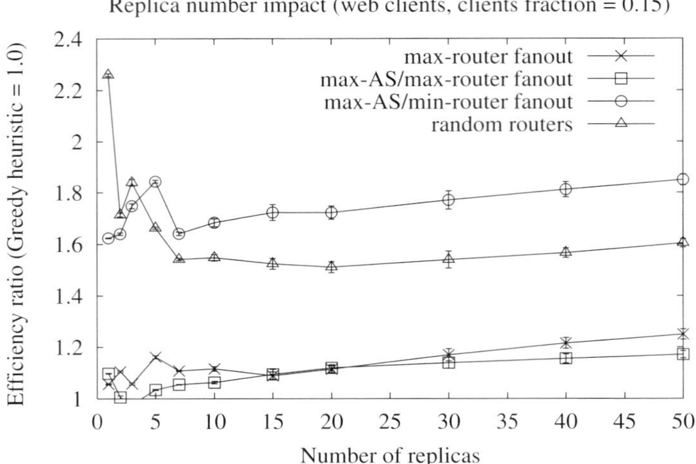

Fig. 4. Internet core: replica placement impact (Web clients).

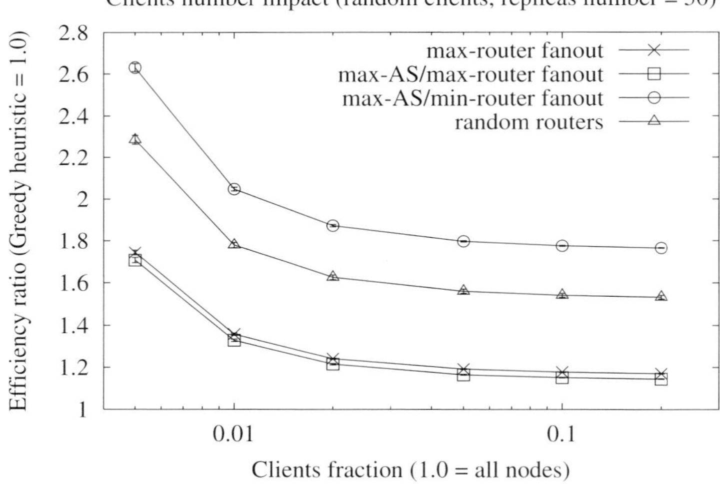

Fig. 5. Internet core: client number impact (random clients).

For moderate and large client number, the fanout-based placements perform much better, as expected[8]. Another observation we can make is that the performance difference is larger with extreme affinity of the clients. This result is not unexpected, because when all clients are clustered together in some part of the network, there is relatively low probability that there will be a node with large fanout in their proximity that will be selected

[8] The *random* and *max-AS/min-routers* placement performance for extreme disaffinity of the clients as a function of the client population size may seem a little bit unusual because it is not monotonically increasing or decreasing. This behavior can be explained by the fact that the results can be influenced significantly by various factors if the number of clients is very small (on the order of the number of replicas.)

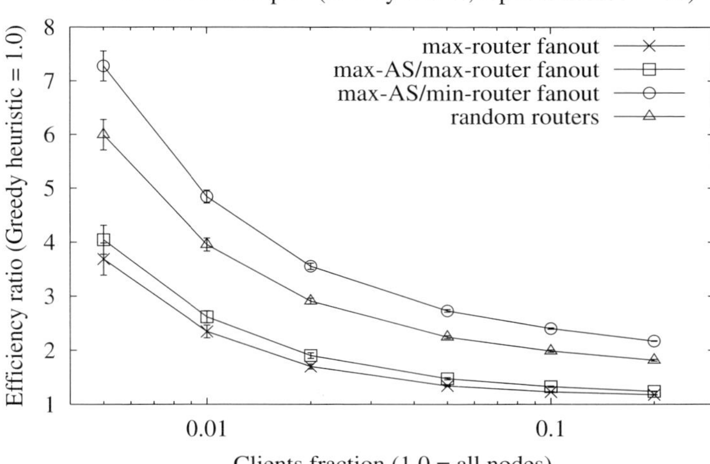

Fig. 6. Internet core: client number impact (extreme affinity clients).

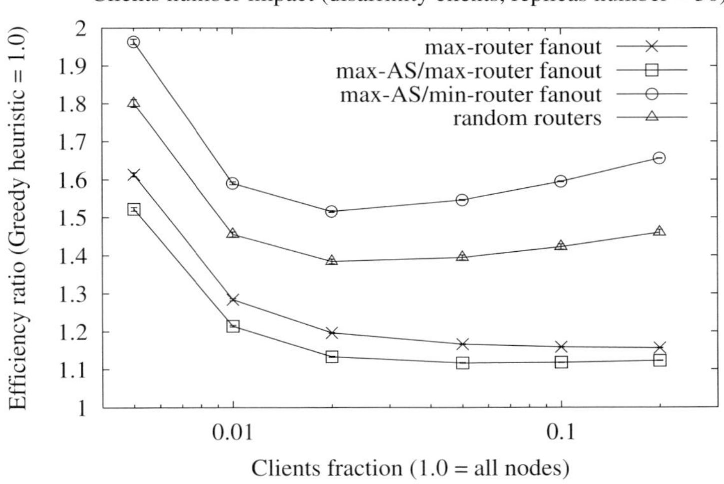

Fig. 7. Internet core: client number impact (extreme disaffinity clients).

as a replica (unless the number of clustered clients is very large and altogether they cover a notable fraction of the network). From the above results we can see that the client population size has impact on performance only when the number of clients is small. Only then the fanout-based placements do not perform as well as the greedy placement.

4.3.4. Network topology impact

The next factor we consider that may have impact on performance is the type of topology. First, we repeat the same simulations with two different types of generated topologies. The first one is a random graph (see Table 1 for some of its metrics, as well

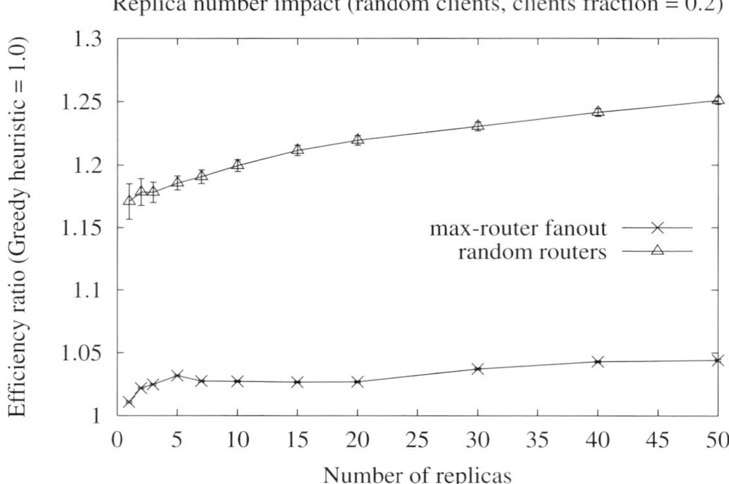

Fig. 8. Random graph: replica placement impact (random clients).

for the metrics of the other topologies), generated by the GT-ITM topology generator [3]. The second one is a power-law graph [9] created by a generator based on the algorithm described in [1]. A recent study shows that this topology qualitatively resembles both the AS and the router-level topologies [21]. Obviously, we do not have ASs over the generated topologies, therefore we have to use shortest-path routing; for the same reason we cannot apply the *max-AS/max-router* or the *max-AS/min-router* replica placement methods.

The results for the random graph with randomly placed clients (20% of all nodes) when we vary the number of replicas are on Fig. 8. We can see that the difference between the greedy placement and the *max-router fanout* placement is even smaller (within a factor of 1.05). On the other hand, even random replica placement can perform within a factor of 1.25 which is much lower compared to the Internet-core results.

The results for the the power-law graph are on Fig. 9. As expected, the fanout-based placement performs very well, while the random placement performs notably worse. We tried also a real-world AS-level topology itself [4], and the results were very similar to the results for the generated power-law graph.

For all topologies, the extreme affinity and extreme disaffinity client placement results were similar to the random client placement results.

However, we should note that this result is not universal. When we tried the Mbone [14] overlay topology [22], we found that the *max-router fanout* replica placement is not better than the random placement. In fact, in most cases it was even worse. We believe the reason is that the connectivity of the Mbone topology is very sparse compared to the other topologies we have considered (compare the topology size, topology diameter and average inter-node distances of all topologies on Table 1). As a result, the average distance from a well-connected node to the rest of the nodes is relatively large, therefore such node is not a good choice to be a replica.

[9] One of the characteristics of the power-law graphs is that the node fanout distribution can be described by a power law: $f_d \propto d^{\beta}$ where f_d is the frequency of out-degree d, and β is a constant.

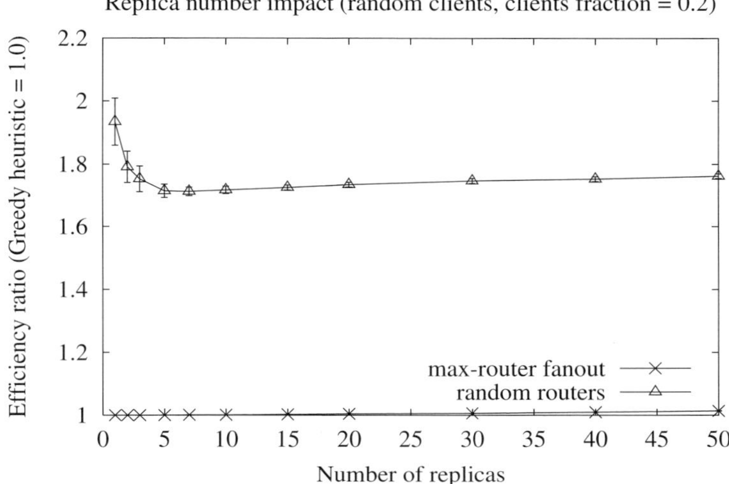

Fig. 9. Power-law graph: replica placement impact (random clients).

Finally, we should note that when we repeated the Internet-core simulations with using shortest-path routing instead of the approximated AS-policy routing, we did not see any notable difference. From this we can conclude that the impact of the routing on relative performance is insignificant.

4.4. Results discussion

In this section we discuss our findings, and try to explain the reasons behind some of them.

Our main finding is that the fanout-based placement methods can perform remarkably well. Unlike more sophisticated methods such as the greedy placement that takes into account the client locations to compute the appropriate replica placement, the fanout-based placement does not require any knowledge about expected client locations. This is a very significant simplification, because it basically suggests that we do not need a dynamic and adaptive replica placement that requires knowledge about expected client locations. In other words, as long as the replicas are placed in some 'key' locations in the network, then the expected performance would be reasonably good.

If we abstract from the particular replica placement methods and ask the question "if we had to select a single node as a replica, what would be the best node to select", the answer would be the node that is as close as possible to all clients. Typically, if a node has a large fanout, it means that it is a one-hop away from a large number of nodes, and therefore probabilistically it is close to a large number of clients as well. The AS and the Internet topologies have the characteristics of power-law graphs [7,19]. One of the characteristics of those topologies is that they have a small number of nodes with very large fanout which nodes are apparently just few hops away from all other nodes. In other words, the high-fanout nodes are the 'key-location' nodes for the power-law graphs that in most cases are very close to the rest of the nodes.

Here someone may ask the question why did we get similar results for the random graph which is not a power-law graph? The answer to that question may be in the fact that the majority of the nodes in the random graph have similar fanout, while overall random graphs have very high *topology expansion* (defined as the growth of neighborhood size as a function of distance) [19]. The combination of these two factors eventually means that all nodes are just few hops away from each other, and then choosing any node to be a replica will be a good solution. This observation also explains why the random replica selection performs much better for random graph compared to power-law graph (see Figs. 8 and 9).

Another observation is that a two-level fanout-based placement such as the *max-AS/max-router* placement method can perform very well. One possible speculation here may be that the AS fanout is the factor that matter, i.e. that choosing any node within an AS with a large fanout will be a good solution. However, the results for the *max-AS/min-router* replica placement show that router selection based on the AS-level fanout only is not sufficient: the router-level fanout must be considered as well. One possible explanation to this is as follows. Typically, an AS with large fanout has inside a large number of nodes, and some of those nodes may not be very well connected [10]. Therefore, choosing such not well connected node as a replica may not be beneficial at all to reduce client latency or network overhead.

Finally, we should note that in most cases the *max-AS/min-router fanout* replica placement performs slightly better compared to the *max-router fanout* placement. The reason for this, we believe, is that the *max-AS/min-router fanout* placement spreads the replicas among a number of ASs, by placing no more than one replica inside each AS. On the other hand, the *max-router fanout* placement does not have this property, therefore it may place a number of replicas very close to each other without adding significant benefit to the clients.

5. Conclusions and future work

In this paper we consider the problem of replica placement for Content Distribution Networks. In particular, given a number of replicas and a network topology, where should we place them such that the average client latency and the overall network overhead are minimized. Previous studies have proposed a simple greedy placement algorithm that performs very well (within a factor of 1.1–1.5) compared to the optimal solution. Unfortunately, this algorithm requires knowledge about expected client locations, and all pairwise inter-node distances.

We look into few other replica placement methods and compare them with the greedy placement. Interestingly, fanout-based placement methods that choose the nodes with the maximum fanout perform very well (within a factor of 1.1–1.2) compared to the greedy placement. Unlike the greedy placement, the fanout-based placements do not require knowledge about client locations, and do not need detailed network topology information. The only information needed is the set of nodes with the largest fanout (including eventually, in case of Internet, the AS-level fanout as well). Further, unlike the greedy

[10] Indeed, when we compared the number of nodes assigned to each AS versus the AS fanout, on average the relation can be approximated with a straight line on the log–log scale, which means that each of the few ASs with the largest fanout contains a large number of nodes inside.

placement solution, a fanout-based solution does not tend to change significantly even on a long-range time scale.

The implication of those finding is not that we want to add various replicas to the high-fanout routers to achieve good performance. Typically, those routers are very busy, and it may be technically impossible to add any services to them. One possible solution would be to build a cluster of replicas that are connected to the network in a point that is as close as possible to a high-fanout router. An interesting problem then would be to investigate how the addition of such clusters of replicas would change the traffic volume at the high-fanout routers and at the rest of the network, and how the change in traffic may have impact on performance.

Someone may argue that CDN providers may possess detailed topology information, and may have reasonable estimation about expected client location, therefore to compute the replica locations a greedy algorithm would be preferred. While it may be true, it is not difficult to imagine that in many situations that information may not be available, or may be inaccurate (e.g., right after major topology or routing reconfiguration). In that case, the fanout-based heuristic can be a quick and easy solution, and that solution could be refined later with the help of more sophisticated algorithms.

The fanout-based placement methods are not universal. They do seem to perform very well on power-law and random graphs, but may not be a good solution if most of the nodes have similar, relatively low fanout. Investigating in more details the particular network topology characteristics that may have impact on the fanout-based replica placement performance is part of our future work.

Acknowledgments

Hongsuda Tangmunarunkit suggested the *Max-AS/min-router fanout* replica placement, and provided us with the AS-level overlay mapping for the Internet-core topology. The Internet-core topology was obtained from the SCAN project [22]. The AS-level information was obtained from the NLANR server [4], which itself collected it from the University of Oregon Route Views Project [16]. Finally, we would like to thank the anonymous reviewers as well for their valuable comments.

References

[1] W. Aiello, F. Chung, and L. Lu. A Random Graph Model for Massive Graphs. In *Proc. of the 32nd Annual Symposium on Theory of Computing*, 2000.

[2] Akamai. http://www.akamai.com/.

[3] K.L. Calvert, M.B. Doar, and E.W. Zegura. Modeling Internet Topology. *IEEE Communications Magazine*, June 1997.

[4] UCSD/San Diego Supercomputer Center. The NLANR Project. http://moat.nlanr.net/Routing/rawdata/

[5] Pierluigi Crescenzi and Viggo Kann (Editors). A compendium of NP optimization problems. http://www.nada.kth.se/~viggo/problemlist/

[6] Digital Island. http://www.digitalisland.com/

[7] Michalis Faloutsos, Petros Faloutsos, and Christos Faloutsos. On Power-Law Relationships of the Internet Topology. In *Proceedings of the ACM SIGCOMM'99*, Cambridge, MA, USA, August 1999.

[8] Ramesh Govindan and Hongsuda Tangmunarunkit. Heuristics for Internet Map Discovery. In *Proceedings of the IEEE Infocom 2000*, Tel-Aviv, Israel, March 2000.

[9] James Gwertzman. Autonomous Replication in Wide-Area Internetworks. BA thesis, Harvard College, Cambridge, MA, 1995.

[10] Inktomi. http://www.inktomi.com/.

[11] Sugih Jamin, Cheng Jin, Anthony R. Kurc, Danny Raz, and Yuval Shavitt. Constrained Mirror Placement on the Internet. In *Proceedings of the IEEE Infocom 2001*, Anchorage, Alaska, USA, April 2001.

[12] P. Krishnan, Danny Raz, and Yuval Shavitt. The Cache Location Problem. *IEEE/ACM Transactions of Networking*, 8(5): 568–582, October 2000.

[13] Bo Li, Mordecai J. Golin, Giuseppe F. Italiano, Xin Deng, and Kazem Sohraby. On the Optimal Placement of Web Proxies in the Internet. In *Proceedings of the IEEE Infocom 1999*, pages 1282–1290, New York, USA, March 1999.

[14] Michael R. Macedonia and Donald P. Brutzman. MBone Provides Audio and Video Across the Internet. *IEEE Computer*, April 1994.

[15] Katia Obraczka and Fabio Silva. Network Latency Metrics for Server Proximity. In *Proceedings of the IEEE Globecom 2000*, San Francisco, CA, USA, November 2000.

[16] University of Oregon Route Views Project. http://www.antc.uoregon.edu/route-views/.

[17] Graham Phillips, Scott Shenker, and Hongsuda Tangmunarunkit. Scaling of Multicast Trees: Comments on the Chuang-Sirbu scaling law. In *Proceedings of the ACM SIGCOMM'99*, Cambridge, MA, USA, August 1999.

[18] Lili Qiu, Venkata N. Padmanabhan, and Geoffrey M. Voelker. On the Placement of Web Server Replicas. In *Proceedings of the IEEE Infocom 2001*, Anchorage, Alaska, USA, April 2001.

[19] Pavlin Radoslavov, Hongsuda Tangmunarunkit, Haobo Yu, Ramesh Govindan, Scott Shenker, and Deborah Estrin. On Characterizing Network Topologies and Analyzing Their Impact on Protocol Design. Technical Report 00-731, University of Southern California, Dept. of CS, February 2000.

[20] Hongsuda Tangmunarunkit, Ramesh Govindan, Scott Shenker, and Deborah Estrin. The Impact of Routing Policy on Internet Paths. In *Proceedings of the IEEE Infocom 2001*, Anchorage, Alaska, USA, April 2001.

[21] Hongsuda Tangmunarunkit, Ramesh Govindan, Scott Shenker, Sugih Jamin, and Walter Willinger. Network Topologies, Power Laws, and Hierarchy. Work in progress.

[22] USC/ISI. The SCAN Project. http://www.isi.edu/scan/.

[23] Vijay Vazirani. *Approximation Methods*. Springer-Verlag, 2001.

[24] Tina Wong and Randy Katz. An Analysis of Multicast Forwarding State Scalability. In *Proceedings of the 8th IEEE International Conference on Network Protocols (ICNP 2000)*, Osaka, Japan, November 2000.

Web Caching and Content Delivery
A. Bestavros and M. Rabinovich (Editors)

A Novel Approach to Managing Consistency in Content Distribution Networks

Zongming Fei [1]

Laboratory for Advanced Networking, Department of Computer Science, University of Kentucky, 773 Anderson Hall, Lexington, KY 40506, USA

Abstract

Content distribution network (CDN) is a technique deployed to push content from the origin server to geographically distributed replicas, usually located at the edge of the network where the clients are attached. One of the important problems in CDNs is how to manage the consistency of content at replicas with that at the origin server, especially for those documents changing dynamically. In the traditional propagation approach the updated version of a document is delivered to all replicas whenever a change is made to the document at the origin server. It may generate significant levels of unnecessary traffic if documents are updated more frequently than accessed. Another approach is invalidation, in which an invalidation message is sent to all replicas when a document is changed at the origin server. This approach does not make full use of the distribution network for content delivery and each replica needs to fetch an updated version individually at a later time. This can also lead to inefficiency in managing consistency at replicas. In this paper, we propose a novel hybrid approach that will generate less traffic than the propagation approach, *and* the invalidation approach. The origin server makes the decision of using either propagation or invalidation method for each document, based on the statistics about the update frequency at the origin server and the request rates collected by replicas. We develop a technique that can reduce the burden of request rate collection at replicas and get rid of the implosion problem when replicas send the statistics to the origin server. Extensive simulations are performed to examine how the traffic generated and freshness rate at replicas are affected by various parameters. We experiment with a wide range of request rate, update frequency, and the number of replicas. The results show that our approach can take advantage of content distribution network and significantly reduce the traffic generated.

Keywords: Content distribution network; Consistency; Caching; Propogation; Invalidation

1. Introduction

Over the past few years we have witnessed an unprecedented growth in the number of Internet users. Perhaps even more impressive is the rate at which new 'content' is being added to the Web each day. Moreover, there doesn't appear to be any end in sight to

[1] E-mail: fei@cs.uky.edu

the addition of new web content. Making information available to a rapidly growing user population is quickly becoming a challenging problem, which has been attacked from both the client side and the content provider side.

- On the client side, the *caching* technique has been employed to store documents accessed by clients and serve the future accesses to the same documents without having to retrieve the document from the origin server. A web cache can be maintained at each client or can be shared by a group of clients via a caching proxy. It is also possible to organize caches hierarchically.
- On the content provider side, the *replication* technique has been used to equip a farm of servers and the load of client requests is distributed. More recently, the *Content Distribution Network* (CDN) is used to push the content from the origin server to geographically distributed replicas, which bring content to the edge of the network where the clients are attached.

Our focus is on the CDNs and how content at the origin server is delivered to replicas. The two common approaches to this problem are to deliver the data over (1) N unicast channels or (2) over an application-level (tunneled) multicast tree that connects the replicas [1,2]. Clearly the unicast approach wastes network bandwidth and can cause congestion at bottleneck links, while application-level multicast approaches are more efficient in delivery (although not as efficient as native IP multicast). Though currently more deployed CDNs use unicast over multicast, there are increased interests in designing (application layer) multicast for the content delivery. We believe the multicast approach will be finally adopted because of its efficiency. In this paper, our discussion will be based on the assumption that there is some multicast delivery network established between the origin server and replicas, either native multicast or application layer multicast.

The efficiency of delivery schemes depends on the characteristics of documents. Roughly speaking, documents requested by clients can be divided into three categories.

- Static documents. Such documents usually do not change at the origin server, or if they do change, do so at very large time scales.
- Dynamic documents. These are documents that change at a relatively high rate. They can generate large amounts of update traffic if not kept in check.
- Dynamically generated documents. These documents are generated on-the-fly by the server, or replica, based on the information provided by clients.

For dynamically generated documents, the server typically needs to run some 'cgi' code to produce the document and thus cannot be implemented with the caching approach. However, in CDNs, the replica, like the origin server can be instantiated with the appropriate code to generate these documents dynamically. The information used to generate the documents may change frequently or infrequently like other standard web documents and thus this information is dealt with just like dynamic or static web content.

The update of static documents is not a problem because it is, in most cases, one time effort and thus does not generate too much traffic. This is not the case for updating dynamic document. It involves generating much higher levels of traffic. It is the goal of this paper to design an efficient scheme for updating dynamic documents and maintaining consistency of documents at replicas with the origin server. There are two ways to update dynamic documents:

- Propagation. Whenever an object is changed at the origin server, it is propagated to all replicas.

- Invalidation. Whenever an object is changed, an invalidation message is sent to all replicas. Each replica will fetch the new version of the object individually at a later time, if necessary.

Unfortunately, the propagation approach often generates significant levels of unnecessary traffic if documents are updated more frequently than they are requested. On the other hand, the invalidation approach may fail to make full use of the delivery network and can degrade to unicast delivery from the origin server to each individual replica. More importantly, the response time will also suffer because the object has to be fetched from the origin server after the request arrives at the replica. This is not true of the propagation approach, where an object is always fresh at replicas.

In this paper, we propose a novel hybrid approach that will generate less traffic than the propagation approach, *and* the invalidation approach. The origin server makes the decision of using either propagation or invalidation method for each document, based on the statistics about the update frequency at the origin server and the request rates collected by replicas. We develop a technique that can reduce the burden of request rate collection at replicas and get rid of the implosion problem when replicas send the statistics to the origin server. Extensive simulations are performed to examine how the traffic generated and the freshness rate at replicas are affected by various parameters. We experiment with a wide range of request rate, update frequency, and the number of replicas. The results show that our approach can take advantage of content distribution network and significantly reduce the traffic generated, compared with the propagation approach and the invalidation approach.

The remainder of this paper is organized as follows. Section 2 provides an overview of our architectural model and assumptions. Section 3 describes schemes for managing consistency of documents at replicas with the origin server. In Section 4 we present extensive simulations to evaluate the performance of various delivery schemes. Related work is discussed in Section 5 and we conclude the paper in Section 6.

2. Architectural overview

In this section we briefly outline the architectural model and assumptions. The Internet can be described as a set of interconnected, autonomous domains (see Fig. 1). A domain may have zero or more content providers (called *origin servers*), which can be fully or partially replicated in other domains. An origin server can specify whether it is replicable or not, and similarly, a domain may have policies about whether it allows replicas in the domain or not.

In the example in Fig. 1, domain D_1 contains an origin server S, which has seven replicas (R_2, R_3, R_4, R_5, R_8, R_9, R_{11}) located in different domains. We assume that a delivery infrastructure (or *delivery network*) has been established from the origin server to the replicas. For example, an application layer multicast [1] protocol may have set up unicast tunnels from S to R_2, from R_2 to R_3, R_4, R_5, from R_4 to R_8, R_9, and from R_5 to R_{11}. This delivery network can be used to propagate information from the origin server S to all replicas. Information collected by replicas can be combined along the way when they are sent back to the origin server through this delivery network.

We view the establishment of replicas as an incremental process. When a new replica is set up, we need to decide how to fill up its content (all or partial). Later when a change

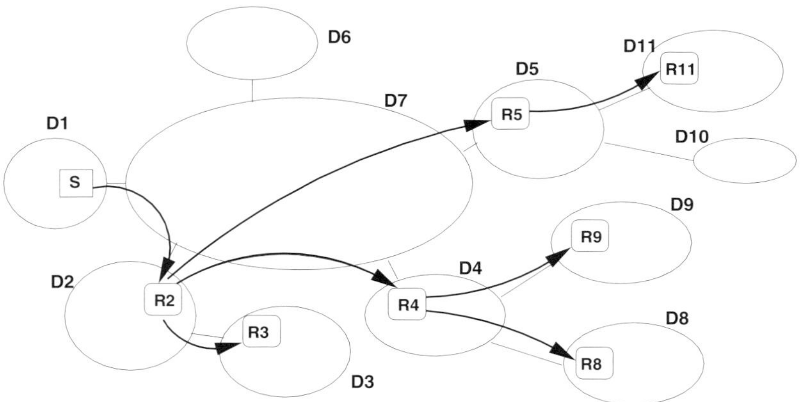

Fig. 1. Architecture for Content Delivery.

is made to a document at the origin server, we need to decide how the update will be made aware to all replicas. Our goal is to guarantee that any object served by any replica to clients is always fresh.

We assume all client requests will be directed to some replica. Which specific replica will be chosen for a request by a client is the server selection problem. Different schemes for server selection may result in different response time of clients and the traffic generated from clients to replicas. Because server selection is not the focus of this paper, we ignore the traffic generated from the clients to replicas. The traffic we are interested in and used as one of performance measures is the traffic generated for delivering content from the origin server to replicas. In the following sections, we will describe several consistency management schemes, which will generate different levels of traffic.

3. Schemes for managing consistency

3.1. Propagation

Propagation is an approach often used in CDNs. Whenever an object is changed at the origin server, it is propagated to all replicas through the delivery network by multicast. This can guarantee that an object is always up to date at any replica when it is requested from a client. We assume that the propagation will not take too long, so we ignore the temporal state in which a request for a document is processed at a replica when the document has been changed at the origin server and is being propagated towards replicas. In these cases a client will get a copy of document different from the one at the origin server, but we still consider it fresh. Under this assumption, we know that the documents served by replicas are always the newest version.

For a newly established replica, all documents at the origin server will be delivered to it by unicast. This will guarantee that each replica has an up-to-date version of all objects at the origin server when it is set up.

3.2. Invalidation

Another approach is invalidation, in which an invalidation message is delivered to all replicas through the delivery network by multicast when an object is changed at the origin server. Each replica will mark the object invalid upon the reception of this invalidation message. When a request for the object is processed at the replica at a later time, the replica will send a request to the origin server, which will use unicast to deliver the object to this replica. We also ignore the temporal state in which an invalidation is being delivered from the origin server to replicas and consider the copy served by replica during the time fresh. Though a document in a replica may be invalid for a certain period of time, the copy served by the replica to clients will always be the newest version.

In the invalidation approach, a newly established replica can simply assume that all objects are invalid. The replica will be filled up as it gets more requests from clients and tries to fetch a fresh copy from the origin server.

3.3. Our approach

We propose a hybrid approach based on the observations of problems existing in the propagation and invalidation approaches. With propagation, a document is propagated to replicas even if it is not accessed at all. This may generate extra traffic and we find that if a document is not accessed frequently enough, it should not be propagated.

In the invalidation approach, a document may be delivered to replicas through unicast because it is invalidated by the origin server and each replica fetch the document individually. Thus the traffic is more than it could have been if the multicast delivery is used. The observation is that if a document is accessed frequently enough, we should use multicast to deliver it to replicas, rather than let each replica fetch it by unicast.

In addition to the access frequency (or *request rate*), another factor is the *update rate* of documents at the origin server. It determines how frequently a document is propagated or invalidated and thus, the traffic for propagation or unicast fetching. Actually it is the relative values of the request rate and the update rate that determine what method we should use. It is simple in the caching scheme because we can use propagation if the request rate is greater than the update rate, otherwise use invalidation. We cannot generalize this to CDNs by simply comparing the rate of requests and updates, because we have to take into account that the methods of transmitting documents from the origin server to replicas are different, propagation using multicast and invalidation using unicast. Therefore, we need to factor in the relative efficiency of unicast and multicast.

Relations between unicast and multicast transmissions were first studied in [3] and recently validated by empirical studies [4,5]. Assume that L_m is the total number of multicast links in the distribution tree and L_n is the total number of unicast hops for distribution from the source to all replicas. Then we have

$$\frac{L_m}{L_n} = 1 - \delta \qquad (1)$$

where δ represents the percentage gain in multicast efficiency over unicast. We can have an estimate of δ in terms of the number of receivers, N and an associated *efficiency factor*, ε. That is, $\delta = 1 - N^{\varepsilon}$. The value of ε tends to range between -0.34 and -0.30 [5]. In our simulations we set $\varepsilon = -0.3$.

We consider a specific object, assuming its update rate at the origin server is U and the total request rate is R. As discussed above, we focus on the traffic generated for transmission of the document from the origin server to replicas. Assume that the document size is s and time we measure the traffic is t. (Actually s and t will later be removed from the inequality because they appear at both sides.) If we use propagation, the traffic generated is $T_p = U \times L_m \times s \times t$.

In the invalidation approach, we ignore the traffic generated for sending invalidation messages for now (because they are relatively small) and focus on unicast fetch by replicas. The request rate by each replica is $\frac{R}{N}$ and the average number of hops from the origin server to each replica is $\frac{L_n}{N}$. Therefore, the traffic generated by invalidation[2] is $T_i = \left(\frac{R}{N} \times \frac{L_n}{N}\right) \times s \times t \times N = R \times L_n \times s \times t/N$.

Our strategy is based on the relative value of T_p and T_i. Use propagation if $T_p < T_i$; use invalidation if $T_p > T_i$. With the power law relation (1) between L_m and L_n, we can get our final decision rule:

$$\text{For each object, if } U \times N^{1+\varepsilon} < R, \quad \text{use propagation;} \qquad \text{otherwise} \quad \text{use invalidation.}$$

where U is the update rate, R is the total request rate, N is the number of replicas, and ε is the efficiency factor ($-0.34 \leq \varepsilon \leq 0.30$).

The number of replicas is available at the origin server. The update rate for each object can be calculated based on the history. The main problem is to get the total request rate at the origin server, while all requests are made to replicas. The simple solution is that each replica collects statistics about the request rate and periodically pushes the data to the origin server. The implosion problem may occur if the number of replicas is large. Our solution is to make use of the delivery network existing between replicas and the origin server. Rather than let replicas push the statistics directly to the origin server, we let the origin server periodically send poll messages to those replicas directly connected in the multicast distribution tree. When a replica receives a poll message, it sends a poll message to replicas directly connected to it downstream, if any. If a replica does not have any replica connected to it downstream, it will send a reply with request rate information to its upstream replica (or the origin server). Those replicas having sent out poll messages will calculate the aggregate request rate for each object after it receives all replies to its poll messages. Then these aggregate rates are sent further upstream. The origin server will get the total request rate information after it receives replies from all replicas directly connected to it. This request rate collection process will take place in the time frame of hours. So the traffic generated is not significant compared to the volume of traffic generated for shipping objects from the origin server to replicas. The collection process is similar to the concast in the context of active networking [6,7], but we can deploy the algorithm in our distribution network without requiring the network being active.

One way to reduce the size of request rate information is that we can ignore those objects requested less than or equal to a threshold value. For example, if we set the threshold value to 1, we can ignore objects requested once or not requested at all. Actually the number of these objects may be large and the size of the reply messages can be made

[2] Note that traffic generated by the invalidation approach is usually less than T_i because it is the worst scenario value.

much smaller. It is up to the origin server whether to make adjustment to the final result, if such optimization takes place at replicas. For example, if the threshold value is 1, we can let the origin server add N/2 to the request rate of each object.

One remaining problem is how to deal with the newly established replica. Our solution is based on the statistics currently available at the origin server. Those documents satisfying $U \times N^{1+\varepsilon} < R$ will be delivered to the replica by unicast, and all other documents will be marked invalid at the replica.

4. Performance evaluation

4.1. Simulation setup

We use GT-ITM [8] to generate 1600 node transit-stub graphs. The origin server is randomly located in one of stub domain. We experiment with 10, 50, 90 replicas, which are located in different stub domains at the node directly connected to transit domain. These replicas and the origin server are connected by a multicast delivery network, which is established by first calculating a complete distance graph for replicas and the origin server and then generating a spanning tree. This tree is used for delivering propagation and invalidation messages. We assume that the average size of objects is 10 KBytes and the size of an invalidation for each object is 100 Bytes.

Assume that there are ten thousand objects at the origin server and the total request rate to these objects is either 0.1, 1 or 10 million times per day. We assume the distribution of requests to different objects follows the Zipf distribution [9,10]. If we order the objects from 1 to 10,000 according to their popularities, the probability of requesting objects $1, 2, 3 \ldots$ will be proportional to $\frac{1}{1}, \frac{1}{2}, \frac{1}{3}, \ldots$. Each request will be made to one replica selected randomly.

Next problem is to determine the *inter-update time* (the inverse of the update rate) of each object. Previous research has shown that there is no direct relationship between the request rate to an object and its inter-update time [10]. We use a random allocation scheme to set the inter-update time for each object. We first choose an average inter-update time of all objects, τ. The inter-update time of an object is randomly chosen from $(0, 2 \times \tau)$. We experiment with τ ranging from 1 to 200 hours. Note this is average inter-update time. The real inter-update time of an object can be very close to 0 and thus the update frequency can be very high.

We have two performance measures. The first one is *traffic generated* during one day. If an object of size s goes through n hops, the traffic generated is counted as $s \times n$. This is used in both multicast and unicast delivery. Another interesting measure is the *freshness rate*, which is the percentage of objects that are fresh when a request arrives at the replica. We want to emphasize that if a replica finds an object is not fresh, it will fetch a fresh copy from the origin server and deliver this new copy to the client. Therefore, all objects served by replicas are always consistent with that in the origin server, even if the freshness rate is less than 100%. The freshness rate only measures the probability that replicas can serve directly without resorting to the origin server. Therefore, the higher the freshness rate, the shorter the response time.

4.2. Results

We compare three approaches: (1) the propagation approach, (2) the invalidation approach, and (3) our hybrid approach. We first experiment with the request rate of one million per day and let the average inter-update time change from 1 to 100 hours. We always use 50 replicas in the following simulations, unless we explicitly specify otherwise. The traffic generated by each approach is shown in Fig. 2. When the average inter-update time is less than 10, the propagation approach generates extremely high volume traffic because of high frequency of blind propagation. When the inter-update time increases from 1 to 100, the traffic generated by all three approaches decreases. The propagation approach decreases faster than the invalidation approach, because it takes advantage of multicast delivery network while the invalidation approach relies on unicast fetching by replicas from the origin server. When the average inter-update time is larger than 35, the propagation approach generates less traffic than the invalidation approach. Our approach chooses different methods for different kinds of objects and can always generate less traffic than both the propagation approach and the invalidation approach. Fig. 3 shows the freshness rate at replicas. The propagation approach always has 100% freshness rate. Our approach has a significantly higher freshness rate than the invalidation approach. The freshness rate is greater than 90% when the average inter-update time reaches 19, at which point the propagation approach generates more than twice as much traffic as ours and the invalidation approach has a freshness rate less than 70%.

Fig. 4 and 5 give the traffic and the freshness rate when the average inter-update time changes from 100 to 200. We get a closer look and can find that the traffic generated by our approach is still significantly less than that generated by both the propagation approach and the invalidation approach, while the freshness rate of our approach is much closer to 100% and the freshness rate of the invalidation approach is almost always less than 90%.

Figs. 6 and 7 give the traffic and the freshness rate when the request rate is 0.1 million per day. The traffic generated by the invalidation approach and our approach is much

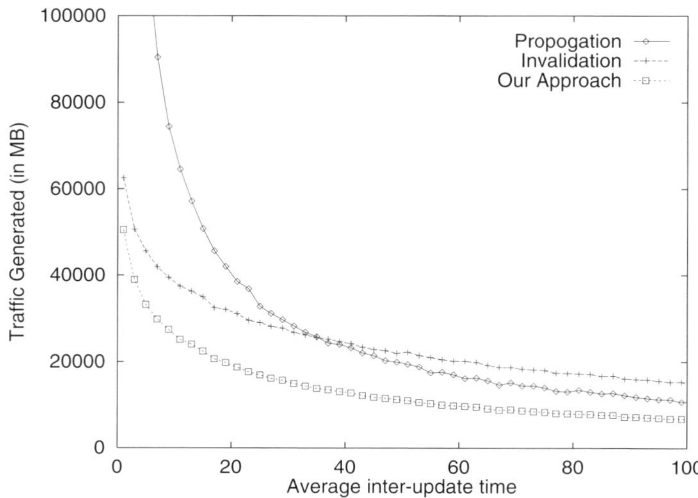

Fig. 2. Traffic generated (request rate = 1M).

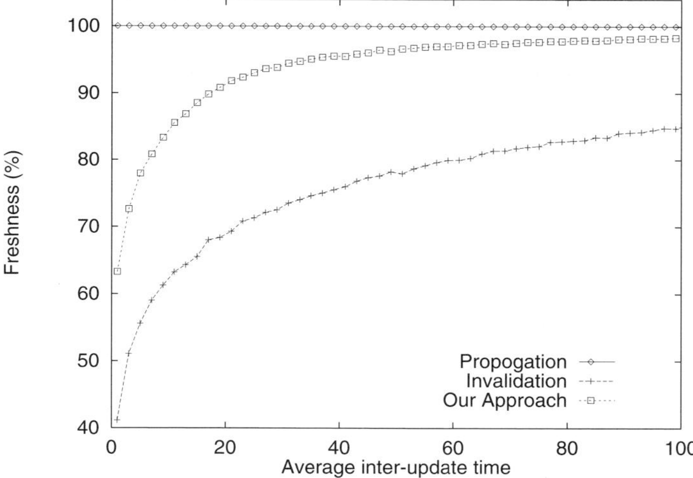

Fig. 3. Freshness rate (request rate = 1M).

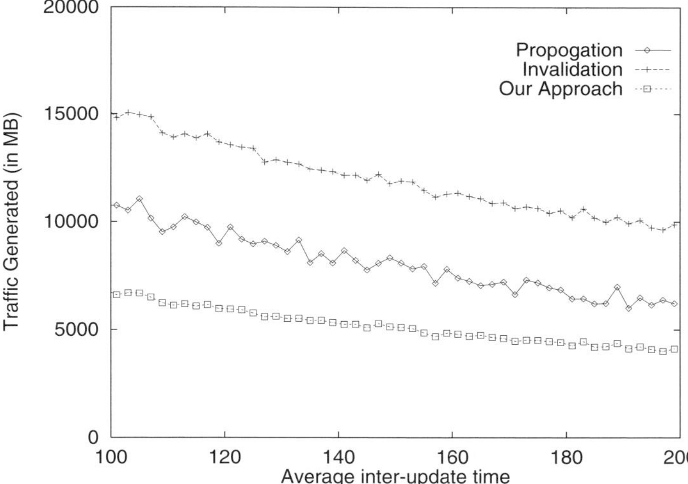

Figs. 4. Traffic generated (request rate = 1M, average inter-update time > 100).

less than in the previous 1M request rate case. They also come closer, and the difference between them and the propagation approach becomes larger. The freshness rate of our approach is always 20% higher than the invalidation approach.

We increase the request rate to 10 millions per day in Figs. 8 and 9 The traffic generated by the three approaches is all higher than in the 1M request rate case. This time the traffic generated by the invalidation approach is significantly higher than both the propagation approach and our approach. This tells us that in these relatively high request rate case, propagation is more appropriate. At the same time, the freshness rate of our approach is very close to 100% and much better than that of the invalidation approach.

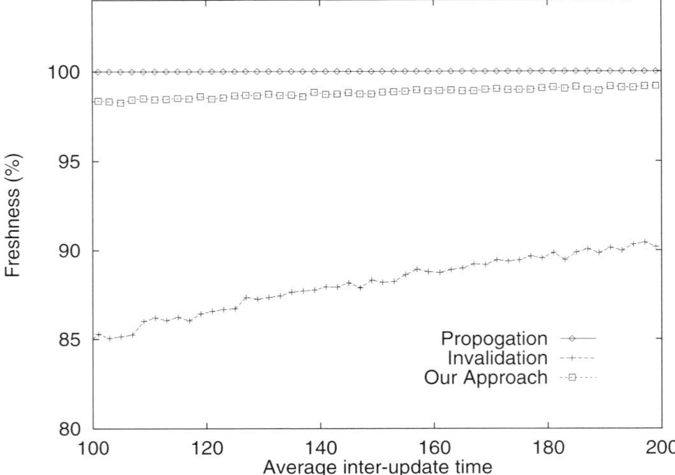

Fig. 5. Freshness rate (request rate = 1M, average inter-update time > 100).

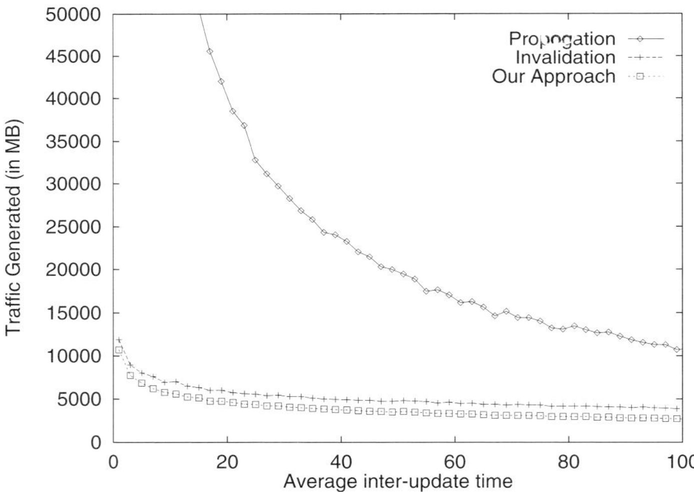

Fig. 6. Traffic generated (request rate = 0.1M).

Next we examine the effect of the number of replicas. We set the request rate to one million. In Figs. 10 and 11, we have 10 replicas. All three approaches generate less traffic than the previous 50 replica case in Figs. 2 and 3. The cross point of the propagation approach and the invalidation approach shifts left. It changes from 35 in the 50 replica case to 10. Also the freshness rate is higher than in the 50 replica case. Figs. 12 and 13 show the traffic and the freshness rate when the number of replicas is 90. As expected, all three approaches generate more traffic than the 50 replica case and the cross point increases to 53. The freshness rate is lower than in the 50 replica case.

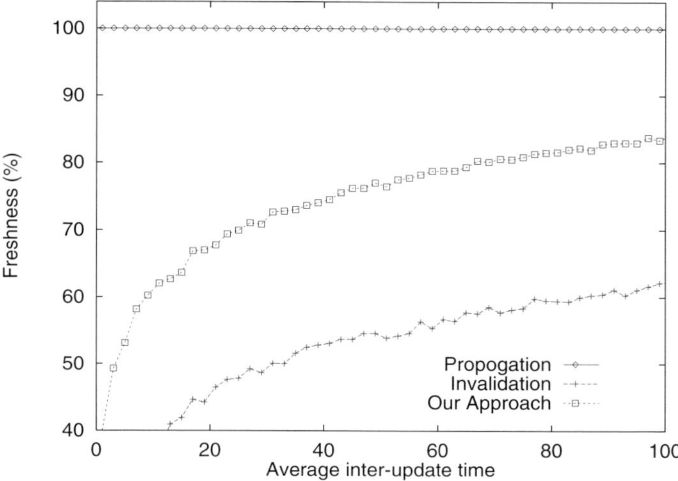

Fig. 7. Freshness rate (request rate = 0.1M).

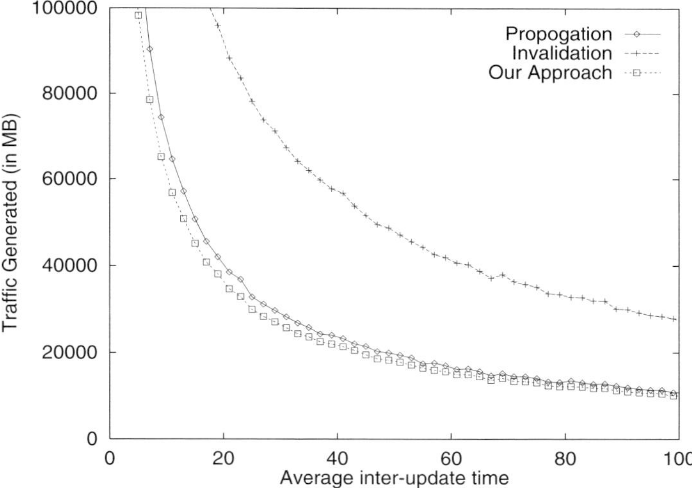

Fig. 8. Traffic generated (request rate = 10M).

5. Related work

Efficient delivery of content to clients has attracted much attention over a decade. The interests in it are also exemplified by the commercial development of delivery network [11–13]. The design and techniques used in these systems are mostly proprietary.

Early research on content delivery concentrates on using native multicast to push the content to the clients directly [14,15]. These schemes are most efficient when the content is changed at a high frequency [16]. It is not an easy task to determine whether a document should be multicast or not. The lack of native multicast support leads people to design

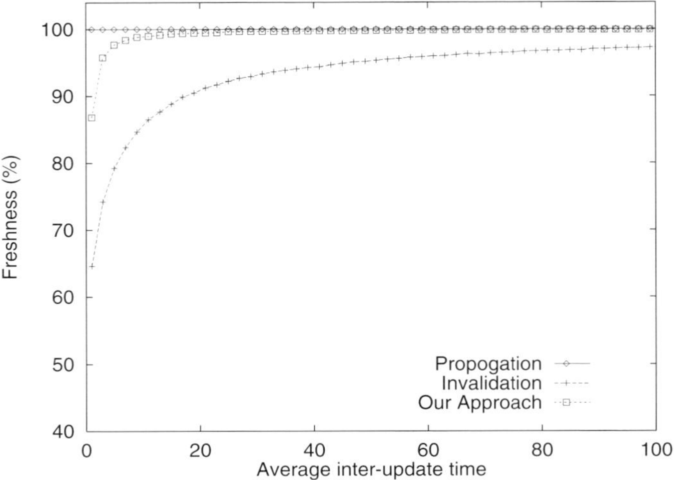

Fig. 9. Freshness rate (request rate = 10M).

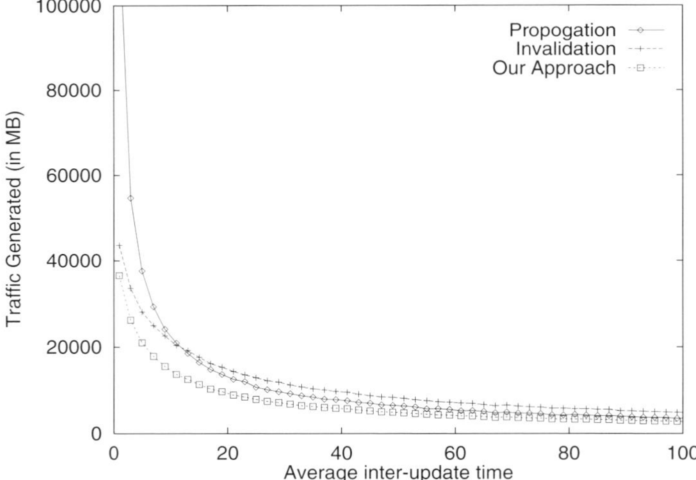

Fig. 10. Traffic generated (10 replicas).

alternative ways for delivery. Prominent among them are application layer multicast schemes: Yallcast [2], end system multicast [1], and scattercast [17]. Basically they run an auto-configuration protocol to establish a delivery structure of tunneled topology among participating members. These unicast connections are used for delivery of content from the origin server to participating nodes. While the Yallcast set up tunnels directly among members, the end system multicast and the scattercast build a mesh topology first and then run the spanning tree algorithm to establish a delivery tree. While the self-organization topology setup mechanism complements our work, these schemes do not discuss how to update dynamic content efficiently.

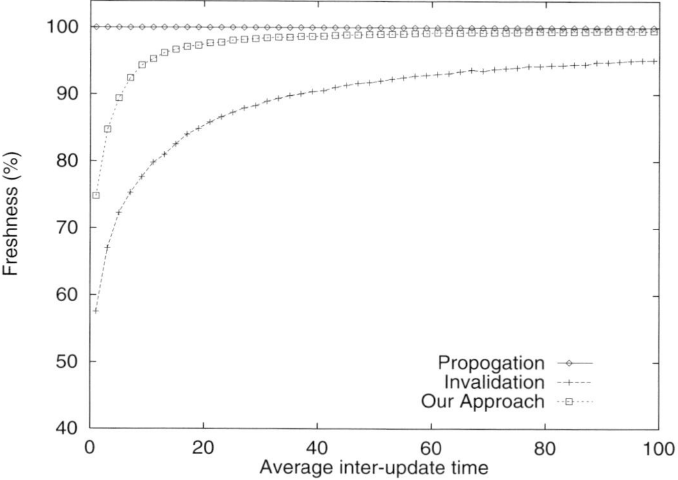

Fig. 11. Freshness rate (10 replicas).

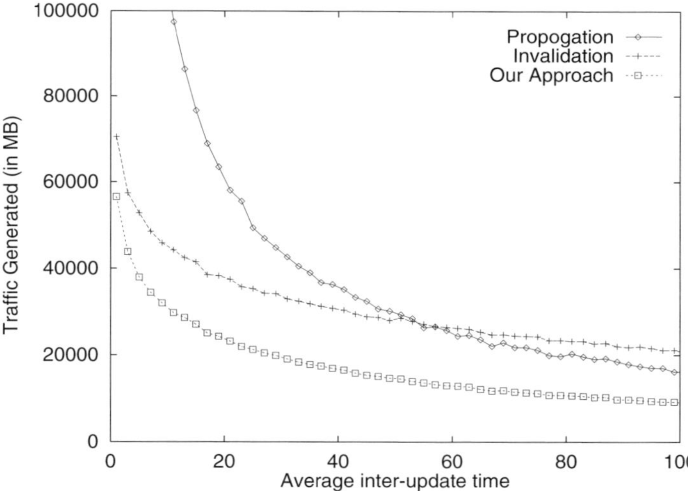

Fig. 12. Traffic generated (90 replicas).

Caching is an area closely related to content delivery. Harvest [18] is an earliest proposal trying to establish a hierarchical caching structure, in which the bandwidth can be more efficiently used and the popular web pages can be pushed closer to the clients. Other hierarchical schemes are adaptive web caching [19], access driven cache [20]. The problem with caching schemes is how to maintain the freshness of the content stored in the cache. There are several proposals dealing with this problem. A simple way to guarantee the freshness is that the cache always check with the origin server. Using IMS, a cache can get the reply from the origin server that the page is fresh, or get a fresh page itself. There are some heuristic schemes to determine the freshness by observing

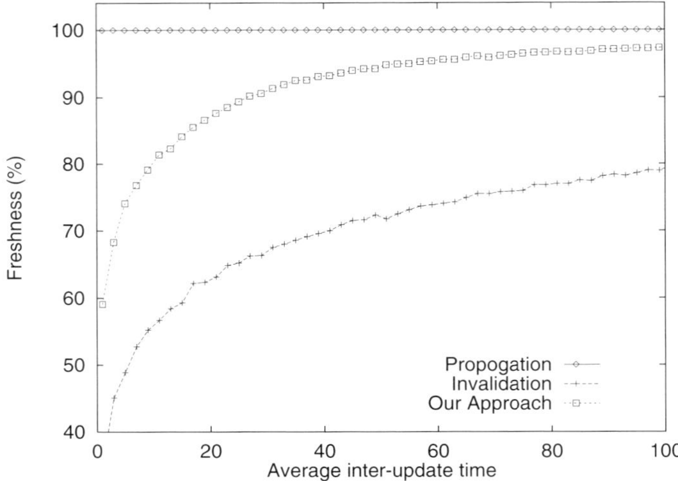

Fig. 13. Freshness rate (90 replicas).

the life time of a page [21]. The longer a page has not been modified, the longer it will not be modified in the future. However, these adaptive schemes cannot guarantee the freshness of a page. The invalidation scheme was proposed to deal with the problem [22]. Unfortunately, requiring a server to contact a huge number of caches is simply not feasible from a scalability standpoint. In CDNs, the invalidation can be used because knowledge about replicas is available and the delivery network can be used to forward the invalidations.

Invalidation can be used most efficiently when combined with propagation and other approaches in CDNs. SPREAD architecture [23] analyzed the tradeoff among client validation (by using IMS), invalidation, and propagation (called replication in that paper). It analyzed the effects of different update distributions on the determination of the thresholds that decide which method to use. The discussion was based on the translucent proxying architecture that achieves transparency to clients by intercepting SYN of a TCP connection and using IP tunneling. The paper used a trace-driven simulation to show the benefits of the threshold-based approach with unicast validation, invalidation and propagation in terms of consumed bandwidth and client latency. There is a brief discussion about multicast extension to the architecture. MMO protocol [24] proposed to use multicast for delivery and invalidation of updates. Whenever an object is changed at the origin server, an invalidation is sent to all replicas by multicast. The new version is immediately delivered to a multicast group, through which all subscribed replicas can get the updated version of an object. A decision is made at each replica whether to join the multicast group or not, based on a threshold W. If there is no request during previous W invalidation periods, the replica does not join; otherwise, it does. The paper shows the performance gain of the protocol without details about how to determine the threshold and how it is related to the inter-update time of an object.

The focus of this paper is on the impact of multicast delivery on the decision making at the origin server whether to use propagation and invalidation. We design a very simple decision rule to select the best strategy on the per object basis. Equipped with our efficient scheme for access rate collection, our approach makes propagation and invalidation perform in a way to generate maximal benefit from each of them, and achieves the goal of reducing the traffic for consistency management.

6. Concluding remarks

Content distribution network can be deployed to improve client performance by pushing the content towards the edges of the network and closer to clients. One of the key problems in CDN is how to manage the consistency of content at replicas with the origin server, especially for those documents changing dynamically. This problem will become more prominent when more web sites use CDNs. In this paper, we proposed a novel approach in which the origin server determines the best way for each document. We explored the impact of multicast delivery network on our decision making process. By using the power law relation between multicast and unicast distributions, we can more accurately determine the traffic generated and make a right decision. The process of collecting request rates is made scalable to a very large number of replicas by aggregating information at the intermediate replicas. We performed extensive simulations to explore the effects of the request rate, the average inter-update time and the number of replicas. The simulations demonstrate that our approach can generate significantly less traffic than both the propagation approach and the invalidation approach.

One question we can further investigate is what the results will be affected if the demand for an object is not uniform across all replicas. One way to deal with it is that we can form multiple multicast groups with each group for a set of objects closely related. Each replica will be associated with those groups having objects that the replica has a high request rate. The decision will be made at the origin server for each group based on the number of replicas in the group and information collected from those replicas. We will study issues of how to divide objects into groups and how replicas will be associated with them in the future.

Acknowledgments

The author would like to thank Dr. Jim Griffieon for his discussions of the subject and anonymous reviewers for their comments on the paper.

References

[1] Y. Chu, S. Rao, and H. Zhang, A case for end system multicast, in *Proceedings of ACM Sigmetrics*, June 2000. Santa Clara, CA.

[2] P. Francis, Yallcast: Extending the Internet multicast architecture. http://www.yallcast.com

[3] J. Chuang and M. Sirbu, Pricing multicast communication: A cost based approach, in *Proceedings of INET'98*, July 1998. Geneva, Switzerland.

[4] G. Phillips, S. Shenker, and H. Tangmunarunkit, Scaling of multicast trees: Comments on the Chuang-Sirbu scaling law, in *Proceedings of ACM SIGCOMM'99*, August 1999. Cambridge, Massachusetts.

[5] R.C. Chalmers and K.C. Almeroth, Modeling the branching characteristics and efficiency gains in global multicast trees, in *Proceedings of INFOCOM'2001*, April 2001.

[6] K. Calvert, J. Griffioen, A. Sehgal, and S. Wen, Concast: Design and implementation of a new network service, in *Proceedings of 1999 International Conference on Network Protocols, Toronto*, Ontario, November 1999.
[7] K. Calvert, J. Griffioen, A. Sehgal, and S. Wen, Implementing a concast service, in *Proceedings of the 37th Annual Allerton Conference on Communication, Control, and Computing*, September 1999.
[8] K. Calvert, M. Doar, and E.W. Zegura, Modeling Internet topology, *IEEE Communications Magazine*, June 1997.
[9] G. Zipf, ed., *Human Behavior and the Principle of Least Effort*. Reading, MA: Addison-Wesley, 1949.
[10] L. Breslau, P. Cao, L. Fan, G. Phillips, and S. Shenker, Web caching and zipf-like distributions: Evidence, and implications, in *Proceedings of INFOCOM'99*, March 1999.
[11] Akamai, http://www.akamai.com.
[12] Digital Island, http://www.digitalisland.net.
[13] Inktomi Corporation, http://www.inktomi.com.
[14] J. Nonnenmacher and E. Biersack, Asynchronous multicast push: AMP, in *Proceedings of ICCC'97*, pp. 419–430, Nov. 1997. Cannes, France.
[15] Rodriguez and E. Biersack, Continuous multicast push of web documents over the Internet, *IEEE Network Magazine*, vol. 12, pp. 18–31, March–April 1998.
[16] P. Rodriguez, E.W. Biersack, and K.W. Ross, Improving the www: Caching or multicast?, in *Proceedings of the 3rd International Web Caching Workshop*, June 1998. Manchester, England.
[17] Y. Chawathe, S. McCanne, and E.A. Brewer, An architecture for Internet content distribution as an infrastructure service, Feb. 2000. Available at http://www.cs.berkeley.edu/yatin/papers/scattercast.ps
[18] A. Chankhunthod, P.B. Danzig, C. Neerdaels, M.F. Schwartz, and K.J. Worrel, A hierarchical Internet object cache, in *Usenix'96*, January 1996.
[19] S. Michel, K. Nguyen, A. Rosenstein, L. Zhang, S. Floyd, and V. Jacobson, Adaptive web caching: Towards a new caching architecture, *Computer Network and ISDN Systems*, Nov. 1998.
[20] J. Yang, W. Wang, R. Muntz, and J. Wang, Access driven web caching. UCLA Technical Report 990007.
[21] J. Gwertzman and M. Seltzer, World-wide web cache consistency, in *Proceedings of the USENIX Conference*, Dec. 1996. Copper Mountain Resort, CO.
[22] H. Yu, L. Breslau, and S. Shenker, A scalable web cache consistency architecture, in *Proceedings of ACM Sigcomm'99*, August 1999.
[23] P. Rodriguez and S. Sibal, SPREAD: Scalable platform for reliable and efficient automated distribution, in *Proceedings of the 9th International World Wide Web Conference*, May 2000. Amsterdam.
[24] D. Li and D.R. Cheriton, Scalable web caching of frequently updated objects using reliable multicast, in *Proceedings of 2nd USENIX Symposium on Internet Technologies and Systems (USITS'99)*, October 1999. Boulder, Colorado.

Panel 1 – Resolved: Publish No More Papers on Web Cache Replacement Policies

Moderator: Jeffrey Mogul, *Compaq Western Research Lab*

Panelists: Martin Arlitt, *Hewlett-Packard Laboratories*
Pei Cao, *Cisco Systems*
Alex Rousskov, *The Measurement Factory*
Carey Williamson, *University of Saskatchewan*

Web Caching and Content Delivery
A. Bestavros and M. Rabinovich (Editors)

Content Services Network: The Architecture and Protocols

Wei-Ying Ma [a,1], Bo Shen [b,2], Jack Brassil [b,3]

[a] *Microsoft Research China, China*
[b] *Hewlett-Packard Laboratories, 1501 Page Mill Road, Palo Alto, CA 94304-1126, USA*

Abstract

Content delivery networks (CDNs) can be viewed as application-specific overlay networks that make web caching an infrastructure service accessible to any content provider. As the Internet continues to evolve with increasing diversity and heterogeneity, we see a growing demand for extending the capabilities of network intermediaries to provide additional services such as content adaptation, personalization, watermarking and location-aware data insertion.

A content services network (CSN) is proposed in this paper to make content transformation and processing an infrastructure service accessible to its subscribers. One can think of CSN as another layer of network infrastructure built around CDNs. This layer interacts collaboratively with user-agents, content servers, and other network intermediaries including ISPs' caching proxies and CDNs' surrogates in the content delivery process to provide value-added services. Furthermore, a CSN provides network resources that are used as a 'service' distribution channel for value-added services providers to make their applications an infrastructure service.

To demonstrate the utility of our proposed CSN model, we describe the prototype implementation of a video segmentation and keyframe selection system as an infrastructure service that can be used by content providers or end users to enhance the way video is delivered over the Internet.

Keywords: Content delivery network; Internet proxy services; Internet Content Adaptation Protocol; Internet service delivery

1. Introduction

In the past two years we have seen a huge industrial effort devoted to the research and development of content delivery networks (CDNs). One can think of CDNs as an overlay network of a large number of caching proxies deployed at the network edge and used as a distribution channel to push content closer to the end user. CDNs handle many issues that used to be a technical burden to the content provider, such as scalability (service automatically scales up while the client requests increase), reliability (content is always available), and flash crowd control. CDNs enable content providers to avoid having to provision and manage their own networks and servers to handle the above issues.

[1] E-mail: wyma@microsoft.com
[2] E-mail: boshen@hpl.hp.com
[3] E-mail: jtb@hpl.hp.com

Table 1. Comparison of CSN and CDNs

	Content services network (CSN)	Content delivery networks (CDNs)
System overview	An overlay network of application proxies	An overlay network of caching proxies
Services	Processing	Storage and caching
Resource types	CPU and processor	Memory and disk
Protocol	Simple object access protocol (SOAP) and Internet service delivery protocol (ISDP)	Internet content adaptation protocol (iCAP)
Distribution channel for	Value-added services and applications	Web contents
Customers	Content providers, end users, ISPs, and CDNs	Content providers or ISPs

In CDNs, caching is the primary intermediary service performed between clients and servers. That is, CDNs only replicates content and makes sure it is delivered reliably and promptly to end-users. They do not modify the content by adding value to it. As the Internet continues to evolve with increasing diversity and heterogeneity, we see a growing demand for extending the capabilities of network intermediaries to provide additional services such as content adaptation, personalization, watermarking and location-aware data insertion. Due to the lack of network support, these problems are being ignored or resolved in an ad-hoc manner. For instance, to make content created for desktop PCs appear appropriately on handheld devices with smaller form factor, content providers typically re-author the content and create multiple versions for different devices. This process is not only time-consuming but also complicates content management.

To make content services an Internet infrastructure service, we propose a new architecture called 'content services network (CSN)'. One can think of content services network as another layer of network infrastructure (an overlaid network) built around CDNs. This layer interacts collaboratively with user-agents, content servers, and other network intermediaries including ISPs' caching proxies and CDNs' surrogates in the content delivery process to provide value-added services.

A CSN provides network resources that are used as a 'service' distribution channel for value-added services providers to make their applications an infrastructure service. In many aspects, the benefit a CSN offered to value-added service providers are similar to what CDNs have offered to content providers. The services of a CSN can be subscribed and used by content provider, end user, ISP or even CDNs who pay for the service. For example, a content provider may request a content adaptation service from a CSN, and its content will be automatically adapted at the network edge before delivered to clients.

A brief comparison between CSN and CDNs is provided in Table 1. This comparison reflects a trend described by Katz [11], "the new Internet will be shaped by the ability to manage computation and storage deep inside the network, connected by application-specific overlay networks, all on behalf of end user applications. This is what we call services . . . " One can think of CDNs as application-specific overlay networks for storage and web caching. In comparison, CSN moves one step further and makes computation (processing and transcoding) an infrastructure service through the development of another overlay network around CDNs.

The technical issues a CSN needs to address are:

(1) How to manage a large scale of computational resources and network services;

(2) How to make the value-added services an infrastructure service that is accessible to its customers which could be content provider, end user, ISP or CDNs;

(3) How to make a CSN interact with other existing network elements collaboratively and seamlessly so that the service model does not undermine the success of end-to-end nature of Internet client/server interactions.

1.1. Related works

The problem of adaptive content delivery in a heterogeneous network environment has been studied quite extensively in the past few years. Example works include Spyglass [14], ProxiNet [16], Intel QuickWeb [15], IBM Transcoding proxy [20], UC-Berkeley TranSend [12], Digestor [18], Mobiware [17], and Smart Client [21]. However, these works did not deal with the problem from the perspective of infrastructure service. Instead, they looked into the deployment of content adaptation technology at an origin server or a transcoding proxy.

In web caching and content distribution community, a number of Internet-Drafts have been proposed to address the problem of extending the functionality of a caching proxy for providing additional services that mediate, modify, and monitor object requests and responses. The IETF Working Group on Open Pluggable Edge Services (OPES) [23] and the Internet Content Adaptation Protocol (iCAP) [7] are the works closely related to our proposed CSN. We use some of the extended functions in their proposed future caching proxy as a foundation to build CSN.

Here we summarize the novel contributions of our work:

(1) The idea of content services network (CSN) is proposed first time in the literature. We describe its system architecture and discuss two network protocols used by CSN to interact with other network elements for performing value-added services.

(2) CSN provides an application framework in which SOAP Simple Object Access Protocol (SOAP) [31] or iCAP operates, so we are able to investigate the issues such as control of policy. We propose a new Internet service delivery protocol (ISDP) which supplements these two protocols.

(3) As an example of our CSN's service, we turn a video segmentation and keyframe selection system into an infrastructure service that can be used by content providers or end users to enhance the way video is delivered over the Internet.

2. System architecture

The architecture of content services network (CSN) consists of the following three basic elements as shown in Fig. 1. They are:

Application proxy (AP) servers: host the software of value-added services for content delivery. These application proxy servers are deployed at the edge of the Internet backbone, providing computational resources to process content on behalf of content providers (content servers) or end users (clients). If the service is provided to ISPs, it is considered performed on behalf of end-users. If the service is provided to CDNs who may resell it as a value-added service in addition to content delivery service,

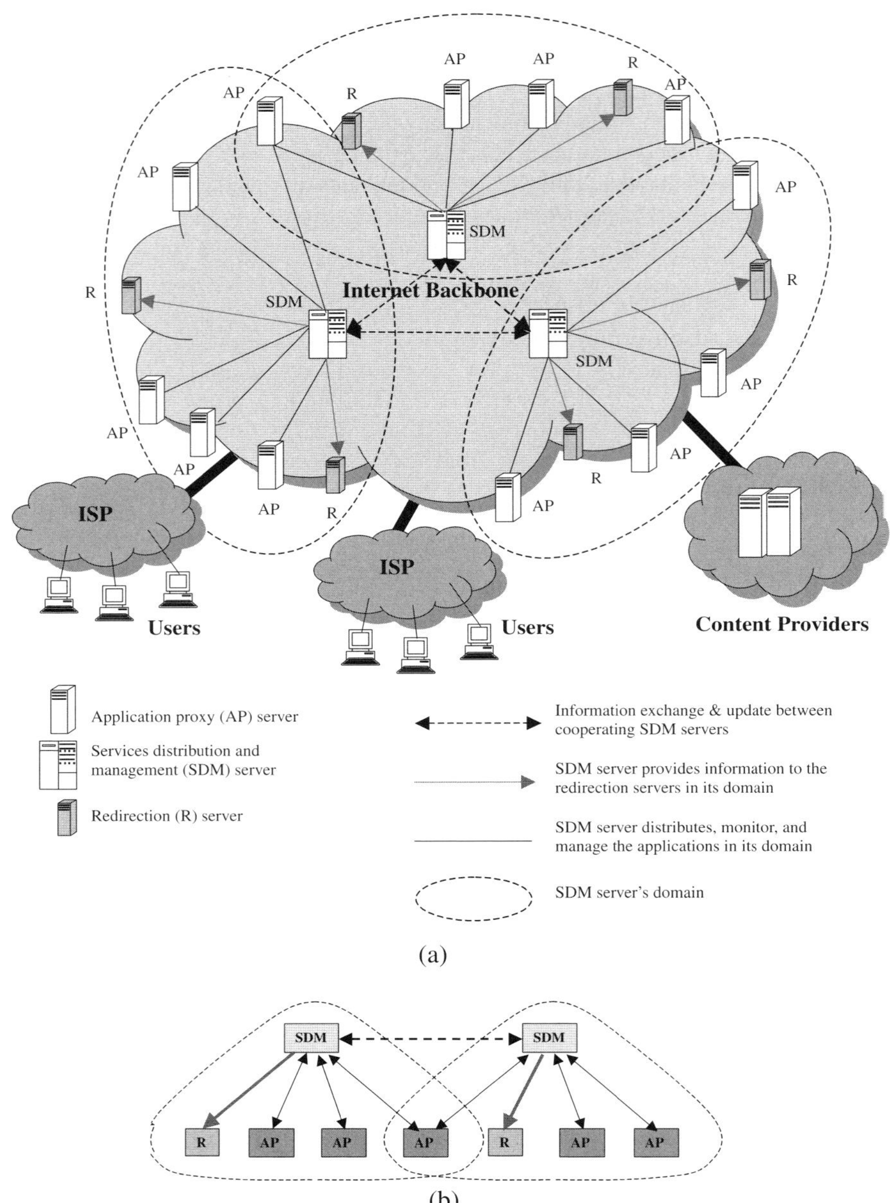

Fig. 1. The system overview of content services network (CSN).

it is considered performed on behalf of content providers. Application proxy servers have a variety of operational modes depending on how the service is performed. They may behave like transcoding proxy servers, remote callout servers, or surrogate servers (with processing and special hosting capability). We will discuss the various service modes in each service mode in Section 4.

Services distribution and management (SDM) servers: are responsible for the following tasks:

(a) they maintain static information about the service execution environment and the location of the applications,

(b) SDM servers register and distribute the services (applications) provided by value-added services providers. They take into account a set of metric that measures the demand of services, the history of servers' load, demography of clients etc, and decide a set of application proxies to remotely install applications.

(c) After initial service registration and distribution, SDM servers continue to monitor the performance of each service and dynamically adapt the scale of distribution and deployment of the service according to its demand.

(d) SDM servers aggregate the information about usage pattern, availability and location of each deployed service, and then provide the information back to the redirection servers. The redirection servers use this information to perform service discovery, network and server load balancing and etc.

(e) SDM server also provides management, accounting and billing functionalities to value-added service providers who use the CSN as service distribution channel. For example, value-added service providers may temporarily bring down their applications for maintenance or upgrade. They may want to know who have used their services and how much they have used so they can bill them.

(f) Each SDM server is responsible for collecting information about its domain and periodically exchanges the information with other cooperating SDM servers. This information exchange can be triggered automatically if there is a change in the system. To reduce bandwidth consumption for information exchange, each SDM server may build a spanning tree that propagates the information efficiently to other SDM servers. Fig. 1(b) shows the information exchange between two cooperating SDM servers.

Redirection servers: direct a service request to an application proxy server according to a number of attributes and measurements. Note that redirection servers receive information from SDM servers so they are able to perform services discovery and network and server load balancing while directing service requests to an application proxy that is close to it in the network. The redirection servers are deployed at the edge of the network. When a service request is sent to a CSN, it is first directed to a redirection server that is close to it in the network. This redirection server then checks various attributes and measurements and further redirects the request to an application proxy server.

Note that CSN is developed as another layer of network infrastructure around CDNs. From the inside, this layer manages its network resources and applications (value-added services) to enhance the way content is distributed. From the outside, it defines interfaces and protocols to handle a variety of system interactions occurring in different types of service request and rendering. We will discuss the role of the application proxy server and its interaction with caching proxies in the next section. The protocol issues will be discussed in Section 4. The redirection problem is covered in Section 5.

3. Open pluggable edge services (OPES)

In today's Internet, caching is the primary intermediary service performed between clients and servers to improve performance for web page access. As Internet continues to evolve with increasing diversity and heterogeneity, there is a need to extend the capabilities of network intermediaries for performing additional services that cannot be provided directly on clients or servers. The OPES has been formed to define protocols and APIs for a broad set of services that facilitate efficient delivery of complex content and services related to content [6].

Note that the most basic building component in a CSN is the application proxy server. In order to make CSN an open framework and architecture for distributing and executing value-added services developed by third-party companies, the application proxy servers should implement the protocols and APIs defined by OPES.

The current architecture of OPES supports two types of services; one is co-located with the transit intermediary (i.e. caching proxy) and the other is located on other cooperating servers (i.e. remote callout servers). For co-located services, OPES is defining the 'service environment caching proxy' (referred as '*OPES proxy*' hereafter) which extends the functionality of a traditional caching proxy, making it capable of executing additional services that mediate, modify, and monitor object requests and responses. For remote callout services, OPES may use protocols like SOAP [31] or iCAP [7] that handle transport of objects to cooperating servers and back.

The OPES proxy is equipped with message parsers, rule modules and a proxylet library for general services. Its services can be extended through the downloading of rule modules and proxylets from user agents and content servers. While messages flow through an OPES proxy, they are parsed and matched against the rules specified in the rule modules. The matching of a rule causes a service to be performed on the message. The execution of the service may be performed by a local proxylet or by a remote callout server via a transport protocol.

Although one can think of the application proxies in a CSN as the remote callout servers in OPES, CSN and OPES have very different view of the world with respect to how content services may be distributed, subscribed and rendered. This difference reflects how the service path is formed and handled. OPES is very caching-proxy centric, and it assumes caching proxy continuously to be the center of the system, coordinating all the participating network elements. This setting limits its capability to address the services (and business models) that may require a more flexible arrangement of service path and system interaction among participating parties. In contrast, CSN shifts the focus to the 'application proxy'. CSN considers many possible service scenarios and defines a variety of service modes (i.e. service paths) to characterize the way the service may be subscribed and rendered. We will discuss the various service modes in Section 4.

Fig. 2 shows the relationship between the OPES framework and the CSN architecture. Note that the application proxy is able to communicate directly with content servers and user agents to position itself at the right injection point in the service path to provide services. Keep in mind that the rendering of the service (processing) does not necessarily happen right after the service subscription stage. This is particularly true for post-distribution services such as personalization and insertion of regional data that are rendered at the network edge (more detail in Section 4). A typical scenario is that content servers or user agents may subscribe to the desired services from one application proxy

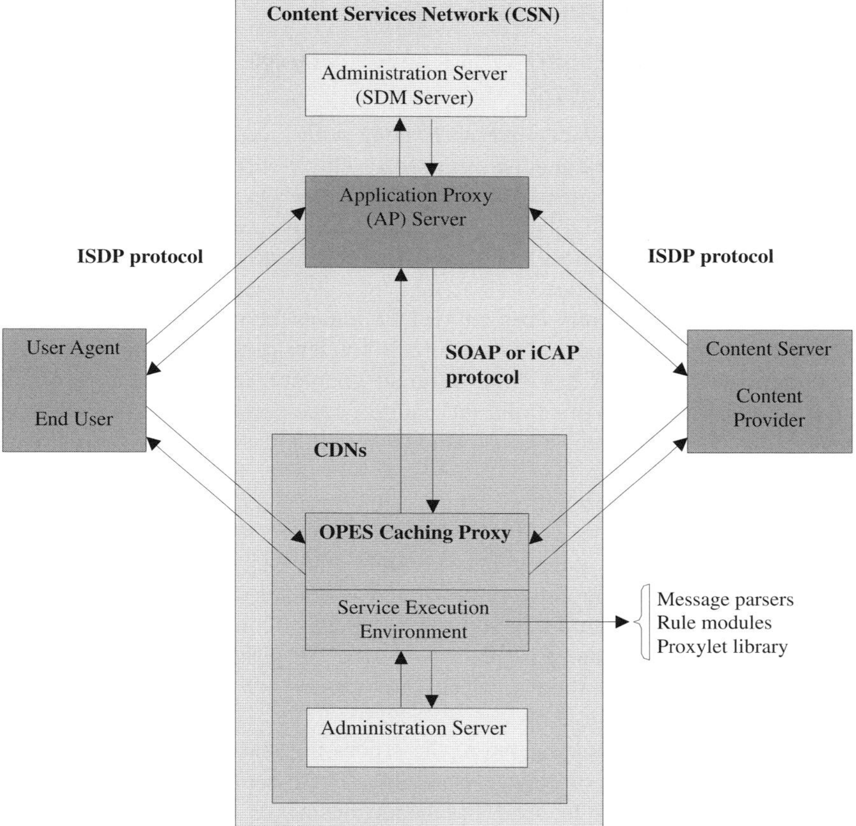

Fig. 2. The relationship between OPES proxies and the CSN architecture.

server and receive the services rendered from the other application proxy server at a later time. In this case, a certificate containing the description of the subscribed services and authentication information is first given to content servers or user agents. This certificate is distributed with the target object or the client request, instructing other network elements (e.g. OPES caching proxy) to perform functions (e.g. running a proxylet) or take actions (e.g. transporting objects to an application proxy via SOAP or iCAP protocol in order to receive value-added services).

4. Internet service delivery protocol

Fig. 2 shows two network protocols used in CSN. The SOAP and iCAP protocols provide an interface for CDNs and any caching proxy that supports OPES to communicate with a CSN for service delivery. One can think of SOAP or iCAP as a protocol for executing a 'remote procedure call' on HTTP messages for some sort of adaptation. Basically, the SOAP or iCAP client sends a request along with a target object (like POST method in HTTP/1.1) to the application proxy server for transformation or value-added services. An example iCAP URI might look like:

```
icap://ms1.csn.hp.net/video_services/
        summarization_and_keyframe_selection
```

The SOAP and iCAP protocols are used along with a certificate issued by CSN for providing content services at the edge of network. This certificate represents a service to be performed on behalf of content providers or end users. On the other hand, the Internet Service Delivery Protocol (ISDP) provides an interface for content servers and user agents to request and receive the services from CSN. This certificate is part of the ISDP protocol to enable post-distribution service.

The Internet Service Delivery Protocol (ISDP) defines the interface between the application proxy (AP) servers and CSN's customers for service subscription and rendering. In our current design, ISDP has three different operation modes based on whom the service is performed on behalf of and the nature of the service. Note that each service mode corresponds to a different service path and system interaction between participating network elements.

A service could be performed on behalf of end-users (clients) or content providers (content servers). If the service is provided to ISPs, it is considered performed on behalf of end-users. If the service is provided to CDNs who may resell it as a value-added service in addition to content delivery service, it is considered performed on behalf of content providers. For the service performed on behalf of content providers, it is further distinguished based on whether it is 'pre-distribution' or 'post-distribution'. As the terms indicate, one way to compare these services is to look at when and where the value-added processing is conducted.

Pre-distribution services correspond to the processing that does not need to differentiate, for example, end-user or client's capability. These services are performed before content is distributed over the Internet, and the responsible AP server acts like a surrogate (reverse proxy) to the origin content server. Pre-distribution services are usually performed once for an object and the result is reused for all subsequent requests. Watermarking [2] and logo-insertion are typical services of this type.

Post-distribution services correspond to the processing that requires a special handling on the object for individual client request. These services are subscribed first and rendered later at the edge of network. Post-distribution services are performed after content is distributed over the Internet, and the responsible AP server acts like an interception proxy or a remote callout server and is usually located in the client's proximity. Post-distribution services may take into account the situation of each request, such as its location, end-user's preferences and device's capability, and then adapt the response accordingly. Example services of this type include content adaptation, insertion of regional data, customization and personalization.

Table 2 shows the classification of a number of example proxy services described in [4] based on our service framework. We now describe how ISDP is operated in different service mode.

4.1. Pre-distribution service performed on behalf of content provider

Fig. 3 depicts the service path for pre-distribution service performed on behalf of content provider. To set up a service path like this, the content server first sends an ISDP

Table 2. The classification of example proxy services into the three service modes defined by a CSN. Mode I: pre-distribution service performed on behalf of content provider, Mode II: post-distribution service performed on behalf of content provider, Mode III: service performed on behalf of end user

Example Proxy Services	Mode		
	I	II	III
Content adaptation for alternate web access devices		×	×
Insertion of Ad banners	×	×	
Insertion of regional data	×	×	
Language translation		×	×
Content adaptation for limited client bandwidth		×	×
Virus scanning			×
Content adaptation for alternate browser types		×	×
Adaptation of streaming media		×	×
Personalization and customization of web pages		×	×
Request filtering and content filtering			×
Watermarking	×		
Data hiding for enabling new applications	×		
Progressive multi-resolution image delivery (e.g., JPEG-2000)	×		

request to a CSN for a service for its object. This request is routed to a designated application proxy (AP) server through redirection. After receiving the request and knowing what service is needed, the designated AP server sends an ISDP response back to the content server. The ISDP response contains information such as digital signature for authentication and the IP address of the designated AP server for configuring the content server to use this AP server as its surrogate [1,5] for that object. Depending on the implementation, this step may involve rewriting the object's URL on content server to point directly to the designated AP server.

In this mode, the designated AP server serves request for that object on behalf of the origin server, performing necessary processing to add value to the object before it is delivered over the Internet. Note that the service relationship between the AP server and the origin server is transparent to other network entities. That is, other network elements should send the requests for this object to the AP server as if it were the origin server. If CDN's surrogate proxies (for web caching and replication) are also used to accelerate content delivery for the origin server, they should talk to the designated AP server to get that object.

The processing for pre-distribution service is usually performed once and the result is cached for reuse. The designated AP server makes sure the result of processing remains fresh. It may fetch the object from origin server and run the processing again if the result has been expired or the object has been outdated.

The AP server performing this service mode is often equipped with a special server for hosting the value-added content as part of the service. For example, a web content provider may have a database of satellite images and aerial photographs that are typically large in size (in the order of 1000×1000 pixels). It is best rendering those images progressively and interactively, e.g. allowing users to zoom in a region of an image without downloading the whole image. The content provider can ask a CSN to provide the service that converts images into a special format, e.g. JPEG-2000, and then host them with progressive and interactive delivery capabilities.

Note that in this case, the communication between caching proxy and CSN's appli-

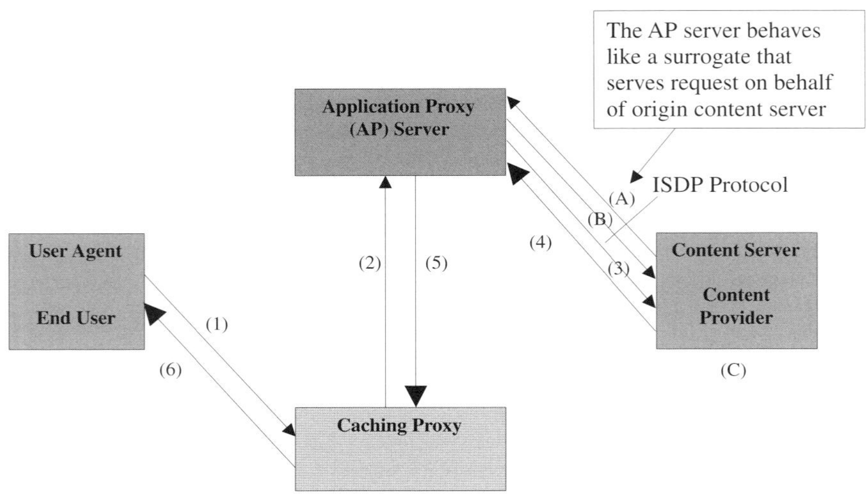

(A)	Content server sends an ISDP request to CSN to subscribe a service for its object. This request is routed to a designated AP server through redirection
(B)	The designated AP server sends an ISDP response back to the content server. The ISDP response contains information such as digital signature for authentication and the IP address of the designated AP server fo r configuring the content server to use this designated AP server as its surrogate for that object
(C)	The configuration may involve rewriting the object's URL on content server to point directly to the designated AP server. Note that the service relation between the AP server and the origin server is transparent to other network entities. That is, other network elements should send the requests for this object to the AP server as if it were the origin server.

(1)	A client sends a HTTP request for that object. The request goes to a caching proxy to see if there is a cache hit
(2)	Assuming no cache hit or the cached version has expired, the caching proxy forwards the request to the AP server because it thinks the AP server is the origin content server fo r the requested object
(3)	Assuming the object has not been value -added yet or the result of previous processing has expired, the AP server sends a request to fetch the object from the content server
(4)	The object is delivered to the AP server. The AP server run the subscribed processing on that object
(5)	The AP server sends the value -added object with expiration time to the caching proxy which may decide to cache it
(6)	The value-added object is delivered to the client

Fig. 3. Pre-distribution service performed on behalf of content provider (content server).

cation proxy is a regular HTTP connection, and the caching proxy does not need to be 'OPES-enabled'.

4.2. Post-distribution service performed on behalf of content provider

Fig. 4 depicts the system interaction occurred in the post-distribution service performed on behalf of content provider. Note that the service subscription and service delivery are conducted at different application proxy (AP) servers. In contrast to the previous mode, this type of service requires the collaboration of caching proxies at the edge of network

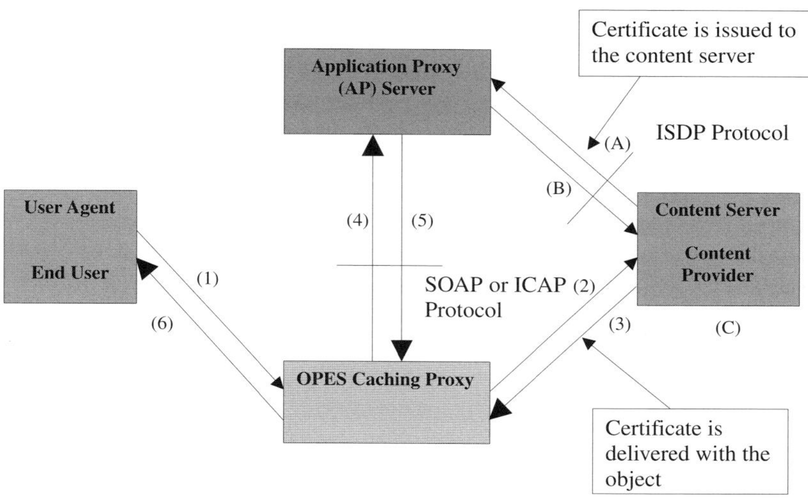

(A)	Content server sends an ISDP request to CSN to subscribe a service for its object. This request is rou ted to a designated AP server through redirection
(B)	The designated AP server sends an ISDP response back to the content server. The ISDP response contains a service certificate which describes the requested service and rules to perform it as well as a d igital signature necessary for performing authentication by the OPES proxy and the AP server
(C)	This certificate is distributed together with the object

(1)	A client sends a HTTP request for that object. The request goes to an OPES caching proxy to see if there is a cache hit
(2)	Assuming no cache hit or the cached version has expired, the OPES proxy forwards the request to the origin content server
(3)	The object along with the certificate is delivered to the OPES proxy
(4)	The OPES proxy sees t he certificate and knows the object needs additional services. Based on the information provided in the certificate, the OPES proxy uses the SOAP or ICAP protocol to upload the object to the AP server for value -added services.
(5)	After the AP server per forms the subscribed processing, the value -added object with expiration time is sent back to the OPES caching proxy. The OPES caching proxy may decide to cache it
(6)	The value-added object is delivered to the client

Fig. 4. Post-distribution service performed on behalf of content provider (content server).

to help render the service. That is, it needs the caching proxy to be 'OPES-enabled'. The CSN's AP server behaves like the remote callout server described in OPES.

To set up a service path like this, the content server first sends an ISDP request to CSN for a service for its object. After the redirection, one AP server responds the request by sending a certificate back to the content server. This certificate contains the description of the requested service and rules to perform it as well as the digital signatures necessary for performing authentication by the OPES proxy and the AP server which renders the service. This certificate is distributed together with the object. This certificate is used by the OPES caching proxies to determine when to perform a service, what kind of service to perform, and from where. An example ISDP certificate issued to a content provider might look like this:

```
<subscriber = "content provider">
  <name>www.example.com</name>
<object>http://www.example.com/video/financial_result_Q2.mpg
</object>
  <rule>
    <property name="user-agent" matches="HP Jornada|Win CE">
<action>icap://ms1.csn.hp.com/video_services/
  summarization_and_keyframe_selection</action>
      <signature>AA%#&*!@!G%N</signature>
    </property>
  </rule>
</subscriber>
```

In the above example, the content provider (e.g. www.example.com) has subscribed a service (e.g. icap://ms1.csn.hp.com/video_services/summarization_and_keyframe_selection) for its object (e.g. http://www.example.com/video/financial_result_Q2.mpg). The certificate describes the requested service, the target object and the condition to perform the service (e.g. when the client device is a HP Jornada or a handheld computer with Win CE operation system).

The IETF OPES working group is currently standardizing an XML-based rule specification language for proxy services [3]. This certificate should comply with the format specified by OPES in the future.

In the above example, the OPES proxy requests a video service for the content provider when it receives a client request from a handheld computer. CSN routes the request to one of its AP servers which performs the necessary processing on the video object and returns the result back to the OPES proxy. The OPES proxy then sends the result to the client, and it may decide to cache the result if appropriate.

4.3. Service performed on behalf of end user

Fig. 5 depicts a typical system interaction for the service performed on behalf of end user. The user agent (or client's proxy) first subscribes to the service from a CSN using the ISDP protocol. Then an application proxy server in the client's proximity responds the ISDP request by sending a certificate back to the user agent (or the client's proxy). This certificate is delivered together with the client's request, instructing other network elements to perform necessary actions on behalf of the end user.

The certificate may only need to be delivered once to the responsible OPES caching proxy. This certificate may contain service instructions at different granularity depending on who initiates the service. If initiated by proxies of enterprises or ISPs, the certificate usually specifies the common services for a group of users. If initiated by end users, it usually specifies the services for a particular user. An example ISDP certificate issued to a group of end users might look like this:

```
<subscriber = "end user">
  <user ip-address="15.4.91.*"/>
  <service name ="adaptive and interactive video delivery">
    <rule>
      <property name="MIME-type" matches="video/mpeg">
```

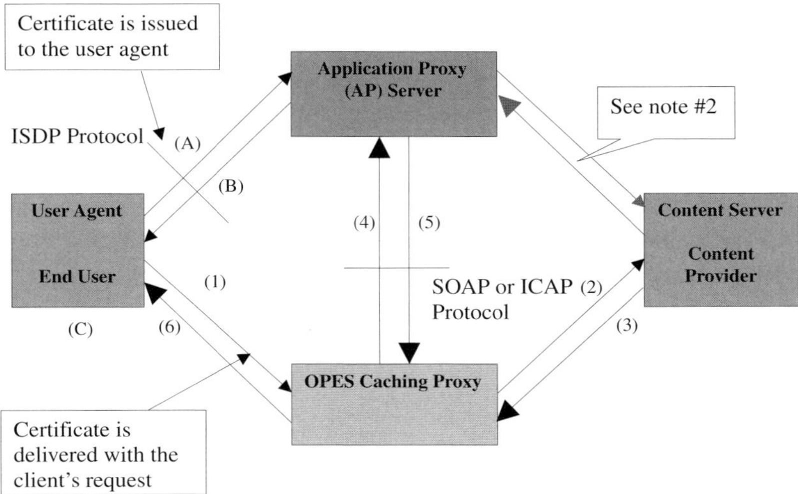

(A)	A client sends an ISDP request to CSN to subscribe a type of service such as adaptive content delivery. This request is routed to a designated AP server through redirection
(B)	The designated AP server sends an ISDP response back to the client. The ISDP response contains a service certificate which describes the requested service and rules to perform it as well as digital signature necessary for performing authentication by the OPES proxy and the AP server
(C)	This certificate is delivered together with the client's request, instructing other network elements the request and respons e pass through to perform necessary actions on behalf of the client. The certificate may only need to be delivered once to the responsible OPES proxy

(1)	A client sends a HTTP request for that object. The request goes to the OPES caching proxy to see if there is a cache hit
(2)	Assuming no cache hit or the cached version has expired, the OPES proxy forwards the request to the origin content server
(3)	The requested object is delivered to the OPES proxy
(4)	The OPES proxy sees it needs to perform cert ain actions on that object for the client. Based on the information provided in the certificate, the OPES proxy uses the SOAP or ICAP protocol to upload the object to the AP server for value -added services.
(5)	After the AP server run the subscribed proc essing, the value-added object with expiration time is sent back to the OPES caching proxy. The OPES caching proxy may decide to cache it
(6)	The value-added object is delivered to the client

Note:

1. The service subscription (A -C) may be performed by ent erprises or ISPs on behalf of their users.
2. The OPES proxy may skip (2)(3)(4) by asking the AP server to directly fetch the content from the content server. This reduces potential time delay and bandwidth waste for passing big objects back and forth between an OPES proxy and an AP server.

Fig. 5. Service performed on behalf of end user.

```
<action>icap://ms1.csn.hp.com/video_services/
  summarization_and_keyframe_selection</action>
        <signature>AA%$#&*!@!G%N</signature>
      </property>
    </rule>
  </service>
</subscriber>
```

In the above example, a group of end user (e.g. ip-address = 15.4.91.*) has subscribed to a video summarization service from a CSN. This certificate indicates that video summarization should be performed when a user from the group downloads a MPEG video from the Web.

Although not indicated in Fig. 5, the OPES proxy may ask the AP server to directly fetch the content from origin server instead of obtaining the content and passing it to the AP server for value-added services. This reduces the potential time delay and bandwidth consumption for passing a big object back and forth between an OPES proxy and an AP server.

5. Redirection

The requests sent to a CSN are redirected to one of the application proxy (AP) servers according to the following consideration:

(1) Locality – direct the request to the AP server that is close to it in the network
(2) Server load – perform load balancing among the AP servers in a local domain
(3) Type of service – direct the request to the AP server that has the corresponding service

Our current redirection scheme is a two-stage process. The first stage deals with network locality (item #1) and is achieved by anycast routing which routes the request to the nearest redirector. The second stage deals with server's load balancing and service discovery (item #2 and #3) and is performed by the redirector that further redirects the request to an AP server in its control domain. We have studied the problem of redirection in a wide-area network in [24]. We briefly summarize the technique used in our CSN prototype in the following.

5.1. Redirection based on administratively provisioned anycast

In a CSN, the redirectors of each domain (see Fig. 1) are associated with the same anycast address. Although IP-anycast service is not ubiquitously deployed, it can be provisioned administratively [26]. Assume a CSN's domain resides in a network domain with A/20 Classless Inter-Domain Routing (CIDR) prefix and an anycast address A*/32 from the A/20 CIDR block is assigned to the redirectors in the domain. To enable anycast service within the domain, the redirectors announce host route for shared address A*/32 through routing daemons such as *gated* [27] or *zebra* [28]. First-hop routers then propagate A*/32 routes through intra-domain routing protocols such as IGP [29]. With the anycast service provided through IGP, network routers can deliver shared-address A*/32 packets to the nearest redirector within the domain naturally. The anycast address A*/32 is advertised to outside domains by BGP [29] together with other A/32 unicast addresses in the A/20 CIDR block. As such, packets sent to A*/32 from other domains could be folded in with the network route and finally reach the nearest redirector through IGP routing [25].

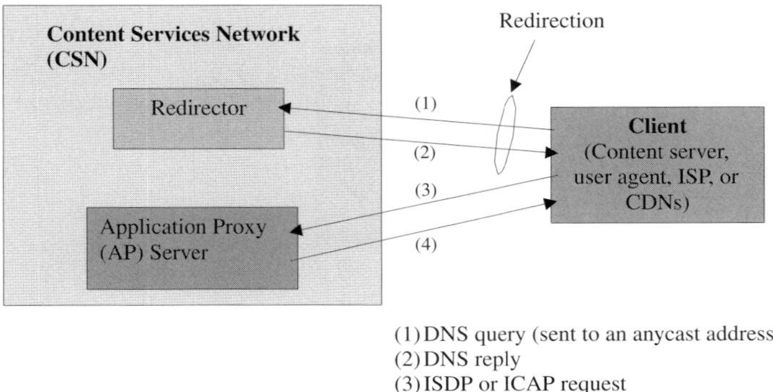

Fig. 6. Redirection performed by A CSN's redirector.

5.2. Redirection based on DNS

After the request reaches the nearest redirector, it is further redirected to an AP server that fulfills the request. We use domain name server (DNS) to perform this second-stage redirection. Essentially, the redirectors are the authoritative name servers for a CSN. This is accomplished by placing DNS 'NS' and 'A' records in the primary domain name server to identify host with A*/32 address as the authoritative name server for the CSN's domain, e.g. 'csn.hp.net'. Therefore, when a client requests a service from a CSN's server, e.g. 'ms1.csn.hp.net', it triggers the client's local DNS server to issue a recursive DNS query to discover the IP address of 'ms1.csn.hp.net'. This DNS query is routed to the nearest authoritative name server (it is also a redirector) through the first-stage redirection. Because informed by the SDM servers, the redirectors have knowledge and information about the AP servers in its domain. After determining which AP server should serve the request, the redirector sends the IP address of the designated AP server as DNS reply to the client. Fig. 6 shows the steps involved in our redirection scheme.

6. Current status

In the process of building a prototype, we decided to use a video analysis technique developed in HP Labs [8,9] as our first CSN's service. This technique has been used in our previous adaptive content delivery system [13] to perform information abstraction and modality transform. It has also been used in our recent interactive video caching and delivery system [10]. We believe this video service represents a richer set of services that other researchers have not considered [4].

The performed video analysis includes shot boundary detection, keyframe selection and face detection and tracking. The result of analysis is used to enhance the way video is delivered over the Internet, as a value-added service provided by a CSN. For instance, upon the client's request, the video server can send the meta-data resulted from the analysis that describes the structure and summarization of the video along with the selected keyframe images to the client, so the user can start browsing video immediately without downloading it. In most scenarios, the summary contains sufficient information

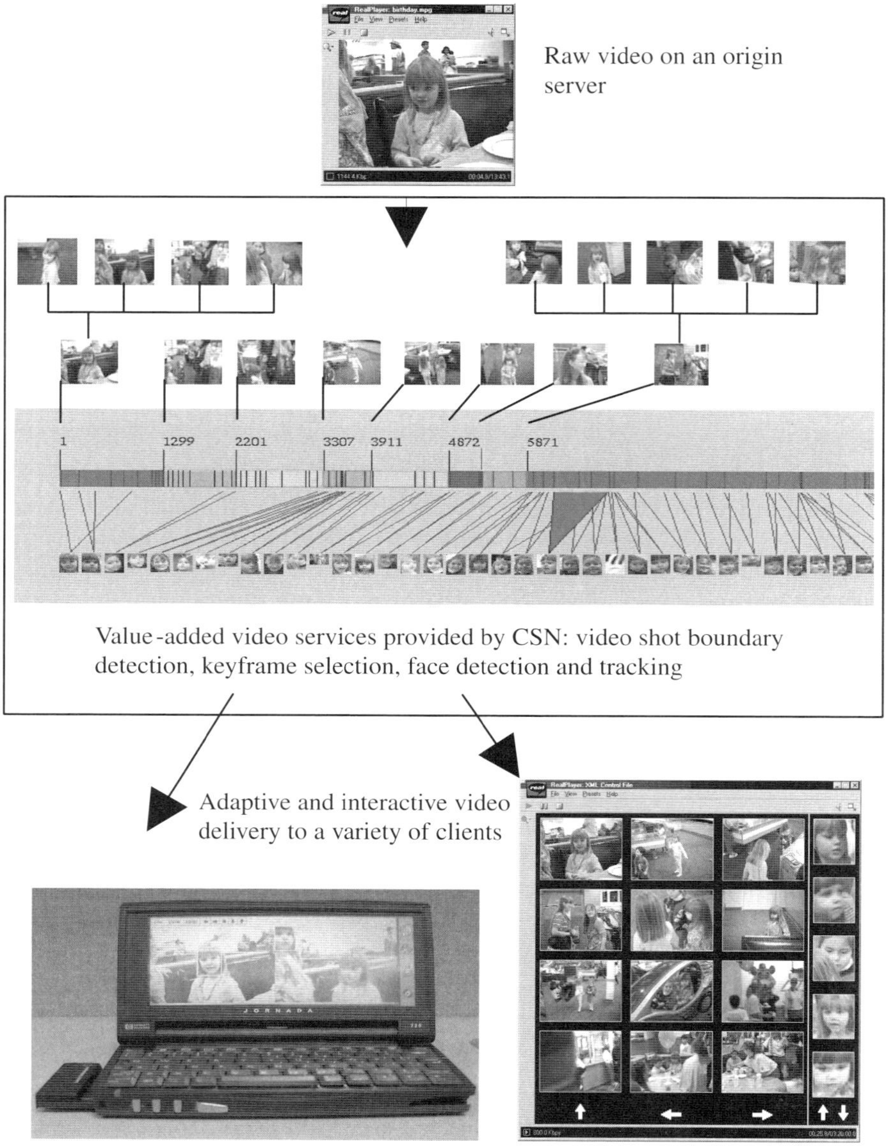

Fig. 7. As an example service provided by our CSN, we turned a video segmentation and keyframe selection system into an infrastructure service that can be used by content providers or end users to enhance the way video is delivered over the Internet. This example shows the result of video content analysis performed by the application proxy server. The video is segmented into shots that can be managed separately. The keyframes from each shot are selected and clustered to form a hierarchical representation that can be used to provide interactive video delivery. (a) Video delivered to a desktop PC. (b) Video delivered to a handheld computer with wireless LAN connection.

for the user to decide whether to download or stream any part of a video so that bandwidth and power consumption are saved. This summary also improves the way the user interacts with a video. For example, the user can navigate the content and choose to jump directly to the beginning of a particular shot of interest.

In a bandwidth constraint environment, the above video analysis and the corresponding interactive delivery are valuable services for content providers and end users. Therefore, we have deployed the service in two different modes: mode-I and mode-III as described in Section 4. Based on the service mode-I, content providers can simply put raw video on their servers and ask a CSN to perform video analysis and host the video for them. The AP servers are equipped with the special video streaming server which can render the video in an adaptive and interactive manner.

Based on the service mode-II, end users (and their corporations and ISPs) can subscribe to the service from a CSN. In this case, the video is first retrieved by the OPES caching proxy and then handed over to a CSN for value-added services. Fig. 7 shows the video analysis and the interactive video delivery as a result of the value-added video service provided by our CSN.

7. Conclusions and future work

Content services network (CSN) broadens the scope of services that have been dealt with by content delivery networks (CDNs) and represents the beginning of an important research area in the future. In this paper, we outlined the architecture of a CSN and the network protocols it uses to interoperate with existing network infrastructures and elements. A new Internet service delivery protocol (ISDP) is proposed to characterize a variety of system interactions necessary to perform different types of service subscription and service rendering. The ISDP protocol supplements many functions not addressed by the iCAP protocol.

We also demonstrated an example service that turned a video segmentation and keyframe selection system into an infrastructure service that can be used by content providers or end users to enhance the way video is delivered over the Internet.

We envision the ‘plain’ content delivery service that CDNs currently offers will soon become a basic service that is no longer a concern. What drives and differentiates the market will be the appearance of new value-added services that fulfill the increasing expectation of Internet users and content providers. Through the development of this new Internet infrastructure, media technologies will find their deserved opportunities to revolutionize the Internet. By making them part of the Internet infrastructure services that can be easily accessed and used like commodity by anyone at anywhere and anytime, content service networks will bring the Internet to the next level that remains to be defined.

Many important and challenging research problems for a CSN remain to be investigated. For example, issues such as security, billing and accounting, service distribution and management are still left open. Our proposed Internet service delivery protocol may need to be revised or extended to encapsulate service scenarios we have not considered. Also, we envision in the future multiple CSNs may coexist and service-peering issues may arise much like the content-peering issues currently happening among CDNs [30]. It is therefore more important that a standardized service delivery protocol is defined and agreed upon. We will continue to work on these issues in the future.

Acknowledgments

We are thankful to Shuheng Zhou for the study of redirection problem performed during her internship with HP Labs. We are also thankful for the comments from the reviewers.

References

[1] Mark Nottingham, On defining a role for demand-driven surrogate origin servers, *Computer Communication*, vol. 24, no. 2, pp. 215–221, Feb. 2001.
[2] C-H. Chi, Y. Lin, J. Deng, X. Li, T.-S. Chua, Automatic proxy-based watermarking for WWW, *Computer Communication*, vol. 24, no. 2, pp. 144–154, Feb. 2001.
[3] A. Beck and M. Hofmann, PSRL: a rule specification language for proxy services, Internet-Draft draft-beck-opes-irml-00.txt, work in progress, Feb. 2001.
[4] M. Hofmann and A. Beck, Example services for network edge proxies, Internet-Draft draft-hofmann-esfnep-00.txt, September 2000.
[5] I. Cooper, I. Melve, and G. Tomlinson, Internet web replication and caching taxonomy, Internet-Draft, RFC-3040, January 2001.
[6] G. Tomlinson, H. Orman, M. Condry, J. Kempf, and D. Farber, Extensible proxy services framework, Internet-Draft draft-tomlinson-epsfw-00.txt, July 2000.
[7] J. Elson et al. ICAP the Internet content adaptation protocol, Internet-Draft draft-elson-opes-icap-01.txt, Aug 2001.
[8] W.Y. Ma and HongJiang Zhang, An indexing and browsing system for home video, *X European Signal Processing Conference* (invited paper), Finland, September 2000.
[9] HongJiang Zhang and W.Y. Ma, Structured and content-based video browsing, *Proceedings of the 32th Asilomar Conference on Signal, System and Computers*, Pacific Grove, CA, 1998.
[10] S.J. Lee, W.Y. Ma, and B. Shen, Interactive video caching and delivery using video abstraction and summarization, *Proc. International Workshop on Web Caching and Content Distribution (WCW'01)*, June 2001.
[11] Randy H. Katz, The Post-PC Era: It's All About the New Services-Enabled Internet, a presentation given to HP Labs in 2000, http://www.cs.berkeley.edu/~randy.
[12] A. Fox, S.D. Gribble, Y. Chawathe, and E.A. Brewer, Adapting to network and client variation using active proxies: lessons and perspectives, *IEEE Personal Communication*, Vol. 5, No. 4, pp. 10–19, August 1998.
[13] W.Y. Ma, I. Bedner, G. Chang, A. Kuchinsky, and H.J. Zhang, A framework for adaptive content delivery in heterogeneous network environments, *SPIE Multimedia Computing and Networking 2000*, pp. 86–100, San Jose, January 2000.
[14] Spyglass-Prism. http://www.spyglass.com.
[15] Intel QuickWeb. http://www.intel.com/quickweb.
[16] ProxiNet. http://www.proxinet.com.
[17] O. Angin, A.T. Campbell, M.E. Kounavis, and R.R.-F. Liao, The Mobiware Toolkit: Programmable support for adaptive mobile networking, *IEEE Personal Communications*, Vol. 5, No. 4, August 1998, pp. 32–43.
[18] T. Bickmore and B. Schilit, Digestor: Device Independent Access to the World Wide Web, *Proceedings of the Sixth International World Wide Web Conference*, Santa Clara, California, 1999.
[19] B.D. Noble, M. Satyanarayanan, D. Narayanan, J.E. Tilton, J. Flinn, and K.R. Walker, Agile application-aware adaptation for mobility, *Proceedings of the 16th ACM Symposium on Operating System Principles*.
[20] J. Smith, R. Mohan, and C. Li, Scalable multimedia delivery for pervasive computing, ACM Multimedia, 1999.
[21] C. Yoshikawa et al, Using Smart Clients to Build Scalable Services, *Proc. Winter 1997 USENIX Tech. Conf.*, January 1997.
[22] The Internet Content Adaptation Protocol (iCAP). http://www.i-cap.org.
[23] Open Proxy Extension Services. http://www.cs.utah.edu/~horman/opencache.html.

[24] Shuheng Zhou, Wide-area redirection, HP Technical Report, 2000.
[25] C. Partridge, T. Mendez, and W. Milliken, Host anycast service, RFC-1546, November 1997.
[26] Steve McCanne, *Enabling Internet TV With Intelligent Network Infrastructure*, mcast 2000, San Francisco, February 2000.
[27] Merit GateD Consortium: http://www.gated.org.
[28] GNU Zebra – routing software: http://www.zebra.com.
[29] Christian Huitema, *Routing in the Internet*, Prentice Hall PTR, 2000.
[30] Content Bridge Alliance. http://www.content-bridge.com.
[31] Simple Object Access Protocol (SOAP). http://www.w3.org/TR/SOAP.

Web Caching and Content Delivery
A. Bestavros and M. Rabinovich (Editors)

Enabling the Internet to Deliver Content-Oriented Services

André Beck [1], Markus Hofmann [2]

Bell Laboratories/Lucent Technologies, 101 Crawfords Corner Rd., Holmdel, NJ 07733, USA

Abstract

Increasing Web traffic has led to the deployment of network intermediaries at the edges of the network. In particular caching proxies and content delivery surrogates have been very successful in accelerating Web content delivery and reducing the load on origin Web servers. Today, however, users and content providers are demanding faster distribution of Web content to end users. Also, many users are looking to their ISPs to provide additional content-oriented services, including filtering, security, personalization, and transformation services. At the same time, ISPs and other service providers are facing increased competition – which drives slimmer margins for basic access and data transport services. These recent developments suggest utilizing the existing network edge infrastructure as a platform for a new class of intelligent services. These services provide tangible benefits for the end user and incremental revenue opportunity for the service providers. This article explains a flexible and open architecture to enable network edge intermediaries to host a variety of content-oriented services. Special emphasis is put on the representation and processing of rules leading to the invocation of these services. This article also describes a research prototype implementation of a service-enabled intermediary and several example services.

Keywords: Content delivery and distribution; Content-oriented services; iCAP; Intelligence at the network edge; Rule engine; Remote callout; Service execution environment; Service invocation rules; Web caching

1. Introduction

The Internet as of today is still mostly governed by the 'end-to-end' principle [11] which demands that the network itself is to be kept as simple as possible and that all intelligence resides at the end-systems. This principle proved to be very successful and benefical for the evolution of the Internet. Despite its success, we have recently seen more application-specific functionality moving into the network, in particular to the edges of the network. Deployment of network caches and content-aware switches are probably the most widely known examples for this kind of functionality. It helps accelerating the

[1] E-mail: abeck@bell-labs.com
[2] E-mail: hofmann@bell-labs.com

delivery of static Web pages by moving content closer to the user. However, margins for such basic delivery services are getting slimmer. Service providers have to take advantage of opportunities to provide new value-added content services for differentiation and additional revenue. Examples for such services include, but are not limited to, content filtering, content adaptation, dynamic and personalized content assembling, ad insertion and virus scanning.

While most of these services could also be installed on and provided at the client machine itself in order to adhere to the end-to-end principle, there are reasons to move them to the network edge. The typical Internet user of today, for example, can be best described as a non-technical consumer who wants to use the latest Internet technology without having to worry about technical matters like software installations or updates. Furthermore, new types of Internet access devices like PDAs and mobile phones may not always have the processing power that is necessary to run the software for providing value-added services. Other Internet appliances may only be capable of running hard-coded software so that software upgrades would not be possible at all.

Rather than developing a service-specific infrastructure from scratch, this article outlines the extension of the existing network edge infrastructure towards a flexible and open platform for a variety of new content services. It makes use of and extends existing intermediary devices, such as caching proxies and content-aware switches, enabling them to perform specific tasks on the application-layer content that is routed through them. Although this might look like a violation of the end-to-end principle, it is somewhat restored by the requirement that one or more of the parties participating in a content transaction must authorize the performed services.

The article is structured as follows: Section 2 describes the overall service platform architecture. In the following section, a rule specification language and the rule engine component of the service platform architecture are discussed in more detail. Section 4 describes a prototype implementation of the proposed service platform and several example services. Section 5 presents the results of performance measurements obtained from experiments with this prototype. Related work is shortly discussed in Section 7 and the final section summarizes the results of this work.

2. Platform architecture

The service enabling architecture evolves around a common network intermediary such as a caching proxy by adding new components, in particular a rule engine, a service invocation dispatcher, a local and remote service execution environment, and a message callout client and server. Fig. 1 shows these components and their interaction in a service-enabled caching proxy and a remote service execution server. The following sections describe how these components help fulfill the requirements of a network edge service platform.

2.1. Service-enabled intermediary

In order to support the execution and installation of value-added service modules, a network intermediary must be augmented by additional components. Service modules may operate on the request/response message stream passing through the intermediary.

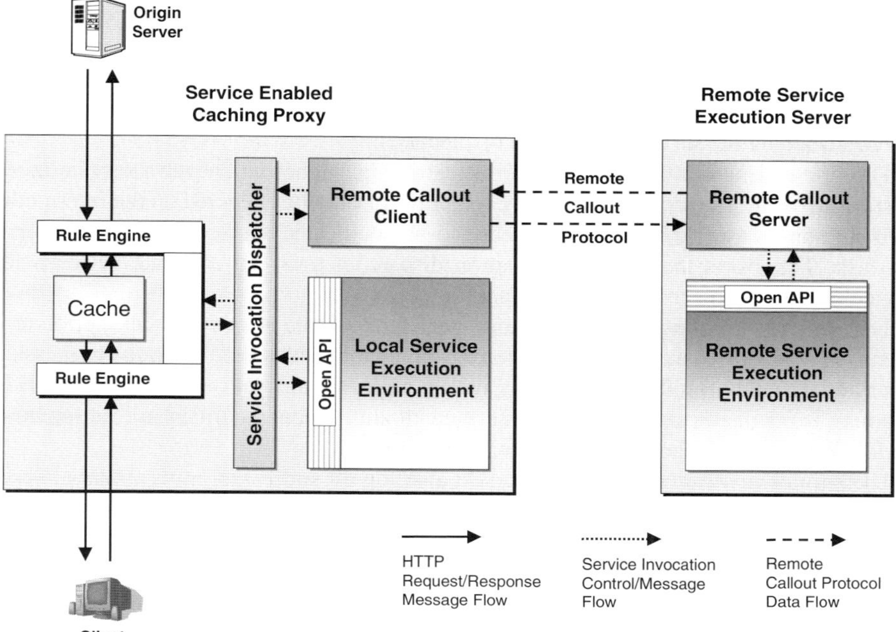

Fig. 1. Service platform architecture.

They may modify or satisfy user requests or modify server responses. One example would be a content adaptation service which adapts requested HTML pages so that they can be viewed with small Internet appliances like PDAs.

It is important to note that more than one service module may operate on any given message stream, although only one service module can modify a message stream at a time. For example, an advertisement insertion service could insert an advertisement banner into a requested Web page and a content adaptation service could adapt the same Web page to the user's Web access device.

Rule engine. Since it may not be desirable to invoke installed service modules for all user requests received by a service-enabled intermediary, there must be a mechanism to trigger the execution of service modules if certain conditions are met.

Alternatively, this decision could be left to the service module. This would require, however, that all installed service modules are invoked for every request/response message passing through the intermediary. Obviously, this approach would introduce a significant delay in requests and responses for which no service modules should be executed. This is especially unacceptable if we assume that only a small fraction of all Web transactions require the invocation of a service module.

Therefore, it is necessary for the parties for which service modules may be executed to provide rules that specify the conditions under which an incoming user request should trigger the execution of a service module. The rule engine component must also provide a secure interface through which authorized rule authors or system administrators can install, modify, and delete rules on the caching proxy.

Service invocation dispatcher. Once the rule engine has determined that a specific service must be applied to a user request or server response, the appropriate service module must be invoked. The invoked service module must then be provided with an interface to the corresponding request or response message stream so that it can modify it. These tasks are accomplished by the service invocation dispatcher.

The rule engine notifies the service invocation dispatcher whenever a service module must be invoked. Service modules, however, may not only be executed on the intermediary itself. In some cases, it makes more sense to use dedicated service execution server for this task. Therefore, the service invocation dispatcher must differentiate between local service modules and service modules on a remote server.

The service invocation dispatcher also performs simple security checks prior to the execution of a service module in order to prevent unauthorized modifications of messages. A service module provided by cnn.com, for example, should not be executed for a HTTP response from disney.com because a service module by cnn.com is not authorized to modify Web objects other than those from cnn.com.

The service invocation dispatcher should also log all successful invocations of service modules in order to provide accounting and billing information to the providers of value-added services so that they can charge their customers for each successful service invocation.

Local service execution environment. The local service execution environment holds and executes service modules on the caching proxy. It must also be able to monitor and limit the use of resources by service modules during their execution. Service modules should not be able to significantly slow down the normal operation of a service-enabled intermediary. Therefore, resource intensive service types, e.g. virus scanning, may not be appropriate for the local service execution environment. These services should rather be hosted by a remote service execution server (see below).

The service execution environment must also provide a secure interface through which authorized parties such as content providers, access providers, and clients can install, update, and delete service modules.

2.2. Remote service execution server

As mentioned before, the remote service execution server is a separate server dedicated to hosting and executing service modules that need more processing power and system resources than are available on a caching proxy, for example a virus scanning service.

Since the service modules on this remote server need to modify the request/response messages which pass through the intermediary, it is desirable to place the remote service execution server as close to the intermediary as possible.

The communication between the caching proxy and a remote service execution server requires a special protocol which we refer to as 'remote callout protocol' since its primary purpose is to efficiently forward request/response messages and information about the service to be executed from the intermediary to the remote service execution server. A service-enabled intermediary may use this protocol to communicate with any number of remote service execution servers on which it wants to execute a service module. This approach also increases the scalability of the proposed service platform. If one service execution server alone cannot handle all service requests, the service platform operator may simply add another service execution server and configure the rules on the caching proxy in a way that balances the load on both service execution servers. This approach requires, however, that remote service execution servers regularly report their current load level to the caching proxy.

The hardware platform of a remote service execution server should be optimized to support the fast execution of service modules. Therefore, it may be desirable to build specialized remote service execution servers which can accelerate the execution of service modules. For example, a Java virtual machine (JVM) built into the hardware of a service execution server could increase the performance of service modules written in Java.

Remote callout client/server. The remote callout client is a component on the caching proxy which talks to the remote callout server component on the service execution server. They communicate through the remote callout protocol in order to exchange request/response messages that may be modified by service modules on the remote service execution server. The remote callout client also sends information about the type of the forwarded message (request/response) and the expected behavior of the service module which is to be executed on the remote service execution server.

Remote service execution environment. The remote service execution environment is similar to its local pendant on the intermediary with the exception that in this execution environment the restrictions on the available resources are not as strict. It is still desirable, though, to enforce the usage of resources so that the available resources are shared equally among running service modules.

3. Service activation rules

3.1. Rule engine requirements

Performance is of paramount importance in an intermediary like a caching proxy whose main purpose is to accelerate the Web access of its users. Even though a service-enabled intermediary offers additional value-added services to its users, this should not affect the performance of the normal operation of the intermediary, at least not significantly. It is not acceptable, for instance, that users who do not want to use these additional services are penalized for using a service-enabled intermediary instead of a regular intermediary.

The rule engine component of a service-enabled intermediary ensures that service modules are invoked only for those user requests or server responses that match certain rules. These rules are provided by the entities for which services can be executed. In the case of HTTP, these include at least content providers, access providers, and clients. Access providers are ISPs, enterprises, CDN service providers, and other organizations operating network edge devices like caching proxies, switches, and surrogates.

The rule engine component of a network edge service platform should meet the following requirements:

- It should be optimized for performance so that user requests for which no service modules are executed are not slowed down.
- It should accept rules in a standardized format from different external rule authors. This is necessary so that the parties for which service modules can be executed have a means to control when service modules are executed.

- Rules should allow rule authors to specify rule conditions on a very fine grained level, for instance on the message property level. This ensures that service modules are not invoked in cases where this is not absolutely necessary. For example, a virus scanning service should only be invoked for Web objects which can possibly contain a virus.
- The rule engine should execute services according to the intended service execution order of rule authors but also be able to find a 'sensible' service execution order among rules from different rule authors.
- The rule engine should take the dynamic message modifications of service modules into consideration. For example, a content adaptation service may under certain circumstances convert images from the JPEG into the GIF graphics format. A subsequent service, however, may not be able to process GIF images and does therefore not have to be executed any more.
- The rule engine should allow for service modules to be executed at different points within the round-trip message flow. This may be necessary, for instance, for services that only need to operate on messages that are served from the origin server and not from cache.

3.2. A rule specification language

In order to simplify and standardize the exchange of rules between rule authors and service platforms, rules should be specified in a standardized rule specification language. [9] describes an XML rule specification language for this purpose. In a caching proxy rules can be processed up to four times for each Web transaction so that service modules can modify messages at different points within the message flow. The following section describes these four rule processing and service execution points.

Rule processing points. Fig. 2 shows the typical HTTP data flow between a client, a caching proxy, and an origin server. The four processing points (1–4) represent locations in the round trip message flow where rules can be processed and service modules can be executed. Note that the message flow may skip points 2 and 3 after point 1 if the requested object can be served from cache.

Point 1 – Client Request: A request from a client has been received. A possible cache lookup has not yet occurred.

Point 2 – Proxy Request: The requested Web object cannot be served from the cache and the origin server is about to be contacted for the HTTP resource.

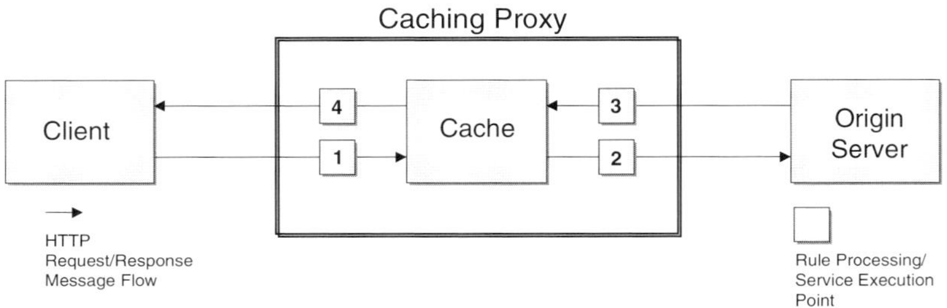

Fig. 2. Rule processing/service execution points.

Point 3 – Origin Server Response: The response from the origin server has been received. It has not yet been stored in the cache.

Point 4 – Proxy Response: The response from the cache or the origin server is about to be sent back to the client.

Depending on the service type, rules may be processed and services may be executed at any of the four points outlined in Fig. 2. A virus scanning service for instance should be executed at point 3 in Fig. 2 in order to scan all Web objects for viruses before they can be stored in the cache. A URL-based request filtering service on the other hand should be executed at point 1 and an ad insertion service will probably be executed at point 4.

We can imagine that in the future there will be a need to have more processing points (at a finer granularity) than the ones mentioned above. It is also important to note that processing points are device-specific. A content-aware switch, for instance, has different processing points than a caching proxy.

Intermediary rule markup language. The Intermediary Rule Markup Language (IRML) [9] allows rule authors to specify rules for network edge services in a standard format. It is important to create a standard rule format that will be supported by vendors of service-enabled caching proxies/surrogates so that rules can be distributed to different service platforms owned by different access providers in the same standard format.

The Intermediary Rule Markup Language also facilitates the exchange and discussion of network edge service rules between and within groups of rule authors.

IRML is an application of XML. Thus, its syntax is governed by the rules of the XML syntax as defined in [2], and its grammar is specified by a DTD, or Document Type Definition.

Valid and well-formed IRML documents consist of one or more rule modules. Each rule module contains a set of rules and information about the rule module provider. Rule modules are provided by a content provider, an access provider, or by a client (although usually indirectly through an access provider). In the future, however, rule modules may also be provided by other parties. On the content provider side, for example, one could differentiate between content hosters and content owners.

The rules contained in rule modules each consist of a number of conditions and a number of consequent actions that must be executed if the conditions are met. The conditions within a rule refer to message properties in the request or response of a given Web transaction. They are met if the property value matches the pattern specified in the condition.

3.2.1. Order of service execution

The order in which service modules on the caching proxy are executed may influence the final result of a Web transaction. For example, an ad insertion service executed against the result of a Web page translation service may produce a different result than a reverse execution order.

A natural processing order for rule modules would be one that reflects the message flow from the user via the intermediary to the origin server and back. According to this order, up to three rule modules would have to be processed by the rule engine of an intermediary per transaction. For incoming requests at points 1 and 2 in Fig. 2, rule modules would be processed in the order: client rule module, access provider rule module, content provider rule module.

For outgoing responses at points 3 and 4, rule modules would be process in the opposite order: content provider rule module, access provider rule module, client rule module.

Within a single rule module, the caching proxy must process and execute all rules and actions in the order they are specified in the rule module (both within 'property' and 'rule' elements). If the rule processor determines that an action must be executed, it must do so before continuing the rule matching process since service modules may modify message property values. This may influence the result of subsequent pattern matches.

3.3. Rule engine architecture

Fig. 3 illustrates the architecture of a complex rule engine that can process rules specified in IRML. It consists of a message dispatcher and parser component, a message context, an XML parser, a rule module optimizer and validator, a rule module repository, and a rule module processor.

XML parser. IRML rule modules are XML documents which have to be distributed to the network edge service platforms on which they should be processed. The XML parser component in the rule engine is invoked whenever a new rule module is received. It parses the received IRML rule module and creates an internal tree representation of the XML elements and values. It then forwards this data structure to the rule module optimizer.

Fig. 3 also shows a secure interface on the XML parser component. Although not a part of the rule engine itself, this interface must be provided to rule authors so that they can distribute their rule modules to network edge service platforms.

Rule module optimizer/validator. The rule module optimizer and validator component of the rule engine pre-processes rule modules once they have been parsed by the XML parser. This component can detect inconsistencies in rule modules, for instance references

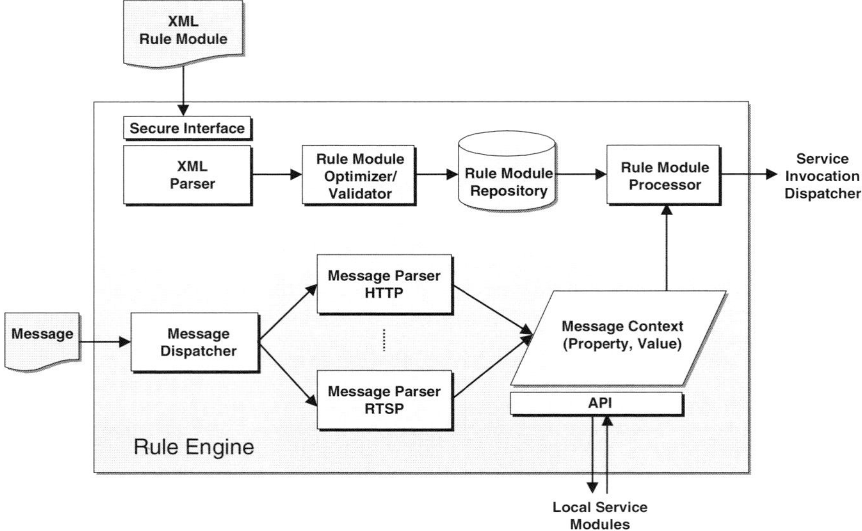

Fig. 3. Rule engine architecture.

to non-existing service modules. It also optimizes the internal representation of rule modules so that they can be processed more efficiently. The goal should be to minimize the number of pattern matches when rule modules are processed. Pattern matches, especially if regular expressions are involved, can be very expensive operations. The rule module optimizer and validator is invoked once for each new rule module and forwards the result of its operation to the rule module repository.

Rule module repository. The rule module repository holds all current rule modules in their optimized internal representation. The rule modules can be accessed by the rule processor when they need to be processed and they are added to the repository by the rule module optimizer. A new version of an existing rule module replaces an older version when it is added to the repository. The rule module owner, name, and version information are used in order to manage these rule module updates.

Message dispatcher/parser. A service-enabled network device is not limited to HTTP applications. It may also support other message-based protocols, for example RTSP [12]. The rule engine may therefore require more than one message parser for each supported protocol.

The message dispatcher is invoked once for each incoming or outgoing message. The message dispatcher directs the message to the appropriate message parser. For example, an incoming HTTP request is forwarded to the HTTP message parser while an outgoing RTSP message is forwarded to the RTSP message parser. The protocol-specific message parser extracts name/value pairs from the headers of the processed message. The property names and values are then stored in the message context. This procedure ensures an important performance requirement; each message is parsed only once in a single pass. It is necessary to parse all message headers because it is not known in advance which property values will be modified by service modules.

Message context. The name/value pairs of the request and response messages of a specific Web transaction are stored in the message context. When the rule engine is invoked for the first time (at processing point 1), the message context contains only the request properties because a response message has not yet been received by the service platform at this point in the message roundtrip flow.

The message context offers an interface to other components whereby message property values can be read and modified. This interface is used by service modules which are executed in the local service execution environment and by the rule processor component (see below) in order to access message property values. The message context also contains the additional properties defined in IRML which cannot be directly mapped to message headers, for instance a user ID.

Rule module processor. The rule module processor is the core component of the complex rule engine. The rule processor decides which service modules are invoked at which points in the roundtrip message flow of a Web transaction. Depending on whether a request is served from cache or the origin server, the rule processor is invoked at two or four of the processing points described in Section 3.2.

When the rule processor is invoked, it retrieves appropriate rule modules from the rule module repository and processes them in the correct order. Rules within rule modules are matched in the order in which they are specified. Whenever a rule is matched, the rule processing stops and the service invocation dispatcher is called in order to execute the specified service module.

The rule processing continues after the execution of the service module which may have modified message property values. In the case of local service modules, these modifications are made directly in the message context through the message context API. The local service execution environment provides an interface to these functions. In the case of remote service modules, however, the modified message properties are contained in the remote service execution server response. Therefore, the remote callout client on the service platform parses the remote callout response and updates the message context after each remote callout transaction.

4. Prototype implementation

Our prototype implementation of the proposed generic service platform follows the architecture presented in the previous sections, but only the core functionality is supported. The service platform prototype consists of a service-enabled proxy with no caching capabilities and a remote service execution server. iCAP [4] is used as the remote callout protocol. Our prototype currently supports an older version of iCAP, but we are currently updating the prototype to support the latest iCAP version. The service platform does not have a local service execution environment. All service modules are hosted by the remote service execution server.

Our service platform is implemented on top of an existing non-caching proxy server for the FreeBSD operating system. The open-source proxy server is written in C. The non-caching proxy server was chosen for its simple design which facilitated the implementation of the service platform. Most of the proxy code could be reused, but had to be modified in various parts. Because some of our service prototypes require the caching of Web objects, we simulate a cache by storing Web objects on a local Web server. Our prototype implementation contains a simple rule engine and supports the remote execution of service modules. These components are explained further in the following sections.

4.1. Rule engine implementation

Our prototype implementation has a simpler rule engine than the one described in Section 3. The rule engine in our prototype maintains a list of rules which are limited to the following properties: index, status, client IP address, request URL, service module name, and iCAP mode. Table 1 shows a list of five example rules. The index property controls the order in which the rules are processed and the status property indicates whether a rule is active or inactive. Only active rules are processed by the rule engine.

The client IP address specifies for which user(s) a particular rule must be processed. This field may also contain a wildcard if a rule should be processed for all users. The request URL field contains the URL that must match the URL in a user request in order to trigger the execution of a service. The request URL property can also be specified in

Table 1. Example Rules

Index	Status	Client IP	Request URL	Service	iCAP Mode
1	Enabled	*	*://*/*	reqfiltering	Resp. Mod.
2	Enabled	*	http://yahoo.de/*	adinsertion	Resp. Mod.
3	Enabled	*	http://*/*	translation	Resp. Mod.
4	Enabled	155.145.123.23	http://*/*	translation	Negative

a pattern which may contain wildcards in each component of the URL: the protocol, the domain name/port number, and the request path. An example using all three wildcards is given in rule number 1 in Table 1.

The name of the service module that must be executed if a rule matches is specified in the field 'service module'. The 'iCAP mode', finally, tells the rule engine which of the two iCAP modes must be used for the specified service module. The iCAP mode field may also contain the value 'negative'. In this case, the rule is to be interpreted as a negative rule meaning that the specified actions must not be executed if the rule matches. Since negative rules always overrule positive rules, they allow for the exclusion of certain values when they are used in combination with wildcards in a corresponding positive rule. Example rule 4, for instance, excludes the user whose client IP address is 155.145.123.23 from the corresponding positive rule number 3.

For each Web transaction the rule engine processes all rules and compiles a list of actions which is then passed to the service invocation dispatcher to execute triggered service modules in the specified order and iCAP modes.

Rule configuration. The rule sets on a caching proxy effectively control which services are executed for which HTTP transactions. A service-enabled caching proxy must therefore provide an open rule configuration interface to entities for which services may be executed. In our prototype implementation, we have implemented a Web interface for this purpose. It allows authorized users to add, modify, and delete rules. It is also possible to enable or disable rules and to change the order of rules. We use basic HTTP authorization as defined in [5,6] to restrict the access to this Web interface.

4.2. iCAP implementation

Our iCAP client implementation is integrated into the non-caching proxy server on top of which our service platform is built. The proxy server is augmented by an iCAP client which can compose, receive, and parse iCAP messages. The iCAP client uses existing, slightly adapted functionality of the proxy server, for instance in order to forward user requests to an iCAP server within an iCAP request.

The iCAP server is also implemented in C and on the FreeBSD operating system. An existing simple HTTP server provides the skeleton for a remote service execution server. The HTTP parser of the Web server is modified so that it can parse the additional iCAP-specific headers and behave in accordance with the iCAP specification.

4.2.1. Service execution interface

In the existing prototype, service modules on the implemented remote service execution interface are invoked through a CGI interface on the iCAP server. We are currently in the process of adding other standard Web server interfaces to the iCAP server such as FastCGI or the Java Servlet API which offer better performance than the CGI interface.

4.3. Service prototype implementations

We have implemented demo prototypes of four different example services in order to test our service platform prototype. All service prototypes have been implemented as CGI programs for the remote service execution server and are described in the following sections.

4.3.1. Language translation service

The translation service translates Web pages to the user's preferred language with the help of a freely available language translation program (Altavista's BabelFish). The user's preferred language is derived from the 'Accept-Language' header [6]. The translation service translates a Web page if there is a mismatch between the user's preferred language and the document language.

4.3.2. Background translation service

The background translation service is similar to the language translation service with the exception that it returns the original Web page to the user and prepares a translation for this page while the user views the original page. After having viewed the original page the user can decide whether he wants to see a translation for this page or not. He can request the translation by clicking on a link which the background translation service added to the original page. The translation can then be served to the user very quickly (possibly even from the intermediary's cache if the background translation service can pro-actively cache the translation).

4.3.3. Web access control service

This service restricts Web access by analyzing requested Web content. All HTTP response messages are forwarded to the Web access control service if it is enabled. Once invoked the service module scans the message for a list of words. If the service module finds a 'forbidden word' in the requested Web page, it returns an HTML error message to the iCAP client instead of the original Web page. The proxy then forwards this error message to the user. Otherwise, the original HTTP message is returned to the iCAP client and from there to the user.

4.3.4. Personalization service

The personalization service reduces the Web access latency for personalized Web pages. It satisfies certain user requests by assembling personalized news pages on the network edge rather than on the origin server. In this prototype, the user can customize a news page through a Web interface in which he can select the news categories he is interested in. These settings are then saved in a cookie variable on the user's machine. Whenever this user requests his personalized news page, the value of the previously set cookie variable is sent along with his request. Thus, the personalization service module can obtain this cookie variable from the user request and assemble the news page accordingly.

5. Performance evaluation

5.1. Rule engine performance

With this performance experiment we measure the additional delay that is introduced by the rule engine for requests that do not trigger any services. We therefore measure the performance penalty a user has to pay for using a service-enabled intermediary instead of a standard intermediary.

The test environment consists of our service-enabled proxy implementation with the simple rule engine design as described in Section 4. There are 10 rules configured, but none of them fire a service for our test request which retrieves a 1.4 kbyte Web page from a co-located local Web server in order to rule out any external effects on the measurements. In order to obtain comparative data we have also installed a copy of our prototype implementation on the same server, but disabled the rule engine in that version.

The performance metrics in this experiment are:

(1) the time from the beginning of the Web transaction until a connection to the proxy is established (Connect)

(2) the time from the beginning of the transaction until the first bit of the server response is received by the client (First Response)

(3) the time it takes to complete the Web transaction (Complete)

For the first test run in this experiment we configure the service-enabled proxy in our browser and request the sample Web page. For the second test run we configure the modified service proxy in which the rule engine is disabled. We then request the same sample Web page. The results shown in Table 2 are average values from 50 identical requests with each proxy version. The variance between the measured values was very low.

The results show that the 'connect' value is almost identical with both proxies which is not surprising because the rule engine has not even been invoked when this value is measured. The 'first response' and 'complete' values both show an additional delay of approximately only 0.5 ms for the proxy where the rule engine is enabled. These results demonstrate that the additional delay introduced by the processing time of the simple rule engine is neglectable considering that average Web transactions take hundreds of milliseconds.

It must be emphasized, however, that this value can increase when the rule engine has to process hundreds of rules instead of only ten rules. A more sophisticated rule engine like the complex rule engine described in Section 3 also may have to match more message properties per rule than just the request URL and the client IP address and may be invoked up to four times for each Web transaction. The additional delay of a more complex rule engine may be offset, however, by a more efficient implementation.

Table 2. Rule engine delay

	Connect	First Response	Complete
Standard Proxy	1.511 ms	16.167 ms	18.450 ms
Service-Enabled Proxy	1.519 ms	16.652 ms	18.907 ms

6. Service introduced delay

This performance experiment examines the additional delay which is introduced by value-added services like the background translation and the Web access control service. These services do not reduce the access latency of Web requests but modify or filter server responses as they pass through the service-enabled intermediary.

The test environment consists of our service-enabled proxy server and a co-located iCAP server on which the background translation and Web access control service modules are installed. The client is located in the same LAN in order to reduce the influence of any network congestions. In each test run, the client is configured to use the proxy server and requests a very small Web page (391 bytes) from a co-located Web server. We want to measure the additional delay introduced by the background translation and Web access control service modules.

In the first test run, all rules are disabled and the client receives the original Web page. In the second test run, the background translation service is enabled and adds a translation image link to the Web page before it is sent to the client. It is important to note that the background translation service does not translate the requested Web page or wait for its translation. Instead, the service only makes a small modification to the original Web page by inserting a new HTML link.

The Web access control service is enabled in the third test run and scans the Web page for illegal content. Both service modules are enabled in the fourth test run which means the original page is first modified by the background translation service and then scanned by the Web access control service. The last test run was conducted with no proxy configured in order to obtain some reference data. The results shown in Table 3 are average values from 50 identical requests in each test run. The performance metrics are the same as in the previous experiment. The variance between the measured values was low.

The results show that the 'connect' value is comparable for all test runs with the exception of the last test run where no proxy was used. The lower value for this test run indicates that the Web server can handle incoming requests faster than the service-enabled proxy. This is understandable because we have used a pre-forking Web server for these tests while the proxy server on top of which we implemented our service platform spawns a new process for each incoming request.

The additional delay introduced by the background translation and Web access control services is for both services approximately 110 ms. This value can be determined if we subtract the 'first response' or 'complete' value of the first test run where no services are triggered from the corresponding values of the second or third test run. The remainder

Table 3. Service introduced delay

Services Enabled	Connect	First Response	Complete
None	5.810 ms	21.407 ms	27.846 ms
Background Translation	5.854 ms	137.506 ms	144.178 ms
Web Access Control	5.828 ms	134.777 ms	141.311 ms
Both	5.833 ms	246.275 ms	253.214 ms
No Proxy	3.698 ms	6.261 ms	10.725 ms

equals the service delay introduced by the execution of each service since all three test runs were conducted under otherwise equal conditions. An additional access delay of 110 ms is quite significant even though average Web transactions last hundreds of milliseconds. However, the poor performance of the service executions can be explained partly by the limitations in the used prototype: The implemented service modules use the CGI interface which means that a new process is forked for each service invocation. Also, the implemented older iCAP version did not yet have support for chunked encoding and persistent connections between iCAP client and server.

The fourth test run in which both services are executed one after the other clearly shows that the service introduced delay has doubled as well. This becomes obvious if the 'first response' and 'complete' values of the first run are subtracted from the corresponding values in the fourth test run. The result, ca. 220 ms, equals twice the introduced delay from test runs 2 and 3. These numbers suggest that a mechanism that allows for the execution of multiple service modules during a single iCAP transaction may decrease the service introduced delay. In the current design, two service executions on the same iCAP server require two separate iCAP transactions even when they both operate in the same iCAP mode like the background translation and Web access control service.

7. Related work

The idea of intelligent networks is not new. In the past, there have been different approaches to intelligent networks. A lot of research has been done on 'active networks' [14,13]. The active networks approach, however, is not restricted to the edges of the network and also operates on lower levels of the protocol stack (i.e. on a packet-by-packet basis). Active networks have not yet received widespread support.

Many different applications for network edge intermediaries, particularly for (caching) proxies, have already been suggested and explored in past publications. For example, in [3], Deng and Chi present a dynamic active proxy for local Web advertisement insertion and its benefits. The concept of content transcoding or transformation performed on caching proxies has been discussed for a long time. More recently, the focus in content transformation has shifted to the requirements of mobile Web access. In [8] and in [1], for example, the authors present a transcoding proxy for mobile Web browsing.

The just recently started IETF activity Open Pluggable Edge Services (OPES) attempts to create a standardized network edge service platform. The OPES initiative has incorporated several Internet Drafts. Among them are the Internet Draft that defines the Intermediary Rule Markup Language (IRML) [9] and an Internet Draft which presents service examples [10]. Another Internet Draft named 'Extensible Proxy Services Framework' [15] describes a network edge service framework similar to the one explained in this article but from a rather high-level perspective. OPES is also considering to develop the current version of iCAP [4] into a standardized remote callout protocol.

With the exception of the IETF activity OPES, related work in this area appears to be focused on specific applications for network edge intermediaries. Some service ideas like ad insertion or content transformation have been explored and also applied before, but the notion of a standardized full-fledged, multi-purpose service platform at the network edge is new.

8. Conclusion

In this article, we have presented the benefits of value-added, intelligent services operating on intermediaries at the edges of the Internet. We have presented a generic service platform architecture with special emphasis on the rule engine component. Our prototype implementation of a simple service platform and four example services proved the general concept proposed in this article and also demonstrated that a variety of different service modules can be implemented on top of a generic service platform with very little efforts. Our performance measurements have shown potentials for future design and implementation improvements, but also confirmed that intermediary services and the additional components of a service-enabled intermediary (in particular the rule engine) do not necessarily introduce a significant additional delay to Web transactions passing through such a service-enabled intermediary.

This article has also shown the required complexity of a generic service platform. Open issues not addressed in this article will therefore be subject of future work. Within the rule engine component, for example, this includes the rule module distribution process and the resolution of rule conflicts.

References

[1] H. Bharadvaj, A. Joshi, and S. Auephanwiriyakul. An active transcoding proxy to support mobile web access. *Proceedings of the 17th IEEE Symposium on Reliable Distributed Systems*, 1998.

[2] T. Bray, J. Paoli, C.M. Sperberg-McQueen, and E. Maler. Extensible Markup Language (XML) 1.0 (Second Edition). W3C Recommendation, W3C, Oct. 2000.

[3] J. Deng and C. Chi. Local Web Advertisement Through Dynamic Active Proxy. In *ICME00*, page TP11, 2000.

[4] J. Elson et al. ICAP, the Internet Content Adaptation Protocol. Internet Draft, Internet Engineering Task Force, Jan. 2000.

[5] R. Fielding, H. Frystyk, and T. Berners-Lee. Hypertext Transfer Protocol – HTTP/1.0. Request for Comments 1945, Internet Engineering Task Force, May 1996.

[6] R. Fielding, J. Gettys, J. Mogul, H. Frystyk, and T. Berners-Lee. Hypertext Transfer Protocol – HTTP/1.1. Request for Comments 2616, Internet Engineering Task Force, June 1999.

[7] L. Gong, M. Mueller, H. Prafullchandra, and R. Schemers. Going Beyond the Sandbox: An Overview of the New Security Architecture in the Java Development Kit 1.2. In *Proceedings of the USENIX Symposium on Internet Technologies and Systems*, pages 103–112, 1997.

[8] R. Han, P. Bhagwat, and R.L. et al. Dynamic adaptation in an image transcoding proxy for mobile WWW browsing. *IEEE Personal Communication*, 5(6): 8–17, Dec. 1998.

[9] M. Hofmann and A. Beck. IRML: A Rule Specification Language for Intermediary Services. Internet Draft, Internet Engineering Task Force, Mar. 2001.

[10] M. Hofmann, A. Beck, and M. Condry. Example Services for Network Edge Proxies. Internet Draft, Internet Engineering Task Force, Nov. 2000.

[11] J. Saltzer, D. Reed, and D. Clark. End-to-end arguments in system design. *ACM Transactions in Computer Systems 2*, pages 277–288, November 1984.

[12] H. Schulzrinne, A. Rao, and R. Lanphier. Real time streaming protocol (RTSP), request for comments 2326, Apr. 1998.

[13] D.L. Tennenhouse, J.M. Smith, W.D. Sincoskie, D.J. Wetherall, and G.J. Minden. A survey of active network research. *IEEE Communications Magazine*, 35(1): 80–86, Jan. 1997.

[14] D.L. Tennenhouse and D.J. Wetherall. Towards an active network architecture. *Computer Communication Review*, 26(2), Apr. 1996.

[15] G. Tomlinson et al. Extensible Proxy Services Framework. Internet Draft, Internet Engineering Task Force, July 2000.

Web Caching and Content Delivery
A. Bestavros and M. Rabinovich (Editors)

Synopsis

Multicast Injection for Application Network Deployment

Oscar Ardaiz [1], Felix Freitag [2], Leandro Navarro [3]

Computer Architecture Department, Polytechnic University Catalonia, Barcelona, Spain

Abstract

Introduction of new services on the Internet is a laborious, time-consuming task. Application networks, applications being serviced through multiple interconnected service nodes disseminated across the Internet, are as well costly to set up. This paper investigates dynamic deployment mechanisms to realize application network service introduction on the Internet.

1. Introduction

Application networks, such as content distribution networks, have been shown to improve service performance, availability and fault tolerance. Today application networks are provisioned either by individual resource providers replicating services uncoordinatedly or by centralized management stations activating services on every managed node. In the first case service providers are not able to control service quality, whereas the management station model is not scalable and does not consider shared third party resources. Introduction of application network services by dynamic deployment mechanisms aims at providing services with a predefined service level making a cost-effective use of shared resources.

2. Application network deployment

Application network deployment is defined as the process of setting up or creating an application network service. It includes all steps from service specification up to making it available to users. Deploying a service requires: obtain service specifications, map specifications to resources, discover resources, gather resources, configure resources, activate service, and provide a management interface.

We implement this functionality making use of an architecture composed of resource agents at resource providers' nodes and deployment managers at service providers' nodes. Resource agents are responsible for publishing resources, mediating between

[1] E-mail: oardaiz@ac.upc.es
[2] E-mail: felix@ac.upc.es
[3] E-mail: leandro@ac.upc.es

resources and service providers' deployment managers, configuring resources, activating services, and returning management interfaces. Deployment managers are responsible for obtaining service specifications, mapping specifications to resources, discovering resources, gathering resources, trading with resource agents on behalf of service providers, and managing overall deployment operation.

Service providers input the following service characteristics to create service spec: service type (static content, streaming content, servlet, etc.), service name, per surrogate storage, network coverage (AS or IP-subnet list), per region expected traffic, maximum distance between clients to surrogates (num hops, RTT, bandwidth, etc.), number of surrogates providing service, service duration and service start time.

Deployment mechanisms make service deployers discover and gather resources, plus activating services on appropriate nodes. Agents at those nodes activate services by configuring local surrogates, installing servlets, etc. Deployment managers obtain nodes location to configure redirection subsystems.

3. Multicast injection

Dynamic deployment mechanisms have to discover and gather resources in a subset of all available nodes, instead of in every node, to be cost-effective. A first solution is the SNMP management station based method, in which a centralized entity monitors, chooses and configures resource agents. It is not scalable nor caters for contention at shared third party resources. Our approach is to use multicast based mechanisms to achieve scalability, adaptability, and simple agents. Multicast injection considers resource agents as active entities that can decide autonomously whether to accept or discard a service activation request based on local policies and information they announce to each other. Periodic refreshes and soft state ensures adaptability to demand and network variations.

Multicast injection deployment takes the following steps:

(1) Deployer injects application service specifications in a global multicast channel.
(2) Resource agents map those specifications to its resource capabilitities and availability, if they can provide service to some regions they allocate resource and announce their intention to start service in a service multicast channel.
(3) After a short random interval, if they have not listened to other agents indicating willingness to provide service with better characteristics, they activate the service.
(4) Periodically: They announce a service active plus resources available message. If they do not receive similar messages from enough nodes they conclude there are not enough resources and cancel service. If other nodes provide best service for equal regions they stop it.

We have performed simulations [1] to compare with centralized deployment how cost-effectively proposed mechanisms scale and adapt to demand and network variations.

4. Related work

Xbone [3] dynamically deploys IP overlays with topology constraints by computing centralized allocations at overlay managers. Cluster reserves [2] perform centralized CPU-time resource allocations for geographically distributed Web servers on non-shared resource nodes. Our proposal aims at designing mechanisms to allow any entity to deploy application networks, or to provide resources for third party application activation.

References

[1] Ardaiz O., Freitag F., Navarro L., Multicast Injection for Application Network Deployment. UPC-DAC-2001-18.

[2] Aron M., Druschel P., Zwaenepoel W. Cluster reserves: A mechanism for resource management in cluster-based network servers. *Proc. ACM SIGMETRICS 2000.*

[3] Touch J., Dynamic Internet Overlay Deployment and Management Using the X-Bone. *Proc. ICNP 2000.*

Web Caching and Content Delivery
A. Bestavros and M. Rabinovich (Editors)

Synopsis

Expanding the Scope of Prefetching through Inter-Application Cooperation

Amy S. Hughes [1], Joseph D. Touch [2]

USC/Information Sciences Institute, 4676 Admiralty Way, Suite 1001, Marina del Rey, CA 90292-6695, USA

Prefetching Web documents is a way to reduce user-perceived latency. Web prefetching works best when Web caches (browsers and proxies) have information to predict which documents should be preloaded into the cache. Inter-application cooperation can increase the amount of predictive information available to a cache. Web context can drive Web prefetching, or can be used to drive prefetching in related caches for different semantic domains,*e.g.*, the DNS [1,2]. Although this is similar to hinting, where one application pushes information to another, other means of sharing are possible. Such inter-application cooperation expands DNS prefetching beyond the use of DNS hints alone, providing entirely new predictive information. In turn, inter-application cooperation, can help increase the amount of predictive information available to Web caches. This work presents an example, under development, of e-mail-driven Web prefetching.

Inter-application cooperation means cooperation between different applications in different semantic domains, e.g., Web and e-mail, rather than between different application programs for the same semantic domain. Most examples of cache cooperation involve caches of the same type, e.g., a Web proxy cache hierarchy. *Intra-application cooperation* creates a larger, distributed cache in the same semantic domain. In contrast, caches that belong to different applications (e.g., Web caches and DNS caches) can cooperate with benefits to one or both caches. When the two caches cooperate, new information is available to drive prefetching.

Prefetching requires some form of predictive information. This information can be derived from user behavior, though Web documents are special because inline links make them self-referential. These links represent requests that the user might make in the future. Even when a specific Web page cannot be prefetched because it cannot be cached, other related items, such as DNS records, can still be prefetched. This is useful because there are a large number of Web documents for which prefetching is not productive, such as dynamic pages. While DNS prefetching relies heavily on Web context, it is not Web prefetching. Instead, information from Web documents is used to predict future use and trigger prefetching across semantic domains. The Web cache provides predictive information that was previously unavailable to the DNS. Cooperation with the Web cache widens the scope of the DNS cache and enables prefetching as a new optimization.

[1] E-mail: ahughes@isi.edu
[2] E-mail: touch@isi.edu

Like a DNS cache, a Web cache can find new predictive information by including new information sources in its search. To do so, it must consider all sources of URLs that are available to the user. They fall into three categories: URLs directly available to the browser, URLs available elsewhere in the host, and URLs received completely out of band (out-of-the-blue guess, watching TV, reading a newspaper, seeing a billboard). Some of these sources are inaccessible to the cache and each source has a different probability of yielding documents that might be good candidates for prefetching.

Of the URLs available in a host, many are found in documents such as e-mail messages and word processing documents. E-mail messages contain URLs that users are likely to request. By their nature, these URLs should be cacheable, because they generally point to static documents. The time between downloading an e-mail message and accessing a URL within it should provide ample time to prefetch the document. In an effort to assess the utility of such cooperation, we have instrumented the Mozilla browser to collect trace logs of URLs within e-mail messages, and to track how the user interacts with these URLs. The information provided by the traces will allow us to characterize the benefits of cooperation. Eventually we will extend the browser to prefetch these URLs to evaluate the effectiveness of intra-application cooperation.

This work examines inter-application cooperation and its applications to Web caching. Web–DNS cooperation is an example of this idea in use. E-mail–Web cooperation is under development. Inter-application cooperation may extend to new situations as the use of caches to improve user-perceived latency increases.

An extended version of this paper is available as a technical report. For a copy, please contact the authors. The modified Mozilla software, which creates the traces to analyze, can be obtained at http://www.isi.edu/~ahughes/cachecooperation.html.

References

[1] E. Cohen and H. Kaplan. Proactive caching of DNS records: Addressing a performance bottleneck. In: *Proceedings of the Symposium on Applications and the Internet*, January 2001, to appear.

[2] A. S. Hughes and J. Touch. Cross-Domain Cache Cooperation for Small Clients. In: *Proceedings of NetStore '99*, Seattle, Washington, October 1999.

Web Caching and Content Delivery
A. Bestavros and M. Rabinovich (Editors)

Instantaneous Offloading of Transient Web Server Load

Vsevolod V. Panteleenko [1], Vincent W. Freeh [2]

Department of Computer Science and Engineering, University of Notre Dame, Notre Dame, IN 46556, USA

Abstract

A modern Web-hosting site is designed to handle load that is sometimes an order of magnitude greater than the average load. Such a site can be expensive and is underutilized most of the time. We describe a design and performance study of the *Web booster* architecture, which reduces Web server load during peak periods. A Web booster, inserted between client and server, instantaneously decreases server processing costs for requests to static documents while keeping the processing on the origin server. Fast reaction to the load change and the fact that the booster does not hold resources during inactive periods allows a Web booster to be time-shared among multiple Web domains that physically reside on different servers.

A *Web accelerator* module on a Web server interacts with the Web booster. It uses network packet caching, optimizing the TCP protocol and offloading of computation to increase the rate at which a server can process client requests. This paper describes the Web booster architecture and our implementation of the accelerator, which decreases the Web server load by more than a factor of three.

Keywords: Web server; Load balancing; Web booster

1. Introduction

Traffic to a Web server domain is unpredictable and very peaky. Request rate peaks can be up to ten times the average rate [27]. To avoid losing or alienating clients, Web-hosting sites are overbuilt to handle the peak load. While some of the sites are built as Web server clusters that host multiple Web domains, many of the sites require each domain to reside on dedicated servers for security or other reasons.

This paper introduces the *Web booster* architecture, a new load distribution mechanism for Web hosting sites that utilize dedicated servers for each Web domain. This mechanism temporarily and instantaneously decreases the request processing cost for static and cached dynamic documents on a Web server in response to transient peaks in load (Fig. 1). During normal operation, client requests are delivered directly to the servers of the target domain. When the load on a domain approaches the maximum capacity of the servers, client requests are redirected to a Web booster, which pre-processes requests and

[1] E-mail: vvp@cse.nd.edu
[2] E-mail: vin@cse.nd.edu

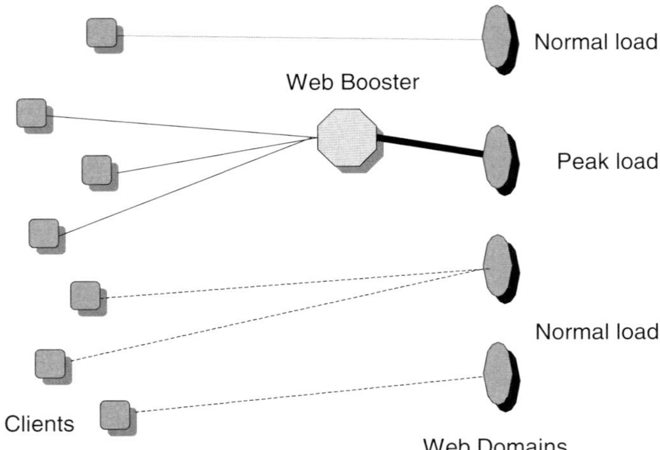

Fig. 1. Web booster.

forwards them to the corresponding servers in an optimized request stream. On a Web server, the *accelerator* kernel module receives requests from the booster. It can service requests itself at a decreased processing cost or pop the request up to the user-level HTTP server for general processing. Replies from the Web server are sent back to the booster, which delivers them to the clients.

The fact that the load may be decreased instantaneously enables effective time-sharing of the Web booster among multiple Web domains that have low correlation among load peaks. A Web booster serves one or few overloaded domains at a time, which prevents it from become a bottleneck for the hosting site. The actual document processing is kept on the origin Web servers.

Compared to accepting and processing requests directly from clients, using a Web booster reduces the load on the origin server in several ways. First, the Web booster communicates with a Web server using an optimized TCP/IP, which decreases the network protocol processing cost on a Web server. Second, the accelerator module caches documents in the form of network packets avoiding data copying, checksumming and network buffer management. Third, some request processing may be migrated to the Web booster, such as parsing HTTP headers.

Caching is a good mechanism for permanently expanding the capacity of a Web server. But it is not a good solution for providing temporary capacity needed for handling transient loads because this mechanism have a long 'warm-up' period while acquiring the resources necessary to share the load. Additionally, a cache has to be kept consistent with the original domain, whereas in the booster model, the original domain retains control of all document content. Furthermore, because all requests go to the origin server, it has the final decision as to how to handle the request.

We implemented the Web accelerator as a kernel module that runs on top of the Linux operating system without any modification to the operating system or device drivers. We also used a modified SURGE [5] Web workload generator to emulate the Web booster. Experiments show that the Web booster architecture decreases Web server load by more than factor of three.

Next section overviews related work. Section 3 gives the performance measurements for the user-level Web server and identifies techniques we used to decrease the request processing cost on a Web server. Section 4 describes the design of the accelerator software which resides on the origin sever. We measure the performance effects of using the accelerator in Section 5. Section 6 discusses the design issues for the Web booster. The following Section 7 talks about possible extensions and the last section concludes.

2. Related work

Several existing systems use the Internet infrastructure to migrate processing from subscribed Web servers. One such commercial system, Akamai, provides a set of high performance Web servers distributed throughout the Internet [3]. Subscribed Web servers upload large files, such as multimedia, on these dedicated servers, which in turn deliver them to the clients. Origin Web servers accept client requests for some documents, while Akamai servers perform file transfers that require high processing and network resources. In this way, Web providers completely control their Web sites without owning or maintaining high-performance hardware.

Another popular way to offload Web servers is using proxy caching and Web accelerators (different from our accelerator). The former are used on behalf of clients and might cache documents requested from any server. The latter are used to cache documents only for a specific set of servers. There is a large body of work that studies different aspects of Web proxy caching such as Web traffic characteristics from the viewpoint of the proxy caches [1,7,11,14] and cooperative caching [30,12,20,28]. These studies show that the effectiveness of caching is limited by such factors as document changes and number of non-cacheable documents.

There has been a lot of research done in the area of load balancing and request routing inside a single Web server cluster. Several works analyze content-based request distribution policies [24,32]. Others study mechanisms for redirecting requests to a particular Web server, including DNS-based [10], TCP splicing [15,13,31], TCP hand-off [2,24] and distributed redirection [4].

There are multiple studies that analyze the performance of Web servers and the effects of different design choices. Pai et al., looked into performance of different server architectures in context of one implementation: the Flash Web server [25]. Lava caching server shows the effect of using a specialized operating system and building the server as integrated software [22]. Two in-kernel Web server daemons [19,29] attempt to decrease the overhead of user–kernel context switches. The latter also implements zero-copy send operation by using gather/scatter network buffer implementation and hardware checksumming. Levi, et al., describes the design and performance of a Web accelerator deployed as the front end to a set of Web servers [21].

Several works analyze the cost of different operations of a busy Web server. Some of these studies use a simulated workload [18,5], while others study server behavior under real-life workload [23,12,9]. These studies show the importance of reproducing such workload characteristics as request inter-arrival time, network delays, and a large number of simultaneously open connections.

There are several areas in operating systems design that are important for Web server performance. U-Net proposed a user-level interface that virtualizes the network datalink layer and allows the implementation of network protocols at the user level [16]. Its design makes it possible to tailor the protocols and network buffer management for a particular application. Active Messages integrate communication with computation by allowing a received message to run user code as the handler on the stack of the running computation [17]. This avoids scheduling overhead for such computation and unnecessary data copying. IO-Lite introduces a unified I/O buffering and caching system [26]. It allows applications, inter-process communication, the file system, the file cache and the network subsystem to share a single physical copy of data. Protection and security are maintained through a combination of access control and read-only sharing.

3. HTTP request processing

Before describing the Web accelerator architecture, we present a brief overview of how request processing is performed by a regular HTTP server running on top of a general-purpose operating system. Quantitative analysis of the request processing cost, which is based on our experiments, will help us to identify possible targets for decreasing such cost.

The cost of request processing on a general-purpose Web server may be roughly subdivided into the four components described below.

User-level processing. The processing cost includes HTTP header parsing, header generation, request decoding and bookkeeping, and data cache management (if a user-level cache is used). It is accomplished in the context of one or more HTTP server processes or threads.

Kernel-level, process context. Most data sending is accomplished in this context. This includes copying data from user level into network buffers, calculating checksums, and sending or queuing data to the network device driver. The copy of the received data from the buffers to the user level is accomplished in this context as well. Another component of request processing performed in this context is the small part of the connection management, mostly related to *accept* and *close* system calls. The event synchronization necessary for an event-based Web server, and usually performed by *select* or *poll* system calls, is done here too.

Hardware interrupts. A network device driver processes received network packets in the hardware interrupt context. It also uses hardware interrupts to release the packets that have been sent by the network adapter.

Software interrupts (deferred procedure calls). The remainder of the network protocol processing is accomplished in software interrupts. This work includes most of the receive processing, checksumming received packet, sending acknowledgements to the received data, retransmitting, and sending queued packets. It also includes most of the connection management processing.

To identify possible ways to decrease the request processing cost, we study the performance of the Flash Web server, one of the fastest servers reported in the literature that runs on top of many general-purpose operating systems [25]. Most of the objects in our measurements are delivered from the main memory.

The test platform is a 650MHz Intel processor with 512MB of the main memory running Linux v2.4 operating system. The Flash Web server was driven by the workload generated by SURGE toolkit [5]. We varied the number of requests per second to obtain

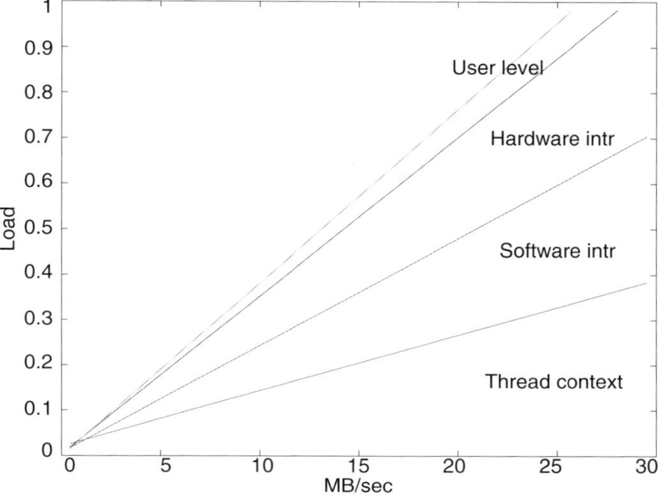

Fig. 2. Cost breakdown: Flash HTTP server.

data that covers the range of the server load. The measured data were approximated by a linear polynomial using the least-square method. We will give more detailed description of the experimental setup, workload characteristics and the measurement methodology in Section 5, which describes the performance measurements of the accelerator using the same techniques.

Fig. 2 gives the graph of approximated data for different cost components. From this graph, we can see that the major cost of request processing is related to network protocol overhead. About one-third of the overall cost is due to the hardware interrupts. This cost does not depend on the size of the packets processed, but rather on the number packets, because the device driver processing does not touch the packet data. Additionally, more than one-third of the overall cost is spent in the kernel mode in process context, which mostly involves data copying, checksumming and buffer management.

To decrease the overall cost of the request processing, we target the following cost components.

- **Send data copying and checksumming**. Using network packet caching in the accelerator makes it possible to perform these operations only once on a cache miss.
- **Network buffer management.** The packet cache also avoids network buffer management overhead.
- **Connection management.** Opening several network connections from the booster to the origin server and sending all requests through them eliminates connection management overhead and decreases the corresponding cost of hardware and software interrupts.
- **Number of network packets processed**. Delaying acknowledgements from the booster further decreases the number of network packets processed and the corresponding cost of hardware and software interrupts.

The next section describes the design of the accelerator that enables these optimizations.

4. Web accelerator

The Web accelerator resides on the origin Web server and optimizes HTTP request processing. It is a kernel module that is able to completely process HTTP requests for static documents. Requests to dynamic documents or to those that require special processing are redirected to a regular HTTP server that runs in user space. The Web booster communicates with the origin server using TCP/IP. The accelerator is active even when Web booster is not used, and the origin server accepts requests directly from clients.

The accelerator uses three techniques to decrease the cost of packet processing. First, it avoids data copying, checksumming and network buffer management by caching documents as the network packets. Second, it communicates with the Web booster using optimized TCP, which avoids network connection/teardown management and decreases the number of processed network packets. Lastly, it may offload some of the HTTP request processing to the Web booster.

Fig. 3 shows the design of the accelerator. It consists of the two main parts: the accelerator core, which handles the request processing, and the packet cache. The accelerator uses a regular socket read to receive requests from the Web booster or directly from the clients. If the request misses the packet cache, the accelerator reads files directly from the file system and builds the network packets that it stores in the packet cache. Partial checksums on the packet data are pre-computed and stored with the packet. After the packets are built or found in the cache, the accelerator uses a special entry point into the TCP module to send or queue the packets to the socket. If the request has to be delivered to the user-level HTTP server, the accelerator writes an unmodified request to a separate socket that is used by user-level the HTTP server to read requests.

The MTU of clients can vary greatly. For example, according to the study of the Web server under real workload [27], only 32% of all clients advertised MSS value of 1460, which corresponds to Ethernet MTU, and 60% of them advertised a value less than 1024. The packet caching technique only can be used within a range of the MTU's that are used for connection to the Web booster or clients. If the size of the packets for a requested document is larger than MTU of the connection, the packets have to be fragmented, which implies copying and checksumming. If the size is smaller, transmission of such packets

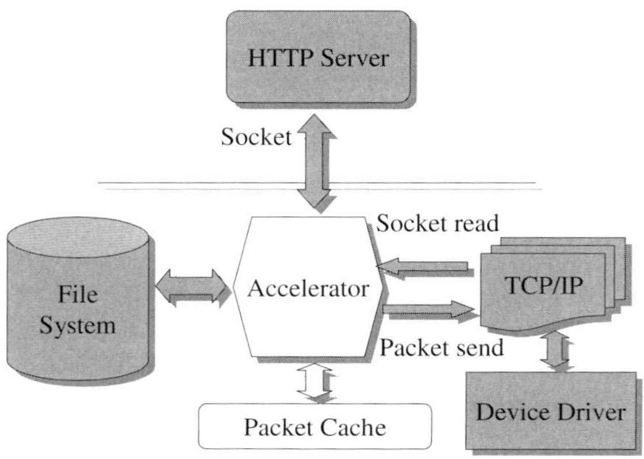

Fig. 3. Accelerator design.

unnecessarily increases the number of processed network packets and the corresponding cost of request processing. When the accelerator communicates with a Web booster, the packet cache can be built for the single MTU of the booster connections. If the accelerator receives requests directly from clients, it deals with a wide range of MTU, which makes the packet cache significantly less efficient.

The Web accelerator uses an unmodified TCP/IP stack to communicate with the Web booster. The booster opens several TCP connections and sends all requests through them. Such set up avoids connection open and close overhead, which is usually incurred when clients send requests directly to the accelerator. Also smaller number of concurrent connections decreases the cost of packet de-multiplexing, which may significantly affect the overall performance [9].

The Web booster delays acknowledgements in order to decrease the overhead of network packet processing. When a booster and an origin server are connected in a local area network, the rate of packet loss is low. In this case it is possible to send acknowledgements from the booster for the sent data less frequently than for every two packets, as the TCP specification requires. Such technique significantly decreases the number of packets processed on the origin server. This in turn decreases the number of hardware and software interrupts and the corresponding cost of the request processing. The TCP module of the Web booster has to be modified to utilize this method, but not the origin server.

One potential problem with this approach is the slow start of the origin server's TCP. Delaying the acknowledgments during this phase would prevent the origin's server TCP to leave slow start quickly and, by this, it would limit the throughput of the connection. Therefore, the Web booster enables delayed acknowledgements only after the slow start.

Although the accelerator is able to completely process HTTP requests, it may offload some computation for HTTP header parsing to the Web booster. In this case, the Web booster parses and extracts the requested URL from the HTTP request, but it sends this URL together with the original header. The accelerator then decides whether to process the request or to redirect it to the user-level HTTP server, in which case the original HTTP header is used. Previous section showed that the cost of the HTTP request parsing is not significant compared to the overall processing cost, so the usefulness of this technique depends on whether HTTP header parsing on the Web booster is required for other reasons, such as those described in Section 7.

The accelerator requires the following support form the operating system and the network protocol stack.

- **Memory management**. The accelerator requires non-paged memory allocation that is possible to use as network buffers.
- **Packet queuing**. The TCP implementation must export an entry point that allows one to send or queue built network packets, avoiding the regular data copying and packet creation mechanism.
- **File system access**. Although it is possible to use the regular file read operation exported to user-level processes, it is more efficient to read file data directly into the accelerator memory, avoiding file buffering.

Most modern operating systems provide such support for the kernel modules, including Linux, which was used as our implementation platform.

In the current design, cached documents are used only by the accelerator and are cached directly as the network packets. When files are read from the file system, the page cache is avoided, so that there is only one cached copy of the file in the memory. Nevertheless, we envision that there might be a situation when the file data have to be both available to the accelerator in forms of network packets and mapped to a user-level process as memory pages. Using two caches is possible but doubles the memory consumption.

It is possible to have only one copy of the file data in the memory if the operating system and the network device driver support multiple non-contiguous buffers for one packet (gather/scatter). In this case a page cache where the file is read is used to create a network packet consisting of two non-contiguous buffers: the packet header built in a separate memory pool and the packet data that are just part of the unmodified page. This page may be also directly mapped into user-level space as read-only page if necessary.

Although some of the processing optimizations described in this section are applicable to the stand-alone configuration when the origin Web server accepts requests directly from the clients, the Web booster is required in order to:

- avoid connection management overhead,
- use delayed acknowledgement technique,
- fully utilize the packet cache (because a single MTU is used), and
- offload some request processing to the Web booster.

5. Performance results

We used Linux kernel v. 2.4 as our implementation and test platform. The accelerator was implemented as a kernel module. For experiments, we used a machine with Intel 650MHz processor equipped with 512MB of main memory and connected to the test clients with three 100Mbps Ethernet cards.

The SURGE simulation toolkit [5] generates the workload. It uses a statistical model to simulate the inter-arrival time, distribution of document sizes, request sizes and temporal locality of the real life HTTP clients. The number of so called 'user equivalents' defines the level of the workload, which are modeled after the real life clients that generate series of HTTP requests separated by off-time.

To measure the cost of request processing in different parts of the kernel and the accelerator, we wrote a kernel profiling tool that uses Intel processor hardware counters to precisely measure the time spent in different parts of the kernel. It takes into account process context switches and interrupts when measuring the time.

5.1. Measurements

We ran four sets of tests in which we enabled different optimization techniques described in previous section. Each set consisted of three runs with different number of SURGE 'user equivalents': 1200, 2400 and 3600. Because the SURGE toolkit generated workload that has some distribution over time, we measured the load and other test parameters averaged over 0.5-second intervals.

Table 1 shows different test parameters for the configuration with all and none of the optimization enabled. The optimized configuration experiences about one-fourth as many hardware interrupts per requests as the unoptimized configuration. This reduction is primarily because there are almost seven times fewer received packets processed in optimized configuration.

Table 1. Test parameters

	Unoptimized	Optimized
Average request size	11.4 KB	11.4 KB
Sent packet/request	12.9	9.31
Received packet/request	9.41	1.41
Hardware intr/packet	0.51	0.22
Software/hardware intr	0.53	0.54

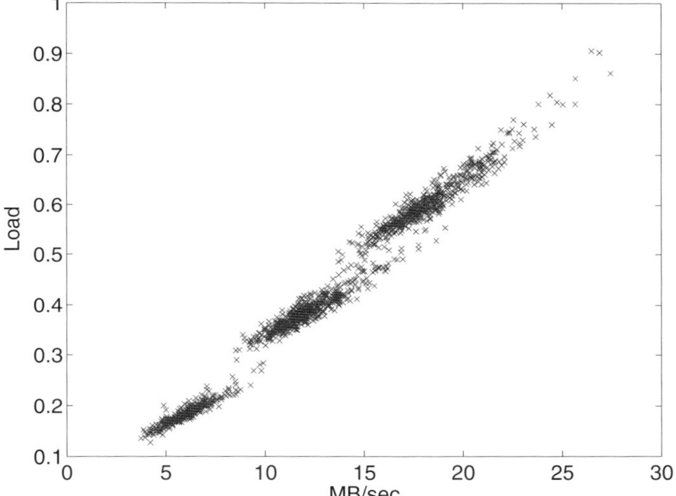

Fig. 4. Load vs. send data rate.

Fig. 4 shows the measurements of the load plotted against the send data rate for the accelerator configuration with no optimizations enabled (which is comparable to a kernel HTTP server). In this case, a new TCP connection is opened for every request. Each point corresponds to 0.5-second interval. Fig. 5 shows the same data plotted against request rate. We can see that the data in the first figure grouped closer to the linear graph, while in the second graph data are more scattered. This indicates that the send operation is the major contributing factor for the overall processing cost, while the additional overhead per request does not have significant influence. Furthermore, when the network cards are nearly saturated (30MB/sec), the load on the server approaches 100%.

We measured the contributions of hardware and software interrupts to the overall processing cost. Further we break down the request processing cost in the context of the accelerator thread into the cost of copying and checksumming and the cost of the rest of the processing. The latter includes a small part of the cost of connection management, which is mostly accomplished in context of software and hardware interrupts.

Fig. 6, 7, 8 and 9 show the approximation of the measurement data with a linear polynomial using least-square method. Fig. 6 is the same configuration with no optimizations as discussed above. Hardware interrupts, software interrupts, and copying-checksumming contribute the most to the cost of the processing. Fig. 7 shows the configuration when

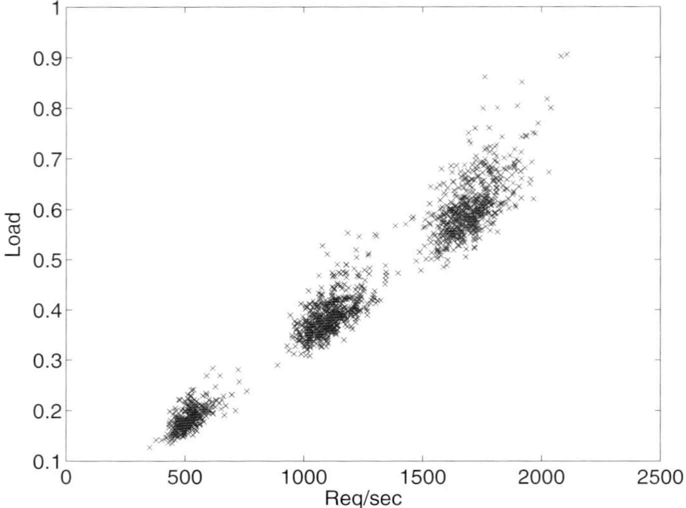

Fig. 5. Load vs. request rate.

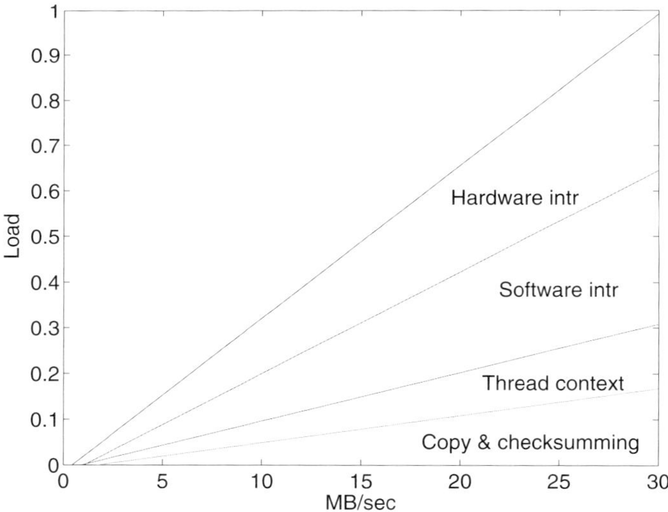

Fig. 6. Cost breakdown: unoptimized.

the packet cache is enabled. This optimization eliminates copying and checksumming and decreases the thread context processing cost. Its overall processing cost is approximately 75% of the unoptimized configuration.

The next test enables connection management optimization in addition to packet caching, which is shown in Fig. 8. The connection cost performed in the context of an accelerator thread is a minor amount of load. However, this greatly reduces interrupts, which cuts the cost of hardware and software interrupts in half.

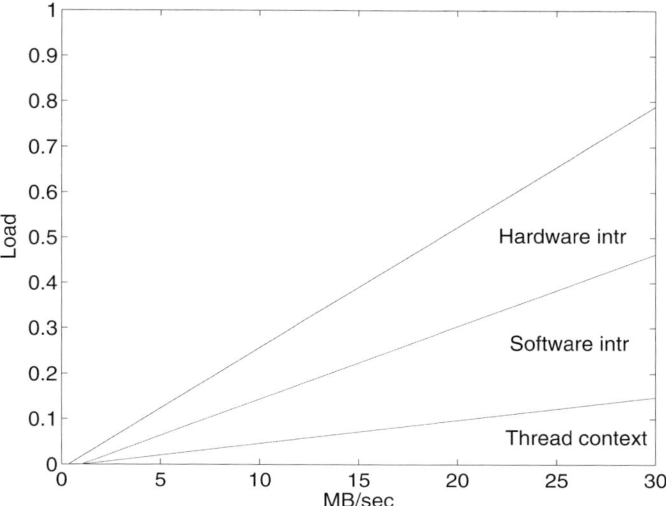

Fig. 7. Cost breakdown: packet cache.

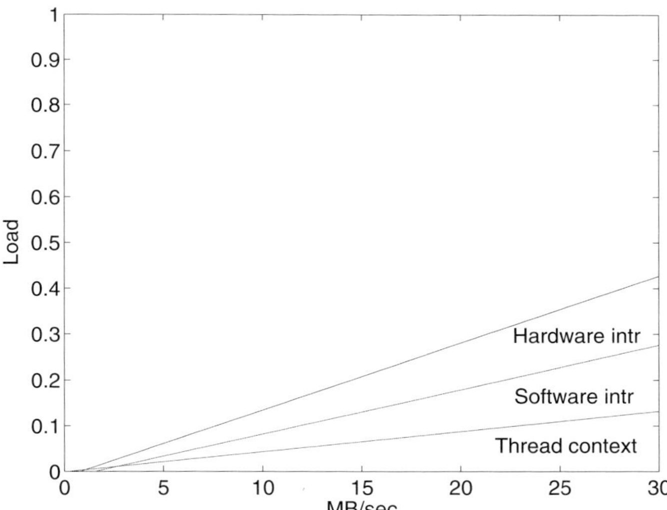

Fig. 8. Cost breakdown: no connections.

Finally, Fig. 9 shows the effect of delaying acknowledgements sent from the booster to the server. This shows the effect of all the optimizations discussed in this paper. The use of delayed acknowledgements again halves the cost of hardware interrupts.

Fig. 10 shows the overall load measurements for all four configurations discussed above. This graph plots the data rate vs. load and uses linear least-square approximation that is superimposed on the measured data. The axes of the graph are reversed from the previous graphs, so in this graph a steeper curve is better (more optimizations enabled).

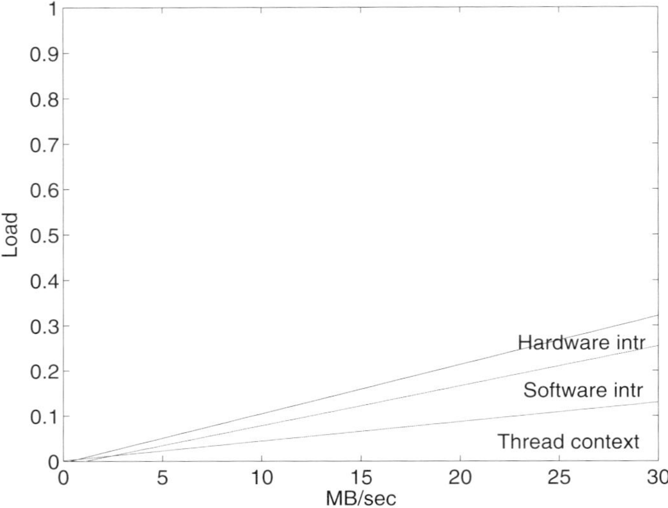

Fig. 9. Cost breakdown: delayed ack's.

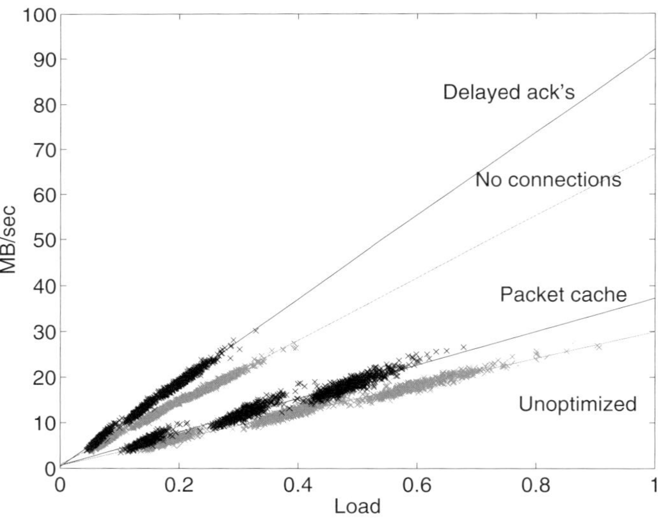

Fig. 10. Maximum data rate.

The graph shows that on the current test platform the extrapolated maximum data rate is about 90MB/sec, which is about 9000 req/s for 10KB objects. This is about 3 times higher than the rate for unoptimized configuration. Recall that unoptimized configuration performs slightly better than Flash user-level Web server.

We compared the performance of the accelerator to the performance of the TUX Web server [29] built as an in-kernel module. This server also avoids data copying and checksumming during data send operation but relies on gather/scatter packet buffer support, provided by Linux 2.4 kernel and some network device drivers, and on hardware packet checksumming. We run tests with TUX enabling the same types of optimizations as with the accelerator including delivering requests through a small number of permanently opened connections and delaying acknowledgements. TUX performance is similar to that of the accelerator, with less than 5% difference. The accelerator design does not require any special support from the operating system or network card such as hardware checksumming. In fact, it was originally implemented on 2.2 Linux kernel without any such support.

6. Web booster

The Web booster has to terminate client TCP connections and route data from/to clients on separate TCP connections opened to Web servers. This requires handling double the traffic of a served domain, because the booster sends to the clients approximately the same amount of data as it receives from the origin server. At the same time, the Web booster does not have to scale with the size of the hosting site, since it is used only for one or few overloaded domains at a time. In fact, the Web booster can be a more powerful and expensive machine than any of the domain servers since the whole site shares its cost. The booster can be easily replicated to increase the maximum throughput.

Unlike the Web accelerator, which has to run within a general-purpose operating system, the Web booster is a dedicated machine. This fact allows the customization of the operating system, network device drivers and adapters. The Web booster has to contain the following functional components.

- Run-time environment exporting basic memory management, scheduling and interrupt processing functionality.
- Network buffer management facility that enables in-place packet processing where possible.
- TCP/IP stack that is integrated with the buffer management facility.
- Network device driver integrated with the protocol stack.
- HTTP parsing engine.

To handle the network traffic requirements of the Web server, the Web booster software can use a couple of techniques. First, it can use in-place packet processing. Many modern network adapters enable non-contiguous (gather/scatter) packet buffers and hardware checksumming. The device driver should utilize these features to build new client packets out of the packets received from the Web server with possibly different MTU without doing copying and software checksumming. Second, the Web booster can use network adapter polling. Polling is more efficient than processing interrupts when a system is busy.

Pai et al. [24] describe layer-7 switch that implements similar functionality to what Web booster has to implement. They indicate that such a switch implemented on general-purpose hardware and software can handle the traffic of approximately ten Web servers on typical Web workload.

7. Possible extensions

There are several ways of extending the proposed model. First, a Web booster can handle secure channels between the Web servers and the clients. If secure channel is required between the booster and the origin server, the packet cache stores already encrypted data. It would be decrypted at the booster and encrypted for each client. Caching encrypted data is not useful for direct client-server transfers because each client has a different key.

Second, most of the existing commercial and research Web servers have coarse resource management. This leads to denial of service attacks when a malicious principal overloads the system with processing. The current design of general-purpose operating systems makes this problem hard to solve [8]. The Web booster may provide a way of enforcing the resource allocation policy by filtering requests that are sent to the Web servers, enabling more fine-grained resource accounting. Because the Web booster itself can be built using a customized operating system, the same problem could be easier to solve there than in the general-purpose operating system.

8. Conclusion

In this work, we described the Web booster infrastructure that is used as a shared resource by Web domains residing on separate servers to temporarily offload the request processing from the Web domain that experiences the peak load. This makes it possible to plan for a smaller infrastructure that handles the same load as a more expensive and often under-loaded infrastructure. To achieve the above goal we: (i) introduced the Web booster model that decreases the HTTP request processing costs on the origin Web server during peak load without removing processing from it; (ii) measured the performance of one the fastest known Web server that runs on top of a general-purpose operating system and identified that the main cost of the request processing is related to the data copying/checksumming and interrupt processing; and (iii) designed, implemented, and measured the performance of the accelerator software, which decreases server load by more than factor of three when compared to direct client request processing.

Acknowledgments

We would like to thank David Cohn for his contributions to the idea and comments on a draft of this paper. The IBM University Partnership Program Award and the JPL HTMT project sponsored this work.

References

[1] V. Almeida, A. Bestavros, M. Crovella, and A. de Oliveira. Characterizing reference locality in the WWW. Technical Report 96-011, Boston University, June 1996.

[2] M. Aron, P. Druschel, and W. Zwaenepoel. Efficient Support for P-HTTP in Cluster-based Web Servers. In *Proceedings of the 1999 USENIX Annual Technical Conference, Monterey*, CA, June 1999.

[3] Akamai Technologies, Inc. http://www.akamai.com.

[4] M. Aron, D. Sanders, P. Druschel, and W. Zwaenepoel. Scalable Content-aware Request Distribution in Cluster-based Network Servers. In *Proceedings of the 2000 Annual USENIX technical Conference*, San Diego, CA, June 2000.

[5] P. Barford and M.E. Crovella. Generating Representative Web Workloads for Network and Server Performance Evaluation. In *Proceedings of Performance '98/ACM SIGMETRICS '98*, Madison, WI, 1998.

[6] A. Bestravos, M. Crovella, J. Liu, and D. Martin. Distributed Packet Rewriting and its Application to Scalable Server Architectures. In *Proceedings of the 6th International Conference on Network Protocols*, Austin, TX, Oct. 1998.

[7] L. Breslau, P. Cao, L. Fan, G. Phillips, and S. Shenker. Web Caching and Zipf-like Distributions: Evidence and Implications. In *Proceedings of IEEE INFOCOM '99*, March 1999.

[8] G. Banga, P. Druschel, and J.C. Mogul. Better Operating System Features for Faster Network Servers. In *Proceedings of the Workshop on Internet Server Performance (WISP)*. Madison, WI, June 1998.

[9] G. Banga and J.C. Mogul. Scalable Kernel Performance for Internet Servers Under Realistic Loads. In *Proceedings of the USENIX Annual Technical Conference*, New Orleans, LA, June 1998.

[10] T. Brisco. DNS support for Load Balancing. Technical Report RFC 1974, Rutgers University, April 1995.

[11] R. Caceres, F. Douglis, A. Feldmann, G. Glass, and M. Rabinovich. Web Proxy Caching: The Devil is in the Details. In *Workshop on Internet Server Performance*, June 1998.

[12] A. Chankhunthod, P.B. Danzig, C. Neerdaels, M.F. Schwartz, and K.J. Worrell. A Hierarchical Internet Object Cache. In *Proceedings of the 1996 USENIX Technical Conference*, San Diego, CA, Jan. 1996.

[13] A. Cohen, S. Rangarajan, and H. Slye. On the Performance of TCP Splicing for URL-Aware Redirection. In *Proceedings of the 2nd USENIX Symposium on Internet Technologies and Systems*, Boulder, CO, Oct.1999.

[14] F. Douglis, A. Feldmann, B. Krishnamurthy, and J. Mogul. Rate of Change and Other Metrics: a Live Study of the World Wide Web. In *Proceedings of the 1st USENIX Symposium on Internet Technologies and Systems*, Dec. 1997.

[15] D. Dias, W. Kish, R. Mukherjee, and R. Tewari. A Scalable and Highly Available Web Server. In *Proceedings of the 1996 IEEE Computer Conference (COMPCON)*, Feb. 1996.

[16] T. von Eicken, A. Basu, V. Buch, W. Vogels. U-Net: A User Level Network Interface for Parallel and Distributed Computing. In *Proceedings of the 15th ACM Symposium on Operating System Principles*, Copper Mountain Resort, CO, Dec 1995.

[17] T. von Eicken, D. Culler, S. Goldstein, and K. Schauser. Active Messages: a Mechanism for Integrated Communication and Computation. In *Proceedings of the 19th International Symposium on Computer Architecture*, Gold Coast, Australia, May 1992.

[18] J.C. Hu, S. Mungee, and D.C. Schmidt. Techniques for Developing and Measuring High-Performance Web Servers over ATM Network. In *Proceedings of the INFOCOM '98 Conference*, San Francisco, March–April 1998.

[19] Khttpd Linux HTTP Accelerator. http://www.fenrus.demon.nl.

[20] D. Krager, T. Leighton, D. Lewin, and A. Sherman. Web Caching with Consistent Hashing. In *Proceedings of the 8th Int. World Wide Web Conference*, May 1999.

[21] E. Levy-Abegnoli, A. Iyengar, J. Song, and D. Dias. Design and Performance of a Web Server Accelerator. In *Proceedings of IEEE INFOCOM'99 Conference*, New York, NY, March 1999.

[22] J. Liedtke, V. Panteleenko, T. Jaeger, and N. Islam. High-Performance Caching With The Lava Hit-Server. In *Proceedings of the 1998 USENIX Annual Technical Conference*, New Orleans, LA, June 1998.

[23] C. Maltzahn, K.J. Richardson, and D. Grunwald. Performance Issues of Enterprise Level Web Proxies. In *Proceedings of the ACM SIGMETRICS '97 Conference*, Seattle, WA, June 1997.

[24] V.S. Pai, M. Aron, G. Banga, M. Svendsen, P. Druschel, W. Zwaenepoel, and E. Nahum. Locality-Aware Request Distribution in Cluster-based Network Servers. In *Proceedings of the 8th Conference on Architectural Support for Programming Languages and Operating Systems*, San Jose, CA, Oct. 1998.

[25] V.S. Pai, P. Druschel, and W. Zwaenepoel. Flash: An Efficient and Portable Web Sever. In *Proceedings of the 1999 USENIX Annual Technical Conference*, Monterey, CA, June 1999.

[26] V.S. Pai, P. Druschel, and W. Zwaenepoel. IO-Lite: A Unified I/O Buffering and Caching System. In *Proceedings of the 3rd Symposium on Operating System Design and Implementation*, New Orleans, LA, Feb. 1999.

[27] W.R. Stevens. TCP/IP Illustrated, Volume 3: TCP for Transactions, HTTP, NTTP, and the UNIX Domain Protocols. Addison-Wesley, 1996.

[28] R. Tewari, M. Dahlin, H. Vin, and J. Kay. Design Considerations for Distributed Caching on the Internet. In *Proceedings of the 19th IEEE Int. Conference on Distributed Computing Systems*, May 1999.

[29] TUX Web Server 2.0. http://www.redhat.com/products/software/tux.

[30] A. Wolman, G.M. Voelker, N. Sharma, N. Cardwell, and H.M. Levy. On the Scale and Performance of Cooperative Web Proxy Caching. In *Proceedings of the 17th ACM Symposium on Operating System Principles (SOSP '99)*, Kiawah Island, SC, Dec. 1999.

[31] C.-S. Yang and M.-Y. Luo. Efficient Support for Content-Based Routing in Web Server Clusters. In *Proceedings of the 2nd USENIX Symposium on Internet Technologies and Systems*, Boulder, CO, Oct. 1999.

[32] X. Zhang, M. Barrientos, J.B. Chen, and M. Seltzer. HACC: An Architecture for Cluster-Based Web Servers. In *Proceedings of the 3rd USENIX Windows NT Symposium*, Seattle, WA, July 1999.

Web Caching and Content Delivery
A. Bestavros and M. Rabinovich (Editors)

The Cyclone Server Architecture: Streamlining Delivery of Popular Content

Stanislav Rost [a,1], John Byers [b,2], Azer Bestavros [b,3]

[a] MIT Laboratory for Computer Science, Cambridge, MA, USA
[b] Department of Computer Science, Boston University, Boston, MA, USA

Abstract

We propose a new Webserver architecture optimized for delivery of large, popular files. Delivery of such files currently pose a scalability problem for conventional content providers, which must devote server-side resources in direct proportion to the high multiprogramming level induced by a set of these connections. While use of scalable multicast may remedy this problem some day, multicast is rarely supported in today's wide-area infrastructure. Our approach alleviates many of the most serious scalability problems by developing new server-side mechanisms capable of managing a large set of TCP connections transporting the same content. The strategy we employ relies on the use of fast forward error correcting (FEC) codes to generate encodings of popular content, of which only a small sliding window is cached in memory at any time instant. The concurrent TCP connections then access content only from this shared window, which is globally useful to all clients. Our method hinges on eliminating unscalable TCP retransmission buffers, as we can 'retransmit' fresh encoding packets in lieu of the originals with no performance degradation and with no modifications to client TCP stacks. Ultimately, our Cyclone server capitalizes on concurrency to maximize sharing of state across different request threads while minimizing context switching, disk I/O, thrashing under high load and the cache memory footprint. In this paper, we describe the design and prototype implementation of our approach as a Linux kernel subsystem.

Keywords: TCP; FEC; Webserver; Popularity; Concurrency; Digital fountain; Tornado codes

1. Introduction

Burgeoning demand for content on the World-Wide Web has led to radical changes in the manner in which popular content is delivered over the Internet. Today, through the use of various proactive replication and redirection schemes, requests for popular content are often routed to, and served from, dedicated servers. Whether such replication and redirection schemes are deployed over a LAN, such as within a local Web

[1] E-mail: stanrost@lcs.mit.edu
[2] E-mail: byers@cs.bu.edu
[3] E-mail: best@cs.bu.edu

server cluster, or in the wide-area, such as across a global Content Distribution Network (CDN), the implications are similar – namely, a server must be able to respond to a very large number of requests for a relatively small number of disproportionately popular files.

While various technologies and protocols that enable replication and redirection have been implemented and deployed (reverse proxies, content surrogates, etc.), the architectures of Web servers have not undergone radical changes to accommodate the delivery of very popular content. In this paper, we argue for such a radical departure – namely, in-kernel support for buffer and network stack management that enables a server to efficiently service a massive number of concurrent requests for files which are both *large* and *frequently* requested. It is well known that such files exist on many popular Web sites. Studies on Web traffic characterization indicate that the frequency of Web requests follows a Zipf-like distribution, or in other words, the distribution of total requests for a given file increases according to a power-law relationship with respect to its popularity ranking [4,10]. Similarly, file sizes served by Web servers have also been shown to follow a similar heavy-tailed distribution [4,15]. Taken together, when we have files which reside at the 'tails' of both of these distributions, such as in the case of movies in a video jukebox or zipped files at a software distribution site, we must address the challenge of serving files which are both very large and very popular. Moreover, serving the large, popular files at the tails of these heavy-tailed distributions is often where scalable content delivery services have the most difficulty [32].

Our solution meets this challenge head-on, by dedicating servers to be responsible for delivery of the largest, most popular files, freeing up the other servers in a server farm for smaller, or less intensely popular files. We expect that our approach would naturally be coupled with traffic engineering solutions that concentrate requests for large, popular files to our specially optimized servers.

The premise of the server architecture we propose in this paper is to reduce the storage complexity of serving a massive number of requests for the same content to almost a constant. To achieve this requires (1) a near-optimal sharing of memory between concurrent requests, and (2) a near-stateless network stack. We achieve both of these goals through the conceptual use of an idealized digital fountain [12], which encodes n blocks of original content into $k \cdot n$ encoding blocks for $k \gg 1$; receiving any n distinct encoding blocks allows the complete, efficient reconstruction of the source data. For large files, close approximations to an ideal digital fountain can be achieved with fast forward error correcting codes, such as Tornado codes [22], which we employ. Traditionally, encoded content has been most widely used in multicast applications, where transmission of a redundant symbol enables different receivers to recover from different packet losses. In our setting, encoding the content realizes a a new benefit, namely while it still enables each piece of encoded content to be useful to all clients simultaneously, in so doing, it facilitates the sharing of information and reduces per-client state at the server.

Compared to traditional architectures, the Cyclone Server Architecture (CSA) allows a significant reduction in resource requirements for delivery of content in situations in which a group of clients is concurrently downloading a particular file, without requiring similarity of transfer rates or synchronization of request arrivals among the clients. In CSA, files are encoded into circular arrays of Tornado blocks that are stored on disk prior to their delivery. The benefits result from the ability of CSA to service an arbitrarily large group of clients interested in the same file using a single, fixed-length sliding cache buffer. Such a buffer is replenished with data from the circular encoding on disk at the speed of the fastest client of the group of clients interested in the same content. Connections servicing the group's slower clients draw data from the same buffer at their respective speeds and thus may miss a number of contiguous encoding blocks. However, the slower clients are able to reconstruct the missed content from redundancy contained in other blocks that they receive successfully.

An almost stateless network stack is achieved by elimination of bulky TCP retransmission queues, made possible by high utility of transmission of any block of the erasure encoding not previously sent. CSA employs a modified version of TCP retransmission semantics (no changes to standard client TCP network stacks are needed) that retransmits the next unsent block of the encoding from the shared sliding cache buffer as opposed to drawing the data from a retransmission queue.

Finally, the need for in-kernel implementation is driven by the necessity of precise synchronization of the speed of progression of the shared buffer to that of the connection to the fastest client of the group, and desire to capitalize on the benefits of elimination of the retransmission queues. Although OS kernel support is required in the server, the decoding functionality of the client can be implemented in a straightforward manner at the application level, for instance as a browser plug-in. Based on the above architectural features, we have implemented a Web server subsystem (under Linux), named Cyclone, for use by server applications.

The rest of the paper is organized as follows. Section 2 outlines related work. In Section 3, we describe the design objectives for our method of content delivery. In Section 4, we present an overview of the design of the Cyclone architecture. Section 5 describes our implementation of the Cyclone subsystem in the Linux kernel. Section 6 contains analytical models and results of simulations. And finally, in Sections 7 and 8 we elaborate on future work and provide acknowledgments.

2. Related work

Considerable work has focused on optimizing the delivery of popular content from a single server. A common theme of this related work is to address issues of scale by minimizing resource consumption, often by reducing the marginal cost of serving an additional concurrent request.

2.1. Multicast-based techniques

One widely researched method for delivering popular files with a minimal footprint on a single server leverages network mechanisms such as native multicast. Researchers have built scalable solutions which use non-adaptive, cyclic transmissions over multicast or broadcast channels to provide eventual reliability [1,2], and more sophisticated solutions which employ forward error correction to achieve scalable reliability without a significant performance penalty [12,26]. These solutions scale to large audiences, as the marginal cost of adding an additional client as perceived by the server is near zero.

The main disadvantage of multicast-based content delivery techniques is their reliance on the existence of an end-to-end multicast-enabled infrastructure. As a result, these techniques are better suited for enterprise network environments, as opposed to WAN environments. This is clearly evident in the slow deployment/adoption of such techniques on the Internet, and the emergence of alternative distribution protocols that 'emulate' multicast using unicast-based overlay networks [14,20].

2.2. Unicast-based techniques

To improve the scalability of Internet servers[4] in a unicast environment, recent research efforts have focused on operating system optimizations (e.g. memory subsystem, file system, network stack, etc.) [18,19,25,28,29]. Generally, these optimizations fall under two categories: (1) optimizations that improve resource allocation decisions, and (2) optimizations that boost resource utilization.

Examples of approaches that aim to improve resource allocation decisions include the use of better cache management [8–10,13,21,24] or the use of prefetching [16,27]. Examples of approaches that aim to improve resource utilization include the elimination of unnecessary memory transfers between the various layers in the system (user space, kernel space, network buffers, etc.) [29] and avoiding overloading through proper admission control [33].

2.3. Scalable content delivery engines

To put our work in context, we compare it to recent projects that parallel some aspects of our two-pronged approach to the construction of popular content delivery servers. Recall that our strategy relies on (1) an (almost) perfect sharing of memory between concurrent requests to a server, and (2) an (almost) stateless network stack implementation on the server.

The IO-Lite system [29] is a good example of a recent effort that aim to achieve the first of the above two goals in the context of Internet servers [28]. In that work, Pai, Druschel and Zwaenepoel demonstrate that repeated copying and multiple buffering of data is a major detriment to system performance. Specifically, their work exposed the unnecessary overhead of copying file blocks from the file system in the kernel layer to the application process' memory space, and then duplicating the very same data buffers in the network layers, as done in conventional operating systems. In [29], they propose a unified cache architecture to remedy this problem in which buffers containing file data are shared across the layers of the operating system. This work differs from ours in that it focuses on eliminating redundant data copying among a single service thread and various OS subsystems; in addition to that, our approach enables sharing *across* threads as well.

The Digital Fountain approach described in the introduction is an example of a recent effort that aims to achieve the second of the above two goals in the context of Internet servers. In one instantiation of that approach, Byers, Luby, Mitzenmacher, and Rege propose the use of fast error correcting codes [22] to alleviate the need for per-client state information at the source of a reliable multicast transmission [12]. Another instantiation of this approach uses encoded content to facilitate stateless downloads from multiple mirror sites in parallel [11]. Our work also employs this paradigm. However, while previous

[4] In this paper, we use the term Internet servers to refer to Web servers, caches, proxies, reverse proxies, surrogates, etc.

work primarily attempts to improve the utilization of network resources; our approach targets servers in a unicast environment and aims to improve utilization of a single server's resources.

3. Design objectives: an ideal compact cache

In the scenario described in the introduction, our objective is to efficiently satisfy a massive number of concurrent requests to a small number of popular files. In this scenario, we expect the server's main memory cache space to be a scarce resource whose usage is at a premium, i.e. it is infeasible to cache the entire working set. Nevertheless, the cost of I/O operations, which is orders of magnitude slower than operations to the cache, make optimizing cache utilization essential to delivering the highest performance. Our objective is to eliminate cache misses in the constrained service environment in which a set S of P of popular files of variable length is known fixed in advance, but where the cache memory of size M is of sufficient size to store only a fraction of S. Thus the challenge is to partition the cache across files and efficiently utilize the *compact* cache space apportioned to file F in a manner which is *globally useful* to all request threads for F even as the multiprogramming level grows large. Issues of scale are central to our design, so apportionment should not necessarily be based on the size or popularity of a file. Expressed in another way, the challenge is to design a scalable system in which the marginal cost of serving an additional client requesting a file from the set S is as close to zero as possible.

From the perspective of managing cache resources in the context of delivering a particular large file, an ideal solution would therefore:

- Consume a fixed amount of cache memory regardless of the number of clients interested in the file.
- Allow the amount of cache memory to be considerably smaller than the size of the entire file.
- Provide performance benefits comparable to that which can be achieved by conventionally caching the entire file.
- Admit clients which arrive asynchronously.
- Accommodate heterogeneous client transfer rates without a performance penalty.

To recap, the properties of the ideal solution can be achieved by a delivery method utilizing a sliding buffer that is globally useful. Global usefulness of the buffer implies that its contents always contribute to the transfer progress of all clients downloading the file whose data is in the buffer. We describe our technique for achieving global usefulness and other components of our design in the subsequent section.

4. Design overview

4.1. Achieving compact caching via fast erasure codes

Our strategy for achieving global usefulness of the sliding buffer employs a powerful procedure originally described by Rabin [30]. His Information Dispersal Algorithm (IDA), disperses a file F of length ℓ into n pieces F_i, $1 \leq i \leq n$, each of length ℓ/m such that the original file F can be reconstructed from any m pieces, where $n > m$. This technique, which can be realized in practice with forward error correcting codes, has been widely used to enable a dispersed encoding of a file to be transmitted over a lossy channel to one or many receivers. For this application, even if up to $n - m$ pieces of the encoding are lost in transit to a given receiver, that receiver may recover from the remaining pieces which arrive intact.

In our application, use of a dispersed encoding gives our server considerable freedom, and enables it to maintain cache contents which are globally useful with very high probability, as we shall now describe. First, for a given file F, the server chooses m so that ℓ/m is equivalent in size to maximum packet payload and generates an information dispersed encoding of the file of length $n = cm$, where we refer to c as the *stretch factor* of the encoding, as in [12]. Note that this encoding procedure need only be done once for each file as its output, the encoded content could be stored on disk for future use. Also note that, since dispersed encoding contains redundancy, strict ordering of its blocks is unnecessary and the encoding can be considered *circular*.

Secondly, the server allocates a *sliding cache buffer* able to hold a fixed quantity (k) of contiguous pieces of the encoding and fills it with initial k blocks of encoding of F from disk. All connections transferring F draw data from that cache buffer. In the steady state, the server continually furnishes the next k blocks of the encoding from disk into the cache buffer whenever the fastest connection delivering F transfers exhausts all of the blocks in the buffer. When the server reaches the end of the file storing the dispersed encoding of F, it may wrap around to draw data from the beginning of the file, thus rotating the cache buffer in the circular encoding.

Using this procedure with high concurrency levels, a typical client would arrive asynchronously, access pieces of encoded content from the cache as the sliding window rotates, and ideally receive sufficiently many pieces of the encoding to recover the file before a full rotation through the encoding completes. Note that the replenishment of pieces of the encoding will occur far faster than their retrieval by the slower clients, thus slow clients will typically ‘miss’ many pieces of the encoding, tolerance to which is one of the key points of our design. Another important design consideration is the use of a sufficiently large stretch factor to ensure that most clients do not experience a full rotation, which can induce redundant transmissions and commensurate performance degradation. Details of the fast error correcting codes we use for encoding are discussed in the implementation section.

4.2. The cyclone subsystem

We now provide an overview of the design decisions we have made in building our Cyclone content delivery architecture which achieves the design objectives specified in the previous section. A high-level depiction of the mechanisms this architecture uses to deliver a single source file is provided in Fig. 1.

The functionality of the Cyclone server architecture is made available to server applications by the Cyclone subsystem. The subsystem houses centralized collections of state uniquely pertinent to delivery of a particular file, the *data pumps*. Data pumps are responsible for maintenance of the file-specific cache buffer. Conceptually, a data pump ensures that fresh content from the FEC encoding is serviced to outbound transport connections, or data taps. As depicted in Fig. 1, the data pump employs a sliding window

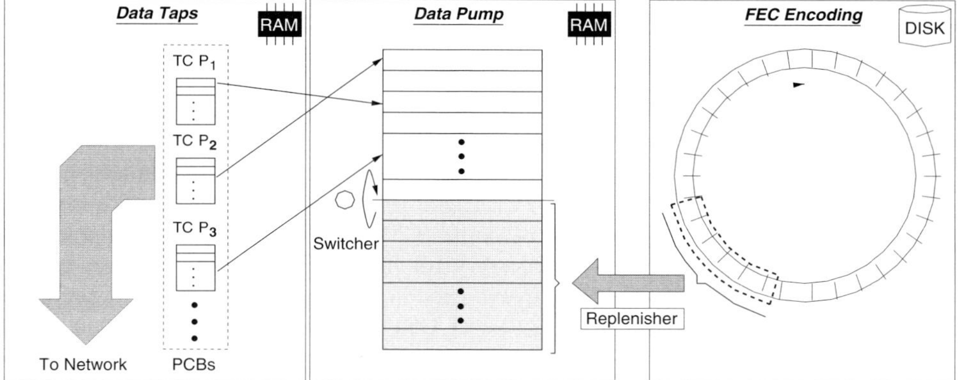

Fig. 1. Delivery of a file in the Cyclone server architecture.

strategy to ensure that fresh content is replenished into the cache. To avoid costs of memory locking while replenishment is occurring, we divide the cache buffer used by a data pump into two *half-spaces*. Each half-space contains pieces of the encoding which are atomically furnished to the data taps (for simplicity, recall that we set the encoding granularity equal to the size of a packet payload). The active half-space is the source of encoding packets to be sent out to the clients. The loading half-space (shaded in Fig. 1) is inaccessible to service threads and can only be accessed by the data pump's *replenisher* thread, whose task is to load encoding packets from disk while packets are being concurrently furnished from the active half-space.

Collections of state which allow connections to interface with the data pump are referred to as *data taps*. A data tap tracks how much of the active half-space content has been transmitted by its parent connection. Service threads, each progressing at the speed driven by the congestion-controlled connection to the client, consult the data taps to determine which encoding blocks to read next and update them to reflect the progress. As soon as any thread exhausts all of the blocks in the active half-space, it requests that the half-spaces be switched. When the switch occurs, the loading and active half-spaces reverse roles, the data pump directs the replenisher thread to fill the new loading half-space, all data taps attached to the pump reset to the first block, and the service threads proceed to seamlessly serve encoding blocks from the new active half-space.

One integrity constraint is imposed on the system to preserve logical separation of the half-spaces. The half-space switch will not be performed until the replenisher thread has finished loading all of the encoding blocks into the non-active half-space. In practice, this constraint does not impose a significant performance cost since there are typically orders-of-magnitude difference between the time required to replenish a half-space and the time needed by a client to exhaust a half-space.

4.3. Interfacing with reliable transport protocols

Of central importance to the design of the Cyclone server is the choice of, and interface to, the transport protocol we use to deliver the content. TCP is the most natural choice, as it is a standard for reliable unicast transfers and it is desirable to employ its congestion control functionality. However, it is highly undesirable to use TCP's stateful retransmission semantics, first because explicit retransmission of data is unnecessary with the encoding framework we use, but more significantly, because retransmission of packets requires undesirable retention of state in the form of a retransmission buffer, which must necessarily be of size proportional to the bandwidth-delay product of the TCP connection.

We propose two methods for circumventing this problem. The conceptually simpler version relies on UDP coupled with TCP-friendly congestion-control mechanisms, as could be provided by the Congestion Manager (CM) architecture [3]. In this scenario, packet retransmissions would be unnecessary for providing reliability, as receipt of a sufficient number of packets from the cyclic encoding would ensure eventual reliability. However, in the contemporary Internet, use of UDP is undesirable, both because many firewalls are configured to block UDP traffic and because many UDP transfers are not congestion controlled and are therefore discriminated against.

Therefore, we rely on a second transport-level approach, in which we make a server-side modification to the TCP packet retransmission algorithms which does not alter TCP timing semantics, but does alter the *content* of TCP retransmissions. In practice, we issue retransmissions which contain a different piece of the encoding than the original transmission. We emphasize that this alteration of TCP, which we call TCP-ERC, or TCP for erasure-resilient content, requires no client modifications, as TCP clients never examine discrepancies between content of an original transmission and a retransmission. Moreover, since our changes do not impact the timing semantics nor the critical path [6] of a TCP transfer, there is no negative performance impact.

Delving into the details of TCP-ERC, all of the flow control and congestion control mechanisms of TCP are retained in full. Conceptually, TCP-ERC differs from regular TCP in only one respect. In a situation in which TCP would retransmit a packet due to loss, TCP-ERC proceeds to transmit a fresh encoding packet (in the Cyclone server, that means simply transmitting the next Tornado block from the active half-space). On the packet level, the sequence number of the retransmitted packet is the same as that of the original lost packet, but a different portion of the encoding is inserted as the retransmitted packet's payload. This approach has the primary advantage that cumbersome (and superfluous) retransmission buffers do not have to be maintained in memory, substantially streamlining the management of TCP connections. At the client side, a client could conceivably observe the fact that TCP-ERC is being used at the sender, i.e. when it receives an original transmission and a retransmission with identical sequence numbers which contain different payloads. However, the TCP specification indicates that duplicate packets (i.e. packets with identical sequence numbers to packets which have already arrived) should be dropped. Thus clients can retain and use their existing TCP stack implementations to receive TCP-ERC transmissions.

4.4. Client support for FEC-encoded content

Transmission of encoded content implies that clients must have the capability to reconstruct the file from the encoded transmission. A client may advertise such a capability in the header of its HTTP request. The ability to reconstruct files from FEC encodings is entrusted to a library of subroutines positioned between the application and the communications protocol. The reconstruction procedure takes over the processing of incoming blocks of the encoding for the application, and supplies the application with a fully reconstructed file. A potential cost of this procedure is that this layer must be able to buffer the entire file prior to decoding. It is also the responsibility of the client to notify the server that it has received enough data to reconstruct the file by closing the connection or transmitting a stop message. The functionality of the reconstruction library can be made available to existing Web browsers as a plug-in for processing of a MIME data type designating erasure-resilient encoding.

4.5. Design summary

At the core of the Cyclone server architecture are files stored as erasure-resilient encodings. The advantage given by such an encoding is the ability to serve pre-encoded file blocks in any order, yet still contribute to the transfer progress of each of its clients with high probability. It is then possible to advance the sliding cache buffer at the speed of the *fastest* client in the group of clients interested in the same file, without waiting for slower clients. Slower clients who receive encoding blocks out of sequence due to an advancing sliding buffer can nevertheless reconstruct the file efficiently. In the event that a client witnesses the sliding buffer traverse the entire encoding, it is likely that this client will receive some redundant transmissions before recovering the file. However, large stretch factors can mitigate the effects caused by this contingency at the expense of increased secondary storage requirements at the server and increased decoding times (for detailed treatment, please see Section 6.3).

The description of the design is now complete. The architecture discussed above achieves both maximization of sharing and cache compactness. However, more details are necessary to provide a full understanding of the Cyclone server architecture implementation.

5. Implementation overview

This section of the paper presents the overview of a prototype implementation of the Cyclone server architecture as an in-kernel subsystem.

5.1. Codes

While the general IDA approach proposed by Rabin is very powerful, a substantial practical limitation is imposed by the computational complexity of encoding and decoding operations. Most authors applying IDA approaches to networking applications have used variants of Reed-Solomon codes (as described in [23]) as their forward error correcting primitive [7,26,31]. These codes rely on cumbersome finite field operations and have $O(n^2)$ encoding and decoding times (where n is the number of source blocks). Thus, while IDA with Reed-Solomon codes works well for reconstructing a file stored as n pieces distributed over n remote sites when n is 14 and m (the number of pieces needed to recover the file) is 10, its decoding inefficiency is prohibitive when transmitting a file spanning 5000 packets encoded with a stretch factor of 10. A partial remedy to this problem, which improves decoding time, is to divide a large file into blocks and to apply Reed-Solomon forward error correction over those smaller blocks [26]. In order to reconstruct the file, this approach necessitates recovery of a set of encoded pieces which together enable the decoding of all blocks. While this approach improves decoding, it limits scalability, as the reconstructor typically must wait a considerable amount of time before receiving the last codeword needed to reconstruct the final incomplete block, especially as the number of blocks grows large, as detailed in [12].

A newly available alternative to Reed-Solomon codes are sparse codes such as Tornado codes [22], which are closely related to low-density parity-check codes. By relaxing the decoding guarantee, i.e. by requiring slightly more than n encoding packets to recover an original file of n packets, and by using randomized encoding and decoding algorithms with fast XOR operations, these codes achieve linear encoding and decoding times. In practice, Tornado codes require reception of $(1 + \epsilon)n$ distinct encoding packets to reconstruct the source data, where ϵ is on the order of 0.05 for files of tens of megabytes or more. We employ these codes for our application, specifically, the family of Tornado Z codes, described in [12], which have an average overhead of roughly 5%, low overhead variance, and decoding times of at most a few seconds for files of tens of MB. A crucial parameter in selecting an appropriate Tornado code is the *stretch factor*, or the ratio between the length of the encoding and the length of the file. Employing a large stretch factor is highly desirable as it enables us to ideally accommodate a wider range of heterogeneous client transfer rates, as we describe momentarily. On the other hand, for our application, increasing the stretch factor causes a commensurate (linear) increase in (a) the disk space needed to store the encoding at the server, (b) the space needed to reconstruct the file at the client, and (c) the decoding time at the client. Unlike blocked Reed-Solomon codes, Tornado codes admit large stretch factors with only a linear degradation in encoding and decoding times and no degradation in overhead, measured as useless packets.

As an example of the tradeoffs, if clients are downloading a 10 MB file at rates varying from 50 kbps to 1 Mbps, the refresh rate of the cache will occur at a rate fast enough to accommodate the fastest client, while a slow client will transfer only about $\frac{1}{20}$ of the packets in a given cache block. In this scenario, a stretch factor of 20 would be needed to ensure that a slow client did not observe a full rotation of the encoding. If a full rotation does occur, this causes performance degradation, as it implies that clients may receive duplicate transmissions. However, the incidence of duplicate transmission will remain low – even with a stretch factor of 10, and assuming pure random transmission of encoding packets (with replacement), the incidence of duplicate packets will remain below 6% using Tornado Z codes. In practice, a stretch factor of 10 is the parameter setting we employ. For further discussion on duplicate transmissions, refer to Section 6.3.

5.2. Overview: Delegation of processing

The Cyclone server subsystem performs the majority of the processing associated with content delivery. The task of the server application is reduced to processing a client's request and then invoking the Cyclone subsystem to deliver the requested content via the existing connection to the client. In the course of content delivery by the Cyclone subsystem, a replenisher thread loads data into the data pump corresponding to the file, and the in-kernel network layer event-driven routines transmit the content and invoke the switching of half-spaces. The process of satisfying a request for content using the Cyclone architecture is depicted in Fig. 2, which we describe now.

The functionality of the Cyclone subsystem is provided to server applications through a system call. After transmitting a response header to the client (Fig. 2a), the server

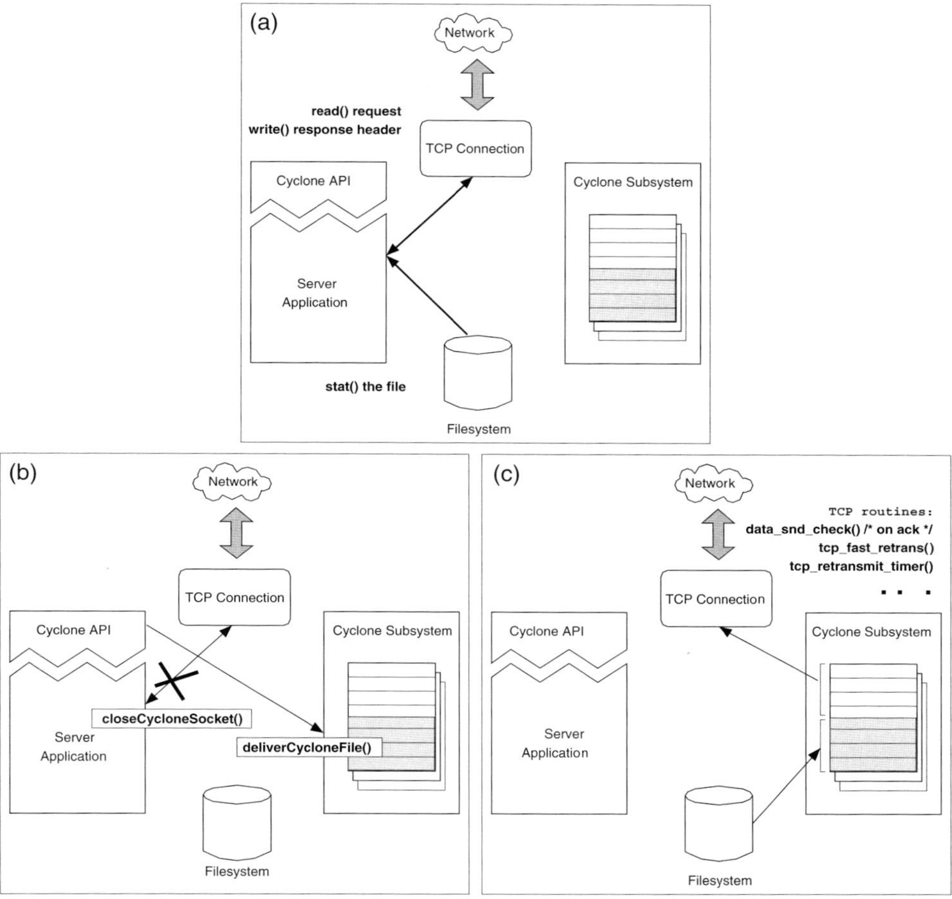

Fig. 2. Satisfying a request for content using Cyclone/Linux.

application invokes the Cyclone system call (Fig. 2b), passing the descriptor to the open socket as well as the name of the file to be delivered as parameters. The system call resolves the file name to the corresponding data pump (creating one if it does not exist yet), create a data tap, integrate it into the socket state, and connect it to the data pump. Once the system call returns, the thread of the server application that invoked it may entirely disregard the remainder of the delivery process and process the next request. Furthermore, it is recommended that the server application should close its socket to conserve per-process resources.

The Cyclone subsystem begins the delivery of encoded content after the system call returns control to the application and the response header has been successfully transmitted. The event-driven kernel routines (Fig. 2c) responsible for the transmission of data in conventional delivery schemes also handle the special-case processing for Cyclone connections, discerning them from regular connections by presence of data taps. Such special-case processing involves procuring data from the pump as opposed to network buffers whenever the kernel routines can transmit or must retransmit.

5.3. Data pump management

As described in Section 4.2, data pumps contain centralized cache buffers, for simultaneous access by multiple threads of service. They must then exist outside of the scope and lifetime of any particular service thread. Additionally, data in half-spaces will be accessed by time-critical kernel routines, and thus must be situated in memory which will not be swapped out to disk. These constraints compelled us to allocate data pumps as well as the hash table for resolving data pumps from file names within kernel–space memory.

Destruction of a data pump is invoked by the server application, and may either be immediate or delayed. In either case, the actual destruction only happens after all of the data taps detach from the pump, but in the case of delayed destruction the existing clients tapped into the data pump are first allowed to finish receiving the file. Note that the costs of creating and destroying data pumps are significant and often it is more beneficial to allow a data pump to idle than to destroy it.

The role of a replenisher thread is to furnish data to a data pump's loading half-space. In our implementation, one replenisher thread is created for every data pump, however, it is possible to improve upon that scheme. Once a replenisher thread fills the loading half-space, it will block until connections exhaust the active half-space and switch the half-spaces to resume loading the data. In practice, due to the difference between the throughput of secondary storage and that of network, the replenisher will often wait for ample periods of time. Instead of blocking, a single thread may be able to assume the role of multiple replenishers for a number of data pumps.

6. Analytical models

The primary benefits of our design result from unified cache and network stack management. Centralized, globally useful cache buffers prevent the amount of cache memory consumed by concurrent service threads from growing with the number of threads. Additionally, using such buffers reduces the cost of operations such as data copying, disk I/O and related system calls which would otherwise be performed by each service thread individually. Aggregation of the network stack with the globally useful cache alleviates the need for bulky send buffers and retransmission queues.

To analyze the resource savings of the Cyclone architecture over a conventional architecture, we will apply the following model. We assume that at an instant in time, a server (either conventional or Cyclone) is serving n asynchronous connections, $C_1 \ldots C_n$, which concurrently deliver a file F of length l bytes to their respective clients. Each connection transmits data at a heterogeneous rate R_i, over a path whose one-way latency is L_i.

6.1. Cache buffer scalability

A conventional server architecture delivers a file F by repeatedly loading a block of size B into a buffer and transmitting its contents.[5] Subdivision of a file into blocks of size B yields $N_B = l/B$ blocks.

[5] Such an assumption is valid regardless of whether the conventional server relies on *write()* or *mmcp()* system calls for file access.

At any instant of time, a connection C_i demands data from one of those blocks, and since connections are asynchronous and independent, we model the mapping of requests to blocks as being mapped independently and uniformly at random. In the event that multiple connections access a common block, we assume that a single instance of the block can be stored in memory and can be shared, as in case of memory-mapped disk access.

Then, for a file of N_B blocks and a multiprogramming level n, total memory consumption in this model is the following occupancy problem: How many blocks are covered by the set of n requests? The probability of a block not being covered is $\left(1-\frac{1}{N_B}\right)^n$. Therefore the expected number of blocks which are covered is $N_B\left(1-\left(1-\frac{1}{N_B}\right)^n\right)$. When n is small relative to N_B, the expected fraction of blocks covered is closely approximated by $\frac{n}{N_B}$, or, coverage grows linearly with the multiprogramming level. As the multiprogramming level becomes large relative to the number of blocks, the limiting behavior is that the entire file is covered. On many modern operating systems, server architectures which do not take advantage of memory mapping cannot share file blocks beyond the boundaries of the file system cache. In such cases, the memory requirements are more simply expressed by $n \cdot B$. On the other hand, in the Cyclone server architecture, total memory consumption is only $2 \cdot H$, where H is the size of a half-space, independent of the number of clients n.

We next analyze the amount of I/O traffic in the two systems. Because of the regulation of TCP send queue sizes by the operating system, a service thread servicing a connection C_i will access the file at a rate ultimately determined by R_i. Thus, in a conventional system, the total rate of disk access for n service threads can be modeled by $\sum_i \frac{R_i}{B}$. Then, assuming transmission rates R_i are independent and identically distributed from some distribution $\mathcal{D}$, where $\mu = \mathbf{E}[R_i]$, the average rate of disk access in the conventional server can be represented as

$$\frac{n \cdot \mu}{B}.$$

In contrast, the Cyclone server's disk access to a file is driven by the rate of transmission of the fastest connection servicing F. The rate of disk access in the Cyclone server architecture can then be expressed as

$$\frac{\max_i R_i}{H}.$$

6.2. Network stack scalability

While our arguments apply to any transmission protocol that buffers content in the server, we also discuss the issues of network stack scalability within the framework of TCP.

The scalability of a server's TCP layer is limited by potentially large quantities of data temporarily residing in send buffers and retransmission queues of TCP stacks of concurrent connections. A TCP buffer can conceptually be subdivided into a send queue and retransmission queue. Content supplied by the application, but not yet transmitted onto the network, resides in the send queue. Content already transmitted, but not yet acknowledged, resides in the retransmission queue. The difference between the application's fill rate and the network connection's transmission rate dictates the size and behavior of the send queue. Many operating systems impose a limit on the send queue size and decelerate the fill rates of applications which exceed such a limit. TCP's sliding window algorithm and retransmission policy limits the size of the retransmission queue of a connection C_i to be at most $2 \cdot R_i \cdot L_i$, with the steady-state limit on the lower bound of the queue size being $R_i \cdot L_i$.

Typical memory demands imposed on a server by a TCP stack can be illustrated with a back-of-the-envelope example. As the Internet technologies evolve, the available bandwidth will increase while propagation delays, dictated by bounds on the speed of light, will likely remain the same. A connection with 100 ms RTT and available bandwidth of tens of Mbps will yield retransmission queue sizes in the range of hundreds of kilobytes per connection.

A TCP-ERC stack coupled with the Cyclone server does not feature a send buffer, but instead draws data from the shared cache buffer. Unlike in the case of TCP retransmission queues, the impact of connection properties on memory requirements of a TCP-ERC stack is negligible. Connection-influenced memory consumption in a TCP-ERC stack occurs primarily due to the need to store per-packet timestamps and selective acknowledgment flags in a lightweight retransmission queue, to ensure proper functioning of TCP. Under Linux, TCP-ERC's lightweight retransmission buffers require 16 bytes per packet as opposed to regular TCP's requirements of $\approx$1600 per socket buffer. By removing timestamps from the TCP-ERC stack and performing timeouts using a constant amount of state, it may be possible to eliminate the need for per-packet state, providing even better memory scalability.

6.3. Duplicate transmissions

One of the factors affecting the performance of the Cyclone server architecture is the potential transmission of duplicate encoding packets. The cyclical manner in which the replenisher retrieves encoding from disk provides for the possibility of slower connections transmitting such packets. Connections may transmit redundant encoding blocks after persisting for more than one rotation of the sliding buffer over the entire length of the encoding.

The performance issues associated with the finite length of the encoding can be mitigated by selecting a large enough value of the stretch factor prior to encoding the content. The choice of the stretch factor's value is crucial for eliminating redundant transmissions, but also impacts storage costs and decoding time.

It is straightforward to calculate the conditions under which a client can reconstruct the source content before a full rotation completes, namely if it has a hit rate of at least $\frac{1+\epsilon}{c}$ (where $1 + \epsilon$ is the reception inefficiency of the Tornado code, and c is the stretch factor) in the first rotation. In the Cyclone server, situations occur in which slower clients miss blocks due to a faster connection's faster advancement of the shared sliding buffer. In the course of delivery of the content in a given half-space, the slower connection C_i will only be able to transmit an $\frac{R_i}{\max_j R_j}$ fraction of the half-space content before the fastest connection will switch the half-space. In fact, on average, C_i will miss a $1 - \frac{R_i}{\max_j R_j}$ fraction of the entire encoding during every revolution of the sliding buffer. Thus it is possible to guarantee that C_i will transmit a sufficient fraction of the encoding to reconstruct the source file before the rotation completes if the following condition holds:

$$\frac{R_i}{\max_j R_j} > \frac{1+\epsilon}{c}$$

The stretch factors needed to realize this guarantee for a wide range of transmission rates are impractically large. In practice, considerably smaller stretch factors can be employed in combination with scalable heuristics aimed to reduce redundant transmissions. One such heuristic ensures that slow clients do not always deterministically send from the front of half-spaces, but rather choose the

$$r = \frac{R_i}{\max_j R_j} \cdot N_h$$

blocks that they send during every 'round' of transmission (with such rounds beginning and ending in a half-space switch) at random. Alternatively, clients might choose a random initial offset from within each half-space. Other, more complicated heuristics may provide better protection against repeated transmissions of identical blocks at the expense of additional memory.

7. Conclusions and future work

We have described an architecture for a scalable content delivery engine dedicated to transmission of large, popular files to a broad audience using TCP transport. The novelty in our design stems from erasure-resilient encoding of the content, which facilitates maximal sharing of transmitted packet payloads across concurrent request threads and keeps per-connection state to a minimum.

We have implemented this Cyclone subsystem in the Linux kernel and have validated the correctness of our version of TCP-ERC implemented in the Linux TCP stack. We have developed server and client APIs suitable for testing the performance of Cyclone transfers. These APIs are integrated into Apache Web server [17] and SURGE, a representative Web workload generator [5].

Currently, we are conducting a series of experiments to demonstrate the performance advantages of Cyclone over traditional server architectures. The initial experiments involve the scenario of a single relatively large, popular file being requested by multiple clients. Such tests allow us to debug, profile and optimize our implementation.

In the future, we would like to test our architecture in multi-file scenarios, in the settings of both local and wide-area networks. We are also exploring various avenues for application of globally useful shared buffers, lightweight network stacks and other components of the Cyclone server architecture.

Acknowledgments

Many thanks to Mark Crovella, Paul Barford, and Bob Frangioso for helpful conversations, useful advice and technical suggestions.

References

[1] S. Acharya and M. Franklin and S. Zdonik. Dissemination Based Data Delivery Using Broadcast Disks. In: *IEEE Personal Communications*, December 1995, pages 50–60.

[2] K.C. Almeroth, M.H. Ammar and Z. Fei. Scalable Delivery of Web Pages Using Cyclic Best-Effort (UDP) Multicast. In: *Proceedings of IEEE INFOCOM*, March 1998.
[3] H. Balakrishnan, H. Rahul and S. Seshan. An Integrated Congestion Management Architecture for Internet Hosts. In: *Proceedings of ACM SIGCOMM '99*, September 1999.
[4] P. Barford, A. Bestavros, A. Bradley and M. Crovella. Changes in Web Client Access Patterns: Characteristics and Caching Implications. *World Wide Web, Special Issue on Characterization and Performance Evaluation*, 2: 15–28, 1999.
[5] P. Barford and M. Crovella. Generating Representative Web Workloads for Network and Server Performance Evaluation. In: *ACM Sigmetrics*, 1998.
[6] P. Barford and M. Crovella. Critical Path Analysis of TCP Transactions. In: *ACM SIGCOMM*, Stockholm, Sweden, August 2000.
[7] A. Bestavros. AIDA-based Real-Time Fault-Tolerant Broadcast Disks. *Proceedings of the 16th Real Time System Symposium*, June 1996.
[8] A. Bestavros, R. Carter, M. Crovella, C. Cunha, A. Heddaya and S. Mirdad. Application Level Document Caching in the Internet. In: *IEEE SDNE'96*, June 1996.
[9] J.-C. Bolot, S. Lamblot and A. Simonian. Design of efficient caching schemes for the World Wide Web. *ITC 15*, Washington DC, June 1997.
[10] L. Breslau, P. Cao, L. Fan, G. Phillips and S. Shenker. Web Caching and Zipf-like Distributions: Evidence and Implications. In: *Proceedings of IEEE Infocom*, New York, NY, March 1999.
[11] J. Byers, M. Luby and M. Mitzenmacher. Accessing Multiple Mirror Sites in Parallel: Using Tornado Codes to Speed Up Downloads. *Proceedings of IEEE Infocom*, New York, NY, March 1999.
[12] J. Byers, M. Luby and M. Mitzenmacher and A. Rege. A Digital Fountain Approach to Reliable Distribution of Bulk Data. *ACM SIGCOMM*, Vancouver, Canada, 1998.
[13] P. Cao and S. Irani. Cost-Aware WWW Proxy Caching Algorithms. In: *Proceedings of the USENIX Annual Technical Conference*, December 1997.
[14] Y. Chu, S. Rao and H. Zhang. A Case for End System Multicast. In: *Proceedings of ACM Sigmetrics 2000*, Santa Clara, CA, June 2000, pages 1–12.
[15] M. Crovella and A. Bestavros. Self-similarity in World Wide Web traffic: Evidence and possible causes. *IEEE/ACM Transactions on Networking*, 5(6): 835–846, December 1997.
[16] L. Fan, Q. Jacobson and P. Cao. Potential and Limits of Web Prefetching Between Low-Bandwidth Clients and Proxies. In: *ACM Sigmetrics*, 1999.
[17] Apache Foundation. Apache Web Server: http://www.apache.org.
[18] J. Hu, S. Mungee and D.C. Schmidt. Techniques for Developing and Measuring High-Performance Web Servers Over ATM Networks. In: *Proceedings of IEEE INFOCOM*, San Francisco, CA, March 1998.
[19] Y. Hu, A. Nanda and Q. Yang. Measurement, Analysis and Performance Improvement of the Apache Web Server. In: Proceedings *of the 18th IEEE International Performance, Computing and Communications Conference (IPCCC'99)*, Phoenix/Scottsdale, AZ, February 1999.
[20] J. Jannotti, D. Gifford, K. Johnson, M.F. Kaashoek and J. O'Toole. Reliable Multicasting with an Overlay Network. In: *Proceedings of OSDI*, San Diego, CA, October 2000.
[21] S. Jin and A. Bestavros. GreedyDual* Web Caching Algorithm: Exploiting the Two Sources of Temporal Locality in Web Request Stream. In: *Proceedings of the 5th International Web Caching and Content Delivery Workshop*, Lisbon, Portugal, May 2000.
[22] M. Luby, M. Mitzenmacher, A. Shokrollahi, D. Spielman and V. Stemann. Practical Loss-Resilient Codes. In: *29th STOC*, May 1997.
[23] F.J. Macwilliams and N. Sloane. *The Theory of Error-Correcting Codes*. North Holland, Amsterdam, 1977.
[24] E.P. Markatos. Main Memory Caching of Web Documents. *Proceedings of the 5th World-Wide Web Conference*, May 1996.
[25] E.N. Nahum, Tsipora Barzilai and Dilip Kandlur. Performance Issues in WWW Servers. In: *ACM Sigmetrics*, 1999.
[26] J. Nonnenmacher, E. Biersack and D. Towsley. Parity-Based Loss Recovery for Reliable Multicast Transmission. In: *Proceedings of ACM SIGCOMM '97*, September, 1997.
[27] V. Padmanabhan and J. Mogul. Using Predictive Prefetching to Improve World Wide Web Latency. *ACM SIGCOMM Computer Communication Review*, July, 1996.

[28] V.S. Pai, P. Druschel and W. Zwaenepoel. Flash: An Efficient and Portable Web Server. In: *Proceedings of the UNENIX Annual Technical Conference*, Monterey, CA, June 1999.

[29] V.S. Pai, P. Druschel and W. Zwaenepoel. IO-Lite: A Unified I/O Buffering and Caching System. In: *Proceedings of OSDI*, 1999.

[30] M. Rabin. Efficient Dispersal of Information for Security, Load Balancing and Fault Tolerance. *Journal of the ACM*, 38: 335–348, 1989.

[31] L. Rizzo. Effective Erasure Codes for Reliable Computer Communication Protocols. *Computer Communication Review*, 2(27): 24–36, April 1997.

[32] E. Schooler and J. Gemmell. Using multicast FEC to solve the midnight madness problem. Microsoft Research, September 1997.

[33] H. Zhu, H. Tang and T. Yang. Demand-driven Service Differentiation for Cluster-based Network Servers. In: *Proceedings of IEEE INFOCOM*, 2001.

Web Caching and Content Delivery
A. Bestavros and M. Rabinovich (Editors)

Synopsis

MPLS-based Request Routing

Arup Acharya [1], Anees Shaikh [2], Renu Tewari [3], Dinesh Verma [4]

Internet Infrastructure and Computing Utilities, IBM T.J. Watson Research Center, Hawthorne, NY 10532, USA

1. Problem scenario

Current high-volume, high-availability data centers and content distribution networks use clusters of Web servers or caches to achieve scalability and reliability. In such environments a front-end dispatcher (or router) directs incoming client requests to one of the server machines. The request-routing decision can be based on a number of criteria, including server load, client request, or client identity. Dispatchers may be broadly categorized into two types: layer-4 dispatchers which base decisions on TCP and IP headers alone, and layer-7 dispatchers which use application layer information (e.g., HTTP headers) to direct clients. Content-based routing, for example, requires the dispatcher to terminate the incoming connection, examine the higher-layer headers, and create a new connection with the appropriate server (or transfer the incoming connection). As Web application requirements evolve, there will be a need for more sophisticated request routing, which implies that examining only transport-layer headers provides insufficient functionality. But layer-7 dispatchers, while more sophisticated, suffer from limited scalability and performance since they must perform connection termination and management for a large number of clients. Ideally, a dispatcher should provide the flexibility of layer-7 forwarding, while maintaining performance levels comparable with layer-4 hardware switches. In this synopsis we describe an approach that, when combined with an intelligent client-side proxy, can implement a dispatcher using commercial, high-performance, off-the-shelf switching hardware, while also providing the flexibility of a content-based router.

2. Solution overview

We leverage the growing migration of networks to Multiprotocol Label Switching (MPLS) to provide flexible routing and sophisticated traffic engineering capabilities. MPLS provides a circuit-switching service in a hop-by-hop routed network by grouping

[1] E-mail: arup@watson.ibm.com
[2] E-mail: aashaikh@watson.ibm.com
[3] E-mail: tewarir@watson.ibm.com
[4] E-mail: dverma@watson.ibm.com

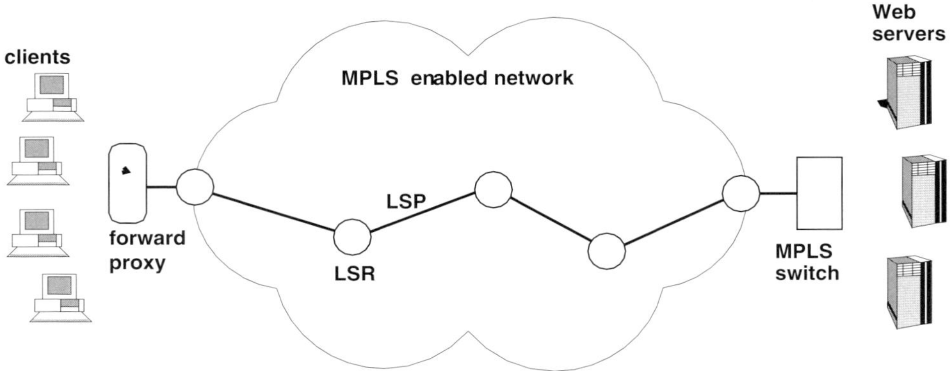

Fig. 1. MPLS-based request routing architecture

related packets using a shared, fixed-size label, allowing the packets to be routed and treated the same way in the network. Though standard usage of MPLS involves establishment of arbitrary label-switched paths (LSPs) for forwarding particular classes of traffic, MPLS labels do not have built-in semantics, in contrast to port numbers or IP addresses, for example. We take advantage of this flexibility by mapping application-layer information onto labels to enable high-performance Web switching, rather than using labels to express routing and forwarding policies. Fig. 1 shows the overall architecture, which consists of an MPLS-enabled client-side proxy, an MPLS network, and a server cluster fronted by a dispatcher which includes a software controller and a standard MPLS switch.

The proxy is responsible for applying labels to packets belonging to client connections. The label applied by the proxy is used at the dispatcher to choose which server should handle the request. We exploit the label stacking feature of MPLS, which allows an inner label to be independent of any outer labels used to route the request through the MPLS network. The mapping of client connections to labels is communicated by the dispatcher to the proxy using a persistent control connection. Depending on the mapping, the dispatcher can support a variety of functions without having to terminate TCP connections, including content-based routing, client-server affinity, client-specific service differentiation, and server load balancing.

This approach has several key advantages over competing solutions that use a front-end Web switch. First, it removes the main bottleneck where all TCP connections are terminated and application-layer information is examined. Second, it lends itself to realization in a standard off-the-shelf MPLS switch, obviating the need for specialized, layer-7 Web switch hardware. Finally, using this approach, many of the functions typically available only with specialized hardware are provided at a much improved price-to-performance ratio. Unlike conventional schemes, this technique assigns some of the dispatch function to the proxy which requires that the proxy is MPLS-aware and that it implements the protocol to receive mapping information from the dispatcher.

Deployment of our scheme relies on wide deployment of MPLS in core networks and access networks, which is supported by reports from several large ISPs and equipment vendors. Also, proxies at the edges of the network must be modified to implement MPLS and support the protocol to communicate with dispatchers in server installations. This is appropriate in settings where proxies and Internet data centers are under a single administrative control, e.g. most large ISPs offer Web hosting service. Similarly, a large corporation with many branch offices and business partners could use the scheme to improve the performance and capacity of its Intranet/Extranet Web servers.

Scalability is a concern if we assume that every forward proxy accessing a Web site participates in this scheme. Instead, we expect that in many cases a relatively small set of proxies contributes the bulk of the traffic to a site, and it is feasible to modify only those proxies. Another scenario that justifies proxy participation is one in which the Web hosting provider wants to provide service level agreements to particular clients. In this case the hosting provider requires proxy participation from those clients as part of the agreement.

For additional information and references please see the project web site at http://www.research.ibm.com/mplsws.

Panel 2 – Content Distribution Internetworking: Vital or Valueless?

Moderator: Mark Day, *Cisco Systems*

Panelists: Lisa Amini, *IBM*
Brad Cain, *Cereva*
Fred Douglis, *AT&T*
Dave Farber, *Digital Island*
Avi Freedman, *Akamai*
Phil Rzewski, *Inktomi*

Web Caching and Content Delivery
A. Bestavros and M. Rabinovich (Editors)

Provably Efficient Stream Merging

E.G. Coffman, Jr. [1], Predrag Jelenković [2], Petar Momčilović [3]

Department of Electrical Engineering, Columbia University, New York, NY 10027, USA

Abstract

We investigate the stream merging problem for media-on-demand servers. Clients requesting media from the server arrive by a Poisson process, and delivery to the clients starts immediately. Clients are prepared to receive up to two streams at any time, one or both being fed into a buffer cache. A multicast mechanism exists that allows multiple clients to receive the same stream. We present an on-line algorithm, the *dyadic stream merging* algorithm, whose recursive structure allows us to derive a tight asymptotic bound on stream merging performance. In particular, let λ be the request arrival rate, and let L be the fixed media length. Then the long-time ratio of the expected total stream length under the dyadic algorithm to that under an algorithm with no merging is asymptotically equal to $3\log\lambda L/2\lambda L$. Furthermore, we establish the near-optimality of the dyadic algorithm by comparisons with experimental results obtained for an optimal algorithm constructed as a dynamic program. The dyadic algorithm and the best on-line algorithm of those recently proposed differ by less than a percent in their comparison with an off-line optimal algorithm. Finally, the worst-case performance of our algorithm is shown to be no worse than that of earlier algorithms. Thus, the dyadic algorithm appears to be the first near optimal algorithm that admits a rigorous average-case analysis.

Keywords: Average-case analysis; Stream merging; Video-on-demand

1. Introduction

At a sequence of random times, clients request content streaming from a given media server, e.g., videos from a video-on-demand server, with delivery for each client to begin immediately. To reduce the potentially heavy traffic burden created by these media streams, it is clearly desirable to combine streams of the same content using multicast techniques. To see how this can be done and still preserve immediate-start delivery, we need the following assumptions: clients can receive two streams in parallel and each has a cache for buffering stream content. Although multimedia streaming embraces video, audio, and data streaming, we will keep with video terminology for simplicity.

[1] E-mail: egc@ee.columbia.edu
[2] E-mail: predrag@ee.columbia.edu
[3] E-mail: petar@ee.columbia.edu

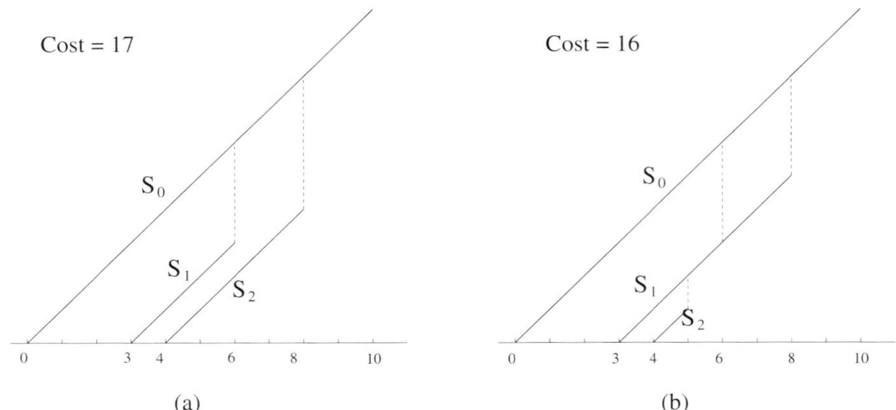

Fig. 1. Stream merging examples.

As an example, consider a situation in which (i) client C_1 arrives at t_1 and requests a video of duration L, and (ii) client C_0 is currently playing the same video from a stream S_0 that began at time $t_0 < t_1$. To minimize duplicate streaming, the video server initiates at time t_1 a stream S_1 to C_1 which it maintains for $\Delta := t_1 - t_0$ time units, and at the same time, it delivers S_0 to both C_0 and C_1, C_0 continues to play from S_0 whereas C_1 caches S_0 while playing the video from S_1. At time $t_1 + \Delta$, C_1 has played the first Δ time units of the video, and, if the video at C_0 was more than half over at time t_1, C_1 has the remainder of the video available in its buffer cache. From this point on, C_1 plays the video from its buffer. If the video playing at C_0 was less than half over at time t_1, then at time $t_1 + \Delta$, the second Δ time units of the video are in C_1's cache and S_0 begins to feed the last $L - 2\Delta$ time units of the video into C_1's buffer. The video segment in the buffer may be thought of as being played from one end and fed at the other. This process is called *stream merging*; in the present case, S_1 was discontinued after being 'merged' at time $t_1 + \Delta$ with the earlier starting S_0.

Note that the total streaming time has been reduced from $2L$, with no merging, to a minimum achievable value of $L + \Delta$. The total streaming time is a simple and effective measure of bandwidth consumption that we will retain throughout the paper.

Stream merging becomes much more involved as we increase the number of streams that are candidates for merging, because then the number of ways in which merging can be done also increases. For example, consider the case of three clients C_0, C_1, C_2 arriving at times $t_0 < t_1 < t_2$ and initiating streams S_0, S_1, S_2 for a video of duration L. Let $\Delta_i = t_i - t_{i-1}$ be the interarrival times. Fig. 1 illustrates an example in which the t_i's are given by 0, 3, and 4, and $L = 10$. Consider just those ways in which we can merge the streams for both C_1 and C_2. For the given parameters, the two possible merging patterns are shown in Fig. 1a and b. In Fig. 1a, S_1 and S_2 are merged independently with S_0 as described earlier: C_1 caches S_0 during $[t_1, t_1 + \Delta_1]$ and C_2 caches S_0 during $[t_2, t_2 + \Delta_2]$; at the end of the respective intervals S_1 and S_2 are merged with S_0.

The second possibility is first to merge S_2 with S_1 and then S_1 with S_0. In this scenario, which is illustrated in Fig. 1b, C_1 plays S_1 and caches S_0 during $[t_1, t_1 + \Delta_1]$. Thereafter, C_1 plays from its buffer which is only fed by S_0 during the last $L - 2\Delta_1$ time units of the video. Client C_2 caches S_1 and plays from S_2 during $[t_2, t_2 + \Delta_2]$, at which point S_2

is discontinued, and play proceeds from C_2's buffer. Client C_2 continues to cache S_1, but in addition, it caches the remainder of S_0 (in a suitably chosen region of the cache where the two buffering operations can not overlap). This continues until $t_2 + \Delta_1 + \Delta_2$ at which point S_1 is shut down and S_0 becomes the only active stream while it is supplying the last $L - 2(\Delta_1 + \Delta_2)$ time units of the video to the buffers of C_1 and C_2. In this process, C_2 has played the first Δ_2 time units of the video directly from S_2, the next Δ_1 time units from a cached segment of S_1 and the last $L - \Delta_1 - \Delta_2$ time units from a cached segment of S_0.

Note that, although the streaming at C_1 is the same as before, S_1 does not terminate at time $t_1 + \Delta_1$ when no longer needed by C_1; the media server must still send S_1 to C_2 until C_2 can switch to S_0, which occurs at $t_2 + \Delta_1 + \Delta_2$. Note also that the cost (sum of stream durations) of the second merging pattern is 16 as compared to the cost 17 of the first pattern. In general, however, the best merge pattern for an arrival at time t depends not only on arrival times before t, but also on the arrival times after t.

The technique of stream merging originated with Eager, Vernon, and Zahorjan [11,12] as a model of the *pyramid broadcasting* scheme introduced by Viswanathan and Imielinski [35,36]. This paradigm provides the multicast basis for sharing streams and is built upon the assumption that clients can receive more bandwidth than they need for play-out. The *skyscraper broadcasting* scheme [15,22,30] is another example of these new techniques. A number of related techniques go under the names of batching [1,9,10], patching [6,16,21], tapping [7,8], and piggy-backing [2,18,19,28] and the general problem has several parameters and useful performance metrics. Other parameters include delay guarantees, receiving bandwidth, server bandwidth, and buffer size [5,13–15,17,20,23–27,29–34]. The maximum number of streams is another metric that is of greater interest in certain circumstances. In this setting, the algorithm of this paper has the properties:

- It is on-line, i.e., the media server does not know arrival times in advance.
- It gives a zero-delay guarantee, i.e., all video requests are satisfied immediately.
- It restricts to at most two the number of streams being received by a client at any one time – the *receive-two* model.
- The buffer size can accommodate up to half of the video.

The last two assumptions are justified in the papers by Bar-Noy and Ladner [3,4], which supply the primary motivation for the work here. In particular, most of the improvement of merging streams is already present in the receive-two model. The $L/2$ buffer size limit comes about because our algorithm does not attempt merging with an existing stream that is already at least half over. As Bar-Noy and Ladner argue, this is not only a convenience, it rules out potential merges that, if implemented, would lead to increased average cost, even for only moderately large arrival rates. For further discussion of the literature on stream merging, we refer the reader to the mini-survey of [3].

Many excellent numerical/experimental studies have appeared in the stream-merging literature, but the absence of mathematical foundations has stood out, at least until the work in [3,4], which focuses on competitive, or worst-case, analysis. Here, we give what appears to be the first rigorous average-case analysis of a near-optimal algorithm.

The paper is organized as follows. In Section 2 we present the *Dyadic Tree* algorithm and state our main results. Section 3 contains numerical experiments that verify the algorithm's performance and conclusions. The proof of the main results can be found in Section 4.

2. Algorithm and results

The problem of stream merging can be posed as a problem on trees (see [3,4]). A *merge tree* is a representation of a stream merging diagram, such as those shown in Fig. 1. Each stream of the merging diagram corresponds to a node in the corresponding merge tree. Thus, the number of nodes in the merge tree is equal to the number of requests placed with the server, i.e., the number of clients. If stream S_j is merged directly to an earlier starting stream S_i, then the node associated with S_j is a child of the node associated with S_i. It is convenient to label the nodes with the arrival times of the corresponding streams.

A *root* stream is merged with no other stream, i.e., it becomes the root in a merge tree. The length of the root stream is always the full length of the video, L. The start rule below provides a simple way to determine which streams are roots. Let $t_0, t_1, \dots$ be the stream starting times.

Start rule: Node t_0 is a root. If t_i is a root, then $t_j = \inf\{t_k : t_k > t_i + L/2\}$ is a root.

In other words, the start rule says that a node will be in a given tree only if the root stream of that tree started less the $L/2$ time units ago. As noted earlier, this constraint simplifies the algorithmics; there is a sacrifice in efficiency, but only when traffic is low. For example, suppose we have a root stream starting at time t_0 and an arrival at time t_1 with $t_0 + L/2 < t_1 \leq t_0 + L$. If t_1 is made a descendant of t_0, then no other node can be merged with t_1 without extending its length to L. Hence, some gain is achieved only if there are no arrivals in the interval $(t_1, t_1 + L]$.

When the arrivals are Poisson, the sequence of merge trees becomes a renewal process. This fact allows us to focus our analysis on a single merge tree rooted at $t_0 = 0$. Let $\{t_n\}_{n=0}^{\infty}$ be a sample path of a Poisson process with rate λ on the non-negative reals, and assume for convenience that $t_0 = 0$. The total length of all streams in a merge tree is defined as

$$T \equiv T(L, \lambda) := \sum_{n=0}^{\infty} l_n \mathbf{1}\{t_n \leq L/2\}, \tag{1}$$

where l_n denotes the length of the stream initiated by the arrival at time t_n. By definition $l_0 = L$. The quantity T will measure the effectiveness of stream merging algorithms.

Our new stream merging algorithm is implicit in the following algorithm for constructing merge trees from a given root.

The Dyadic Tree Algorithm: The input is a sequence of $n > 0$ arrival times $t_0, \dots, t_n$ with $t_0 = 0$, and the output is a tree of n nodes. The arrival at time 0 determines the root. To find the children of the root, first divide the interval $[0, L/2]$ into dyadic subintervals I_i with lengths $2^{-i}L/2, i = 1, 2, \dots$, as shown in Fig. 2. If I_i contains at least one arrival time, then $t_{(i)}$ denotes the earliest such time; otherwise, $t_{(i)} = 0$. Each

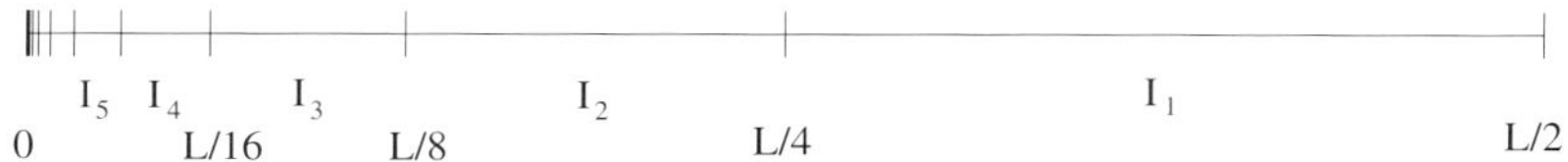

Fig. 2. Dyadic partition of the interval.

$t_{(i)} > 0$ is made a child of the root. Then for each $t_{(i)} > 0$, the algorithm is applied recursively to the interval $[t_{(i)}, 2^{-i}L]$ to determine the subtree rooted at $t_{(i)}$.

It is not difficult to verify that this can be formulated as an on-line algorithm, as we show at the end of this section. In particular, the decision as to whether or not a node t_i should be attached to an existing tree is unaffected by arrivals after time t_i. The following theorem gives our first result, a uniform bound on total stream length. We postpone the proof until Section 4. Throughout, the paper we use log to denote $\log_2$.

Theorem 1. *The total cost of the dyadic tree algorithm satisfies*

$$\frac{1}{4}L\log\lambda L - \frac{1}{4}L \leq \mathbb{E}T(L,\lambda) \leq \frac{3}{4}L|\log\lambda L| + \frac{23}{8}L.$$

The main contribution of the preceding theorem is the upper bound that will be proved to be asymptotically tight in the following theorem. The proof of the lower bound is supplied in order to help the reader in understanding the technique that we use. However, in [11] a slightly better lower bound was obtained

$$\mathbb{E}T(L,\lambda) \geq \frac{1}{2\log e}L\log(\lambda L + 1),$$

there the authors do not assume any restrictions on the clients' buffer space and receiving bandwidth.

For large values of λL Theorem 1 can be strengthened by the following result, which is proved in Section 4.

Theorem 2. *The total cost of the dyadic tree algorithm satisfies*

$$\lim_{\lambda L\to\infty} \frac{\mathbb{E}T(L,\lambda)}{L\log\lambda L} = \frac{3}{4}.$$

In order to consider the worst-case performance we examine a slightly different model. Let time be slotted and let the video have a length of $2n$ time slots, i.e., a merge tree is being built on n slots. In each of the slots at most one stream can be initiated. In [4] it is proved that the worst-case performance of the optimal algorithm is $\Theta(n\log n)$. On the other hand, the total cost for the Dyadic Tree algorithm satisfies $2T(n/2) + n/2 \leq T(n) \leq 2T(n/2) + 3n/2$, with the solution $T(n) = \Theta(n\log n)$. Thus, the Dyadic algorithm is within a constant factor of optimal in worst-case. A more detailed numeric comparison of the Dyadic algorithm and the optimal algorithm is made in the next section.

We conclude this section with a straightforward on-line implementation of the algorithm.

On-line Dyadic Stream Merging: Let S be a stack with `push` and `pop` operations defined for pairs of numbers (t_a, t_r). Each pair corresponds to a stream: t_a is the time at which the stream was initiated and t_r is the time after which newly arrived streams will not be allowed to merge with it.

At time $t = 0$ `push` $(0, L/2)$ onto S. At the time t of a new request, `pop` the pairs (t_a, t_r) from the stack until $t_r > t$. Add the new stream to the stack by performing push (t, t'), where $t' = t_a + (t_r - t_a)\max\{2^{-k+1} : 2^{-k}(t_r - t_a) < t - t_a\}$. The stream started at t is the child of the stream started at t_a.

3. Numerics and conclusions

This section provides a numerical validation of the asymptotic approximation

$$T' \equiv T'(L, \lambda) := L \log \lambda L.$$

The first example investigates the dependency of the total cost on the length of the stream for fixed values of the arrival rate λ. The parameter values are set within the regions that are plausible for real-life systems. In particular, we set $L = 20i$ minutes, $i = 1, \ldots, 9$ and plot the ratio $\mathbb{E}T/T'$ in Fig. 3, where $\mathbb{E}T$ is obtained by simulating 10,000 trees for each set of values. Points marked with '$\circ$', '$+$' and '$\times$' correspond to λ^{-1} equal to 5, 20 and 60 seconds, respectively. Note that for $(\lambda^{-1}, L) = (60\text{ s}, 20\text{ min})$ the merge tree consists of only 11 nodes on average.

In the second example we fix L and look at $\mathbb{E}T(\lambda, L)$ as a function of the first argument. The simulation results of $\mathbb{E}T/T'$ are plotted in Fig. 4. As in the previous case we simulated 10,000 trees for each point. Values of L are set to 120, 60 and 30 minutes and denoted respectively by the symbols '$\circ$', '$+$' and '$\times$'. Using approximation T' with the appropriate multiplicative factor yields excellent engineering estimates for all reasonable values of L and λ.

Finally, we compare the performance of the Dyadic Tree algorithm to the performance of the optimal off-line algorithm. The cost of the latter can be determined by a dynamic program (see [2]). Let $T_{opt}(i, j)$ be the optimal cost of the merge tree for streams initiated

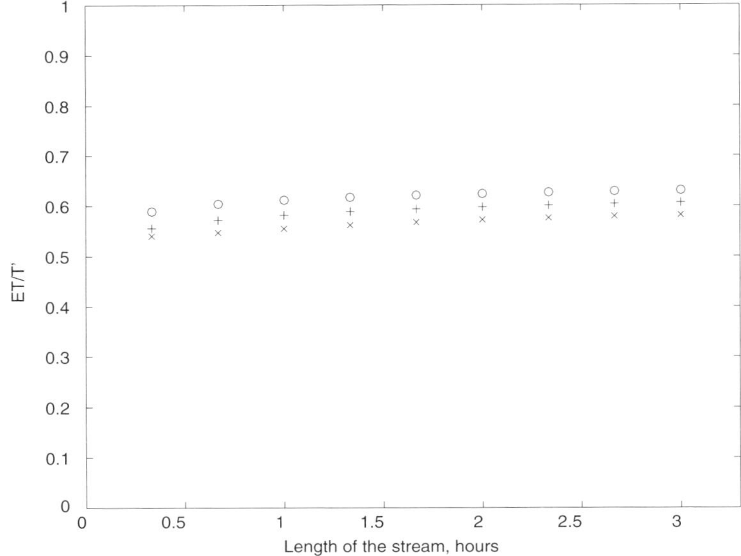

Fig. 3. $\mathbb{E}T/T'$ as a function of the stream length for three values of the arrival rate. Expected interarrival times are 5 s ('$\circ$'), 20s ('$+$') and 60s ('$\times$').

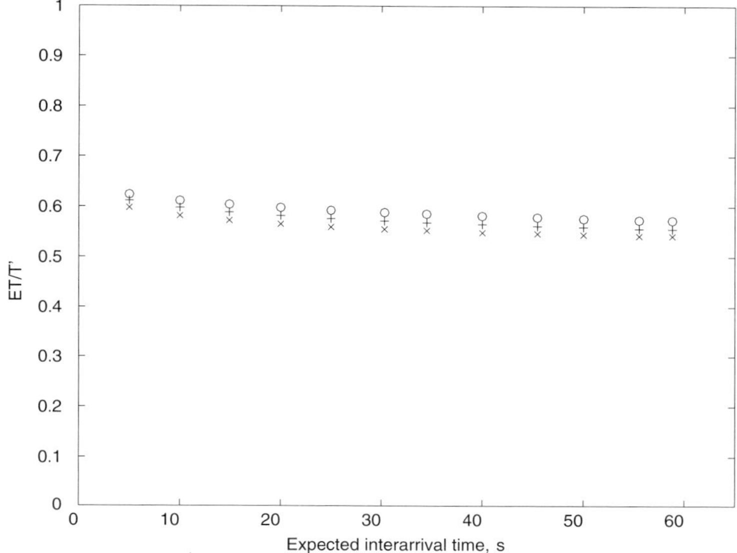

Fig. 4. $\mathbb{E}T/T'$ as a function of the arrival rate for three values of the stream length. The stream length is set to 120 ('$\circ$'), 60 ('+') and 30 ('$\times$') minutes.

at $0 \leq t_i < \cdots < t_j < L/2$. The optimal merge tree satisfies the preorder traversal property [4] and, hence,

$$T_{opt}(0, n) = \min_{1 \leq k \leq n} \left\{ T_{opt}(0, k-1) + T_{opt}(k, n) - (L - 2t_n + t_k + t_0) \right\}$$

with $T_{opt}(i, i) = L$. The last term represents the gain from a merge of optimal trees rooted at t_0 and t_k. We used the fact that the length of the stream t is equal to $2t_l - t - t_p$, where t_p is its parent and t_l is the last stream that merges to it (see [3]).

For numerical comparison, let the length of the video be 2 hours and let the value of the expected interarrival time vary from 5s to 60s in steps of 5s. For every pair (λ, L) we simulated 1000 trees and based on that computed the average cost for two algorithms. The increase in expected cost when using the Dyadic Tree algorithm instead of the optimal off-line algorithm is remarkably small as shown in Fig. 5. For all parameter values the increase did not exceed 8%.

In summary, we have been able to prove the tight average-case asymptotic behavior $\frac{3}{4}L \log \lambda L$ for the dyadic stream merging algorithm, and to show in addition that its average-case and worst-case performance are comparable to those of the best on-line algorithms known to date. Average-case analysis of the stream merging algorithms that arise in other settings is an obvious avenue of further research.

4. Proofs

We start by introducing a recursive procedure for labeling the arrival times in $(0, L/2)$. For the purposes of the proof these labels replace the t_i labels. The procedure can be

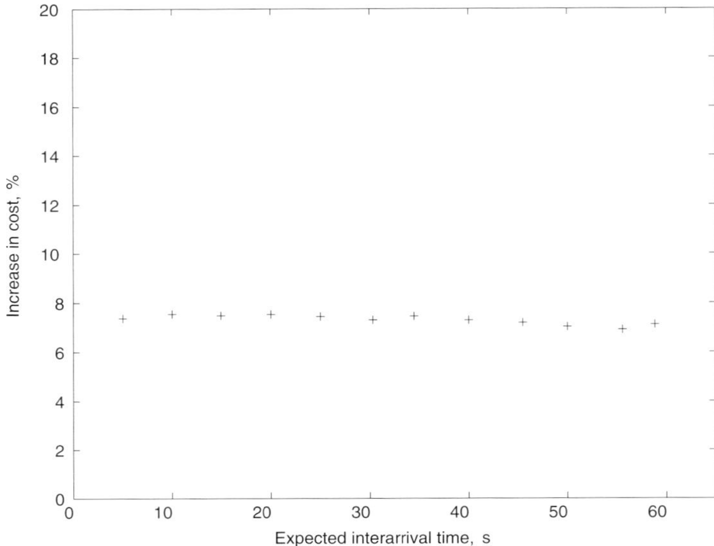

Fig. 5. Performance of the algorithm in comparison with the optimal off-line algorithm. The length of the stream is equal to 2 hours.

thought of as a function $\mathcal{E}_L : \boldsymbol{T} \mapsto \boldsymbol{\omega}$ that maps a set $\boldsymbol{T}$ of arrival times to the space of indices $\boldsymbol{\omega}$. Each index ω consists of a number of digits equal to the depth of the node in the merge tree that corresponds to the given arrival. In general, $\omega = \omega_1\omega_2 \dots \omega_n$, where $\omega_i \in \mathbb{N}$ for $i = 1, 2 \dots$, and the parent of the node labeled ω is a node labeled with the prefix $\omega' = \omega_1 \dots \omega_{n-1}$. The algorithm labels the arrivals as follows. The interval $(0, L/2)$ is divided into dyadic intervals in increasing order from the root as shown in Fig. 2. If a point t is the first point in the subinterval I_i then its label is i. Label the rest of the points in $(t, 2^{-i}L)$ recursively by using the parent's label as a prefix for childrens' labels. An example of how the points are labeled is shown in Fig. 6.

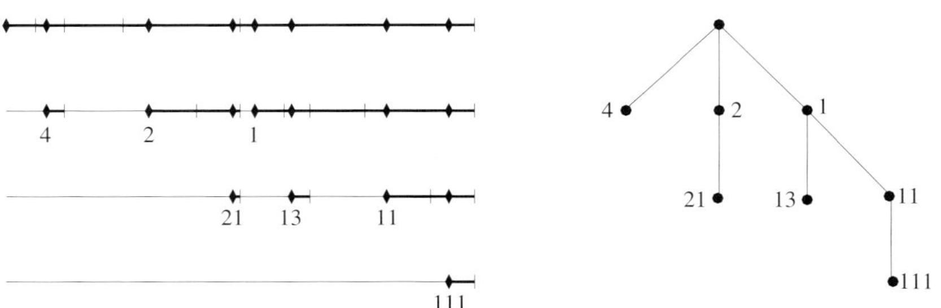

Fig. 6. An illustration of the labeling algorithm. In this example there are seven points that need to be labeled. On the first call of the procedure three points are assigned labels (1, 2 and 4). The recursive algorithm is applied until all points are labeled.

4.1. Proof of Theorem 1

4.1.1. Lower bound:

By applying the above labeling procedure, it is not hard to verify that (1) becomes

$$
\begin{aligned}
T(L,\lambda) &= L + \sum_{n=1}^{\infty} l_n \mathbf{1}\{t_n \le L/2\} \\
&= L + \sum_{n=1}^{\infty} \sum_{\omega=\omega_1\ldots\omega_n} l_{\omega_1\ldots\omega_n}, \qquad (2)
\end{aligned}
$$

where $l_{\omega_1\ldots\omega_n}$ is the length of the stream starting at the point labeled $\omega_1\ldots\omega_n$. If for a particular realization of the Poisson process there is no point with label $\omega_1\ldots\omega_n$, then $l_{\omega_1\ldots\omega_n} = 0$.

Next, we estimate the expected values of $l_{\omega_1\ldots\omega_n}$. Let η, $\{\eta_n\}_{n=1}^{\infty}$ be a set of i.i.d. exponential random variables with mean λ^{-1}, and consider first the streams that are children of the root, i.e., the streams whose indices consist of a single digit. Given that, for a particular realization of the Poisson process, there exists a stream with label ω_1, its length must be at least $2^{-\omega_1}L/2$, since it is at least that much later than the root. Therefore,

$$
\begin{aligned}
l_{\omega_1} &\ge \frac{L/2}{2^{\omega_1}} \mathbf{1}\left\{\exists n : \frac{L/2}{2^{\omega_1}} \le t_n < \frac{L/2}{2^{\omega_1+1}}\right\} \\
&\ge \left(\frac{L/2}{2^{\omega_1}} - \inf\left\{t_n - \frac{L/2}{2^{\omega_1}} : t_n > \frac{L/2}{2^{\omega_1}}\right\}\right)^+
\end{aligned}
$$

so after taking into account the memoryless property of the Poisson process, we conclude that

$$
\mathbb{E} l_{\omega_1} \ge \mathbb{E}\left(\frac{L/2}{2^{\omega_1}} - \eta_1\right)^+.
$$

A node with label of form $\omega_1\omega_2$ is a child of the node with label ω_1. Considering the preceding inequality, the recursive nature of the merging algorithm and the size of the problem in which node ω_1 is the root one obtains

$$
\begin{aligned}
\mathbb{E} l_{\omega_1\omega_2} &\ge \mathbb{E}\left(\frac{\left(\frac{L/2}{2^{\omega_1}} - \eta_1\right)^+}{2^{\omega_2}} - \eta_2\right)^+ \\
&= \mathbb{E}\left(\frac{L/2}{2^{\omega_1+\omega_2}} - \eta_2 - \frac{\eta_1}{2^{\omega_2}}\right)^+.
\end{aligned}
$$

The recursive structure of the merging algorithm shows that for a stream with an arbitrary index $\omega_1\omega_2\ldots\omega_n$,

$$
\mathbb{E} l_{\omega_1\ldots\omega_n} \ge \mathbb{E}\left(\frac{L/2}{2^{\omega_1+\cdots+\omega_n}} - \eta_n - \sum_{i=1}^{n-1} \frac{\eta_i}{2^{\omega_{i+1}+\cdots+\omega_n}}\right)^+
$$

with the understanding that the sum in the above expression is equal to zero if $n = 1$. If $W := \sum_{i=0}^{\infty} \eta_i 2^{-i}$ then the expected value of an individual stream length is further lower bounded by

$$\mathbb{E}l_{\omega_1\ldots\omega_n} \geq \mathbb{E}\left(\frac{L/2}{2^{\omega_1+\cdots+\omega_n}} - W\right)^+. \tag{3}$$

Now observe that the number of indices with a digit sum equal to k is 2^{k-1}, i.e.,

$$\sum_{n=1}^{\infty} \sum_{\omega=\omega_1\ldots\omega_n} \mathbf{1}\left\{\sum_{i=1}^{n} \omega_i = k\right\} = 2^{k-1}, \tag{4}$$

since the above sum is equal to the number of ways one can partition a set of cardinality k. Rearrange the sum in (2), use the bound (3) and apply (4) to find

$$\begin{aligned}\mathbb{E}T(L,\lambda) &= L + \sum_{k=1}^{\infty} \sum_{\sum \omega_i = k} \mathbb{E}l_{\omega_1\ldots\omega_n} \\ &\geq L + \sum_{k=1}^{\infty} 2^{k-1}\mathbb{E}\left(\frac{L/2}{2^k} - W\right)^+ \\ &\geq L + \sum_{k=1}^{\infty} 2^{k-1}\left(\frac{L/2}{2^k} - \frac{2}{\lambda}\right)^+,\end{aligned}$$

where the last step follows from Jensen's inequality. Finally, simple manipulations yield

$$\begin{aligned}\mathbb{E}T(L,\lambda) &\geq L + \frac{L}{4}\sum_{k=1}^{\infty}\left(1 - \frac{2^{k+2}}{\lambda L}\right)^+ \\ &= L + \frac{L}{4}\sum_{k=1}^{\lfloor \log \frac{\lambda L}{4} \rfloor}\left(1 - \frac{2^{k+2}}{\lambda L}\right) \\ &\geq \frac{L}{4}\log \lambda L - \frac{L}{4},\end{aligned}$$

from which we conclude that the lower bound holds.

4.1.2. Upper bound:

Consider the streams that are children of the root. For such streams we have

$$l_{\omega_1} \leq 3\frac{L/2}{2^{\omega_1}}, \tag{5}$$

since stream ω_1 has to be extended to accommodate the requirements of the streams in its subtree. The inequality is tight when there is an arrival right after time $2^{-\omega_1}L/2$ and an arrival just before time $2^{-\omega_1}L$. Next we examine the streams that can be reached from the root in exactly two steps. An upper bound on their length is

$$l_{\omega_1\omega_2} \leq 3\left(\frac{\frac{L/2}{2^{\omega_1}} - \inf\{t_n - \frac{L/2}{2^{\omega_1}} : t_n > \frac{L/2}{2^{\omega_1}}\}}{2^{\omega_2}}\right)^+, \tag{6}$$

whereupon the memoryless property of the Poisson process gives

$$\mathbb{E}l_{\omega_1\omega_2} \leq 3\mathbb{E}\left(\frac{L/2}{2^{\omega_1+\omega_2}} - \frac{\eta_2}{2^{\omega_2}}\right)^+.$$

Note that (5) and (6) are of the same form. In the first inequality the size of the problem is $L/2$ while in the second the size is $2^{-\omega_1}L/2 - \inf\{t_n - 2^{-\omega_1}L/2 : t_n > 2^{-\omega_1}L/2\}$. Since the merging algorithm is recursive, for streams that have depth $n \geq 2$ in the merge tree one can conclude that

$$\mathbb{E}l_{\omega_1\ldots\omega_n} \leq 3\mathbb{E}\left(\frac{L/2}{2^{\omega_1+\cdots+\omega_n}} - \sum_{i=2}^{n}\frac{\eta_i}{2^{\omega_i+\cdots+\omega_n}}\right)^+$$

$$\leq 3\mathbb{E}\left(\frac{L/2}{2^{\omega_1+\cdots+\omega_n}} - \frac{\eta}{2^{\omega_n}}\right)^+. \qquad (7)$$

It is easy to verify that the number of indices with the digit sum k and last digit i is equal to 2^{k-i-1}, i.e., for $1 \leq i \leq k-1$

$$\sum_{n=2}^{\infty}\sum_{\omega=\omega_1\ldots\omega_n}\mathbf{1}\left\{\sum_{j=1}^{n}\omega_j = k,\, \omega_n = i\right\} = 2^{k-i-1}. \qquad (8)$$

The length of the root stream is always L so (5), (7) and (8) yield

$$\mathbb{E}T(L,\lambda) = L + \sum_{\omega_1=1}^{\infty}\mathbb{E}l_{\omega_1} + \sum_{k=2}^{\infty}\sum_{\omega_n=1}^{k-1}\mathbb{E}l_{\omega_1\ldots\omega_n}\mathbf{1}\left\{\sum_{j=1}^{n}\omega_j = k\right\}$$

$$\leq L + 3\sum_{k=1}^{\infty}\frac{L/2}{2^k} + 3\sum_{k=2}^{\infty}\sum_{i=1}^{k-1}2^{k-i-1}\mathbb{E}\left(\frac{L/2}{2^k} - \frac{\eta}{2^i}\right)^+$$

$$\leq \frac{5}{2}L + \frac{3}{4}L\sum_{k=2}^{\infty}\sum_{i=1}^{k-1}2^{-i}\mathbb{E}\left(1 - \eta\frac{2^{k+1-i}}{L}\right)^+.$$

A simple computation shows that

$$\mathbb{E}(1-\eta)^+ = 1 - \lambda^{-1}(1 - \exp(-\lambda))$$

and, therefore, by changing the order of summation one obtains

$$\mathbb{E}T(L,\lambda) \leq \frac{5}{2}L + \frac{3}{4}L\sum_{k=2}^{\infty}\sum_{i=1}^{k-1}2^{-i}\left(1 - \frac{2^{k+1-i}}{\lambda L}\left[1 - e^{-\lambda L 2^{-k-1+i}}\right]\right)$$

$$= \frac{5}{2}L + \frac{3}{4}L\sum_{i=1}^{\infty}\sum_{m=2}^{\infty}2^{-i}\left(1 - \frac{2^m}{\lambda L}\left[1 - e^{-\lambda L 2^{-m}}\right]\right)$$

$$= \frac{5}{2}L + \frac{3}{4}L\sum_{m=2}^{\infty}\left(1 - 2^{m-\log\lambda L}\left[1 - e^{-2^{-m+\log\lambda L}}\right]\right).$$

Finally, straightforward but tedious calculations show that $\sum_{j=1}^{\infty}\left(1 - 2^j\left[1 - e^{-2^{-j}}\right]\right) \leq 1/2$ which in conjunction with the preceding inequality and the monotonicity of the function $1 - 2^x(1 - e^{-2^{-x}})$ yields

$$\mathbb{E}T(L,\lambda) \leq \frac{5}{2}L + \frac{3}{4}L\sum_{j=2-\lceil|\log\lambda L|\rceil}^{\infty}\left(1 - 2^j\left[1 - e^{-2^{-j}}\right]\right)$$

$$\leq \frac{3}{4}L|\log\lambda L| + \frac{23}{8}L.$$

This concludes the proof. □

4.2. Proof of Theorem 2

The upper bound is a direct consequence of Theorem 1. Below we provide the proof of the lower bound. Let $P_\epsilon \equiv P(\lambda, \epsilon) := 1 - e^{-\lambda\epsilon}$ denote the probability of having at least one Poisson arrival in an interval of length ϵ. By conditioning on an arrival in both $(2^{-\omega_1-1}L, 2^{-\omega_1-1}L + \epsilon)$ and $(2^{-\omega_1}L - \epsilon, 2^{-\omega_1}L)$ one obtains

$$\mathbb{E}l_{\omega_1} \geq P_\epsilon^2 \left(\frac{3L/2}{2^{\omega_1}} - 3\epsilon\right)^+ .$$

Extending the above reasoning to the streams with two-digit labels yields a lower bound on their expected lengths

$$\mathbb{E}l_{\omega_1\omega_2} \geq P_\epsilon^3 \left(\frac{3L/2}{2^{\omega_1+\omega_2}} - \frac{3\epsilon}{2^{\omega_2}} - 3\epsilon\right)^+ .$$

In the above inequality we conditioned on the position of the stream $\omega_1\omega_2$, its parent and the last stream that will merge to it. Due to the recursive structure of the algorithm, for a stream with an arbitrary label $\omega_1 \ldots \omega_n$ the lower bound has the following form

$$\begin{aligned}\mathbb{E}l_{\omega_1\ldots\omega_n} &\geq P_\epsilon^{n+1} \left(\frac{3L/2}{2^{\omega_1+\cdots+\omega_n}} - \sum_{i=2}^{n} \frac{3\epsilon}{2^{\omega_2+\cdots+\omega_n}} - 3\epsilon\right)^+ \\ &\geq P_\epsilon^{n+1} \left(\frac{3L/2}{2^{\omega_1+\cdots+\omega_n}} - 6\epsilon\right)^+\end{aligned}$$

Next, the preceding inequality, (1) and (4) result in

$$\begin{aligned}\mathbb{E}T &\geq \sum_{k=1}^{\infty} 2^{k-1} P_\epsilon^{k+1} \left(\frac{3L/2}{2^k} - 6\epsilon\right)^+ \\ &\geq \sum_{k=1}^{\lfloor \log \lambda L \rfloor} P_\epsilon^{k+1} \left(\frac{3L}{4} - 3\epsilon 2^k\right) \\ &\geq \frac{3}{4} P_\epsilon^{\log \lambda L + 1} L \lfloor \log \lambda L \rfloor - 6\epsilon\lambda L\end{aligned}$$

Finally, setting $\epsilon = \lambda^{-1} \log\log \lambda L$ and using $\log e > 1$ yield

$$\lim_{\lambda L \to \infty} P_\epsilon^{\log \lambda L} = \lim_{\lambda L \to \infty} \left(1 - e^{-\log\log \lambda L}\right)^{\log \lambda L} = 1$$

and, therefore,

$$\frac{T}{L \log \lambda L} \geq \frac{3}{4} P_\epsilon^{\log \lambda L + 1} \frac{\lfloor \log \lambda L \rfloor}{\log \lambda L} - 6 \frac{\log\log \lambda L}{\log \lambda L} \longrightarrow \frac{3}{4}$$

as $\lambda L \to \infty$. This concludes our proof. □

Acknowledgments

This work is supported by the NSF Grant No. 0092113.

References

[1] C.C. Aggarwal, J.L. Wolf, and P.S. Yu. On optimal batching policies for video-on-demand storage servers. In *Proceedings of the IEEE International Conference on Multimedia Computing and Systems (ICMCS '96)*, 1996.

[2] C.C. Aggarwal, J.L. Wolf, and P.S. Yu. On optimal piggyback merging policies for video-on-demand systems. In *Proceedings of the ACM SIGMETRICS Conference on Measurement and Modeling of Computer Systems (SIGMETRICS '96)*, pages 200–209, 1996.

[3] A. Bar-Noy and R. Ladner. Competitive on-line stream merging algorithms for media-on-demand. Available at www.cs.washington.edu/homes/ladner/papers.html. A conference version appeared in Proceedings of SODA'01, 2000.

[4] A. Bar-Noy and R. Ladner. Efficient algorithms for optimal stream merging for media-on-demand. Available at www.cs.washington.edu/homes/ladner/papers.html, 2000.

[5] Y. Cai and K.A. Hua. An efficient bandwidth-sharing technique for true video on demand systems. In *Proceedings of the 7th ACM International Multimedia Conference, (MULTIMEDIA '99)*, pages 211–214, 1999.

[6] Y. Cai, K.A. Hua, and K. Vu. Optimizing patching performance. In *Proceedings of the IS&T/SPIE Conference on Multimedia Computing and Networking (MMCN '99)*, pages 204–215, 1999.

[7] S.W. Carter and D.D.E. Long. Improving video-on-demand server efficiency through stream tapping. In *Proceedings of the 6th International Conference on Computer Communication and Networks (ICCCN '97)*, pages 200–207, 1997.

[8] S.W. Carter and D.D.E. Long. Improving bandwidth efficiency of video-on-demand servers. *Computer Networks*, 31(1-2): 99–111, 1999.

[9] T. Chiueh and C. Lu. A periodic broadcasting approach to video-on-demand service. In *Proceedings of the SPIE Conference on Multimedia Computing and Networking (MMCN '95)*, pages 162–169, 1995.

[10] A. Dan, D. Sitaram, and P. Shahabuddin. Dynamic batching policies for an on-demand video server. *ACM Multimedia Systems Journal*, 4(3): 112–121, 1996.

[11] D. Eager, M. Vernon, and J. Zahorjan. Minimizing bandwidth requirements for on-demand data delivery. In *Proceedings of the 5th International Workshop on Advances in Multimedia Information Systems (MIS '99)*, Indian Wells, CA, October 1999.

[12] D. Eager, M. Vernon, and J. Zahorjan. Optimal and efficient mergind schedules for video-on-demand servers. In *Proceedings of the 7th ACM International Multimedia Conference, (MULTIMEDIA '99)*, pages 199–203, Orlando, FL, November 1999.

[13] D.L. Eager, M. Ferris, and M.K. Vernon. Optimized regional caching for on-demand data delivery. In *Proceedings of the Conference on Multimedia Computing and Networking (MMCN '99)*, pages 301–316, 1999.

[14] D.L. Eager and M.K. Vernon. Dynamic skyscraper broadcasts for video-on-demand. In *Proceedings of the 4th International Workshop on Advances in Multimedia Information Systems (MIS '98)*, pages 18–32, 1998.

[15] L. Gao, J. Kurose, and D. Towsley. Efficient schemes for broadcasting popular videos. In *Proceedings of the 8th IEEE International Workshop on Network and Operating System Support for Digital Audio and Video (NOSSDAV '98)*, 1998.

[16] L. Gao and D. Towsley. Supplying instantaneous video-on-demand services using controlled multicast. In *Proceedings of the IEEE International Conference on Multimedia Computing and Systems (ICMCS '99)*, 1999.

[17] L. Gao, Z. Zhang, and D. Towsley. Catching and selective catching: efficient latency reduction techniques for delivering continuous multimedia streams. In *Proceedings of the 7th ACM International Multimedia Conference, (MULTIMEDIA '99)*, pages 203–206, 1999.

[18] L. Golubchic, J.C.S. Liu, and R.R. Muntz. Reducing I/O demand in video-on-demand storage servers. In *Proceedings of the ACM SIGMETRICS Conference on Measurement and Modeling of Computer Systems (SIGMETRICS '95)*, pages 25–36, 1995.

[19] L. Golubchic, J.C.S. Liu, and R.R. Muntz. Adaptive piggybacking: A novel technique for data sharing in video-on-demand storage servers. *ACM Multimedia Systems Journal*, 4(3): 140–155, 1996.

[20] K.A. Hua, Y. Cai, and S. Sheu. Exploiting client bandwidth for more efficient video broadcast. In *Proceedings of the 7th International Conference on Computer Communication and Networks (ICCCN '98)*, pages 848–856, 1998.

[21] K.A. Hua, Y. Cai, and S. Sheu. Patching: a multicast technique for true video-on-demand services. In *Proceedings of the 6th ACM International Conference on Multimedia (MULTIMEDIA '98)*, pages 191–200, 1998.

[22] K.A. Hua and S. Sheu. Skyscraper broadcasting: A new broadcasting scheme for metropolitan video-on-demand systems. In *Proceedings of the ACM SIGCOMM '97 Conference on Applications, Technologies, Architectures, and Protocols for Computer Communication*, pages 89–100, 1997.

[23] L. Juhn and L. Tseng. Fast broadcasting for hot video access. In *Proceedings of the 4th International Workshop on Real-Time Computing Systems and Applications (RTCSA '97)*, pages 237–243, 1997.

[24] L. Juhn and L. Tseng. Harmonic broadcasting for video-on-demand service. *IEEE Transactions on Broadcasting*, 43(3): 268–271, 1997.

[25] L. Juhn and L. Tseng. Staircase data broadcasting and receiving scheme for hot video service. *IEEE Transactions on Consumer Electronics*, 43(4): 1110–1117, 1997.

[26] L. Juhn and L. Tseng. Enhancing harmonic data broadcasting and receiving scheme fo popular video service. *IEEE Transactions on Consumer Electronics*, 44(2): 343–346, 1998.

[27] L. Juhn and L. Tseng. Fast data broadcasting and receiving scheme for popular video service. *IEEE Transactions on Broadcasting*, 44(1): 100–105, 1998.

[28] S.W. Lau, J.C.S. Liu, and L. Golubchic. Merging video streams in a multimedia storage server: complexity and heuristics. *ACM Multimedia Systems Journal*, 6(1): 29–42, 1998.

[29] J. Pâris, S.W. Carter, and D.D.E. Long. A low bandwidth broadcasting protocol for video on demand. In *Proceedings of the 7th International Conference on Computer Communication and Networks (ICCCN '98)*, pages 690–697, 1998.

[30] J. Pâris, S.W. Carter, and D.D.E. Long. A hybrid broadcasting protocol for video on demand. In *Proceedings of the IS&T/SPIE Conference on Multimedia Computing and Networking (MMCN '99)*, pages 317–326, 1999.

[31] J. Pâris and D.D.E. Long. Limiting the receiving bandwidth of broadcasting protocols for video-on-demand. In *Proceedings of the Euromedia Conference*, pages 107–111, 2000.

[32] J. Pâris, D.D.E. Long, and P.E. Mantey. Zero-delay broadcasting protocols for video on demand. In *Proceedings of the 7th ACM International Multimedia Conference, (MULTIMEDIA '99)*, pages 189–197, 1999.

[33] S. Sen, L. Gao, and D. Towsley. Frame-based periodic broadcast and fundamental resource tradeoffs. Technical Report 99-78, University of Massachusetts Amherst.

[34] Y. Tseng, C. Hsieh, M. Yang, W. Liao, and J. Sheu. Data broadcasting and seamless channel transition for highly-demanded videos. In *Proceedings of the 19th Annual Joint Conference of the IEEE Computer and Communications Societies (INFOCOM '00)*, 2000.

[35] S. Viswanathan and T. Imielinski. Pyramid broadcasting for video-on-demand service. In *Proceedings of the SPIE Conference on Multimedia Computing and Networking (MMCN '95)*, pages 66–77, 1995.

[36] S. Viswanathan and T. Imielinski. Metropolitan area for video-on-demand service using pyramid broadcasting. *ACM Multimedia Systems Journal*, 4(3): 197–208, 1996.

Web Caching and Content Delivery
A. Bestavros and M. Rabinovich (Editors)

The Potential Costs and Benefits of Long-Term Prefetching for Content Distribution

Arun Venkataramani, Praveen Yalagandula, Ravindranath Kokku,
Sadia Sharif, Mike Dahlin [1]

Department of Computer Sciences, University of Texas at Austin, Austin, TX, USA

Abstract

This paper examines the costs and potential benefits of long-term prefetching for content distribution. In traditional short-term prefetching, caches use recent access history to predict and prefetch objects likely to be referenced in the near future. In contrast, long-term prefetching uses long-term steady-state object access rates and update frequencies to identify objects to replicate to content distribution locations. Compared to demand caching, long-term prefetching increases network bandwidth and disk space costs but may benefit a system by improving hit rates. Using analytic models and trace-based simulations, we examine algorithms for selecting objects for long-term prefetching. We find that although the Zipf-like popularity distribution of Web objects makes it challenging to prefetch enough objects to significantly improve hit rates, systems can achieve significant benefits at modest costs by focusing on long-lived objects.

Keywords: Web caching; Prefetching; Content distribution

1. Introduction

In spite of advances in Web proxy caching techniques in the past few years, proxy cache hit rates have not improved much. Even with unlimited cache space, passive caching suffers from uncacheable data, consistency misses for cached data and compulsory misses for new data. Prefetching attempts to overcome these limitations of passive caching by proactively fetching content without waiting for client requests. Traditional short-term prefetching at clients uses recent access history to predict and prefetch objects likely to be referenced in the near future and can considerably improve hit rates [7,8,15,16,25].

In this paper we examine a technique more appropriate for large proxies and content distribution networks (CDNs), namely long-term prefetching. Rather than basing prefetching decisions on the recent history of individual clients, long-term prefetching seeks to increase hit rates by using global object access patterns to identify a collection of valuable objects to replicate to caches and content distribution servers.

[1] E-mail: dahlin@cs.utexas.edu

As hardware costs fall, more aggressive prefetching becomes attractive making it possible to store an enormous collection of data at a large content distribution site. For example, in March 2001 an 80 GB disk drive cost about \$ 250 [1]. However, maintaining a collection of hundreds of gigabytes or several terabytes of useful Web data incurs not just a space cost but also a bandwidth cost: as objects in the collection change, the system must fetch their new versions. It must also fetch newly created objects that meet its selection criteria. Due to the Web's Zipf-like access patterns, a large number of objects must be actively prefetched to improve hit rates significantly [7]. Maintaining such a collection appears to be challenging. In particular, bandwidth expenditure will be the primary constraint in a long-term prefetching strategy. For example, in May 2001 a 1.5 Mbps T1 connection cost about \$ 1000 per month [3].

In this paper, we present a model for understanding steady-state cache behavior in a bandwidth-constrained prefetching environment. Our hypothesis is that by prefetching objects that are both long-lived and popular, we can significantly improve hit rates for moderate bandwidth costs. The key contribution of our work is a threshold algorithm for long-term prefetching that balances object access frequency and object update frequency and that only fetches objects whose probability of being accessed before being updated exceeds a specified threshold.

Using synthetic and real proxy trace based simulations we establish that our algorithm provides significant hit rate improvements at moderate storage and bandwidth costs. For example for a modest-size cache that receives 10 demand requests per second, long-term prefetching can improve steady state hit rates for cacheable data from about 62% (for an infinite demand-only cache) to above 75% while increasing the bandwidth demands of the system by less than a factor of 2. More generally, we quantify the trade-offs involved in choosing a reasonable prefetch threshold for a given object access rate. Based on our trace based simulation, we conclude that the key challenge to deploying such algorithms is developing good predictors of global access patterns. Although we leave development of such predictors as future work, we provide initial evidence that even simple predictors may work well.

The rest of the paper is organized as follows. Section 2 provides some background information about prefetching and our prefetching model. Section 3 presents the algorithms that we consider for long-term prefetching. Section 4 discusses the methodology we use to evaluate long-term prefetching. Section 5 discusses the results of our simulations and provides insights about how long-term prefetching works. Section 6 discusses related work. Section 7 summarizes our conclusions.

2. Prefetching model

Prefetching schemes can be categorized as short-term and long-term. In the short-term model, objects that are likely to be referenced in the near future are prefetched based on the client's recent access history. In the long-term model, objects are prefetched and updated based on long-term global access and update patterns.

We envision a hierarchical structure for a CDN, with caches at higher levels in the hierarchy using long-term prefetching to maintain a collection of objects, to maximize the global hit rates of the CDN for a given bandwidth cost. The caches at the lower levels in the hierarchy can further use short-term prefetching to efficiently service client requests, but we do not consider this optimization here. In the rest of the paper, we focus on the long-term prefetching model.

A content distribution system using long-term prefetching, should address the following challenges:

Statistics tracking. It should keep track of various statistics such as access patterns and object lifetimes. Maintaining these estimates is a key challenge to deploying a long-term prefetching based system, and various strategies could be used to gather and maintain this information. For example, a distributed federation of caches and content distribution nodes could gather local object access distributions and report these statistics to a central aggregation site which would distribute the aggregate statistics to the caches and nodes [19].

Object selection criteria. Based on the collected statistics, it should select a good set of objects for prefetching, that can result in significant improvements in hit rate at modest costs.

Distribution of updates. Updates must be distributed to all the caches that include the modified object in their collection of replicated objects. We assume a push-based system in which updates to replicas are sent immediately to caches that are 'subscribed' to the object in question.

In this paper, we focus on object selection. We assume the presence of required statistics and a push-based update system.

Prefetching increases system resource demands in order to improve response time. Maintaining a collection of hundreds of gigabytes or several terabytes of useful Web data incurs not just a space cost but also a continuous bandwidth cost: as objects in the collection change, the system must fetch new versions of changed objects and must fetch newly created objects. This places a constraint on our long-term prefetching model in that the benefits of our prefetching model should justify the continued cost incurred in terms of bandwidth.

Prefetch algorithms often explicitly calculate the probability that a candidate for prefetching will be used in order to control the resource demands. For such algorithms, it is natural to specify a prefetch threshold and to prefetch objects whose probability of use exceeds the prefetch threshold. This approach limits the excess resources consumed by prefetching to a factor of at most $\frac{1}{threshold}$ times more resources than a demand system.

Several factors support the position that aggressive prefetching can be justified even if it 'wastes' system resources. (i) If bandwidth is cheap and human waiting time is expensive, prefetching can be justified even if it significantly increases bandwidth demands and only modestly improves response times [10,15]. (ii) technology trends favor increased prefetching in the future. The prices of computing, storage, and communications fall rapidly over time, while the value of human waiting time remains approximately constant. (iii) prefetch requests may be less expensive to serve than demand requests for the same amount of data. For example, servers may schedule prefetch requests to be handled in the background [12].

We conclude that if aggressive prefetching can be shown to significantly improve response time, the required infrastructure can be built to accommodate it.

3. Prefetching algorithms

A naive popularity-based algorithm identifies the k most popular objects in the universe and maintains copies of them in the cache. Whenever any one of these objects is updated (or a new object joins the set of the most popular k objects), the system fetches the new object into the cache immediately.

This algorithm does not work well in presence of popular objects that change frequently. As we explain in [29], to increase hit rate by 10% the popularity algorithm might consume 1000 times more bandwidth than a demand cache. This paper does not consider the simple popularity-based algorithm any further.

3.1. Threshold

The Threshold algorithm that we focus on in this paper, balances object access frequency and object update frequency and only fetches objects whose probability of being accessed before being updated exceeds a specified threshold. In particular, for object i, given the object's expected lifetime $lifetime_i$, the probability that a request will access that object P_i, and the total request rate of demand requests to the cache *requestRate* and assuming that object references and updates are independent, the probability that a cache will access an object that it prefetches before that version of the object dies is

$$P_{goodFetch} = 1 - (1 - P_i)^{lifetime_i \cdot requestRate} \tag{1}$$

where $lifetime_i \times requestRate$ is the total number of requests to the cache expected during the object lifetime, and $(1 - P_i)^{lifetime_i \cdot requestRate}$ is the probability that none of these requests access object i.

The Threshold algorithm prefetches the collection of objects whose $P_{goodFetch}$ exceeds a specified threshold. This definition of threshold is similar to that used by several short-term prefetching algorithms [15], and it provides a natural way to limit the bandwidth wasted by prefetching. For each object prefetched, we will consume at most $\frac{1}{threshold}$ times bandwidth accessing that object than a demand system. Note that the total amount of wasted bandwidth typically remains significantly below this value because some objects will attain a higher useful prefetch fraction than enforced by this threshold.

In [29], we show that the above selection criterion is indeed optimal to within a constant factor of approximation. More formally, given a set of n objects, with a popularity distribution P_i and a lifetime distribution λ_i, $1 \leq i \leq n$, a total bandwidth constraint B and an infinite demand cache, the problem is to select a suitable subset of objects S to keep updated locally in order to maximize hit rate. We show that this problem can be reduced to the Knapsack problem and that the threshold strategy is equivalent to the value-density heuristic for the Knapsack problem.

4. Methodology

We performed a cost–benefit analysis of the Threshold algorithm in terms of improvement in hit rate, bandwidth consumption and cache size through two sets of experiments – (i) an analytical evaluation based on a synthetic workload of a billion objects and

(ii) a trace based simulation that compares the performance of different predictors for assessing object popularities. A key benefit of using a synthetic workload is that it allows us to model global object popularities with a known distribution. Thus popularities for all objects are known, even for those which are not seen during a particular simulation run. On the other hand the proxy trace based experiments analyze the performance of adaptive versions of the Threshold algorithm that use various popularity predictors on smaller but realistic workloads. Such workloads exhibit temporal locality between accesses to the same object, have representative object size distributions, and exhibit burstiness in request traffic as observed in real proxy workloads.

4.1. Analytic model

In this section we develop expressions for calculating the steady state hit rate for a demand cache as well as steady state hit rate, cache size and bandwidth consumption for a prefetch cache with a specified threshold. Due to space constraints we show only the first two derivations. We use a workload model based on a Zipf-like popularity distribution for object popularities where $p_i = \frac{C}{i^\alpha}$ represents the popularity of the ith object and C is a normalization constant [5,7,13,17]. We assume that object lifetimes follow an exponential distribution [8] with l_i representing the average lifetime of object i. Each object i is assumed to have a fixed size s_i. For simplicity, we assume the demand request arrivals follow a Poisson distribution with a mean of a requests per second.

4.1.1. Steady state demand hit rate

Let $P_{A_i}(t)$ represent the probability that the most recent access to object i was t time units back, and $P_{B_i}(t)$, the probability that no updates were done to object i since its last access t time units in the past. Now, the probability of a hit on a request to a demand cache is

$$P_{hit_d} = \sum_i p_i \int_0^\infty P_{A_i}(t) P_{B_i}(t)\,\mathrm{d}t, \tag{2}$$

Suppose $P_{(a,t)}(k)$ is the probability that k requests occur in any interval of length t given an access arrival rate of a. With the assumption of request arrivals following Poisson distribution, the probability of k arrivals occurring in t seconds is $P_{(a,t)}(k) = e^{-at} \cdot \frac{(at)^k}{k!}$. The probability of no accesses to object i in this time t is

$$\begin{aligned} P(0 \text{ accesses to object } i \text{ in } t \text{ time}) &= \sum_{k=0}^{\infty} P(k \text{ requests in } t)\ P(\text{none of } k \text{ requests is for } i) \\ &= \sum_{k=0}^{\infty} \left(e^{-at} \frac{(at)^k}{k!} \right) (1 - p_i)^k \\ &= e^{-(ap_i)t}, \end{aligned}$$

The above equation implies that the inter arrival times to object i follow an exponential distribution with mean $(1/ap_i)$. Hence, the probability of an access to an object i occurring t time units after the most recent access to it is $(ap_i)e^{-(ap_i)t}$, which by definition is $P_{A_i}(t)$. Hence,

$$P_{A_i}(t) = (ap_i)e^{-(ap_i)t} \tag{3}$$

Given that the lifetimes of an object i are exponentially distributed with an average l_i, the probability of no updates to that object happen in time t is

$$P_{B_i}(t) = e^{-t/l_i} \tag{4}$$

From Equations (2), (3) and (4), the probability of hit on an access will be

$$\begin{aligned} P_{hit_d} &= \sum_i p_i \int_0^\infty \left((ap_i)e^{-(ap_i)t}\right)\left(e^{-t/l_i}\right) \mathrm{d}t \\ &= \sum_i p_i(ap_i)\left(\left.\frac{e^{-(ap_i+1/l_i)t}}{-(ap_i+1/l_i)}\right|_0^\infty\right) \\ &= \sum_i p_i\left(\frac{ap_il_i}{ap_il_i+1}\right) \end{aligned} \tag{5}$$

The term $\frac{ap_il_i}{ap_il_i+1}$ represents the fraction of hits among accesses to the object i. We call this the *freshness factor* of object i and denote it by $ff(i)$.

4.1.2. Steady state prefetch hit rate

In the Threshold algorithm, if an object qualifies for prefetching, i.e. its $P_{goodFetch}$ as calculated in Equation (1) is greater than the chosen threshold value T then every access to it results in a hit. For other objects the fractional hit rate remains same as calculated before and is $ff(i)$. Hence, the steady state hit rate in a prefetch based scheme with threshold value T is

$$P_{hit_p}(T) = \sum_i p_ih_i$$

where

$$h_i = \begin{cases} 1 & \text{if } P_{goodFetch}(i) > T \\ \dfrac{ap_il_i}{ap_il_i+1} & \text{otherwise} \end{cases}$$

4.1.3. Steady state cache sizes

Proceeding as above, it is straightforward to show that the steady state demand cache size $Csize_{ss_d}$ is given by

$$Csize_{ss_d} = \sum_i s_i\frac{ap_il_i}{ap_il_i+1} \tag{7}$$

When using the Threshold algorithm for prefetching with threshold value T, the estimated total (prefetch + demand) cache size is calculated as

$$Csize_{ss_d} = \sum_i s_i * f_i,$$

where

$$f_i = \begin{cases} 1 & \text{if } P_{goodPreFetch}(i) > T \\ \dfrac{ap_il_i}{ap_il_i+1} & \text{otherwise} \end{cases}$$

4.1.4. Steady state bandwidth

The estimated steady state bandwidth consumed by just demand fetches is

$$BW_{ss_d} = \sum_i s_i \big(1 - ff(i)\big) ap_i \tag{9}$$

For the Threshold algorithm based prefetch strategy, the steady state bandwidth consumed by both prefetch and demand fetches is

$$BW_{ss_d} = \sum_i s_i * h_i, \tag{10}$$

where

$$h_i = \begin{cases} 1/l_i & \text{if } P_{goodFetch}(i) > T \\ ap_i\big(1 - ff(i)\big) & \text{otherwise} \end{cases}$$

The detailed proofs for all of the above derivations may be found in [29].

4.2. Analytic model parameters

Our analytic results assume a set of 1 billion objects that exhibit a Zipf-like popularity distribution with the Zipf parameter $\alpha = -0.982$ [7,13]. The sizes of the objects are assumed to follow a distribution given by a *log-normal* body [2] and a *pareto* [3] tail as explained in [6]. We assume that there is no correlation between object sizes and their popularities. The distribution of object lifetimes was taken from [14], again assuming no correlation with popularity or size. This distribution shows a mean lifetime of about 1.8 months and a median of 12.8 days for HTML files, and a mean of 3.8 months and a median of 63.9 days for image files. The analytic results are obtained by numerically evaluating the expressions derived in Section 4.1, given these parameters.

All data is considered to be cacheable. This assumption is justified because we are concerned only with the improvement in hit rate due to prefetching, and uncacheable data affects both demand and long-term prefetch caching alike. We also speculate that efforts such as active caches [9], active names [27], and ICAP [26] will support execution of server programs at caches and content distribution nodes. Moreover, efforts to improve cache consistency semantics [11,20,23,30] will enable caching of much currently uncacheable data.

Our analysis has several limitations. It ignores burstiness of the request traffic and approximates it by a fixed average arrival rate. This assumption directly affects the number of consistency misses as seen by a demand cache. Burstiness of request traffic can also hurt prefetching at a proxy since there may not be any bandwidth available for prefetching at the peak points of demand traffic. On the other hand prefetching can also help by smoothing out demand [12] network traffic. Ignoring temporal locality in the synthetically generated trace underestimates the hit rate seen by the demand cache.

4.3. Proxy trace simulation

The trace based simulator uses a 12 day trace logged by the Squid proxy cache [4] at NCSA, Urbana Champaign between Feb. 27 and Mar. 10 2001. The trace consists of

[2] $p(x) = (1/x\sigma\sqrt{2\pi})e^{-(\ln x-\mu)^2/2\sigma^2}$, $\mu = 9.357$, $\sigma = 1.318$.
[3] $p(x) = \alpha k^{\alpha} x^{-(\alpha+1)}$, $k = 133K$, $\alpha = 1.1$.

about 10 million records and accesses to 4.2 million unique objects. We simulate an LRU based demand cache and a prefetch cache implementing the Threshold algorithm using two simple predictors for assessing object popularities. Query URLs (with a '?' in them) are considered as both uncacheable and unprefetchable.

The sizes of the objects are used as logged in the trace. However, as in the analytic model, lifetimes are generated synthetically from the distribution given in [14], because the traces do not contain object update information. Since our prefetch strategy is sensitive to object lifetimes, this distribution could directly and significantly affect our results. Hence we also perform a sensitivity analysis of the performance of the Threshold algorithm with respect to median object lifetime by shifting the probability distribution curve of the lifetimes by several orders of magnitude along the lifetime axis.

We use a simple statistical model to estimate the popularities of the objects. The simulator maintains a running count of the number of accesses to each object and computes object popularity by dividing this number by the total number of accesses seen. At any access the simulator computes the $P_{goodFetch}$ of the object as defined in Equation 1 and checks if it exceeds the threshold, in which case the access is considered to be a prefetch hit. We call this object popularity predictor as *Predictor1*. *Predictor1* is aggressive, as it uses the current access to update the corresponding object's popularity before computing its $P_{goodFetch}$. This predictor can potentially save compulsory misses to an object since it knows an object's popularity even before the first access to it. Such a predictor is feasible in a scenario where popularity information is aggressively pushed out by the server, or is widely shared across several cooperating caches. We also simulate a more conservative predictor known as *Predictor2* that can not prevent compulsory misses. An object has to be seen at least once before its popularity can be used to consider it for prefetching by this predictor. For comparison purposes, we also simulate an oracle EverFresh that gets rid of all consistency misses, i.e., an access is a hit if the corresponding object has been seen before. The hit rate so obtained is the maximum attainable by a cache based on local prefetching alone. Even the oracle cannot prevent compulsory misses or achieve hits to uncacheable objects. For all of the experiments, the cache was allowed to warm up for 8 days. The long period of warm up will prevent inflated estimates of popularities corresponding to accesses in the beginning of the trace.

As part of future work we intend to measure the performance of more aggressive predictors that gather popularity information from several cooperating caches. In such a scenario, it might be possible to considerably reduce compulsory as well as consistency misses.

5. Results

5.1. Analytic evaluation

Fig. 1a plots the hit rates obtained by our prefetching policy for various prefetch thresholds with increasing request arrival rate. Note that demand request arrival rate is a key parameter describing the scale of the content distribution node under consideration and an increase in demand arrival rate increases the set of objects that meet a given threshold. The steady state hit rates for demand cache serve as a baseline for comparing the hit rates obtained by our prefetch policy. The graphs show that the threshold policy

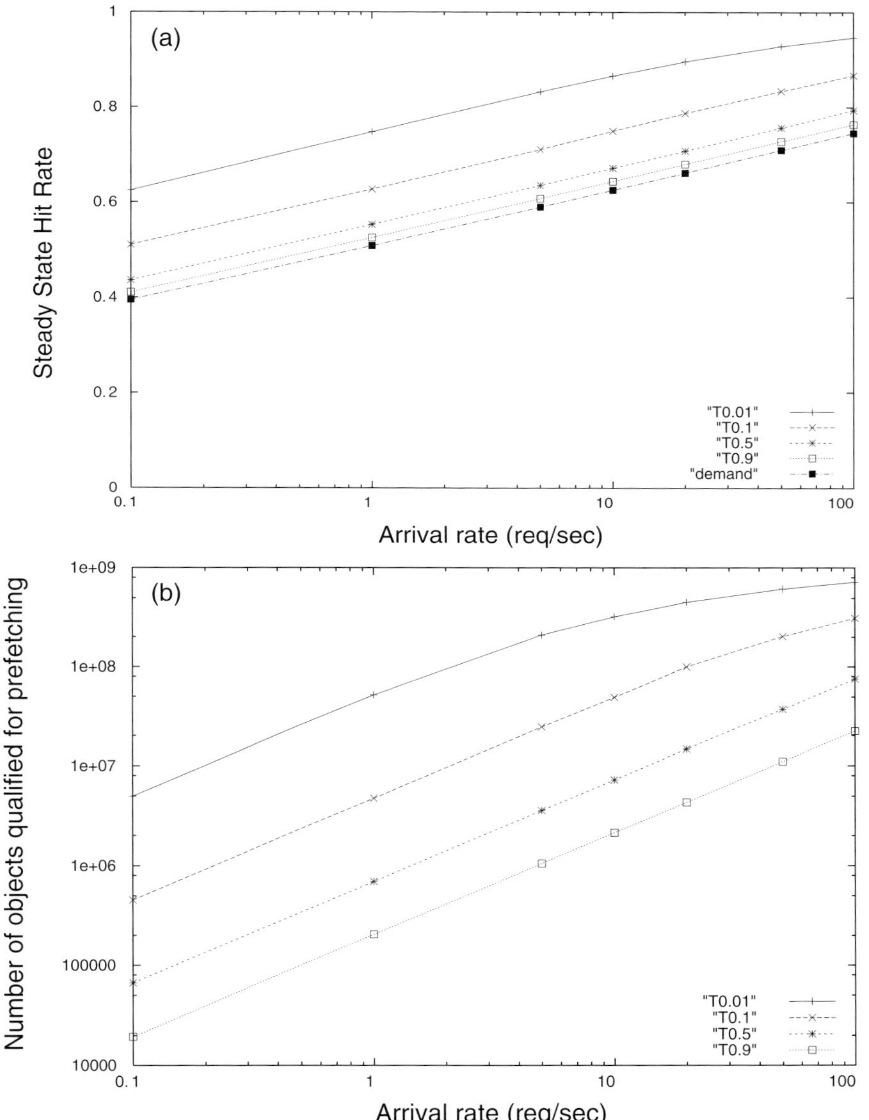

Fig. 1. Prefetching popular long lived objects. Effect of increasing request arrival rates for various thresholds. (a) Steady state hit rate. (b) Number of objects prefetched.

improves hit rates. For example, at an arrival rate of 1 req/sec, for threshold 0.5, we get an overall hit rate of 55% compared to a hit rate of 50% obtained by an infinite demand cache in steady state. For an arrival rate of 10 req/sec, for threshold 0.1, we get an overall hit rate of 75% compared to a hit rate of 62% obtained by the demand cache.

Note that significant improvements are achievable across a broad range of CDN scales. Although lower arrival rates reduce the collection of objects that meet the prefetch

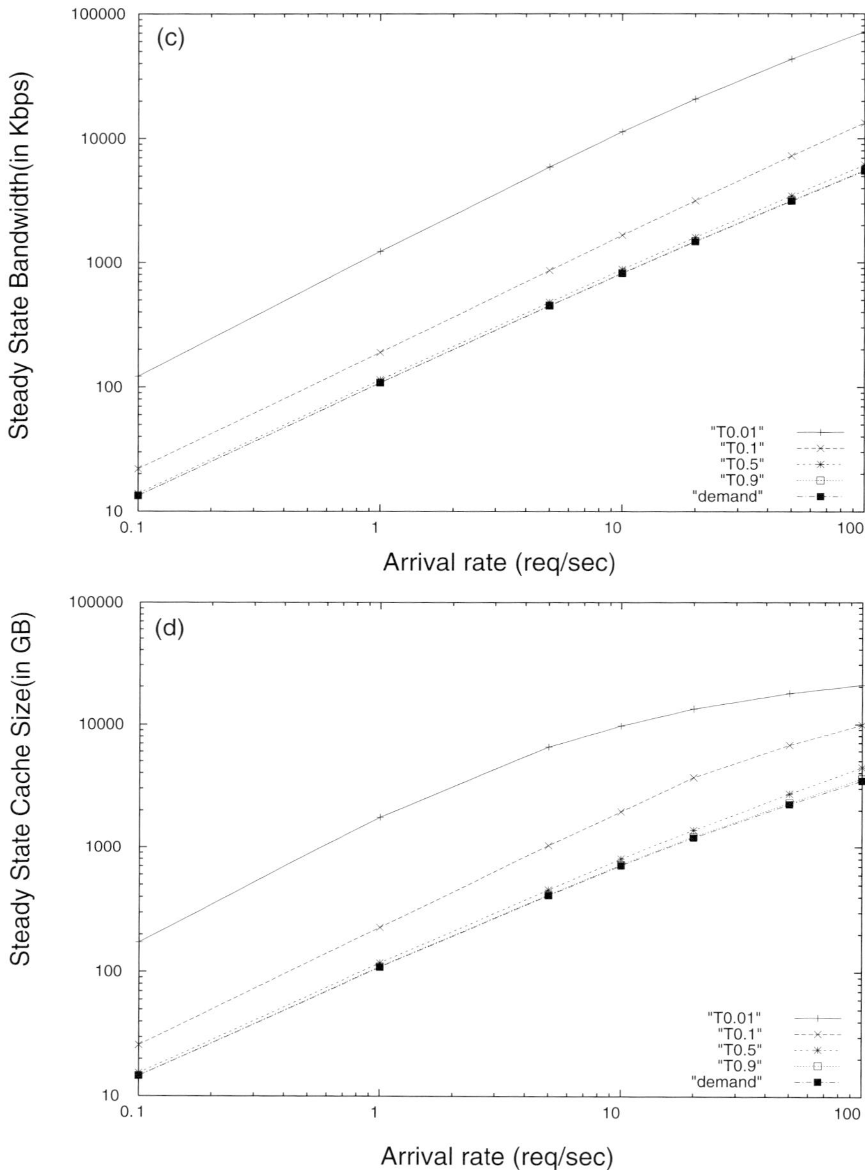

Fig. 1 (continued). (c) Steady state bandwidth consumed. (d) Steady state cache size.

threshold criteria, lower arrival rates also reduce the steady state hit rates achieved by a demand cache.

Fig. 1b plots the total number of objects (from our simulated universe of one billion objects) that qualify to be prefetched at various threshold values with increasing arrival rates. Fig. 1c and 1d plot the amount of prefetch bandwidth and prefetch cache needed to maintain the prefetched objects.

As seen from the graphs, the choice of a threshold value affects the observed hit rate and the overhead. A high threshold implies a better chance of use of the prefetched object but a decreased hit rate since fewer objects will qualify for prefetching. At the same time it implies a reduced bandwidth and prefetch cache size overhead.

Fig. 1c suggests that as the arrival rate increases, even low thresholds would incur a modest bandwidth overhead as compared to demand bandwidth. For example, for an arrival rate of 10 req/sec, a threshold of 0.1 would incur a bandwidth cost of 1.6 Mbps compared to the demand bandwidth of 800 kbps. From Fig. 1a, this would give us a hit rate of 75%.

Fig. 1d helps us in analyzing a typical cache size budget needed at a real world proxy given its request rate. For example, a 10 req/sec request rate, with a threshold of 0.1 would correspond to a 2 TB prefetch cache size. Given today's disk costs, it would cost around \$ 6400 to add a 2 TB disk. From Fig. 1a, a threshold of 0.1 at an arrival rate of 10 req/sec would provide us with a 75% hit rate.

Given falling hardware costs, and the potential to use system-level techniques to decrease cost of handling prefetch requests, even more aggressive prefetching such as $T = 0.01$ might be contemplated in the future.From the graphs, at the cost of 10 TB disk and 10 Mbps bandwidth, we could achieve 87% hit rate which effectively means a decrease in missrate from 45% to 13%.

5.2. Trace based simulations

A simple analysis of the trace showed that out of the 10.9 million requests that the proxy received, approximately 10% were consistency check messages. This implies that even an ideal prefetching strategy that prevents all of the consistency misses cannot give an improvement of more than 10% in hit rate over that of an infinite demand cache, unless, its statistics tracing spans multiple caches, or it allows servers to supply popularity estimates when objects are created.

In our experiments we assume a demand cache of size 28 GB. We allow the cache to be warmed for 8 days and then gather performance measurements over the remaining 4 days.

Fig. 2a, b and c show the change in hit rate, overall bandwidth consumption (demand + prefetch) and overall cache size (demand + prefetch) with varying thresholds. In Fig. 2a, the *EverFresh* algorithm gives a hit rate of about 61%. At a threshold of 0.1 *Predictor2* almost matches this 'optimal' achievable hit rate. *Predictor1*, as expected, gives much higher hit rates since it can avoid compulsory misses as well. Fig. 2c shows that for a threshold of 0.1, the bandwidth blow-up as compared to the demand bandwidth is less than 2×. *Predictor1* shows lesser bandwidth costs because of the smoothing out of prefetched bytes over a larger duration (a typical prefetched object's lifetime) as opposed to the post-warming period of 4 days for Demand and *Predictor2*. Fig. 2b shows that the increase in cache size due to prefetching is nominal as well. Thus, we conclude that we can obtain significant improvements in hit rate at modest bandwidth and cache space costs.

Fig. 2d and e show the attainable hit rate with respect to the bandwidth and cache space costs respectively. These graphs have also been generated from the data obtained from experiments performed by varying the threshold and have been included for ease of reference.

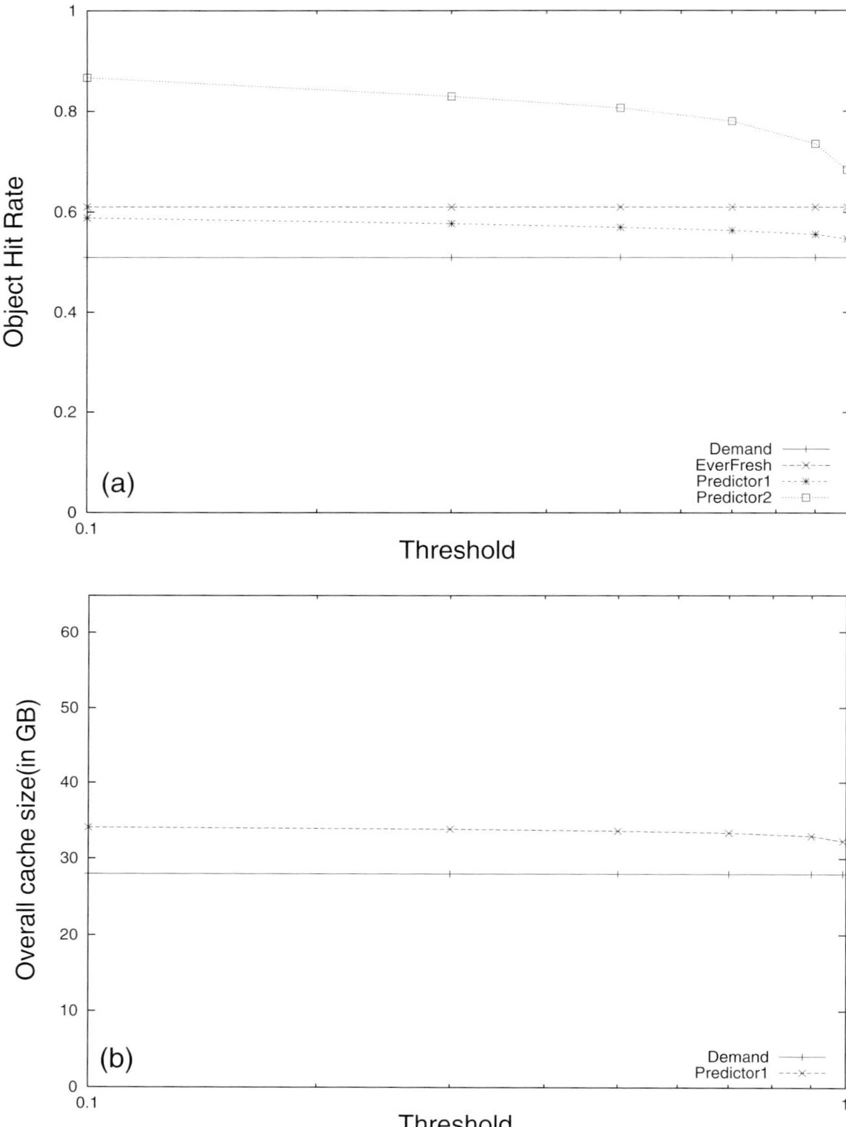

Fig. 2. (a)–(e). Effects of varying Threshold value hit rate and bandwidth; (f)–(h) Sensitivity analysis of results. (a) Object hit rate. (b) Overall cache size.

To test the sensitivity of our results to our assumptions about lifetimes, we vary the mean life time of objects and study its effect. Fig. 2f–2h show our results. The x-axis shows a shift factor s which denotes the horizontal displacement along the lifetime axis (on a log-scale) of the probability density function corresponding to the CDF taken from [14]. This graph varies the mean lifetime of the objects across several orders of magnitude, with each unit representing a change in the average lifetimes by a factor of 10. The graphs

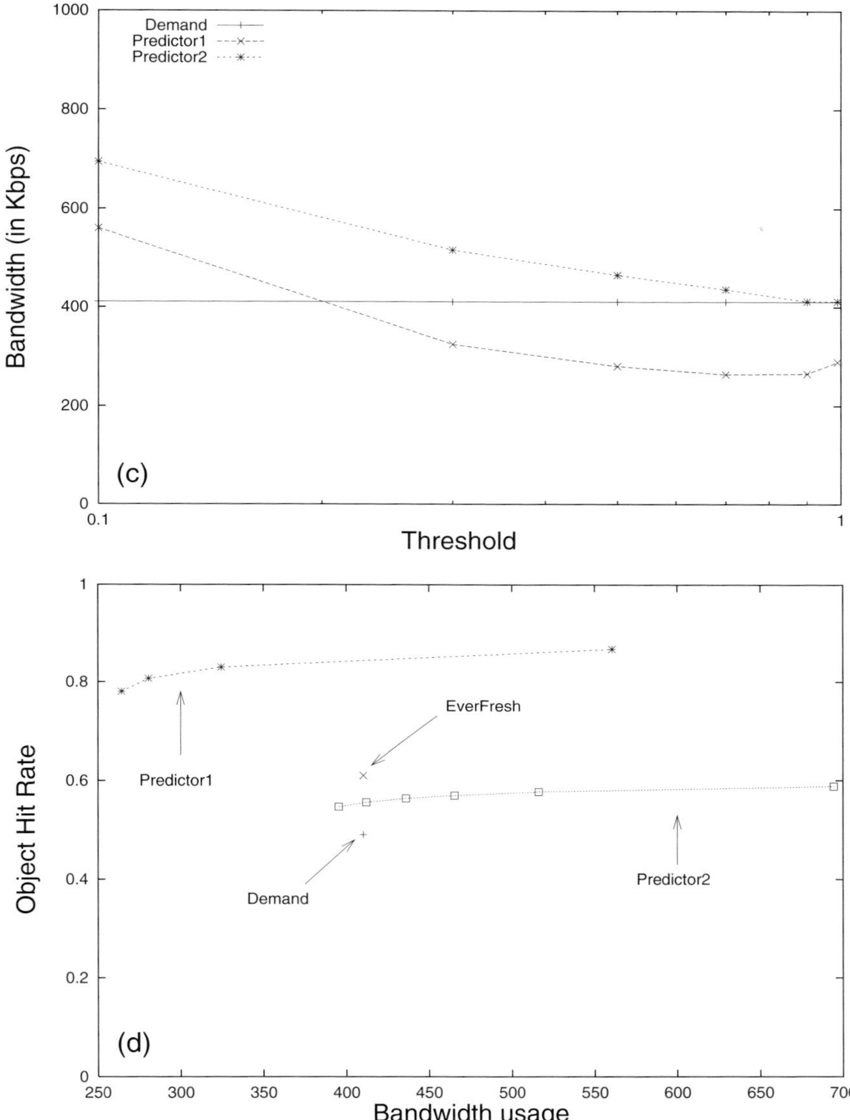

Fig. 2 (continued). (c) Total bandwidth. (d) Hit rate vs. bandwidth.

show that when life times are small, we get less hit rate improvement but at the same time use less prefetch cache size and bandwidth. This result is expected because our algorithm does not select short lived objects. For higher lifetime values, we achieve higher hit rates at a reduced cost of bandwidth and increase in prefetch cache size. The hit rate graphs at high threshold values flatten as the number of unique objects are limited, and almost all the objects would have already qualified for prefetch. This observation holds for a universe of a fixed set of objects; if we are already caching all the objects, then increase in

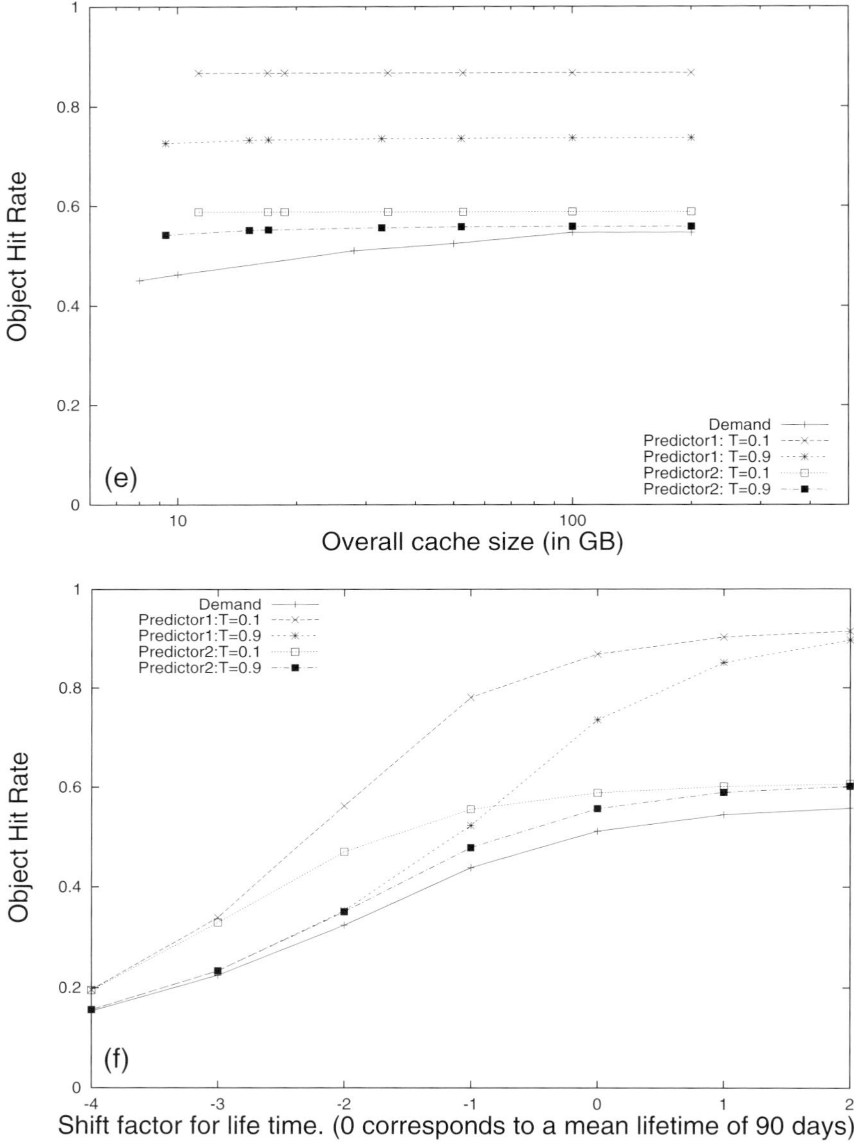

Fig. 2 (continued). (e) Hit rate vs. total cache size. (f) Object hit rate sensitivity.

life times or arrival rates would not alter hit rates. But the bandwidth required to keep the objects refreshed reduces proportionally as the lifetimes increase.

In summary, trace based simulation results show that our prefetch algorithm indeed provides significant hit rate improvements. One limitation of our trace based study is that we chose a medium-sized trace. But given the results we obtained, increasing the trace length would only benefit our results rather than hurt them.

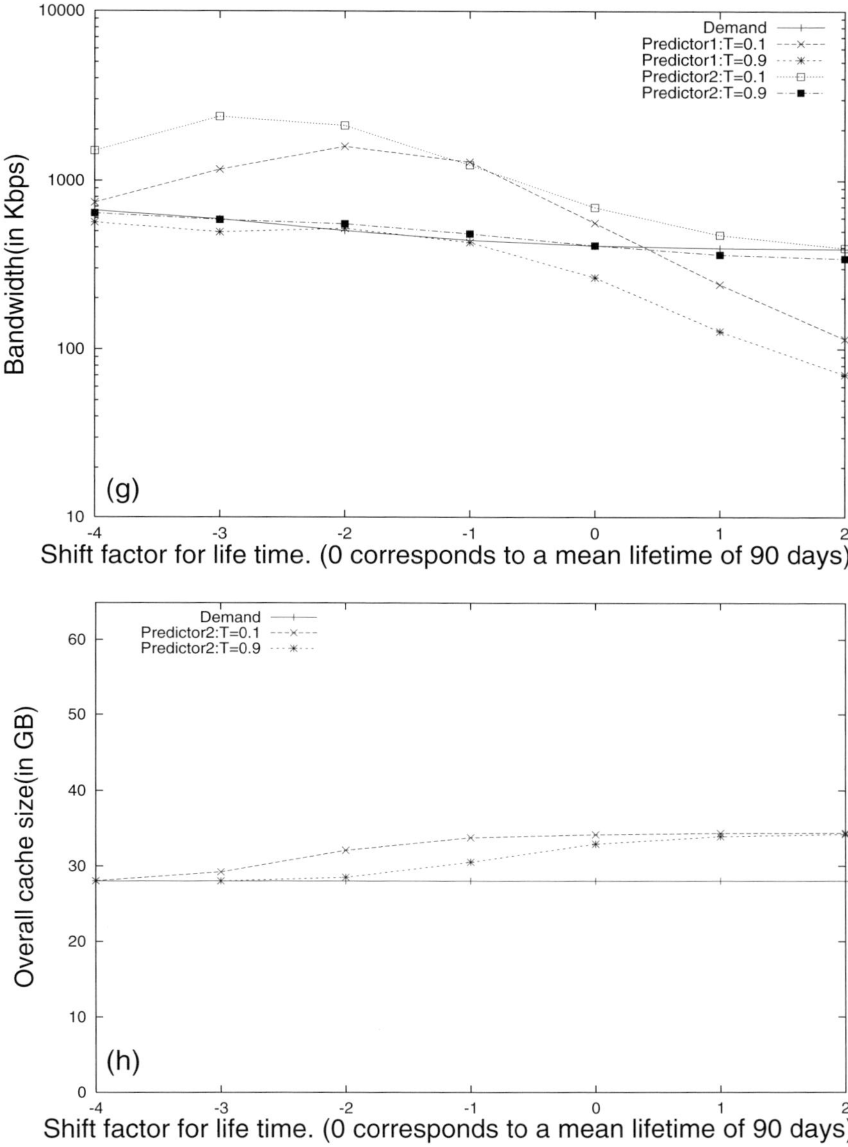

Fig. 2 (continued). (g) Bandwidth sensitivity. (h) Total cache size sensitivity.

6. Related work

The idea of prefetching in the Web has been widely studied by many researchers recently. Most of the research has concentrated on short-term prefetching based on recent access patterns of clients. Duchamp [15] provides a survey of various research contributions relevant to short-term prefetching in the Web: software systems, algorithms, simulations and prototypes [24], and papers that establish bounds [21]. Duchamp [15] proposes to prefetch hyperlinks of Web pages based on aggregate access patterns of clients as observed by the server. This approach gives priority to popular URLs and hence is similar to our popularity algorithm. Our (threshold based) approach is different from the above approaches in that we consider long-term prefetching suitable to CDNs [2] and busy proxies by prefetching objects that are both popular and long lived so that we get long-term benefits.

Gwertzman et al. [18] discuss push caching which makes use of a server's global knowledge of usage patterns and network topology to distribute data to cooperating servers. A number of research efforts support multicast delivery for Web content distribution. Li et al. [22] investigate multicast invalidation and delivery of popular, frequently updated objects to Web cache proxies. These techniques are complementary to our work and can be used to realize the distribution of updates that we assume in our CDN model.

Implementations of cooperating caches are becoming increasingly commonplace. Sharing of popularity information across caches enables not only better estimates of popularity but can also prevent some compulsory misses. Venkataramani et al. [28] develop a provably near optimal algorithm for placing objects in a set of cooperating caches that are constrained by update bandwidth. Given the network distances between the cooperating caches and the predictions of access rates from each cache to a set of objects, the placement algorithms determine where to place each object in order to minimize the average access cost. The algorithm could be used to extend long-term prefetching to a collection of cooperating caches.

7. Conclusion

In this paper, we focussed on a technique called long-term prefetching, which is beneficial for Web proxies and content distribution networks. In this prefetching model, we have explored an algorithm for object selection based on the popularity and lifetime of objects. We evaluated the performance of a long-term prefetching algorithm whose aggressiveness can be tuned by varying a prefetch threshold. For example, our analytical evaluation showed that, for a cache that receives 10 demand requests per second, our prefetching algorithm can improve hit rates by up to 13 percent, while increasing the bandwidth requirements by just over a factor of 2.

The work in this study brings up three key issues which make interesting topics of future research.

(1) Exploring the performance of a two level prefetcher composed of a long-term prefetching module that is useful at the entry level while accessing Web pages, and a short-term prefetcher that can prefetch hyperlinks there onwards.
(2) Exploring mechanisms to estimate the long-term effects of prefetching on the underlying network, and the increased opportunities it offers for traffic shaping. resulting from the smoothening of demand network traffic.
(3) Extending the threshold algorithm to a set of cooperating caches that can share aggregated popularity information.

An in depth understanding of these issues will form the basis for the design of efficient content distribution systems in the future.

References

[1] http://cs.utexas.edu/~dahlin/techtrends/data/diskprices/data.

[2] http://www.akamai.com.

[3] http://www.netdoor.com/info/tiert3pricing.html.

[4] http://www.squid-cache.org.

[5] V. Almeida, A. Bestavros, M. Crovella and A. de Oliveira. Characterizing Reference Locality in the WWW. In: *Proceedings of PDIS'96*.

[6] P. Barford and M. Crovella. Generating representative workloads for network and server performance evaluation, 1998.

[7] L. Breslau, P. Cao, L. Fan, G. Phillips and S. Shenker. Web caching and Zipf-like distributions: Evidence and implications. In: *Proceedings of IEEE Infocom*, 1999.

[8] B.E. Brewington and G. Cybenko. How dynamic is the web? *WWW9/Computer Networks*, 33(1–6): 257–276, 2000.

[9] P. Cao, J. Zhang and K. Beach. Active cache: Caching dynamic contents on the web. Technical Report CS-TR-1998-1363, 1998.

[10] B. Chandra, M. Dahlin, L. Gao, A. Khoja, A. Razzaq and A. Sewani. Resource management for scalable disconnected access to web services. In: *WWW10*, May 2001.

[11] E. Cohen, B. Krishnamurthy and J. Rexford. Improving End-to-End Performance of the Web Using Server Volumes and Proxy Filters. In: *SIGCOMM98*.

[12] M. Crovella and P. Barford. The network effects of prefetching. In: *Proceedings of IEEE Infocom*, 1998.

[13] C. Cunha, A. Bestavros and M. Crovella. Characteristics of WWW Client-based Traces. Technical Report TR-95-010, Boston University, CS Department, April 1995.

[14] F. Douglis, A. Feldmann, B. Krishnamurthy and J.C. Mogul. Rate of change and other metrics: a live study of the world wide web. In: *USITS'97*.

[15] D. Duchamp. Prefetching Hyperlinks. In: *USITS99*.

[16] L. Fan, P. Cao, W. Lin and Q. Jacobson. Web prefetching between low-bandwidth clients and proxies: Potential and performance, 1999.

[17] S. Glassman. A caching relay for the World Wide Web. *Computer Networks and ISDN Systems*, 27(2): 165–173, 1994.

[18] J. Gwertzman and M. Seltzer. An analysis of geographical push-caching, 1997.

[19] G. Karakostas and D. Serpanos. Practical LFU implementation for Web Caching. Technical Report TR-622-00, Department of Computer Science, Princeton University, 2000.

[20] B. Krishnamurthy and C. Wills. Piggyback Server Invalidation for Proxy Cache Coherency. In: *WWW7*, 1998.

[21] T.M. Kroeger, D.E. Long and J.C. Mogul. Exploring the bounds of web latency reduction from caching and prefetching. In: *USENIX Symposium on Internet Technologies and Systems*, 1997.

[22] D. Li and D.R. Cheriton. Scalable web caching of frequently updated objects using reliable multicast. In: *Proceedings of USITS'99*.

[23] C. Liu and P. Cao. Maintaining Strong Cache Consistency in the World-Wide Web. In: *Proceedings of ICDCS 1997*, May 1997.

[24] V.N. Padmanabhan and J.C. Mogul. Using predictive prefetching to improve World-Wide Web latency. In: *Proceedings of the SIGCOMM'96*.

[25] T. Palpanas. Web prefetching using partial match prediction, 1998.

[26] The ICAP Protocol Group. Icap the internet content adaptation protocol. Technical Report draft-opes-icap-00.txt, IETF, December 2000.

[27] A. Vahdat, M. Dahlin, T. Anderson and A. Aggarwal. Active names: Flexible location and transport of wide-area resources. In: *USENIX Symposium on Internet Technologies and Systems*, 1999.

[28] A. Venkataramani, M. Dahlin and P. Weidmann. Bandwidth constrained placement in a WAN. In: *To appear in ACM Principles of Distributed Computing*, August 2001.

[29] A. Venkataramani, P. Yalagandula, R. Kokku, S. Sharif and M. Dahlin. The potential costs and benefits of long term prefetching for content distribution. Technical Report TR-01-13, UT, Austin, 2001.

[30] J. Yin, L. Alvisi, M. Dahlin and C. Lin. Using Leases to Support Server-Driven Consistency in Large-Scale Systems. In: *Proceedings of ICDCS 1998*, May 1998.

Web Caching and Content Delivery
A. Bestavros and M. Rabinovich (Editors)

Assertion: Prefetching With GET is Not Good

Brian D. Davison [1]

Department of Computer Science, Rutgers, The State University of New Jersey, 110 Frelinghuysen Road, Piscataway, NJ 08854 USA

Abstract

The benefits of Web cache prefetching are well understood, and so prefetching has been implemented in a number of commercial products. This paper argues that the current support for prefetching in HTTP/1.1 is insufficient because *prefetching with* GET *is not good.* Existing prefetching implementations can cause problems with undesirable side-effects and server abuse, and the potential for these problems may thwart additional prefetching development and deployment. We make some initial suggestions of extensions to HTTP that would allow for safe prefetching, reduced server abuse, and differentiated Web server quality of service. It is our hope that this paper will restart a dialog on these issues that will move in time into a standards development process.

Keywords: HTTP; Prefetching; Web caching; QOS

---

1. Introduction

Prefetching into a local cache is a well-known technique for reducing latency in distributed systems. However, prefetching is not widespread in the Web today. There are a number of possible explanations for this, including

- the bandwidth overhead of prefetching data never utilized,
- the potential increase in queue lengths and delays from naive prefetching approaches [15],
- the reported bounds on the potential of prefetching [30], and
- the effect on the Internet (e.g. added traffic and server loads) if all clients were to implement prefetching.

Fortunately, the first two objections can be satisfied by more careful approaches, and the third still allows for a significant reduction in latency from prefetching, and only considers proxy-based prefetching. The fourth is still up for debate, but when prefetching occurs over a private connection for objects stored on an intermediate proxy (as in proxy initiated prefetching [23]), this is no longer an issue.

---

[1] New address: Department of Computer Science and Engineering, Packard Lab, Lehigh University, 19 Memorial Drive West, Bethlehem, PA 18015. E-mail: davison@cs.rutgers.edu

This paper will first attempt to define prefetchability and then review how Web prefetching has been suggested by many researchers and implemented in a number of commercial systems. In section 3 we will discuss a number of less-well-investigated problems with prefetching, and with the use of GET for prefetching in particular. In effect we argue that 1) GET is unsafe because in practice, GET requests may have (not insignificant) side-effects, and 2) GET can unfairly use server resources. As a result, we assert that *prefetching with* GET *is not good*. We then propose extending HTTP/1.1 [24] to incorporate methods and headers that will support prefetching and variable Web server quality of service.

2. Background

While some researchers have considered prepushing or presending, this paper is only concerned with client-activated preloading of content. We wish to set aside concerns of how the client chooses what to prefetch (e.g. Markov model of client history, bookmarks on startup, user-specified pages, the use of proxy or server hints), with the understanding that a hints-based model (as suggested in [38,34,20] and others) has the potential to avoid many of the concerns discussed here but may also introduce other problems and likewise lacks specification as a standard.

Therefore, we make the not-unreasonable assumption that a prefetching system (at the client or intermediate proxy) has a list of one or more URLs that it desires to prefetch.

2.1. Prefetchability

Can prefetchability be defined? Let us start with prefetching. A relatively early paper [19] defines prefetching as a cache that "periodically refreshes cached pages so that they will be less stale when requested by the user." While this definition does have a Web-specific perspective, it does not reflect current usage of the term as it is specific to cache-refreshment. A more general definition is:

Prefetching is the (cache-initiated) speculative retrieval of a resource into a cache in the anticipation that it can be served from cache in the future. (1)

Typically the resource has not yet been requested by the client (whether user or machine), but the definition applies equally to cache refreshes (when the content has changed). Note that with this definition we can see that:

- Prefetching requires the use of a cache.
- Prefetchability requires cacheability.

Note that not all prefetched resources will be used before they expire or are removed from the cache. Some will never be requested by the client. This implies that:

- Prefetching requires at least idempotence, since resources may end up being fetched multiple times.
- Speculative prefetchability requires safety. Unless we can guarantee that the client will actually use this resource (before removal or expiration), a prefetching system should not perform any action that has unwanted (from either the client or server's perspective) side-effects at the server.

Perhaps now we can propose a working definition:

A Web resource is *prefetchable* if and only if it is cacheable and its retrieval is safe. (2)

Typical concerns for safety (e.g. [25]) are really concerns for idempotency, but idempotency is insufficient for prefetching, as the prefetched response might never be seen or used. Here we are referring to the definition of safe as having no significant side-effects (see section 9.1.1 of the HTTP/1.1 specification included in Appendix B).

2.2. Prefetching research

Prefetching for the Web is not a new concept. Discussions of mechanisms and their merits date back at least to 1994-1995[2]. Many papers have been published on the use of prefetching as a mechanism to improve the latencies provided by caching systems (e.g. [3,11,14,16,20,23,26,27,33,34,38,39,42,44–46]).

2.3. Prefetching in the Web today

A number of commercial systems used today implement some form of prefetching. CacheFlow [10] implements prefetching for inline resources like images, and can proactively check for expired objects. There are also a number of browser extensions for Netscape and Microsoft Internet Explorer as well as some personal proxies that perform prefetching of links of the current page (and sometimes bookmarks, popular sites, etc.). Examples include NetSonic [47], PeakJet 2000 [40], and Webcelerator [22].

3. Problems with prefetching

Even with a proliferation of prefetching papers in the research community, and examples of its use in commercial products, there are a number of well-known difficulties with prefetching as described in the Introduction.

Some researchers even suggest pre-executing the steps leading up to retrieval [12] as one way to avoid some of the difficulties of content retrieval and still achieve significant latency savings. However, as suggested above, researchers and developers are still interested in the performance enhancements possible with speculative data transfer. When prefetching (and not prepushing/presending), the temptation for most system builders is to use the HTTP GET mechanism. Advantages of GET and standard HTTP request headers include:

- GET is well-understood and universally used.
- There are supporting libraries to ease implementation (e.g. for C there is W3C's Libwww [49] and for Perl there is Libwww-perl [1]).
- It requires no changes on the server's side.

However, the use of the current version of GET has some obvious and non-obvious drawbacks, which we discuss in this section. Even from the prefetching client's per-

[2] For one interesting discussion still accessible, see the threads 'two ideas ... ' and 'prefetching attribute' from the www-talk mailing list in Nov.–Dec. 1995 at http://lists.w3.org/Archives/Public/www-talk/1995NovDec/thread.html.

Prefetchability Quiz

```
http://www.cnn.com/
http://www.ibm.com/
http://www.geocities.com/
http://www.microsoft.com/
http://www.napster.com/
http://www.volera.com/
http://www.bn.com/
```

Fig. 1. Which of these URLs are prefetchable? (Answers are in Appendix A.)

spective, there may be some drawbacks. In particular, just like users, a naive prefetcher may not know that the object requested is very large and will take minutes or hours to arrive.

In many cases, however, these drawbacks can be characterized as server abuses, because the inefficiencies and deleterious effects described could be avoided if the content provider were able to decide what and when to prefetch. In the rest of this section we detail the problems with prefetching, with emphasis on the consequences of using the standard HTTP GET mechanism in the current Web.

3.1. Unknown cacheability

One of the differences between Web caching and traditional caching in file and memory systems is that the cacheability of Web objects varies. One cannot look at the URL of an object and *a priori* know that the response generated for that URL will be cacheable or uncacheable (see Fig. 1). Some simple heuristics are known, including examining the URL for substrings (e.g. '?' and 'cgi-bin') that are commonly associated with fast-changing or individualized content, for which caching does not provide much use. However, while a URL with an embedded '?' has special meaning for HTTP/1.0 caching (see the HTTP/1.1 specification [24], section 13.9, excerpted in Appendix B), a significant fraction of content that might be labeled dynamic (e.g. e-commerce site queries) does not change from day to day [48] and should be treated as cacheable unless marked otherwise (as stated by the HTTP/1.1 specification). Only the content provider will know for certain, which is perhaps why the cacheability of a response is determined by one or more HTTP headers that travel with the response.

Some researchers (e.g. [20]) have proposed prefetching and caching data that is otherwise uncacheable, on the grounds that it will be viewed once and then purged from the cache. However, the HTTP specification [24] states that such non-transparent operations require an explicit warning to the end user, which may be undesirable. Since many objects are marked uncacheable just for hit metering purposes, Mogul and Leach suggest something similar in their 'Simple Hit-Metering and Usage-Limiting for HTTP' RFC [35] which states in part (*emphasis added*):

> Note that the limit on 'uses' set by the max-uses directive does not include the use of the response to satisfy the end-client request that caused the proxy's request to the server. *This counting rule supports the notion of a cache-initiated prefetch: a cache*

may issue a prefetch request, receive a max-uses = 0 response, store that response, and then return that response (without revalidation) when a client makes an actual request for the resource. However, each such response may be used at most once in this way, so the origin server maintains precise control over the number of actual uses.

Under this arrangement, the response no longer has to be marked uncacheable for the server to keep track of views and can even direct the number of times that the object may be served.

In summary, though, when a client or proxy prefetches an object that it is not permitted to cache, it has wasted both client and server resources to no avail.

3.2. Server overhead

Even when the object fetched is cacheable, the server may have non-negligible costs in order to provide it. The retrieval will consume some portion of the server's resources including bandwidth and cpu, and logging of unviewed requests. Likewise, the execution of some content retrievals may not be desirable from a content-provider's point of view, such as the instigation of a large database search. In fact, the use of overly aggressive prefetchers has been banned at some sites [41].

As more attention is paid to end-user quality of service for the Web (e.g. [8]), the content provider may want to be able to serve prefetched items at a lower quality of service so that those requests do not adversely impact the demand-fetched requests.

3.3. Side effects of retrieval

According to the HTTP/1.1 specification [24], GET and HEAD requests are not supposed to have a significance other than retrieval and should be considered safe (the relevant portions of the draft standard are included in Appendix B). In fact, the GET and HEAD methods are supposed to be idempotent methods. In reality, many requests do have side-effects (and are thus not idempotent).

Often these side effects are the reason for some objects to be made uncacheable (that is, the side effects are desirable by the content producers, such as for logging usage). More importantly, some requests, when executed speculatively, may generate undesirable effects for either the content owner, or the intended content recipient. Placing an item into an electronic shopping basket is an obvious example — a prefetching system, when speculatively retrieving links, does not want to end up placing the items corresponding to those links into a shopping cart without the knowledge and consent of the user.

This reality is confirmed in the help pages of some prefetching products. For example, one vendor [21] states:

> On sites where clicking a link does more than just fetch a page (such as on-line shopping), Webcelerator's Prefetching may trigger some unexpected actions. If you are having problems with interactive sites (such as e-mail sites, online ordering, chat rooms, and sites with complex forms) you may wish to disable Prefetching.

Idempotency is a significant issue and is also mentioned in other RFCs (e.g. [7,5,6]). It is additionally an issue for pipelined connections in HTTP/1.1 (prefetching or otherwise) as non-idempotent requests should not be retried if a pipelined connection were to fail before completion [3]. The experimental RFC 2310 [25] proposes the use of a new response header called Safe which would tell the client that the request may be repeated without harm, but this is only useful after the client already has header information about the resource. The lack of guaranteed safe prefetching also complicates live proxy evaluation [17].

The HTTP/1.1 specification [24] does note that "it is not possible to ensure that the server does not generate side-effects as a result of performing a GET request." A conscientious content developer would not only need to use POST to access all potentially unsafe resources but to prevent GET access to those resources, as linking to content cannot be controlled on the WWW. There may also be some confusion as to the interpretation of the idempotence of GET as a MUST rather than a SHOULD, and what constitutes safety and its significance (as a SHOULD requirement). In any case, enough content providers have built Web sites (perhaps without thought to prefetching) that do generate side-effects from GET requests that careful developers are unlikely to develop widespread prefetching functionality, for fear of causing problems.

3.4. Related non-prefetching applications

There are other situations in which server resources are potentially abused. These include price-comparison systems that repeatedly retrieve pages from e-commerce sites to get the latest product pricing and availability, and extensive mechanical crawling of a site at too fast a rate [32]. Both of these can cause undue loads at a Web site and affect performance of the demand-fetched responses. While the need for an improved interface between crawlers and servers has been recognized (e.g. [9]), the need for distinguishing between demand– and non-demand-requests has not been suggested. Interestingly, there has been recent work [43] to build crawlers that attempt to access the 'hidden Web' — those pages behind search forms [4], further blurring the semantic distinction between GET and POST methods.

A server may also benefit from special handling of other non-demand requests, such as non-demand-based cache refreshment traffic [13], in which additional validation requests are made to ensure freshness of cached content. From the content provider's perspective, it would be helpful in general to serve non-demand requests of any kind at a different quality of service than those requests that come from a client with a human waiting for the result in real-time.

3.5. User activity conflation

Non-interactive retrieval also has the potential for generating anomalous server statistics, in the sense that a page retrieval is assumed to be represent a page view. Almost certainly some fraction of prefetched requests will not be displayed to the user, and so the logs generated by the server may overestimate and likely skew pageview statistics. This is also the case for other kinds of non-interactive retrievals, such as those generated by Web crawlers. Today, when analyzing server logs for interesting patterns of

[3] HTTP idempotency continues to be significant. For a relatively recent discussion of HTTP idempotency with emphasis on idempotent sequences, see the discussion thread 'On pipelining' from the IETF HTTP working group mailing list archives at http://www.ics.uci.edu/pub/ietf/http/hypermail/2000/thread.html.

usage, researchers must first separate (if possible) the retrievals from automated crawlers [29,18].

Additionally, if the server were maintaining a user model based on history, undistinguished prefetching requests could influence that model, which could generate incorrect hints that would cause additional requests for useless resources which would likewise (incorrectly) influence the server's model of the user, and so on. A server that is able to distinguish such requests from demand traffic would also be able to distinguish them in logs and in user model generation.

4. Proposed extensions to HTTP

The preceding section has discussed the problems with prefetching on the Web using current methods. In this section, we describe the need for an extension (as opposed to just new headers) for HTTP, mention briefly some previous proposals for HTTP prefetching extensions, and then provide a starting point for recommended changes to the protocol.

4.1. Need for an extension

HTTP is a generic protocol that can be extended through new request methods, error codes, and headers. An extension is needed to allow the server to define the conditions under which prefetching (or any other non-demand request activity) is allowed or served.

The alternative to an extension is more appropriate use of the current protocol. One approach, say, to eliminate some wasted effort would be to use range-requests (much like Adobe's Acrobat Reader [2] does) to first request a portion of the document. If the document was small, then there is a chance the whole object will be retrieved. In any case, the headers would be available. A slight variation would be to use HEAD to get meta-information about the resource. That would allow the client to use some characteristics of the response (such as size or cacheability) to determine whether the retrieval is useful. These suggestions do not address the problems of request side-effects and high back-end overhead which would not be visible from headers, and in fact may be exacerbated by HEAD requests (e.g. if the server has to generate a dynamic response to calculate values such as Content-length). Neither do they allow for a variable quality of service at the Web server.

A second alternative would be to classify systems performing prefetching activity as robots, and require compliance with the so-called 'robot exclusion standard' [28]. However, conformity with this non-standard is voluntary, and is ignored by many robots. Further, compliance does not ensure a prevention of server abuse, as there is no restriction on request rates, allowing robots to overload a server at whim.

A third approach would be to incorporate a mechanism to support mandatory extensions to HTTP without protocol revisions. Such a mechanism has been proposed in Experimental RFC 2774 [37], which allows for the definition of mandatory headers. It modifies existing methods by prefixing them with 'M-' to signify that a response to such a request must fulfill the requirements of the mandatory headers, or report an error. If RFC 2774 were widely supported, this proposal might only need to suggest the definition of new mandatory headers that allow for prefetching and other non-interactive requests to be identified.

4.2. Previous proposals

Other researchers have proposed extensions to HTTP to support prefetching in one form or another.

- In his masters thesis, Lee [31] prepared a draft proposal for additional HTTP/1.1 headers and methods. PREDICT-GET is the same as GET, but allows for separate statistical logging (so that logs are not skewed with prefetching requests). PREDICT-GOT is a method equivalent to HEAD, but is to be used as a way for the client to tell the server that the prefetched item was eventually requested by the client. Lee also lists new headers that would specify what kinds of predictions are desired by the client, and the kinds of predictions returned by the server.
- Padmanabhan and Mogul [38] suggest adding a new response header to carry predictions (termed Prediction) that would provide a list of URLs, their probabilities, and possibly their size.
- Duchamp [20] defines a new HTTP header (termed Prefetch) along with a number of directives. The new header is included in both requests and responses to pass information on resource usage by the client and suggested resources for prefetching by the server. The actual retrieval is performed using GET.

Unlike these proposals, we would like to see changes that are independent of a particular prediction technique.

4.3. Recommending changes

Any realistic set of changes will need to be agreed upon by a large part of the Web community, and so it makes sense to develop a proposal for these changes in consultation with many members of that community. However, there are certain aspects to the changes that appear to be sensible with respect to the type of prefetching described in this document.

We argue that a new method is needed. It should be treated similarly to the optional methods in HTTP/1.1. The capability of the server could be tested by attempting to use the new method, or by using the OPTIONS method to list supported methods. A new method provides safety – if a client uses a new method, older servers that do not yet support prefetching would return the 501 Not Implemented status code, rather than automatically serving the request, which would happen with the use of a new header accompanying a GET request. If the server does support these prefetching extensions, it would have the option to serve the request as if it were a normal GET, or at a lower-priority, or to deny the request with a 405 Method Not Allowed status code. When a client receives some kind of error code using the new method, it may choose to re-try the request with a traditional GET, but with the understanding that such action may have undesirable side-effects.

Therefore, we suggest a second version of GET (arbitrarily called `GET2`). A new header (possibly called `GET2-Constraint`) may also be useful to allow the client to specify constraints (e.g. `safe` to guarantee safety of the processing of this request, `max-size` to prevent fetching even a portion of an object that is too large, `min-fresh` to prevent fetching an object that will expire too quickly, `max-resp-time` to not bother if the response will take too long, etc.). Note that some of the `Cache-control` header values may be relevant here (like `min-fresh`), even though `GET2` requests may be made to servers as well as caches. Another header might be useful to allow client-type identification (e.g. interactive for browsers and other clients needing immediate response, non-interactive for prefetching systems that will eventually send this content to users, robot for non-interactive systems that will parse and use content directly, etc.), but it may also be sufficient to assume that `GET2` requests will only be generated by non-interactive systems. In summary, we recommend the development of a protocol extension that, when implemented by non-interactive clients that would otherwise use GET, allows for absolutely safe operation (no side-effects). When implemented by servers, gives them the ability to distinguish between interactive and non-interactive clients and thus potentially provide different levels of service.

5. Summary

The benefits of Web cache prefetching are well understood. Prefetching could be a standard feature of today's browsers and proxy caches. (Older versions of Netscape Navigator even have some prefetching code present, but disabled [36].) This paper has argued that the current support for prefetching in HTTP/1.1 is insufficient. Existing implementations can cause problems with undesirable side-effects and server abuse, and the potential for these problems may thwart additional development. We have made some initial suggestions of extensions to HTTP that would allow for safe prefetching, reduced server abuse, and differentiated Web server quality of service.

Overall, the conclusions we reach about the current state of affairs are the following:

- Prefetching with GET can be applied safely and efficiently between client and proxy under HTTP/1.1 using the `only-if-cached` and `min-fresh` options to the `Cache-control` header. Proxy resources can be abused, however, by a client prefetching content that will never be used, and prefetching effectiveness is limited to the contents of the cache.
- The safety nor efficiency of prefetching from an origin server cannot be guaranteed, as the origin server cannot does not recognize non-demand requests and so must serve every request, including requests for content that is uncacheable or has side effects.
- Proxies and origin servers cannot provide different qualities of service to demand and non-demand requests, again because they cannot distinguish between demand requests and non-demand requests (generated by prefetchers and Web robots).
- Much of the uncacheable content of the Web can be prefetched by clients in the sense that the content can be cached if semantic transparency is allowed to be compromised (although user warnings are still required under HTTP/1.1).

An extension to HTTP could rectify the second and third problems and allow for safe, semantically transparent prefetching for those systems which support it, and 'gracefully' degrade to the existing situation if necessary when the extension is not supported by either the client or the server. It is our hope that this paper will restart a dialog on these issues that will move in time into a standards development process.

Acknowledgments

Thanks are due to Vincenzo Liberatore, Chandresekar Krishnan, Haym Hirsh, and to anonymous referees for valuable suggestions. This work is supported in part by the National Science Foundation under grant NSF ANI 9903052.

Appendix A. Answers to prefetchability quiz in Fig. 1

As defined in Section 2.1, prefetchability depends on the cacheability and safety of the resource. However, only the content provider can determine each of those. Thus, a quiz on prefetchability is a bit of a trick question. Since each of these are home pages, we might get away with the assumption that retrieval of their contents is safe. Thus, we need only concern ourselves with cacheability. Fortunately, cacheability is well-defined, so we can test it (albeit after fetching at least the headers of the content)[4].

- http://www.cnn.com/ is cacheable for private (e.g. single-user) caches for the next 60 seconds. So, this page could be prefetched by a browser, but not by a generic proxy.
- http://www.ibm.com/ does not provide a validator (e.g. `Last-Modified` or `ETag header`) so it cannot be validated (and thus is imprudent to cache). The same can be said for the home pages of www.cacheflow.com, www.netscape.com, www.apple.com, www.inktomi.com, www.spidercache.com, www.google.com, www.eurosport.com, www.cisco.com, www.aol.com, www.att.com, www.f5.com, www.yahoo.com, www.altavista.com, www.redhat.com, and www.news.com.
- http://www.geocities.com/ has been explicitly marked stale, and uncacheable at all by intermediate proxies.
- http://www.microsoft.com/ does not have any explicit caching headers, but does include a validator. Likewise, www.akamai.com, www.netapp.com, www.infolibria.com, www.imimic.com, and www.fireclick.com have validators but no explicit expiration.
- http://www.napster.com/ has an explicit expiration of one day.
- http://www.volera.com/ has an explicit expiration of 15 minutes.
- http://www.bn.com/ is set to expire far in the past, and uncacheable by a proxy.

The moral of course is that one cannot tell the cacheability (let alone prefetchability) of a resource from its URL.

Appendix B. Excerpts from Draft Standard RFC 2616: 'Hypertext Transfer Protocol – HTTP/1.1' [24]

B.1. Safe and idempotent methods

B.1.1. Safe methods

Implementors should be aware that the software represents the user in their interactions over the Internet, and should be careful to allow the user to be aware of any actions they might take which may have an unexpected significance to themselves or others.

[4] These cacheability tests were performed in early June 2001 using the tools available at www.web-caching.com.

In particular, the convention has been established that the GET and HEAD methods SHOULD NOT have the significance of taking an action other than retrieval. These methods ought to be considered 'safe'. This allows user agents to represent other methods, such as POST, PUT and DELETE, in a special way, so that the user is made aware of the fact that a possibly unsafe action is being requested.

Naturally, it is not possible to ensure that the server does not generate side-effects as a result of performing a GET request; in fact, some dynamic resources consider that a feature. The important distinction here is that the user did not request the side-effects, so therefore cannot be held accountable for them.

B.1.2. Idempotent methods

Methods can also have the property of 'idempotence' in that (aside from error or expiration issues) the side-effects of $N > 0$ identical requests is the same as for a single request. The methods GET, HEAD, PUT and DELETE share this property. Also, the methods OPTIONS and TRACE SHOULD NOT have side effects, and so are inherently idempotent.

However, it is possible that a sequence of several requests is non- idempotent, even if all of the methods executed in that sequence are idempotent. (A sequence is idempotent if a single execution of the entire sequence always yields a result that is not changed by a reexecution of all, or part, of that sequence.) For example, a sequence is non-idempotent if its result depends on a value that is later modified in the same sequence.

A sequence that never has side effects is idempotent, by definition (provided that no concurrent operations are being executed on the same set of resources).

B.2. Side effects of GET *and* HEAD

Unless the origin server explicitly prohibits the caching of their responses, the application of GET and HEAD methods to any resources SHOULD NOT have side effects that would lead to erroneous behavior if these responses are taken from a cache. They MAY still have side effects, but a cache is not required to consider such side effects in its caching decisions. Caches are always expected to observe an origin server's explicit restrictions on caching.

We note one exception to this rule: since some applications have traditionally used GETs and HEADs with query URLs (those containing a '?' in the rel_path part) to perform operations with significant side effects, caches MUST NOT treat responses to such URIs as fresh unless the server provides an explicit expiration time. This specifically means that responses from HTTP/1.0 servers for such URIs SHOULD NOT be taken from a cache. See section 9.1.1 for related information.

References

[1] G. Aas. libwww-perl home page. http://www.linpro.no/lwp/, 2001.

[2] Adobe Systems Incorporated. Adobe Acrobat Reader. http://www.adobe.com/products/acrobat/readermain.html, 2001.

[3] D.W. Albrecht, I. Zukerman, and A.E. Nicholson. Pre-sending documents on the WWW: a comparative study. In *Proceedings of the Sixteenth International Joint Conference on Artificial Intelligence (IJCAI-99)*, volume 2, pages 1274–1279, Stockholm, Sweden, 1999. Morgan Kaufmann.

[4] M.K. Bergman. The deep Web: Surfacing hidden value. White paper, BrightPlanet.com, July 2000. Available from http://www.completeplanet.com/tutorials/deepweb/index.asp.

[5] T. Berners-Lee and D. Connolly. Hypertext markup language – 2.0. RFC 1866, http://ftp.isi.edu/in-notes/rfc1866.txt, Nov. 1995.

[6] T. Berners-Lee, R.T. Fielding, and L. Masinter. Uniform resource identifiers (URI): Generic syntax. RFC 2396, http://ftp.isi.edu/in-notes/rfc2396.txt, Aug. 1998.

[7] T. Berners-Lee, L. Masinter, and M. McCahill. Uniform resource locators (URL). RFC 1738, http://ftp.isi.edu/in-notes/rfc1738.txt, Dec. 1994.

[8] N. Bhatti, A. Bouch, and A. Kuchinsky. Integrating user-perceived quality into Web server design. In *Proceedings of the Ninth International World Wide Web Conference*, Amsterdam, May 2000.

[9] O. Brandman, J. Cho, H. Garcia-Molina, and S. Shivakumar. Crawler-friendly Web servers. *Performance Evaluation Review*, 28(2), Sept. 2000. Presented at the Performance and Architecture of Web Servers (PAWS) Workshop, June 2000.

[10] CacheFlow Inc. Active caching technology. http://www.cacheflow.com/technology/whitepapers/active.cfm, 2001.

[11] K.-i. Chinen and S. Yamaguchi. An interactive prefetching proxy server for improvement of WWW latency. In *Proceedings of the Seventh Annual Conference of the Internet Society (INET'97)*, Kuala Lumpur, June 1997.

[12] E. Cohen and H. Kaplan. Prefetching the means for document transfer: A new approach for reducing Web latency. In *Proceedings of IEEE INFOCOM*, Tel Aviv, Israel, Mar. 2000.

[13] E. Cohen and H. Kaplan. Refreshment Policies for Web Content Caches. In *Proceedings of IEEE INFOCOM*, Anchorage, AK, Apr. 2001.

[14] E. Cohen, B. Krishnamurthy, and J. Rexford. Efficient algorithms for predicting requests to Web servers. In *IEEE INFOCOM '99*, New York, Mar. 1999.

[15] M. Crovella and P. Barford. The Network Effects of Prefetching. In *Proceedings of IEEE INFOCOM*, San Francisco, CA, 1998. More detailed version available as Boston University Computer Science Department Technical Report, TR-97-002, February 1997.

[16] C.R. Cunha and C.F.B. Jaccoud. Determining WWW User's Next Access and Its Application to Prefetching. In *Proceedings of Second IEEE Symposium on Computers and Communications (ISCC'97)*, Alexandria, Egypt, July 1997.

[17] B.D. Davison. Simultaneous Proxy Evaluation. In *Proceedings of the Fourth International Web Caching Workshop (WCW99)*, pages 170–178, San Diego, CA, Mar. 1999.

[18] B.D. Davison. Web traffic logs: An imperfect resource for evaluation. In *Proceedings of the Ninth Annual Conference of the Internet Society (INET'99)*, June 1999.

[19] A. Dingle and T. Partl. Web cache coherence. *Computer Networks and ISDN Systems*, 28(7–11): 907–920, May 1996.

[20] D. Duchamp. Prefetching hyperlinks. In *Proceedings of the Second USENIX Symposium on Internet Technologies and Systems (USITS '99)*, Boulder, CO, Oct. 1999.

[21] eAcceleration Corporation. Webcelerator help page on prefetching. http://www.webcelerator.com/webcelerator/prefetch.htm, 2001.

[22] eAcceleration Corporation. Webcelerator home page. http://www.webcelerator.com/webcelerator/, 2001.

[23] L. Fan, Q. Jacobson, P. Cao, and W. Lin. Web Prefetching Between Low-Bandwidth Clients and Proxies: Potential and Performance. In *Proceedings of the Joint International Conference on Measurement and Modeling of Computer Systems (SIGMETRICS '99)*, Atlanta, GA, May 1999.

[24] R.T. Fielding, J. Gettys, J.C. Mogul, H. Frystyk, L. Masinter, P. Leach, and T. Berners-Lee. Hypertext Transfer Protocol – HTTP/1.1. RFC 2616, http://ftp.isi.edu/in-notes/rfc2616.txt, June 1999.

[25] K. Holtman. The safe response header field. RFC 2310, http://ftp.isi.edu/in-notes/rfc2310.txt, Apr. 1998.

[26] Z. Jiang and L. Kleinrock. An adaptive network prefetch scheme. *IEEE Journal on Selected Areas in Communications*, 16(3): 358–368, Apr. 1998.

[27] R.P. Klemm. WebCompanion: A friendly client-side Web prefetching agent. *IEEE Transactions on Knowledge and Data Engineering*, 11(4): 577–594, July/August 1999.

[28] M. Koster. A standard for robot exclusion. Available from: http://www.robotstxt.org/wc/norobots.html, 1994.

[29] B. Krishnamurthy and J. Rexford. Software Issues in Characterizing Web Server Logs. In *World Wide Web Consortium Workshop on Web Characterization*, Cambridge, MA, Nov. 1998. Position paper.

[30] T.M. Kroeger, D.D.E. Long, and J.C. Mogul. Exploring the Bounds of Web Latency Reduction from Caching and Prefetching. In *Proceedings of the USENIX Symposium on Internet Technologies and Systems (USITS '97)*, Dec. 1997.

[31] D.C. Lee. Pre-fetch document caching to improve World-Wide Web user response time. Master's thesis, Virginia Tech., Blacksburg, VA, Mar. 1996.

[32] J.C. Luh. No bots allowed! *Interactive Week*, Apr. 2001. Online at http://www.zdnet.com/intweek/stories/news/0,4164,2707542,00.html.

[33] E.P. Markatos and C.E. Chronaki. A top-10 approach for prefetching the Web. In *Proceedings of the Eighth Annual Conference of the Internet {S}ociety (INET'98)*, Geneva, Switzerland, July 1998.

[34] J.C. Mogul. Hinted caching in the Web. In *Proceedings of the Seventh ACM SIGOPS European Workshop*, Connemara, Ireland, Sept. 1996.

[35] J.C. Mogul and P. Leach. Simple hit-metering and usage-limiting for HTTP. RFC 2227, http://ftp.isi.edu/in-notes/rfc2227.txt, Oct. 1997.

[36] Netscape, Inc. Mozilla source code. Available at http://lxr.mozilla.org/classic/, 1999.

[37] H. Nielsen, P. Leach, and S. Lawrence. An HTTP extension framework. RFC 2774, http://ftp.isi.edu/in-notes/rfc2774.txt, Feb. 2000.

[38] V.N. Padmanabhan and J.C. Mogul. Using predictive prefetching to improve World Wide Web latency. *Computer Communication Review*, 26(3): 22–36, July 1996. Proceedings of SIGCOMM '96.

[39] T. Palpanas. Web prefetching using partial match prediction. Master's thesis, Department of Computer Science, University of Toronto, Toronto, Ontario, CA, Mar. 1998. Available as Technical Report CSRG-376.

[40] PeakSoft Corporation. PeakJet 2000 web page. http://www.peaksoft.com/peakjet2.html, 2001.

[41] J. Pelline. Accelerators cause headaches. *c|net News.com*, Dec. 1996. http://news.cnet.com/news/0,10000,0-1003-200-314937,00.html.

[42] J.E. Pitkow and P.L. Pirolli. Mining longest repeated subsequences to predict World Wide Web surfing. In *Proceedings of the Second USENIX Symposium on Internet Technologies and Systems*, Oct. 1999.

[43] S. Raghavan and H. Garcia-Molina. Crawling the Hidden Web. Technical Report 2000-36, Computer Science Dept., Stanford University, Dec. 2000.

[44] S. Schechter, M. Krishnan, and M.D. Smith. Using path profiles to predict HTTP requests. In *Proceedings of the Seventh International World Wide Web Conference*, Brisbane, Australia, Apr. 1998.

[45] N. Swaminathan and S.V. Raghavan. Intelligent prefetching in WWW using client behavior characterization. In *Proceedings of the Eighth International Symposium on Modeling, Analysis and Simulation of Computer and Telecommunication Systems (MASCOTS)*, 2000.

[46] Z. Wang and J. Crowcroft. Prefetching in World-Wide Web. In *Proceedings of IEEE Globecom*, London, Dec. 1996.

[47] Web 3000 Inc. NetSonic Internet Accelerator web page. http://www.web3000.com/, 2001.

[48] C.E. Wills and M. Mikhailov. Studying the impact of more complete server information on Web caching. In *Proceedings of the Fifth International Web Caching and Content Delivery Workshop*, Lisbon, Portugal, May 2000.

[49] World Wide Web Consortium. Libwww – the w3c sample code library. http://www.w3.org/Library/, 2001.

Panel 3 – Rule-Based Active Edge Services

Moderator: Micah Beck, *University of Tennessee and Lokomo Systems*

Panelists: Markus Hofmann, *Lucent Technologies*
Wei-Ying Ma, *Microsoft Research China*
Mark Nottingham, *Akamai Technologies*

Web Caching and Content Delivery
A. Bestavros and M. Rabinovich (Editors)

Thin-Client Web Access Patterns: Measurements from a Cache-Busting Proxy

Terence Kelly [1]

Electrical Engineering and Computer Science, University of Michigan, Ann Arbor, MI 48109, USA

Abstract

This paper describes a new technique for measuring Web client request patterns and analyzes a large client trace collected using the new method. In this approach a modified proxy intercepts requests and serves all responses to clients marked uncacheable, effectively disabling browser caches and allowing the proxy to record requests that would otherwise result in silent browser cache hits. WebTV Networks used a 'cache-busting proxy' to collect an unusually large and detailed anonymized Web client trace in September 2000. It contains over 347 million requests for over 36 million documents by over 37,000 clients and spans 16 days. By most measures it is two orders of magnitude larger than existing Web client traces. We compare cache-busting proxies with conventional client instrumentation and use the WebTV trace to explore browser cache performance, reference locality, and document aliasing. We present the aggregate browser cache success function (hit rate vs. cache size) of the *entire client population* and discuss design implications for memory- and bandwidth-constrained Web clients. For the workload studied, eliminating redundant data transfers would increase browser cache hit rates by at least 35% to 45% over their current levels. A simple and practical technique for eliminating redundant transfers is described. Document sharing across client reference streams is so strong that the hit rate of a shared proxy cache could exceed 57% even if browser caches were infinitely large.

Keywords: World Wide Web; WebTV; Client trace; Browser trace; Instrumentation; Workload characterization; Duplicate suppression; Hit rates; Cache simulation; Success function; LRU stack distance; Lognormal models

1. Introduction

To design efficient and cost-effective systems we must understand the workloads submitted to them. World Wide Web workload consists of two fundamental components: the universe of data made available by servers, and client requests for these data. This paper deals with the latter aspect of Web workload. We discuss a new technique for measuring Web client request streams and describe how it was used to collect a large and detailed trace at WebTV Networks. The paper also presents a preliminary workload

[1] E-mail: tpkelly@eecs.umich.edu

analysis, including simulation results describing the aggregate hit rate of the entire client population as a function of browser cache size. For the workload studied the potential benefits of eliminating redundant proxy-to-browser transfers are large, and we describe a simple way to obtain these benefits.

Empirical Web caching research is largely based on proxy logs. Implementors and administrators regard these logs primarily as security features; consequently the logging capabilities of most proxies are not well suited to research. Logs rarely record all of the data available to the proxy and typically omit information crucial to accurate trace-driven simulation. In particular, they fail to record cache-related HTTP metadata in reply headers and '`META http-equiv`' tags within HTML files, reply entity-bodies or their hashes, and accurate, high-resolution timestamps. Davison and Cáceres et al. have described the shortcomings of conventional proxy log formats [14,18].

In a few cases researchers have instrumented browsers to collect Web client traces [15, 17]. In principle, such traces support arbitrarily realistic bottom-up explorations of cache hierarchies and shed light on user interactions invisible outside the client. Unfortunately, today most researchers cannot instrument popular browsers because source code is unavailable. Even if it were, it is difficult to deploy an instrumented browser among a large and representative sample of Web users. Furthermore, if such a feat were possible it would still be difficult to synchronize large numbers of client clocks, and without precise event timestamps accurate simulation of a cache hierarchy is impossible. Finally, elaborate browser instrumentation may not be an option in severely memory-constrained client devices.

Another problem with existing proxy and client traces is that most were collected in idiosyncratic environments, e.g., academic computer science departments and computer corporations. Finally, nearly all existing traces were generated by heavyweight clients: full-featured browsers running on desktop PCs or engineering workstations. They may not be representative of workloads on the memory- and bandwidth-constrained browsers that are proliferating as the Web expands onto set-top boxes and wireless handheld devices.

This paper describes a technique that combines the relative ease of proxy logging with some of the advantages of client instrumentation. In this method a 'cache-busting proxy' intercepts requests from unmodified clients and labels all replies uncacheable, thereby disabling browser caches and allowing the proxy to log requests that would otherwise be served silently from browser caches. An informal survey of Web researchers reveals that this technique has been proposed before; it was discussed by a group at Boston University in late 1999 [13] and is described in a recent book by Krishnamurthy and Rexford [24]. However to the best of our knowledge it has never before been used.

In September 2000 WebTV Networks collected a large anonymized trace of client accesses using a cache-busting proxy. The proxy itself ran in non-caching mode; the trace therefore reflects activity in a cacheless system. The proxy furthermore recorded a checksum of every entity-body (data payload) received from origin servers, as well as a checksum of the (possibly different) entity-body served to the client after transcoding by the proxy. All events in this trace are timestamped at microsecond resolution by well-synchronized proxy clocks. The proxy recorded all cache-related HTTP metadata in client requests, server reply headers, and '`META http-equiv`' tags in HTML files. WebTV's trace spans 16 days and records over 347 million requests to over 36 million documents by over 37,000 clients; it is two orders of magnitude larger than any client trace described in the Web caching literature.

This paper presents a preliminary analysis of the WebTV trace and describes how it was recorded. Careful capacity planning based on workload measurement is essential in large-scale deployments of spartan clients, where neither storage nor bandwidth are cheap or abundant. Therefore the relationship between browser cache size and performance is our primary concern. An efficient single-pass simulation algorithm permits us to compute arbitrarily-weighted hit rates at *every* cache size for *each* client in the WebTV trace [23]. It is straightforward to aggregate individual client success functions to obtain hit rate as a function of cache size for the entire client population, and this is the centerpiece of our analysis. Reference locality and document aliasing have performance implications, and we shall explore these issues as well.

Our main finding is that browser cache hit rates would increase substantially if redundant payload transfers resulting from unnecessary cache misses were eliminated, and we describe a simple and practical way to eliminate redundant transfers.

2. Related work

Researchers have investigated in detail the workload placed on *components* of the World Wide Web, e.g., servers, proxies, and networks [4–9,19–21,38,39]. However, little is known about the workload placed on the Web *as a system*, i.e., the universe of available documents and patterns of client requests. Recently Padmanabhan and Qiu have investigated content creation and modification dynamics at a large, busy Web site [34]; this is the only systematic study of available content (not to be confused with *requested* content, i.e., server access patterns) of which we are aware.

The situation is only slightly better at the client end, where true client traces – request streams not filtered by browser caches – are extremely rare. The Web Characterization Repository [1] contains several proxy and server workloads but only a single client trace, collected at Boston University's Computer Science Department in 1995. Catledge and Pitkow recorded a client trace at Georgia Tech's CS department in 1994. Both the BU and Georgia Tech traces are remarkably rich, recording a wide variety of user-interface events unavailable outside the browser. Together these two traces have supported a number of interesting studies [12,15–17]. Unfortunately, as Netscape and Microsoft Internet Explorer displaced the open-source Mosaic browser in the late 1990s it became difficult for researchers to instrument Web browsers, and no true client traces have been collected since 1995 [2].

Table 1 summarizes the aforementioned Web client traces, more recent proxy and server traces used in References [6,7,28,39], an AFS client trace [32] and the WebTV trace that is the subject of this paper. The most striking feature of Table 1 is the large size difference between the early client traces and the more recent proxy and server traces; by nearly every measure the latter are orders of magnitude larger. The difficulty of deploying an instrumented browser on large numbers of clients is largely responsible for the difference.

To summarize, the few existing Web client traces are several years old, reflect the requests of computer science students, and are small in comparison with server and proxy traces. By contrast server and proxy traces are often large and sometimes describe more

[2] A 1999 sequel to the original B.U. study used a trace that did not reflect browser cache hits [10].

Table 1. Traces used in Web and file system research. Dynamic IP addresses prevented a precise count of clients in the Cable Modem trace [3]. The number of distinct documents is not known for the Compaq data [27]

Trace	Type	Begin	End	Clients	Objects	Requests	Requests per Client per Day
CITI AFS	client	20 Oct 93	20 Dec 93	37	N/A	12,192,933	5,402
Georgia Tech.	client	3 Aug 94	24 Aug 94	107	9,452	43,060	19
Boston U.	client	21 Nov 94	17 Jan 95	600	46,830	575,775	17
Cable Modem	proxy	3 Jan 97	31 May 97	≈1000s	16,110,126	117,652,652	
World Cup	server	1 May 98	23 Jul 98	2,770,108	20,728	1,352,804,107	6
Compaq WRL	proxy	1 Jan 99	31 Mar 99	≈25,000	N/A	125,259,641	54
U. Washington	proxy	7 May 99	14 May 99	22,984	≈18,400,000	≈82,800,000	515
Microsoft	proxy	7 May 99	14 May 99	60,233	≈15,300,000	≈107,700,000	286
WebTV	client	7 Sep 00	22 Sep 00	37,169	36,573,327	347,483,200	425

representative user populations but typically omit much information in the original client request streams, e.g., references served from browser caches. Section 3 describes a collection methodology that combines some of the advantages of client and proxy traces and explains how this technique was used to measure Web client workload on a very large scale.

3. Trace collection

With over a million active subscribers WebTV Networks is among the largest ISPs, and its customer base is arguably more representative of the general public than the traditional subjects of Web traces (computer science students and computer industry employees). Furthermore the WebTV system is extraordinarily well integrated, providing essentially everything but the origin server: client hardware, browser software, proxies, and Internet connectivity. Most importantly, WebTV staff constantly monitor and tune the system to improve its performance, frequently adding new instrumentation as new questions arise. For these reasons WebTV is an ideal environment for Web-related research.

WebTV clients represent an interesting intermediate point in design space, midway between the resource-rich PC-based browsers of the early Web and the ultra-thin clients of tomorrow. WebTV employs a relatively inexpensive (often diskless) set-top box to enable Web surfing on a conventional television. Five types of client devices were in use during September 2000; see Table 2. Clients connect to the WebTV service via modem; according to WebTV's measurements, bandwidth to clients varies but is typically roughly 33.6 Kbps.

Our original goal was to collect a client trace using instrumented browsers. WebTV frequently downloads software updates to its client devices, so at first this seemed a straightforward approach. However a combination of logistical difficulties and schedule constraints forced us to seek an alternative approach. Compared with client software modifications, proxy patches are much easier to implement and deploy and are far more frequent in practice. We therefore decided to record unfiltered client requests by disabling the browser cache with a modified proxy.

Table 2. WebTV client devices

Type	Description	Cache size		# in trace	H.R. (%)
		RAM	disk		
FCS	'Classic'	420 KB		8,790	37.64
BPS	No-frills	1240 KB		11,253	41.94
LC2.5	'Plus'	3200 KB		7,370	44.41
LC2	Diskful Plus	1 MB	20 MB	8,535	44.64
ST1	Satellite	3 MB	20 MB	1,221	44.81

A sophisticated centralized service infrastructure compensates for WebTV clients' limitations by transcoding images, re-writing HTML, and maintaining persistent state (e.g., cookies). Sixteen modified proxies collected WebTV's client trace, with the following non-standard features enabled during data collection:

- events were timestamped at microsecond resolution;
- checksums were logged of all entity bodies received from origin servers and all entity bodies served to clients after transcoding;
- all metadata relevant to caching in client requests, server reply headers, and embedded HTML tags were logged;
- all documents were served to clients with an '`Expires: 0`' HTTP header[3];
- the proxy itself was run in non-caching mode.

During normal operations WebTV proxies process every byte of every data payload, so the performance penalty of computing checksums was relatively minor; similarly, the proxies normally parse META tags in HTML. The number of proxy hosts that collected data was twice as large as would normally be used for our sample client population, so the proxies were not overloaded as they recorded the trace. All trace fields related to user identity and requested content are anonymized to protect user privacy.

META tags are necessary for correct browser cache simulations and are furthermore interesting because they illustrate discrepancies between HTML-embedded metadata and HTTP headers. For instance, META expiration dates often disagree with HTTP expirations. Of over 149 million requests issued during 16–22 September, 95,558 have expiration dates in both headers and META tags. Among these requests the META expiration is earlier than the response header expiration 21.8% of the time; ignoring the HTML-embedded expiration could cause consistency violations in some of these cases. In 141,159 cases an expiration is specified only in a META tag; unnecessary revalidations would result from ignoring the embedded metadata in some of these cases.

WebTV proxy host clocks are carefully synchronized using Network Time Protocol [26]. A script queried the proxies with `ntpq` at ten-minute intervals throughout the data-collection period to check their clock synchronization; Fig. 1 shows the distribution of observed NTP parameters. The absolute offset of the proxies with respect to an accurate reference is nearly always under 10 milliseconds.

A sample of client devices was 'attached' to our modified proxy bank throughout the data collection period, i.e., all Web sessions initiated by these devices were handled by the special proxies. WebTV clients communicate directly with origin servers for secure

[3] Caching pre-expired objects is legal in HTTP/1.1 [22], but WebTV clients do not do so.

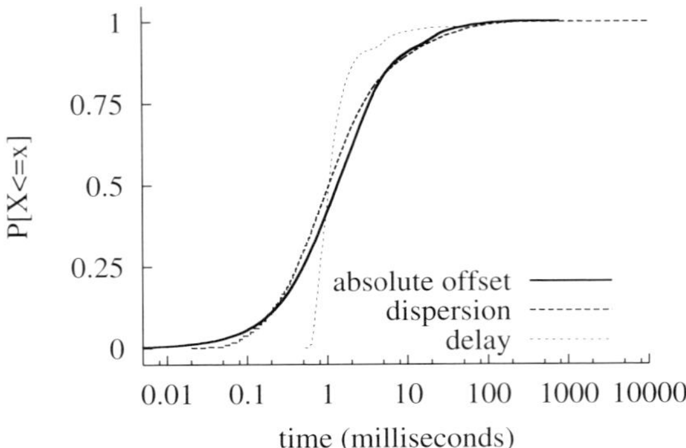

Fig. 1. Distribution of NTP parameters during data collection.

transactions, which are therefore not reflected in our trace. Furthermore the trace contains only HTTP requests; we did not record the small volume of FTP and Gopher traffic handled by the proxies.

We began serving documents pre-expired on 6 September 2000. The number of requests per hour reaching our proxies promptly doubled, as illustrated in Fig. 2. By comparing request volumes from each client device type before and after 6 September we obtain crude estimates of browser cache hit rates; estimates based on requests of 4–5 vs. 11–12 September are shown in Table 2. This technique must be used with care, because our sample browser caches did not cease to operate on 6 September, they merely ceased to cache incoming documents. It is reasonable to suppose that many browser caches remained 'warm' even after our experiment began, serving some fraction of requests from cache. We gain insight into browser cache 'cool down' from the percentage of revalidation requests ('`If-Modified-Since`') reaching our proxies from each device type over time, as shown in Fig. 3.

Rich-client browsers typically use separate regions of memory to hold the currently-viewed document and to cache previously-viewed objects; the contents of the cache therefore change only when new items are cached. In the memory-constrained WebTV client, however, the same region of memory is used as both a 'staging area' for the current

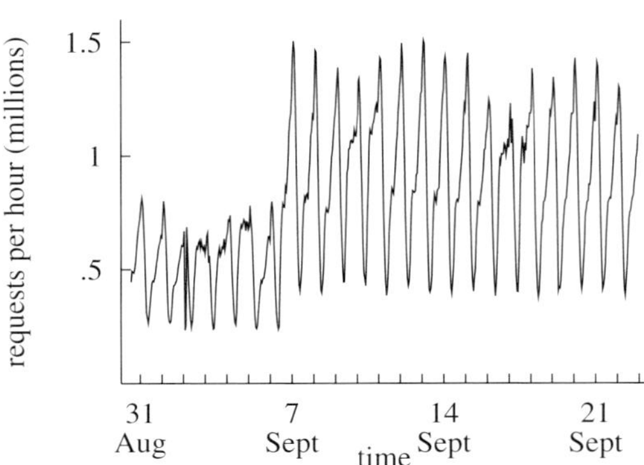

Fig. 2. Hourly request volume.

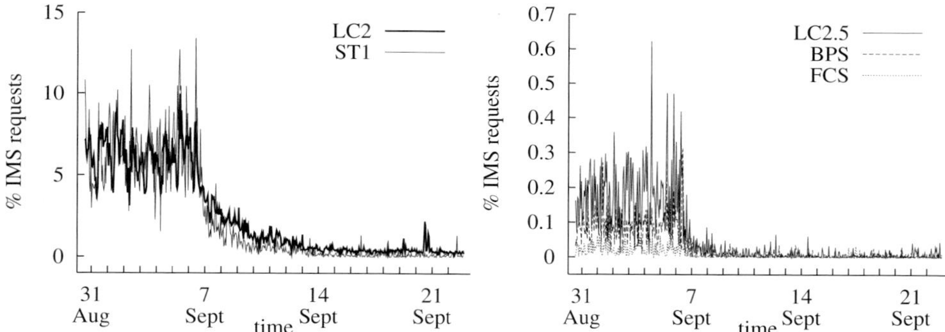

Fig. 3. Percentage of IMS requests from diskful (left) and diskless (right) clients, 1-hour bins. Vertical scales differ.

item and as cache for previously-requested items. Large incoming documents therefore cause cache evictions *even if they are not cached themselves*. This accounts for the rapid decrease in IMS requests in Fig. 3. Collectively, the browser caches in our sample are never flushed completely; even after two weeks IMS requests reach our proxies, possibly from clients with low activity levels. However the fraction of IMS requests quickly falls to negligible levels, particularly for diskless clients. Our estimates of browser cache hit rate are based on proxy request volumes several days after cache busting began, by which time most browser caches have cooled substantially. However it is possible that our estimated hit rates for diskful clients are slightly low.

In retrospect, we realize that we might have obtained better results from a more thorough cache-busting proxy that attempted to forcibly flush browser caches, e.g., by serving an HTML file with a large number of newline characters appended to it. Alternately, we might have served replies with expiration dates equal to the current time plus one second; we would then see IMS requests in most cases that would otherwise be browser cache hits.

Table 3 summarizes the WebTV trace. As noted above, it is roughly as large in most respects as recent proxy traces and substantially larger than mid-90s Web client traces. Furthermore it reflects a client sample comparable to the entire end-user population served

Table 3. WebTV trace summary statistics. All sizes in bytes. Asterisk (*) indicates figures based on successful requests only

Clients	37,169	
Payloads (entity-bodies)	36,573,327	
Total requests	347,483,200	
Successful requests	325,591,889	
Sum of payload sizes	640,177,065,087	
Bytes transferred*	4,376,249,806,158	

	mean	median
Payload size	17,504	5,493
Transfer size*	13,441	2,916
Requests per client*	8,760	3,326

by NLANR's cache hierarchy, which is thought to be under 100,000.[4] The compressed trace occupies roughly 101.6 GB on disk.

4. Preliminary analysis

A thorough workload characterization of the WebTV trace is the subject of ongoing research; this section presents only a brief preliminary analysis. For simplicity and also for computational reasons we focus on the entity-bodies returned by origin servers rather than the URLs and request headers submitted by clients. For brevity we shall often use the terms 'document' or 'payload' instead of 'entity-body.' Throughout this section we consider only successful requests (response code 200); the trace records over 325 million such events (93.7% of the total). We equate a document with its payload checksum and define its size to be the largest document-size-related reply header associated with it; size therefore includes protocol overhead. Fig. 4 shows the distributions of document and transfer sizes.

Fig. 5 shows the percentage of replies containing never-before-seen payloads in non-overlapping windows of 10,000,000 requests for the first 320 million references in the WebTV trace. This is identical to the minimal miss rate of the overall WebTV system, assuming caches so large that capacity misses never occur. The figure shows that in the absence of redundant payload transfers the steady-state hit rate of an infinitely large WebTV proxy serving cacheless clients exceeds 90%; even a cold proxy cache would enjoy an 80% hit rate. In practice, imperfect cache consistency mechanisms and namespace complexities (aliasing) cause unnecessary cache misses and redundant payload transfers. Section 5 describes a simple and practical way to eliminate these problems entirely and raise hit rates to the full potential suggested by Fig. 5.

Client activity levels span a wide range. Fig. 6 shows the distribution of the number of requests and total bytes transferred to clients in the WebTV trace. Graphical evidence

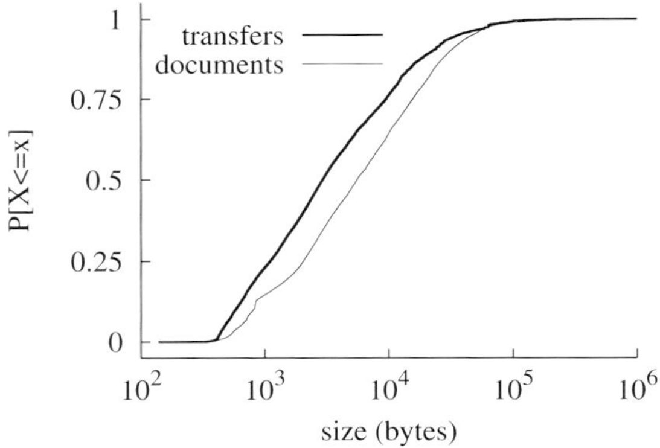

Fig. 4. Distribution of document and transfer sizes.

[4] NLANR caches' `x-forwarded-for` logs recorded 98,144 unique 'leaf' IP addresses during the first 26 days of October 2000 [37]. This may over-estimate the end-user population due to the use of dynamic IP addresses.

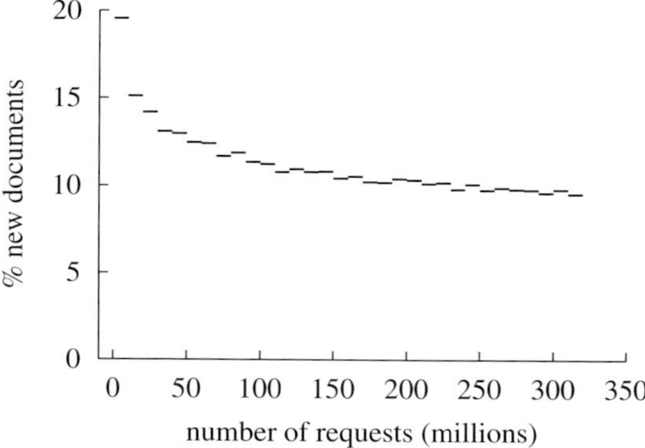

Fig. 5. Percentage of replies containing new documents.

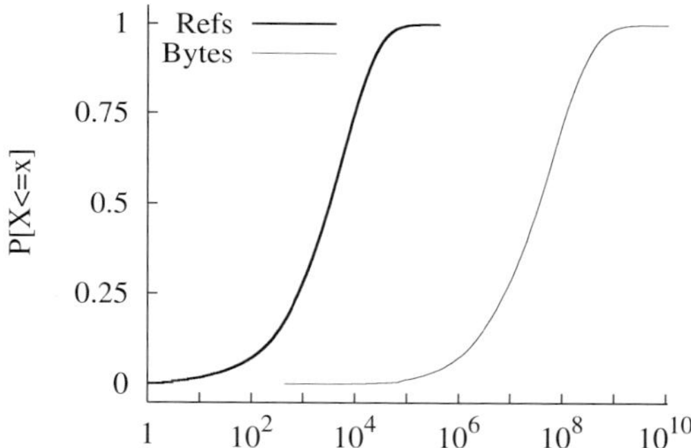

Fig. 6. Distribution of references/client and bytes/client.

suggests that these distributions are roughly lognormal, i.e., the logarithm of requests-per-client and of bytes-per-client appears to be roughly Gaussian, as illustrated in Fig. 7. The figure shows histograms of log-transformed data superimposed over a normal curve defined by sample mean and sample variance.

Similarly, graphical evidence suggests that the distribution of LRU stack distances at the client may be lognormal (Fig. 7, right; the data shown are from a sample of requests from a subset of BPS clients, described below). This distribution is closely related to

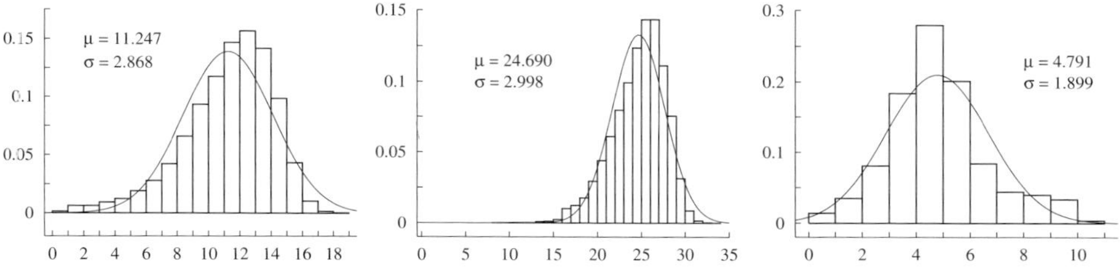

Fig. 7. Histograms of $\log_2$-transformed data: *Left:* references/client. *Center:* bytes/client. *Right:* stack distances in BPS sample.

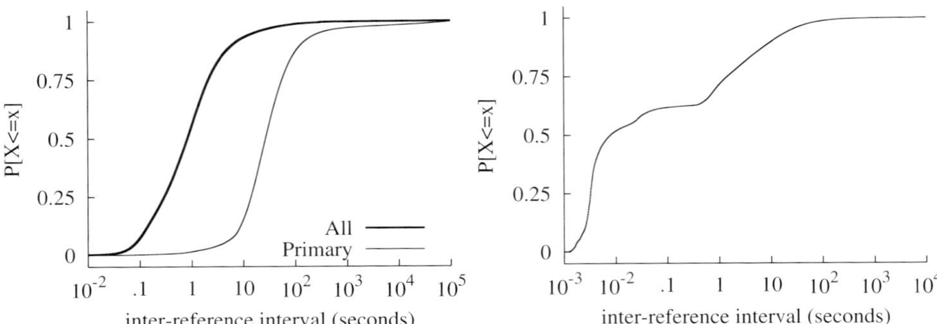

Fig. 8. Distribution of inter-reference intervals in WebTV (left) and Boston University (right) client traces.

the success function of an LRU cache [23,25] and is often used to measure temporal locality in reference streams [2,9]. Almeida et al. report that references reaching *servers* appear to have lognormal stack distance distributions, and that lognormal stack distance models predict cache success functions well [2]. We have not yet tested the usefulness of lognormal models in predicting hit rates for the WebTV data.

We might expect bandwidth-constrained thin clients to 'surf' at different rates than conventional rich-client browsers in academic or corporate environments. Fig. 8 shows the distribution of inter-reference intervals for the last seven days of the WebTV trace and for the Boston University client trace. WebTV requests corresponding to user-initiated actions are marked as 'primary' in the trace, and the distribution of intervals between primary references is plotted separately for WebTV. The Boston distribution is bi-modal due to browser cache hits (compound objects, e.g., HTML pages with embedded images, are *not* responsible; such objects are present in both traces). The WebTV data reflect a cacheless low-bandwidth environment, and therefore it is somewhat surprising that WebTV browsers appear to be operating roughly as fast as Xmosaic: 89.5% of BU requests are served in 10 seconds or less; for WebTV the figure is 93%.

Fig. 9 shows the distribution of maximal browser hit rates under ideal conditions for the observed request sequences, and the distribution of browser cache sizes required to achieve maximal hit rates. 'Ideal conditions' means that the first request that yields a given payload is a miss, but all subsequent requests that would return the same payload

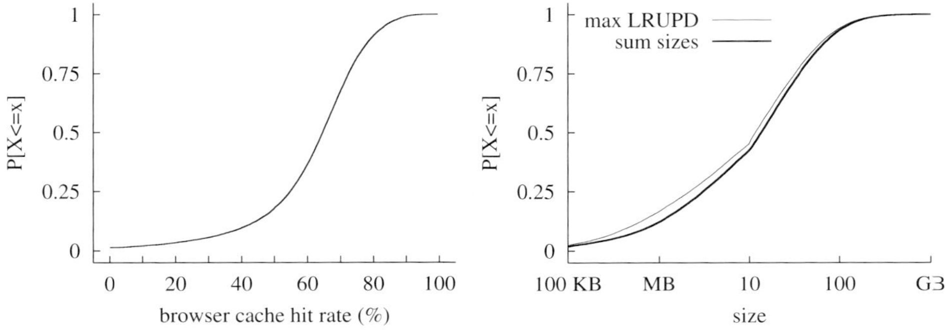

Fig. 9. Distribution of maximal browser hit rates (left) and effectively infinite browser cache sizes (right).

are hits. In other words, no redundant transfers occur, and only compulsory misses occur. This is similar to the 'perfect coherency' cache considered by Mogul [28–30], but it assumes no misses due to aliasing. In Mogul's terminology, we simulate a 'perfect duplicate suppression' cache large enough to store all requested documents. We see from the left-hand subfigure that the median of maximal individual browser hit rates is roughly 65%.

A browser cache attains maximal hit rate if it can store all requested documents; the sum of distinct payload sizes is therefore termed the 'infinite cache size' of a request sequence. However if we assume LRU replacement we can compute the maximal *priority depth* across references in a workload [23]; this is the smallest LRU cache size that experiences no capacity misses. The distribution of infinite cache sizes and maximal LRU priority depths is shown on the right of Fig. 9. For the workloads studied an 11.6 MB LRU cache is effectively infinite for half of clients.

Muntz and Honeyman report that hit rates of shared intermediate caches in network file systems will not exceed 20% if reference streams are filtered by even small client caches [31]. The WebTV data, however, point to a dramatically different conclusion: Assuming *infinite* browser caches and perfect duplicate suppression, 73.4% of requests would be served from browser caches. Of the remaining requests, 57.7% could be served from a sufficiently large shared proxy cache.

We obtain a complete picture of the relationship between browser cache size and hit rate by computing each client's success function (hit rate as a function of cache size) separately, assuming LRU replacement. We now permit capacity misses, but as before no redundant transfers occur. Efficient single-pass simultaneous simulation algorithms for this computation have long been available for the special case where document sizes and miss penalties are uniform [11,33,36] and have recently been generalized to non-uniform sizes and miss costs [23]. Using the Reeves-Kelly algorithm we first compute browser cache hit rates for each client at every cache size. We then aggregate the results into a single success function for the entire client population.[5]

To avoid the confounding effects of cache cool-down (Fig. 3) and cold-start, we also perform the same exercise for a sample of 1,959 modern diskless (BPS) clients with moderately heavy request volumes (between median and 75th percentiles) and moderate locality (maximal browser cache hit rates between the 25th and 75th percentiles). We use each client's first 2,000 references to warm the browser cache and tabulate hit rates based only on its next 1,000 requests. Results for both the BPS sample and the entire client population are shown in Fig. 10; the estimates of actual WebTV browser hit rates from Table 2 are included for comparison. Our results are comparable to the success function presented in Fig. 5 of Bestavros et al., which assumes LFU replacement [12].

Aggregate browser cache success functions are needed in order to make informed tradeoffs between browser functionality and cache hit rates in thin-client systems such as WebTV. New versions of browser software support new features and therefore require

[5] Kelly and Reeves note that fast simultaneous simulation yields correct results only for cache sizes no smaller than the largest document in a trace [23]. This is true for rich-client browsers such as Netscape and IE, in which replies larger than the cache do not alter its contents. The memory-constrained WebTV browser, however, uses the same region of memory as both a cache and a staging area for the document currently being viewed. A reply larger than the cache will therefore flush the browser cache's contents. Stack methods can simulate WebTV-like browser caches at *all* cache sizes.

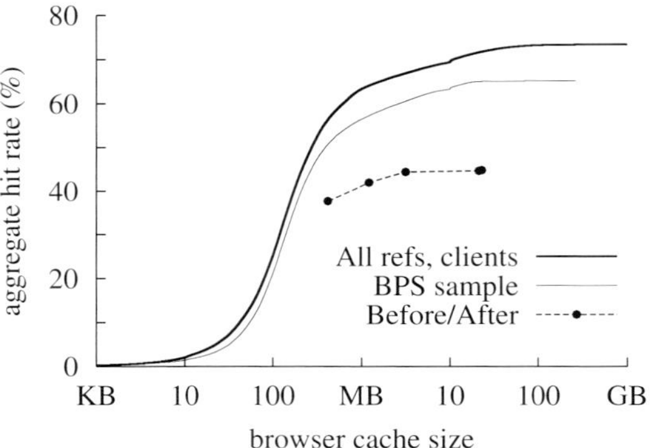

Fig. 10. Aggregate WebTV client success function.

Table 4. Percent relative improvement (R.I.) over current hit rates

Type	Cache Size	Measured H.R. (%)	BPS sample		All clients	
			H.R.	R.I.	H.R.	R.I.
FCS	420 KB	37.6	50.8	35.1	56.4	50.0
BPS	1240 KB	41.9	57.3	36.8	64.1	53.0
LC2.5	3200 KB	44.4	60.6	36.5	66.9	50.7
LC2	21 MB	44.6	65.1	46.0	71.7	60.8
ST1	23 MB	44.8	65.1	45.3	71.8	60.3

more resources, e.g., RAM, but capacity expansion is not possible in the installed base of client devices. One option for browser designers is to steal application memory from the cache. However it is impossible to know the performance implications of such a decision without browser cache success functions obtained through measurement (Table 2) or simulation (Fig. 10).

Table 4 summarizes the relative improvement in aggregate browser cache hit rates that would result from eliminating redundant payload transfers. For each WebTV device type, the table compares simulated hit rates with estimates based on proxy request volumes before and after cache-busting began. The large gap between the simulated and measured success functions in the WebTV data is due to unnecessary misses caused by inefficient consistency mechanisms and aliasing. Section 5 describes a simple and practical way to completely eliminate redundant payload transfers, raising actual cache hit rates to the full potential illustrated by our simulations.

A detailed investigation of aliasing in the WebTV trace is the subject of ongoing work, and presents formidable computational challenges: Mogul reports that 7,400 MB of RAM is required to analyze duplication in a trace containing 80 million events [29]; the WebTV trace is over four times larger. As a first step, we computed the number of payloads in the trace that are aliased, i.e., that are referenced through more than one URL. Roughly 4.98% of payloads are aliased.

Table 5 shows the relative frequency of the most common MIME types observed during one-week periods before and after cache-busting was activated. Several popular types, e.g., PDF, are absent entirely because WebTV browsers do not support them.

Table 5. Most common MIME types before (31 Aug–6 Sept) and after (14–20 Sept) cache busting

MIME type	Before		After	
	number	%	number	%
Image/gif	43,941,647	48.11	96,904,786	64.49
Image/jpeg	17,889,601	19.59	26,037,449	17.33
Text/html	14,150,501	15.49	14,397,016	9.58
(missing)	13,290,676	14.55	9,469,181	6.30
Application/x-javascript	934,997	1.02	1,652,086	1.10
Other	1,131,681	1.24	1,795,913	1.20
Total	91,339,103	100.00	150,256,431	100.00

The large increase in the popularity of GIFs may occur because GIFs are normally extraordinarily cacheable. It is also conceivable that the browser requests multiframe GIFs each time they are displayed; at the time of writing it is unclear whether WebTV browsers do so.

5. Discussion

The main contributions of this paper are a new method for recording Web browser requests, including browser cache hits, and a preliminary analysis of workload data collected with it.

The advantages of the cache-busting proxy technique are that it requires no client modifications and relatively minor proxy modifications. In most situations is it probably easier to use than conventional client instrumentation, especially for collecting large and representative data sets. However the method is not without limitations and disadvantages. One limitation is that it fails to record user-interface events and therefore cannot support the same range of investigations as an instrumented client, which remains the 'gold standard' for trace collection. Furthermore the new method provides event timestamps recorded at the proxy, and these do not necessarily reflect the latency experienced by clients. If documents are served pre-expired as in the WebTV procedure, browsers may continue to serve some requests from cache even after cache-busting begins (Fig. 3), so the technique does not provide a perfect record of client requests. Finally, it is unclear whether cache busting alters user behavior by increasing latency. Nonetheless a cache-busting proxy trace sheds far more light on client access patterns than ordinary proxy logs.

The most interesting result of our workload analysis is the large gap between actual and potential browser cache hit rates for the client population as a whole (Fig. 10). One way to think about the simulated success functions is that they describe performance in a 'trivial namespace' Web, in which a simple one-to-one correspondence exists between URLs and data payloads. To an extent such a namespace is achievable in practice, e.g., by embedding payload checksums in URLs. Content delivery networks do this already: Akamai URLs contain partial MD5 checksums of data payloads. If requests contain payload checksums, replies never expire and stale content is never served from cache; a simple namespace improves the both the performance and the correctness of CDNs.

Unchanging and mnemonic document names are necessary in systems like the Web, however, and this requirement precludes an entirely flat namespace.

Several practical techniques have been proposed to avoid redundant payload transfers, but published 'duplicate suppression' schemes for the Web do not completely eliminate the problem and require that modified servers supply hints to clients. Mogul reports that one such proposal would increase an infinite proxy's hit rate and byte hit rate by 5.4% and 6.2% respectively [29,30].

While the benefits of imperfect duplicate suppression for infinite proxy caches may be modest, WebTV's data show that the benefits of *perfect* duplicate suppression for *finite browser* caches are substantial. Our most conservative simulation data suggest that browser cache hit rates would increase by 35% to 45% over their estimated current levels (Table 4). Fortunately a simple and practical procedure can completely eliminate redundant proxy-to-client transfers in systems such as WebTV:

- The browser caches every data payload it receives, without exception.
- The browser issues ordinary requests to the proxy.
- Before the proxy returns a payload it first sends the payload's checksum.
- The browser compares the checksum to those of items in its cache. A match ends the transaction; otherwise the proxy transmits the full payload.

Several variants of this overall approach are possible: The proxy could transmit a full reply preceded by a payload checksum and halt the transmission at the client's request. Alternately the proxy might wait for an explicit 'proceed/abort' from the client. The former entails no user-latency penalty and does not throttle the proxy or prolong transactions. However it may have little impact in high-bandwidth, high-round-trip-time environments if documents are small (the full payload reaches the client before its 'halt' message reaches the proxy). The latter variant introduces an additional RTT into the transaction but completely eliminates redundant transfers; it may be attractive in low-bandwidth, low-RTT environments.

For purposes of duplicate suppression the proposed approach entirely ignores the namespace (URLs, request headers, etc.) and consistency mechanisms. Unnecessary misses due to aliasing and inappropriate metadata therefore disappear completely; only compulsory and capacity misses occur. The proposed approach could use entity tags as well as payload digests to avoid still more unnecessary transfers, and furthermore could be used as a hop-by-hop mechanism between any two levels in a cache hierarchy. The semantics of existing protocols, e.g., HTTP, are largely unchanged if cached payloads and digests thereof are used to avoid redundant transfers. The above scheme is similar in spirit to Spring and Wetherall's method of eliminating redundant network traffic [35]. Mogul independently conceived a technique essentially identical to the one presented here but has not published it [27].

Re-writing the rules of browser/proxy interaction is difficult in the most general case because different vendors' products must interoperate during migration and backward compatibility with legacy software must be maintained. However in more tightly integrated environments where a single organization controls both browser and upstream service infrastructure, e.g., WebTV and AOLTV, such changes are feasible. These also happen to be bandwidth-constrained environments, where the prospect of transferring compact message digests rather than far larger entity-bodies is particularly attractive.

Acknowledgments

Literally dozens of WebTV personnel helped to collect the anonymized trace described in this paper. My manager, Stuart Ozer, lent resources and his expertise to the project. Arnold de Leon provided a large computer and with Jeff Allen worked out a thousand operational details. Jay Logue modified WebTV's proxy software to log additional data and serve documents pre-expired. Todd Stansell and Jonathan Tourtellot assembled a 1.2-TB storage array and Brad Whisler managed day-to-day data logging. Paul Roy allowed us to run our measurements on a large fraction of WebTV's production system, and Andrea Chien conducted preliminary tests. Jake Brutlag helped me to understand WebTV's complex service architecture and to document WebTV's proxy log format. WebTV client engineers explained the various client devices and the rationale behind their design; Scott Sanders, Monique Barbanson, David Conroy and Wiltse Carpenter were particularly helpful. Finally, Eric Horvitz of Microsoft Research introduced me to the extraordinary research potential of WebTV.

Professor Peter Honeyman guided and funded my research. Jim Rees, Chuck Lever, and Brad Quinn of CITI designed and built a large storage array for me. The U-M Center for Parallel Computing provided computational resources that made my analyses possible; Tom Hacker was particularly helpful and flexible. Jeff Mogul provided valuable guidance on the logging of HTTP metadata. Jim Gray, Geoff Voelker, Martin Arlitt and the anonymous reviewers supplied valuable feedback on early drafts. Duane Wessels provided data on the number of clients served by the NLANR cache hierarchy. Lara Catledge and James Pitkow provided the Georgia Tech client trace, and Boston University supplied the BU trace.

References

[1] Web Characterization Repository. http://researchsmp2.cc.vt.edu/cgi-bin/reposit/index.pl.

[2] V. Almeida, A. Bestavros, M. Crovella, and A. de Oliveira. Characterizing reference locality in the WWW. In *4th Int'l Conf. on Parallel and Distributed Information Systems*, Dec. 1996.

[3] M. Arlitt. Personal communication.

[4] M. Arlitt, L. Cherkasova, J. Dilley, R. Friedrich, and T. Jin. Evaluating content management techniques for Web proxy caches. Technical Report HPL-98-173, HP Labs, Mar. 1999.

[5] M. Arlitt, L. Cherkasova, J. Dilley, R. Friedrich, T. Jin. Evaluating content management techniques for Web proxy caches. In *2nd Workshop on Internet Server Performance*, May 1999.

[6] M. Arlitt, R. Friedrich, and T. Jin. Workload characterization of a Web proxy in a cable modem environment. Technical Report HPL-1999-48, HP Labs, 1999.

[7] M. Arlitt and T. Jin. Workload characterization of the 1998 World Cup Web Site. Technical Report HPL-1999-35R1, HP Labs, Sep. 1999.

[8] M. Arlitt and C. Williamson. Web server workload characterization: The search for invariants. In *SIGMETRICS*, May 1996.

[9] M.F. Arlitt and C.L. Williamson. Internet Web servers: Workload characterization and performance implications. *IEEE/ACM Trans. Networking*, 5(5): 631–644, Oct. 1997.

[10] P. Barford, A. Bestavros, A. Bradley, and M. Crovella. Changes in Web client access patterns: Characteristics and caching implications. *World Wide Web Journal*, 1999.

[11] B.T. Bennett and V.J. Kruskal. LRU stack processing. *IBM J. Res. Dev.*, 19(4): 353–357, July 1975.

[12] A. Bestavros, R. Carter, M. Crovella, C. Cunha, A. Heddaya, and S. Mirdad. Application-level document caching in the Internet. In *2nd Int'l Workshop on Services in Distributed and Networked Environments*, June 1995.

[13] A. Bradley. Personal communication.

[14] R. Cáceres, B. Krishnamurthy, and J. Rexford. HTTP 1.0 logs considered harmful. W3C Web Char'n Group Workshop, Nov. 1998.
[15] L.D. Catledge and J.E. Pitkow. Characterizing browsing strategies in the World-Wide Web. *Computer Networks and ISDN Systems*, 27(6): 1065–1073, Apr. 1995.
[16] M.E. Crovella and A. Bestavros. Self-similarity in World Wide Web traffic: Evidence and possible causes. *IEEE/ACM Trans. Networking*, 5(6): 835–846, Dec. 1997.
[17] C.R. Cunha, A. Bestavros, and M.E. Crovella. Characteristics of WWW client-based traces. Technical Report BU-CS-95-010, Boston U. CS Dept., July 1995.
[18] B.D. Davison. Web traffic logs: An imperfect resource for evaluation. In *9th Conf. Internet Society*, June 1999.
[19] F. Douglis, A. Feldmann, B. Krishnamurthy, and J. Mogul. Rate of change and other metrics: a live study of the World Wide Web. In *USENIX Symposium on Internet Technologies and Systems*, 147–158, Dec. 1997.
[20] B.M. Duska, D. Marwood, and M.J. Feeley. The measured access characteristics of World-Wide-Web client proxy caches, In *USENIX Symposium on Internet Technologies and Systems*, 23–35, Dec. 1997.
[21] A. Feldmann. Continuous online extraction of HTTP traces from packet traces. In *Proc. W3C Web Char'n Group Workshop*, 1999.
[22] R. Fielding, J. Gettys, J. Mogul, H. Frystyk, L. Masinter, P. Leach, and T. Berners-Lee. RFC 2616: Hypertext transfer protocol – HTTP/1.1, June 1999.
[23] T. Kelly and D. Reeves. Optimal Web cache sizing: Scalable methods for exact solutions. *Computer Communications*, 24: 163–173, Feb. 2001.
[24] B. Krishnamurthy and J. Rexford. *Web Protocols and Practice*. Addison-Wesley, May 2001.
[25] R.L. Mattson, J. Gecsei, D.R. Slutz, and I.L. Traiger. Evaluation techniques for storage hierarchies. *IBM Systems Journal*, 9(2): 78–117, 1970.
[26] D.L. Mills. RFC 1305: Network time protocol, Mar. 1992.
[27] J. Mogul. Personal communication.
[28] J.C. Mogul. Errors in timestamp-based HTTP header values. Technical Report 99/3, Compaq WRL, Dec. 1999.
[29] J.C. Mogul. A trace-based analysis of duplicate suppression in HTTP. Technical Report 99/2, Compaq WRL, Nov. 1999.
[30] J.C. Mogul. Squeezing more bits out of HTTP caches. *IEEE Network*, pages 6–14, May/June 2000.
[31] D. Muntz and P. Honeyman. Multi-level caching in distributed file systems. Technical Report 91-3, U. Michigan Ctr. for IT Integration (CITI), Aug. 1991.
[32] D.A. Muntz, P. Honeyman, and C.J. Antonelli. Evaluating delayed write in a multilevel caching file system. In *IFIP/IEEE Int'l Conf. on Dist'd Platforms*, pages 415–429, Feb. 1996.
[33] F. Olken. Efficient methods for calculating the success function of fixed space replacement policies. Technical Report LBL-12370, U.C. Berkeley EECS Dept./Lawrence Berkeley Lab, May 1981.
[34] V.N. Padmanabhan and L. Qiu. The content and access dynamics of a busy Web server: Findings and implications. *SIGCOMM*, Aug. 2000.
[35] N.T. Spring and D. Wetherall. A protocol-independent technique for eliminating redundant network traffic. In *SIGCOMM*, Aug. 2000.
[36] J.G. Thompson. Efficient analysis of caching systems. Technical Report UCB/CSD 87/374, U.C. Berkeley EECS, Oct. 1987.
[37] D. Wessels. Personal communication.
[38] A. Wolman, G. Voelker, N. Sharma, N. Cardwell, M. Brown, T. Landray, D. Pinnel, A. Karlin, and H. Levy. Organization-based analysis of Web-object sharing and caching. In *2nd USENIX Symposium on Internet Technologies and Systems*, Oct. 1999.
[39] A. Wolman, G.M. Voelker, N. Sharma, N. Cardwell, A. Karlin, and H.M. Levy. On the scale and performance of cooperative Web proxy caching. *Operating Systems Review*, 34(5): 16–31, Dec. 1999.

Web Caching and Content Delivery
A. Bestavros and M. Rabinovich (Editors)

Analysis of Web Workloads Using the Bootstrap Methodology

Johnson Lee [1], William Miniscalco [2], Meng Li [3], W. David Shambroom [4], John Buford [5]

Verizon Communications, 40 Sylvan Road, Waltham, MA 02451, USA

Abstract

Modeling the performance of caches requires examining their behavior when subjected to realistic workloads that are created by extracting the essential characteristics of actual Web traffic. We have used the Bootstrap methodology for analyzing response size and file popularity distributions obtained from proxy log files. The Bootstrap is a resampling technique that enables one to estimate both population parameters and their standard errors when no accurate mathematical representations are available for the underlying distributions. For this investigation we used real-world workloads from NLANR and Verizon Laboratories together with a synthetic workload generated by Web Polygraph. The analysis of response size included averages and percentiles, processing and bandwidth costs, and a null hypothesis test for ascertaining the likelihood that different datasets have the same underlying distribution. The file popularity distribution was investigated to assess the degree of Zipf-like behavior. We conclude that the Bootstrap is an effective tool for the analysis of nonparametric distributions that enables one to determine confidence levels and make stronger statements than possible using conventional statistics. It is also valuable for determining how accurately a synthetic workload represents actual traffic.

Keywords: Web caching; Proxy cache; Web workloads; Bootstrap

1. Introduction

An effective implementation of Web caching requires a detailed understanding of the temporal and spatial characteristics of the traffic load together with their impact on cache performance. A network service or content distribution network (CDN) provider with a national or international footprint needs to deploy a widely distributed network of caching proxies to provide the required quality of services. Issues that must be resolved include sizing the caches, loadbalancing of cache clusters, distributing traffic between caches sites, backup/fail-over policies, and managing performance for service level agreements.

[1] E-mail: leezongson@yahoo.com
[2] E-mail: miniscalco@ieee.org
[3] E-mail: meng.li@verizon.com
[4] E-mail: dshambroom@ieee.org
[5] E-mail: buford@alum.mit.edu

The behavior of a distributed system with many clients, servers, and networks depends heavily on the characteristics of its workload [2,6,8,12–14,16]. Thus, one of the first steps in any performance evaluation study is to understand the workload by extracting key characteristics from actual Web workloads.

In order to analyze distributions of important parameters such as file size from workload sources or evaluate the accuracy of a synthetic workload, it is extremely valuable to use a nonparametric statistical method (i.e., one without an assumed mathematical expression for the distribution function). Adequately understanding a distribution normally requires knowledge of more than the mean. In the absence of a mathematical expression for the distribution, however, evaluating statistics poses a problem because for most estimators other than the mean there are no procedures for obtaining the uncertainty of the estimate. In this work we adopt the Bootstrap methodology [9,10] to perform statistical estimates and inferences of Web workload parameters that include estimates of their errors.

The objective of this paper is to use the Bootstrap methodology to investigate the variations of workloads obtained from different sources by comparing their response sizes and popularity distributions. This includes the evaluation of standard errors and the confidence with which a synthetic workload represents measured data. The remainder of this paper is organized as follows: In Section 2 a brief description of the Bootstrap methods is provided. In Section 3 the data collection procedures are discussed. In Section 4 are presented statistical estimates and inferences determined by applying the Bootstrap methods to the datasets. We focus our attention on the response size distributions and the distributions for the file popularity. Finally, a summary is presented in Section 5. In the Appendices the Bootstrap algorithms relevant to this paper are described.

2. The Bootstrap methodology

2.1. Motivation

Since the Bootstrap methodology was introduced in 1979 by Efron [9,10], it has been widely used for statistical problems in a variety of fields [7,11]. The Bootstrap is a computer-based method of inference that can answer many important statistical questions without assuming a particular functional form for the underlying probability density function. One of the goals of the Bootstrap is to provide a mechanism for evaluating inferences such as the variance, the confidence interval, and the significance level.

Many of the distributions encountered in the analysis of Web traffic have no *a priori* functional form. If it is necessary to represent them by mathematical expression (e.g., to generate synthetic workloads for experiments or tests), it is typically done through piece-wise fits with common distribution functions [2] or using a superposition of such functions [18]. Statistics and error estimates calculated using such fits are generally valid only for comparison to the original dataset to assess goodness of fit. Thus evaluating statistics on measured datasets, whether for direct analysis or evaluating a fit, must be done nonparametrically. The explicit recognition of uncertainty is central to statistical analysis, and any statistical estimates that do not include confidence levels or estimated standard errors are of limited utility. However, for nonparametric distributions there are in general no procedures for evaluating the error of an estimate beyond those for the error of a mean. The Bootstrap and some other computer-based techniques, such as permutation tests and nonparametric inferences, play an important role in resolving such difficulties.

The essence of the Bootstrap is to create additional samples of the population by resampling the original dataset with replacement (i.e., allowing a specific datum to be selected more than once). A wide range of statistical problems can be addressed this way, eliminating the need to oversimplify complex problems. The reader is referred to the Bootstrap literature for details of the method [7,9–11].

2.2. Estimating values using the Bootstrap

In this section we illustrate how the Bootstrap is used to estimate values. Appendix A describes how it can be applied to determining the standard errors of these estimates. Let x' be a continuous random variable with values x whose probability density function (pdf) is $f(x)$. The cumulative distribution function (CDF) of $f(x)$ is $F(x)$ and is defined in the usual way as

$$F(x) = P(x' \leq x) = \int_0^x f(x')\,\mathrm{d}x', \tag{1}$$

$$\text{with } F(\infty) = 1, \tag{2}$$

where P is the probability of selecting a value of x' in the range from 0 to x. The complimentary function (CCDF) of $F(x)$ is $\underline{F}(x)$ and is given by

$$\underline{F}(x) = 1 - F(x). \tag{3}$$

Suppose that a random sample $\boldsymbol{x} = (x_1, x_2, \ldots, x_n)$ of size n is drawn from a population whose pdf and CDF are denoted by f and F, respectively. If all n observations x_i are identically distributed and mutually independent of each other, then all of the x_i are described by the same CDF. For the current problem x_i represents a datum (such as response size) from the log file record i. When there is no mathematical model for the CDF, the statistical analysis is nonparametric and uses only the fact that the random variables are independent and identically distributed (iid). An important role is played in nonparametric analysis by the empirical distribution that assigns equal probability $1/n$ to each sample value x_j. The empirical distribution function (EDF), $\hat{F}$, is the corresponding estimate of F, which is defined as the sample proportion

$$\hat{F}(x) = \#\{x_j \leq x\}/n, \tag{4}$$

where $\#\{A\}$ means the number of times the event A occurs in the sample. More explicitly, we may write

$$\hat{F}(x) = \frac{1}{n}\sum_{j=1}^{n} H(x - x_j), \tag{5}$$

where $H(x - x_j)$ is the Heaviside (unit step) function which jumps from 0 to 1 at $x = x_j$. Notice that the values of the EDF are discrete $(0, 1/n, 2/n, \ldots, n/n)$, so the EDF is equivalent to its points of increase, the ordered values $x_{(1)} \leq x_{(2)} \leq \ldots \leq x_{(n)}$. The EDF plays the role of fitted model when no mathematical form is assumed for F.

The sample (dataset) $\boldsymbol{x}$ is used to make inferences about a population characteristic, generically denoted by θ, using a statistic whose value in the sample is t:

$$\theta = t(F), \tag{6}$$

where $t(F)$ is a statistical function that specifies how to compute t from F. Because F is unknown we estimate θ by substituting the EDF for F:

$$\hat{\theta} = t(\hat{F}). \tag{7}$$

The Bootstrap methodology relies upon the above substitution. In Bootstrap terminology this is referred to as the Plug-in Principle. Simple examples of statistics are the mean and the variance of the population, which are defined, respectively, as

$$t(F) = \mu = \int u \, \mathrm{d}F(u), \qquad t(F) = \sigma^2 = \int u^2 \, \mathrm{d}F(u) - \left[\int u \, \mathrm{d}F(u)\right]^2. \tag{8}$$

By applying Equations (5) and (7) to estimate the sample mean, $\overline{x}$, we obtain

$$\hat{\theta} = \overline{x} = t(\hat{F}) = \int u \, \mathrm{d}\hat{F}(u) = \frac{1}{n} \sum_{j=1}^{n} x_j \tag{9}$$

and, similarly, for the sample variance $\overline{\sigma}^2$, we have

$$\hat{\theta} = \overline{\sigma}^2 = \frac{1}{n} \sum_{j=1}^{n} x_j^2 - \left[\frac{1}{n} \sum_{j=1}^{n} x_j\right]^2. \tag{10}$$

It can be shown that μ is equal to $\overline{x}$ and $t(\hat{F})$ is unbiased, while σ^2 is not equal to $\overline{\sigma}^2$ and $t(\hat{F})$ is biased by $\sigma^2 = n\overline{\sigma}^2/(n-1)$. The bias of the sample variance is relatively unimportant in this context because of the large ($n \sim 10^6$) sample size used here. The Bootstrap algorithm for estimating standard errors is presented in the Appendix A. Several authors have suggested implementing Bootstrap programs using the statistical programming languages S and S-plus [7,11]. We implemented the Bootstrap algorithms in both Fortran with IMSL subroutines [17] and S-plus. We used the Fortran versions because of a factor of 10 speed advantage.

3. Data collection

The values of the characteristic parameters of the workload may vary from one server to another due to differences in client populations. Therefore, we extracted workloads from proxy log files obtained from three different sources:

(1) National Laboratory for Applied Network Research (NLANR-bo1) hierarchical cache system, where bo indicates the NCAR site in Boulder, CO [15],
(2) Verizon Laboratories' (VZL) proxy server without caching capabilities [4], and
(3) A Lucent caching proxy subjected to a load generated by the Web Polygraph benchmarking system running the Polymix-3 workload (POLY) [18].

Log files obtained from NLANR-bo1 and VZL represent real-world workloads while those obtained from POLY are synthetic workloads. A test system such as Polygraph does not exactly reproduce an actual Web workload for reasons of computational efficiency and the need to reproduce long-term cache behavior within a restricted test schedule

[19]. Accordingly, it is interesting to analyze the differences between actual and synthetic workloads.

Log entries from all three sources included response size, elapsed time, and a time stamp. From NLANR-bo1 we used five days (September 18–22, 2000) of sanitized cache access logs (from bo1.sanitized-access.20000919.gz to bo1.sanitized-access.20000922.gz) and stored the data in a database with a total of 2.4×10^6 records. Only weekdays were examined to exclude the effect of different behavior on weekends. Similarly, we used one day (June 5, 2000) of VZL data and stored them in a database with 1.4×10^5 records. For the synthetic workload from POLY, we collected a dataset over a period of 160 minutes after the cache server reached steady-state. This generated 5×10^5 records. The full datasets were used in all calculations unless otherwise noted.

4. Analysis of Web workloads

4.1. Distributions for the workloads

To determine a response size distribution, we queried the appropriate database and counted the number of requests (frequency) for each response size fs, independent of file identity. A bin size of $\Delta fs = 1$ byte was used and the distribution was normalized to construct the pdf as a function of fs, $f(fs)$. The CCDF $\underline{F}(fs)$ is determined using Equations (1)–(3). Fig. 1 shows the variation of $\log_{10}[\underline{F}(fs)]$ with $\log_{10}[fs]$ for the NLANR-bo1, VZL and POLY workloads. It is apparent that the real-world workloads

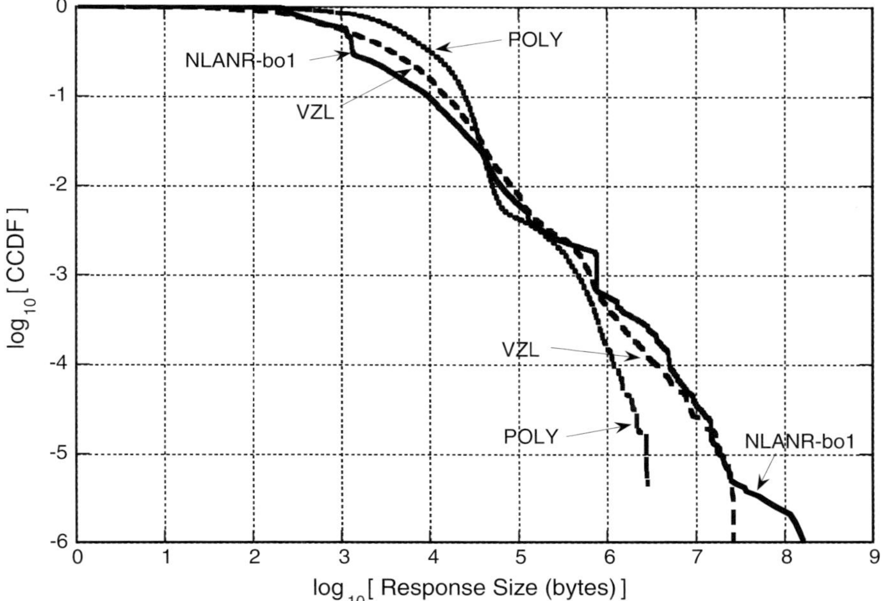

Fig. 1. Complimentary cumulative distribution function versus response size for the NLANR-bo1, VZL, and POLY datasets.

Table 1. Statistical estimates and conclusions

Characteristic	NLANR-bo1	VZL	POLY
(1) Mean File Size (bytes) B [a]	8,080 (±200)	8,398 (±69)	11,027 (±49)
(2) Mean File Size (bytes) CS [b]	8,100 (±200)	8,409 (±67)	11,029 (±48)
(3) Median File Size (bytes) B [a]	1,170.1 (±0.3)	1,407 (±3)	5,235 (±11)
(4) Median File Size (bytes) CS [b]	1,170	1,407	5,234
(5) 99th Percentile File Size (bytes) B [a]	63,660 (±300)	83,880 (±620)	51,120 (±230)
(6) 99th Percentile File Size (bytes) CS [b]	63,700	83,860	51,110
(7) Maximum File Size (bytes)	1.9×10^8	1.6×10^7	3.4×10^6
(8) Bootstrap H_0: F = G	ASL = 48% (Ref)	ASL = 15%	ASL <0.01%
(9) Zipf-like Exponent	0.853	0.902	NA

[a] B indicates value obtained using the Bootstrap.
[b] CS indicates value obtained using conventional statistics.

(NLANR-bo1 and VZL) behave similarly and have much longer tails than the synthetic workload (POLY). This heavy-tailed behavior has been widely noted for file and response size distributions in Web traffic. Statistical techniques for heavy-tailed distributions are discussed in [1].

4.2. Bootstrap estimates and inferences

Table 1 lists statistical estimates, with standard errors in parenthesis, for NLANR-bo1, VZL and POLY obtained using both the Bootstrap and conventional statistical methods. The latter consists of calculating the desired statistic on a single sample from a population and, except for the mean, cannot provide an estimate of error. For convenience we split the discussion of the estimates into four groups: (A) sample means and percentiles, (B) processing and bandwidth cost as a function of response size, (C) Bootstrap's null hypothesis H_0 test, and (D) file popularity distributions. For the analyses we used 500 iterations of the Bootstrap resampling technique (B = 500). The parameters obtained can be used to build or validate workload models to capture the important features and characteristics of the distributions.

4.2.1. Sample averages and percentiles

Row (1) of Table 1 is the mean of the response sizes in bytes with the standard deviation of the sample mean in parenthesis, both calculated using the Bootstrap on the full datasets. POLY has the largest mean response size with the smallest standard deviation, while NLANR-bo1 and VZL have smaller mean response sizes with larger (in the case of NLANR-bo1 much larger) standard deviations because of the heavy tails seen in Fig. 1. The value of mean response size for POLY agrees with the input specification used for Web Polygraph. Row (2) shows the same statistics calculated using conventional methods. The close agreement between the corresponding values in rows (1) and (2) indicate that the Bootstrap adds little value if only the mean of a distribution is required. Rows (3) and (4) are the median response sizes calculated using Bootstrap and conventional statistics, respectively. Rows (5) and (6) are the 99th percentile response sizes determined by both methods, while row (7) is the maximum file size for each dataset. Another indication of how skewed NLANR-bo1 and VZL response size distributions are relative to the synthetic workload is the ratio between their 99th percentile and median response sizes. For the NLANR-bo1 and VZL datasets this ratio is 54, while for POLY it is 9.7. It is important to note that while the median and 99th percentile values calculated by both methods are extremely close, only the Bootstrap provides an estimate of uncertainty.

4.2.2. Processing and bandwidth cost as a function of response size

In assessing the impact on a caching system of a distribution of response sizes, one needs to consider both the file size and frequency with which files of that size are requested. Caching large files can save considerable network bandwidth and load on the origin server, but can consume a significant amount of disk space at the cache and cause long waits on requests for smaller files while a larger file is being processed. This trade-off analysis can be aided by computing the impact of a given file size, which can be done by taking the product of the file size and probability of a request for that file size, $C(fs) = fs \times Pr(fs)$. This provides the marginal cost for processing files of size *fs*. Here we made the simplifying assumption that the bandwidth and processing costs are proportional to the file size. We took a bin size, Δfs, of 100 bytes with a probability, *Pr*, of finding a file of size fs in the bin. Examining the shape of $C(fs)$ plotted versus *fs* is particularly helpful in assessing the cost of very large files.

Statistical estimates for $C(fs)$ were made using the Bootstrap with B = 500 and are plotted in Fig. 2a, b and c for NLANR-bo1, VZL and POLY, respectively. Because the marginal cost is plotted on a logarithmic scale, bins containing no files cannot be displayed and the plots are cutoff at file sizes for which this becomes significant. Both the NLANR-bo1 and VZL data have no clearly defined peak but roll off from maxima at a file size in the region of 1,000 bytes. In contrast, the POLY data cover a significantly smaller range of marginal costs and have a very broad peak at file sizes between 3,200 and 20,000 bytes. The notch in the POLY data just above 3,000 bytes is reproducible and is being investigated further. We conclude that for the actual Web workloads, the marginal costs for processing files of increasing size falls off faster than linearly because the probability of requesting a file of a particular size decreases faster than the file size grows. Because the Polymix-3 workload produces a more uniform marginal cost that is significant to larger file sizes, it gives more weight to large files than the NLANR-bo1 and VZL workloads. Applying these results to a trade-off analysis between storage and bandwidth costs requires quantitative estimates of their respective costs. Additional work on cost analysis is underway.

4.2.3. Null hypothesis h_0 test

The Bootstrap provides a unique method for performing the null hypothesis test for the two-sample problem. Suppose that we examine two independent random samples $\mathbf{z} = (z_1, z_2, \ldots, z_n)$ and $\mathbf{y} = (y_1, y_2, \ldots, y_m)$ drawn from two possibly different CDFs, F and G. Having observed $\mathbf{z}$ and $\mathbf{y}$, we want to test the null hypothesis H_0 that there is no difference between F and G, H_0: $F = G$. The equality $F = G$ means that F and G assign equal probabilities to all sets, $\text{Prob}_F\{A\} = \text{Prob}_G\{A\}$, where A is any subset of the common sample space of $\mathbf{z}$ and $\mathbf{y}$. If H_0 is true, then there is no difference between the probabilistic behavior of a random $\mathbf{z}$ or a random $\mathbf{y}$. This enables us to determine whether two datasets are statistically equivalent. It can also be used to evaluate the accuracy with which a fitted function represents an underlying distribution by applying the test to the original dataset and one calculated using that function.

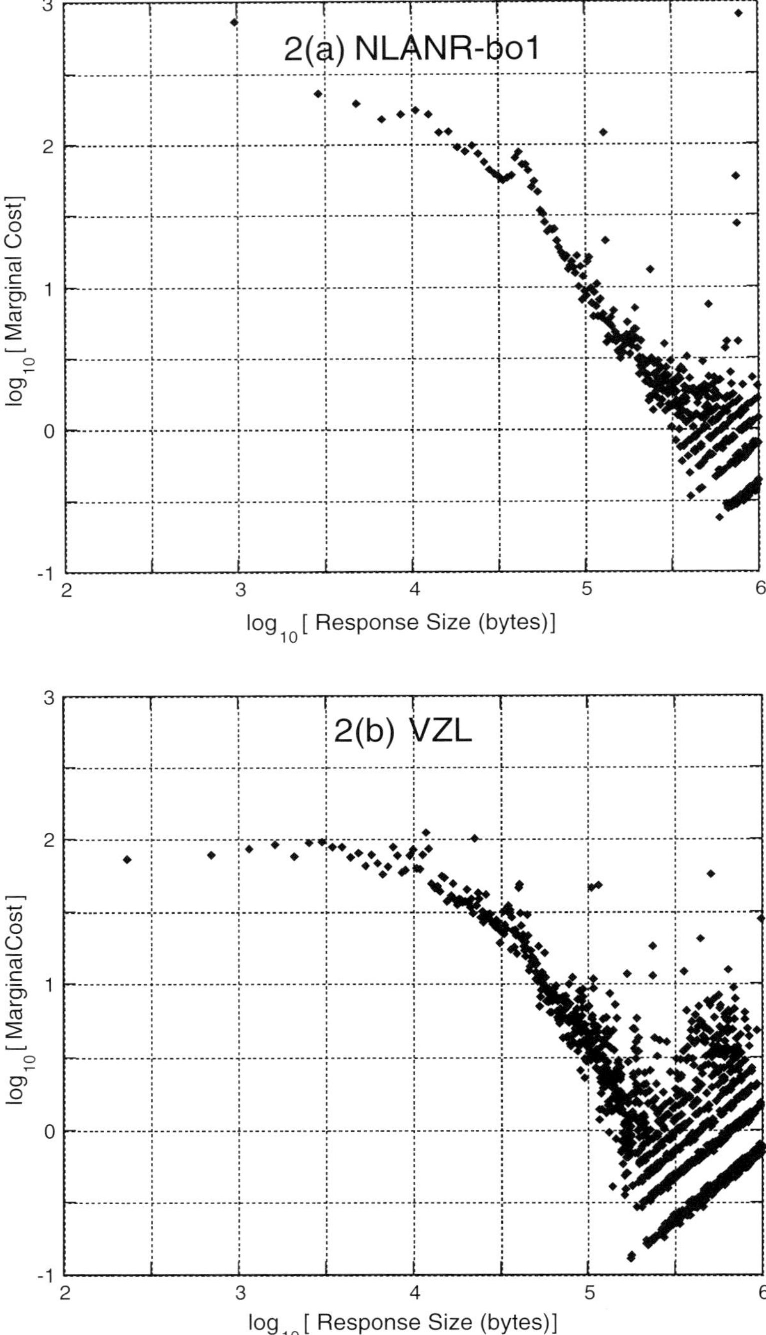

Fig. 2. Estimated processing or bandwidth marginal cost as a function of file size.

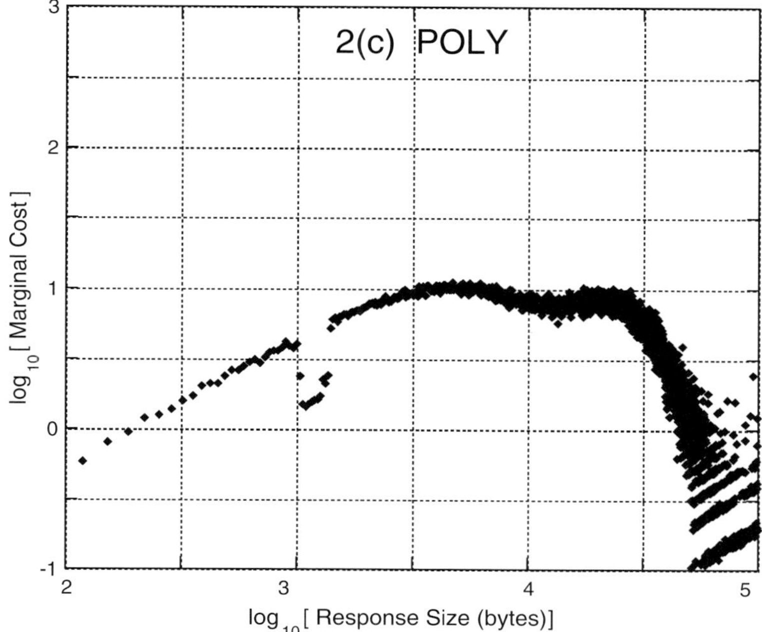

Fig. 2 (continued).

We used the Bootstrap to test the null hypothesis H_0: $F = G$, where F is the NLANR-bo1 response size distribution with a random sample $\boldsymbol{z}$ of size n and G is the VZL or POLY response size distribution with a random sample $\boldsymbol{y}$ of size m. Let $\boldsymbol{x}$ be a combined sample of $\boldsymbol{y}$ and $\boldsymbol{z}$. We seek an achieved significance level:

$$\text{ASL} = \text{Prob}\{t(\boldsymbol{x}^*) \geq t(\boldsymbol{x})\}.$$

The quantity $t(\boldsymbol{x})$ is fixed at its observed value and the random variable $\boldsymbol{x}^*$ has a distribution specified by the null hypothesis H_0. Bootstrap hypothesis testing uses a substitution estimate for the distribution. The EDF of $\boldsymbol{x}$ puts equal probability on each member of $\boldsymbol{x}$. Under H_0, the EDF provides a nonparametric estimate of the common population that gave rise to both $\boldsymbol{y}$ and $\boldsymbol{z}$.

Appendix B describes an algorithm for computing ASL. In this paper, $t(\boldsymbol{x})$ is the difference between two-sample means and is chosen to be the Student's two-sample t-statistic, as described in Appendix B. The theoretical value is expected to be 50% for identical distributions. In row (8) of Table 1, the ASL for NLANR-bo1 is 48% because the NLANR-bo1 workload is the reference. Row (8) shows that NLANR-bo1 and the VZL possess the same response size distribution with a significance level of 15%. In contrast, the significance level for NLANR-bo1 and POLY having the same response size distribution is $<0.01\%$, indicating that they are unlikely to be the same.

4.2.4. Distributions of file popularity

We also investigated the variation of file popularity with popularity rank. File popularity is the relative frequency with which specific files are requested. This property has been extensively discussed in the literature, with some disagreement over whether the distribution is Zipf-like or not. A detailed examination of these issues can be found in Breslau et al. [5] and references therein. Since there has been a report of popularity distributions changing over a period of years [3], our primary objective in this analysis was to compare our more recent data to results reported previously. Using the three log files, the number of requests (frequency) for each specific file was tabulated. Then the files were ordered from the most popular to the least popular and assigned a rank r. The rank is defined such that file r is the rth most popular file with $r = 1$ the most popular file. Fig. 3a, b and c show for NLANR-bo1, VZL and POLY, respectively, the frequency of requests as a function of file popularity rank.

In Fig. 3a and b for the real-world workloads, we see that for ranks larger than a relatively small number the frequency decreases linearly in the log–log plots, revealing inverse power law behavior. The exponents found from the fits shown are -0.853 for NLANR-bo1 and -0.902 for VZL. These values indicate the expected Zipf-like behavior and are similar to those reported previously [3,5]. In Fig. 3a and b the frequency is observed to fall off much slower than Zipf's law for the 10–50 most popular files, which is also consistent with prior work [3,5]. The POLY data in Fig. 3c does not exhibit Zipf-like behavior over any range for the Polymix-3 workload used. According to the Polygraph team, this is done intentionally to provide the required stress to the caches under test [19]. The roll-off in frequency for the least popular files is probably caused by the fixed working set size used by Polymix-3. This causes files to eventual age out of the set that can be requested. From this analysis we conclude that the NLANR-bo1 and VZL datasets have Zipf-like exponents typical of those observed over the past 5 years.

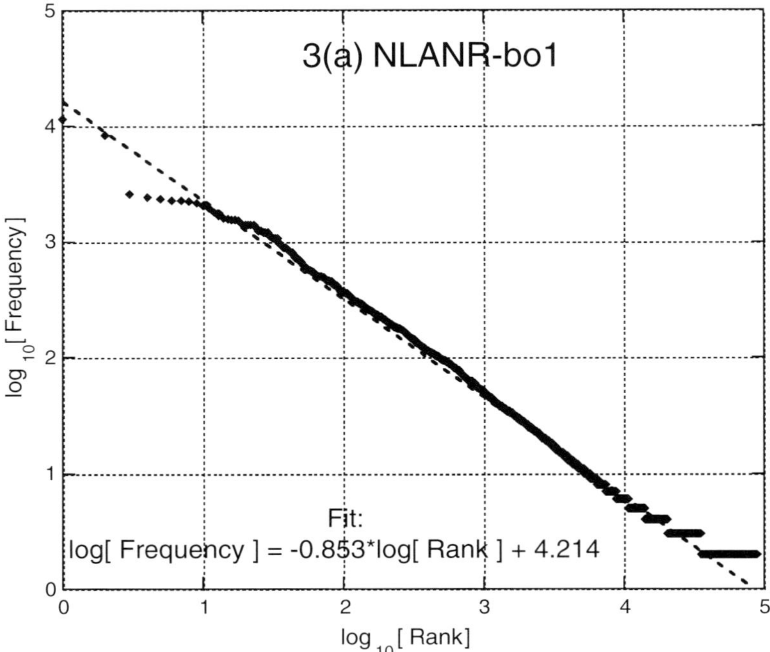

Fig. 3. Frequency for requesting a file (popularity) as a function of file popularity rank.

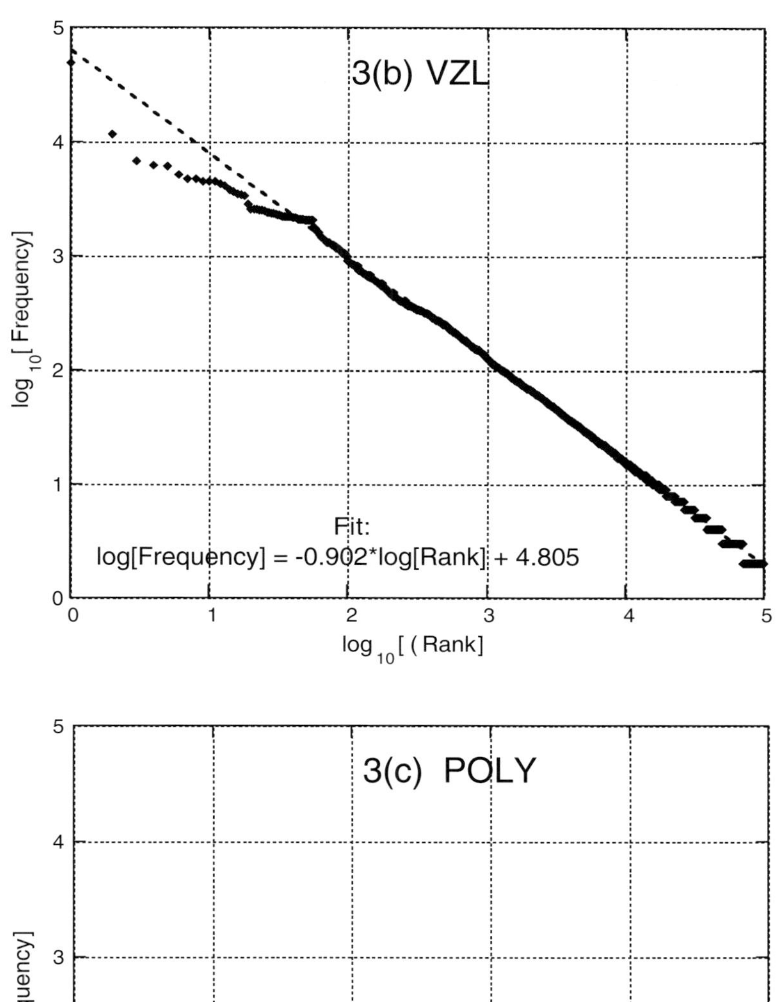

Fig. 3 (continued).

5. Summary

We have used the Bootstrap methodology to analyze response size and file popularity distributions. The chief value of the Bootstrap is that it provides error estimates for statistics evaluated on nonparametric distributions, ones that are not well represented by mathematical expressions. In addition, it can be used to evaluate the statistical significance of how well a parameterized function represents the data. The data were drawn from three different proxies to obtain a measure of how workloads depend upon the client population. Included with the real-world workloads (NLANR-bo1 and VZL) was a synthetic workload generated by Web Polygraph (POLY), a widely used cache benchmarking tool, running Polymix-3.

We found the requested response size distributions for NLANR-bo1 and VZL to have pronounced heavy tails, consistent with previous reports. The NLANR-bo1 dataset had the heaviest tail while the synthetic POLY workload had the lightest tail. An analysis of marginal processing and bandwidth cost found it to fall off rapidly as a function of file size for NLANR-bo1 and VZL, but not for POLY. The Bootstrap null hypothesis test was employed to infer the significance level for the conclusion that the NLANR-bo1 distribution is the same as for the other two populations. We determined that NLANR-bo1 and VZL possess the same response size distributions with a significance level of 15%, where 50% is the maximum value. However, NLANR-bo1 and POLY have <0.01% significance level for having the same distribution. File popularity as a function of popularity rank has strong Zipf-like behavior for the NLANR-bo1 and VZL workloads for popularity ranks larger than 10–50. By design, POLY does not exhibit Zipf-like behavior for the Polymix-3 workload.

From the analysis of proxy log files presented here, we conclude that the Bootstrap is a valuable tool for estimating errors in the values of important characteristics of workloads derived from actual traffic. Moreover, it can be used to evaluate the accuracy with which a synthetic workload represents actual Web traffic.

Acknowledgments

The authors are indebted to S. Zdonik for valuable discussion.

Appendix A. The Bootstrap method for estimating standard errors

Suppose we encounter a common data analysis problem: a random sample

$$\boldsymbol{x} = (x_1, x_2, \ldots, x_n) \tag{A1}$$

from an unknown probability distribution F has been collected and we wish to estimate a parameter of interest $\theta = t(F)$ [see Equation (6)] on the basis of $\boldsymbol{x}$.

The Bootstrap methods depend on the notion of the Bootstrap sample which is defined to be a random sample of size n drawn from $\hat{F}$ [see Equations (4) and (5)]

$$\hat{F} \to \boldsymbol{x}^* = (x_1^*, x_2^*, \ldots, x_n^*). \tag{A2}$$

The star notation indicates that $\boldsymbol{x}^*$ is not the actual data set $\boldsymbol{x}$, but rather a randomized, or resampled, version of $\boldsymbol{x}$. Corresponding to a Bootstrap data set $\boldsymbol{x}^*$ is a Bootstrap replication of $\hat{\theta} = s(\boldsymbol{x})$, i.e.,

$$\hat{\theta}^* = s(\boldsymbol{x}^*). \tag{A3}$$

Note that $s(\boldsymbol{x})$ may be the plug-in estimate $t(\hat{F})$, but does not have to be. It can be defined as a complicated function if users wish to study the Bootstrap estimate bias.

The Bootstrap methods can be used to estimate the accuracy of $\hat{\theta} = s(\boldsymbol{x})$ by evaluating the standard errors. The algorithm is as follows:

(1) Select B independent Bootstrap samples $\boldsymbol{x}^{*1}, \boldsymbol{x}^{*1}, \ldots, \boldsymbol{x}^{*B}$, each consisting of n data values drawn with replacement from $\boldsymbol{x}$ as in Equation (A2). For estimating standard error, the number B is ordinarily in the range 25–200.

(2) Evaluate the Bootstrap replication corresponding to each Bootstrap sample,

$$\hat{\theta}^*(b) = s(\boldsymbol{x}^{*b}), \qquad b = 1, 2, \ldots, B. \tag{A4}$$

(3) Estimate the standard error $\boldsymbol{se}_F(\hat{\theta})$ by the sample standard deviation of the B replications

$$\hat{\boldsymbol{se}}_B = \left\{ \sum_{b=1}^{B} \left[\hat{\theta}^*(b) - \hat{\theta}^*(\cdot)\right]^2 / (B-1) \right\}^{1/2} \tag{A5}$$

where $\hat{\theta}^*(\cdot) = \sum_{b=1}^{B} \hat{\theta}^*(b)/B$.

The limit of $\hat{\boldsymbol{se}}_B$ as B goes to ∞ is the ideal Bootstrap estimate of $\boldsymbol{se}_F\ (\hat{\theta})$. For more details please consult references [7,11].

Appendix B. The Bootstrap statistic for testing $F = G$

(1) Draw B samples of size $n+m$ with replacement from $\boldsymbol{x}$. Call the first n observations $\boldsymbol{z}^*$ and the remaining m observations $\boldsymbol{y}^*$.

(2) Evaluate $t(\cdot)$ on each sample,

$$t(\boldsymbol{x}^{*b}) = \overline{z}^* - \overline{y}^*, \qquad b = 1, 2, \ldots, B.$$

(3) Approximate ASL by $\#\{t(\boldsymbol{x}^{*b}) \geq t_{\text{obs}}\}/B$ where $t_{\text{obs}} = t(\boldsymbol{x})$ the observed value of the statistic.

More accurate testing can be obtained by using a Student statistic. In the above test, instead of $t(\boldsymbol{x}) = \overline{z} - \overline{y}$, we could use

$$t(\boldsymbol{x}) = \frac{\overline{z} - \overline{y}}{\overline{\sigma}\sqrt{1/n + 1/m}},$$

where $\overline{\sigma} = \left\{ \left[\sum_{i=1}^{n} (z_i - \overline{z})^2 + \sum_{j=1}^{m} (y_j - \overline{y})^2 \right] / [n + m - 2] \right\}^{1/2}$.

This is the two-sample t-statistic. Please consult references [7,11] for more information.

References

[1] R.J. Adler, R.E. Feldman and M.S. Taqqu, eds. *A Practical Guide to Heavy Tails, Statistical Techniques and Application*, Birkhauser, Boston Basel Berlin, 1998.

[2] Paul Barford and Mark Crovella, Generating Representative Web Workloads for Network and Server Performance Evaluation, *Proc. of 1998 ACM SIGMETRICS Intl. Conf.*, 1998.

[3] P. Barford, A. Bestavros, A. Bradley, and M. Crovella, Changes in Web Client Access Patterns, *World Wide Web* 2, pp. 15–28, 1999.

[4] S. Belczyk, private Communications.

[5] Lee Breslau, Pei Cao, Li Fan, Graham Phillips, Scott Shenker, Web Caching and Zipf-like Distributions: Evidence and Implications, *IEEE InfoCom*, 1999.

[6] M. Crovella, C. Lindemann and M. Reiser, Internet performance modeling: the state of the art at the turn of the century, *Performance Evaluation* 42, 91–108, 2000.

[7] A.C. Davison and D.A. Hinkley, *Bootstrap Methods and their Application, Cambridge Series in Statistical and Probabilistic Mathematics*, Cambridge University Press, 1997.

[8] J. Dilley, M. Arlitt, Improving Proxy Cache Performance: Analysis of three Replacement Policies, *IEEE Internet Computing*, November/December 1999.

[9] B. Efron, Bootstrap methods: another look at the jackknife, *Ann. Statist.* 7, 1–26, 1979.

[10] B. Efron, Computers and the theory of statistics: thinking the unthinkable, *SIAM Review* 21, 460, 1979.

[11] B. Efron and R.J. Tibshirani, *An Introduction to the Bootstrap, Monographs on Statistics and Applied Probability 57*, Chapman and Hall/CRC, 1993.

[12] J. Kangasharju, K.W. Ross and J.W. Roberts, Performance Evaluation of Redirection Schemes in Content Distribution Networks, *Computer Comm.* 24, 207–214, 2001.

[13] Kihong Park, Gi Tae Kim and Mark E. Crovella, On the Effect of Traffic Self-Similarity on Network Performance, *Proceedings of the SPIE International Conference on Performance and Control of Network Systems*, November 1997.

[14] A. Mahanti, C. Williamson and D. Eager, Traffic Analysis of a Web Proxy Caching Hierarch, *IEEE Network* 14, 16–23, 2000.

[15] National Lab of Applied Network Research (NLANR). Sanitized access log. ftp://ircache.nlanr.net/Traces/.

[16] S. Paul and Z. Fei, Distributed Caching with Centralized Control, *Computer Comm.* 24, 256–268, 2001.

[17] *Visual Numerics*, MSIMSL Math/Library, Visual Numerics, Houston, Texas, 1994.

[18] Web Polygraph, http://polygraph.ircache.net/.

[19] Web Polygraph, http://www.web-polygraph.org/reference/models/realism.html.

Web Caching and Content Delivery
A. Bestavros and M. Rabinovich (Editors)

Analyzing Web Robots and their Impact on Caching

Virgílio Almeida [a,1], Daniel Menascé [b,2], Rudolf Riedi [c,3], Flávia Peligrinelli [a,4], Rodrigo Fonseca [a,5], Wagner Meira Jr. [a,6]

[a] *Department of Computer Science, Universidade Federal de Minas Gerais, Belo Horizonte, MG 31270, Brazil*
[b] *Department of Computer Science, George Mason University, Fairfax, VA 22030, USA*
[c] *Department of Electrical and Computer Engineering, Rice University, Houston, TX 77251, USA*

Abstract

Understanding the nature and the characteristics of Web robots is an essential step to analyze their impact on caching. Using a multi-layer hierarchical workload model, this paper presents a characterization of the workload generated by autonomous agents and robots. This characterization focuses on the statistical properties of the arrival process and on the robot behavior graph model. A set of criteria is proposed for identifying robots in real logs. We then identify and characterize robots from real logs applying a multi-layered approach. Using a stack distance-based analytical model for the interaction between robots and Web site caching, we assess the impact of robots' requests on Web caches. Our analyses point out that robots cause a significant increase in the miss ratio of a server-side cache. Robots have a referencing pattern that completely disrupts locality assumptions. These results indicate not only the need for a better understanding of the behavior of robots, but also the need of Web caching policies that treat robots' requests differently than human generated requests.

Keywords: Performance analysis; Workload characterization; Web cache; Robots; e-Commerce

1. Introduction

Robots play a particularly central role in information economy. Robots automatically search the Internet for information, goods and services on behalf of customers. Indeed, directories and search engines are among the most popular sites of the Internet. At the same time, with the dawn of e-business and time-sensitive information, such as news and financial data, came along a steep growth of dynamic documents on the Web. Thus, search engines require exhaustive crawling work to maintain and update their indices to the

[1] E-mail: virgilio@dcc.ufmg.br
[2] E-mail: menasce@cs.gmu.edu
[3] E-mail: riedi@rice.edu
[4] E-mail: flavia@dcc.ufmg.br
[5] E-mail: rfonseca@dcc.ufmg.br
[6] E-mail: meira@dcc.ufmg.br

increasingly time-sensitive Web content. Currently, publicly indexed documents exceed one billion in numbers [1]. In addition to the general-purpose crawlers, an ever growing number of focused *crawlers* selectively seek out documents that are relevant to a specific pre-defined set of subjects [2]. To obtain information about a product or service requested by a customer (e.g., price, expected delivery time, etc.) might require to query hundreds of sites within seconds. For example, www.shopper.com claims to compare 1,000,000 prices on 100,000 specific products.

The growing popularity of crawlers, shopbots, and other robots on the Web, demands for an understanding of their behavior and their impact on the infrastructure of the Internet, in particular on the performance of Web caching. Towards this end, we analyze three different types of logs from actual Web sites: an online bookstore, servers for the 1998 FIFA World Cup, and the site of the Computer Science Department at UC Berkeley.

The goals of this paper are twofold. We first aim at identifying, characterizing and eventually distinguishing two major categories of robots, namely 'Crawlers' and 'Shop-Bots' solely based on observations at the server. These two classes produce quite distinctively different streams of requests. A typical Crawler will request a site's Home Page, wait for the response, parse it and determine the links present in the page. It then waits for a predetermined amount of time (possibly zero), and sequentially issues requests for each link found, repeating the process for each page received. On the other hand, PriceBots issue requests triggered by human action on a remote site, for example the search for a book by author in a price comparison site. One should expect the arrival process of requests and the popularity of objects requested to differ substantially for the two classes, which is what we set out to show. Second, it is impossible to ignore the impact of Web robots on Web caching. Using a stack distance-based model, we analyze the interaction between robots and server-side caches. Based on actual logs we compute cache hit ratios for different types of robots and analyze their impact on the cache behavior.

There are very few studies on Web robots available. Most concentrate on defining architectures and implementations for crawlers and shopbots. In [8], the authors survey the state-of-the-art of Web robots and discuss robot crawling, a technique for building indices for search engines. In [3], the authors examine the problem of identifying navigational patterns of Web robot sessions using standard classification techniques but do not cover features and statistical characterization of robot accesses. Reference [4] searches for invariants in e-business workloads. The authors studied the workload of two actual e-business sites and found the presence of robots in the workload. They also estimate that robot requests correspond to roughly 16% of the total workload of the sites analyzed.

Section 2 shows our hierarchical approach to characterizing robot workloads and summarizes the main features of the three actual logs used in this study. Section 3 models in detail the robot requests found in the bookstore logs. Section 4 assesses the impact of robots' requests on Web caches. Finally, Section 5 presents concluding remarks.

2. Robot workload modeling

This section describes the approach used for characterizing robot workloads. The resulting characterization not only provides information about the behavior of the various classes of robots but also allows for the determination of the resource demands imposed

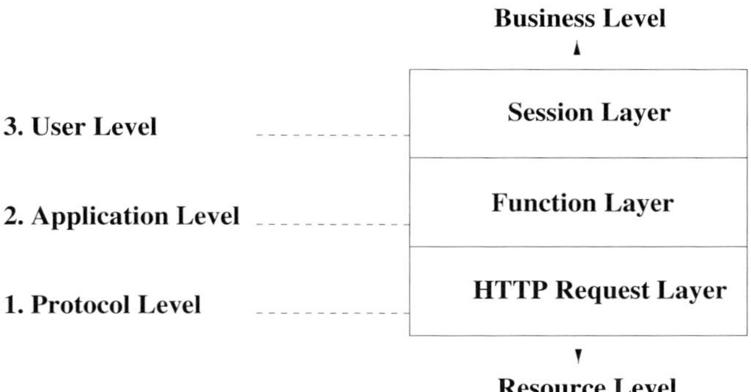

Fig. 1. A hierarchical workload model.

by them. Since not all robots identify themselves to the server, the task of characterizing robot workload is a combination of two highly intervowen sub-tasks: identifying robots for analysis, and an analysis which allows to characterize and thus identify robots. Identification may result from clues as diverse as session length, patterns, and others, as we are about to elaborate on.

Our starting point is the multi-layer hierarchical model proposed by Menascé et al. [4]. The model proposes a three-layer characterization strategy (see Fig. 1) to facilitate the understanding of how business-level decisions impact the resource level. The business strategy of robots is quite simple: gather information from the e-business site for tasks such as indexing or price/product comparison. The session layer focuses on the session length and on the overall behavior of each robot in terms of functions (e.g., search) invoked per session. The function layer specifies features associated with each function, such as their parameters, inter-arrival times, and the number of embedded files (e.g.,images) requested when a function is invoked. The request layer characterizes the individual HTTP requests in terms of an analysis of their arrival process on multiple time scales. Finally, the resource level characterizes all components of the computational platform of the e-commerce server.

Robots behave quite differently from humans; they invoke a smaller variety of functions and exhibit different repetition patterns and search strategies. The major simplification is that we do not expect robots to present a buying behavior, that is, they usually do not select products for later acquisition ('add to cart') and, in consequence, never purchase. However, we expect that the evolution of agent technology will allow such tasks to be performed automatically in the future. On the other hand, the process of robot characterization demands not only the determination of visiting patterns and arrival process, but also the nature of the parameters requested by robots. For instance, a crawler visits each object served by the Web site just once, producing an access pattern that is quite different from human users.

Inspired by Tan and Kumar [3] and Menascé [4] we introduce now several criteria, based on the aforementioned hierarchical model, which allow us to identify robots in real logs. We group these characteristic criteria according to the three layers of the hierarchical model.

2.1. The robot criteria

2.1.1. Session layer

The session-layer criteria for identifying robots are *session length* and *function*. Session length is defined as the number of functions invoked during a session. It is intuitive that thousands of requests within a few hours is highly atypical for a single human user, making session length an obvious criterion for identifying robots. But robots and humans differ also in terms of the type and variability of functions they invoke. For instance, some robots perform only searches and others visit systematically all the pages of a site, whereas humans typically follow some procedure of narrowing the search and potentially 'buying'.

2.1.2. Function layer

The criteria used at the function layer are the execution of *human-like functions* and the occurrence of *embedded files* in the request stream. The 'human-like function criterion' discards sessions in which products are bought or added to a shopping cart as being non-robotic. This criterion might fall short of being accurate in the future as robots start to buy on behalf of human customers. Robots usually do not request embedded files, since their goal is to obtain the textual information resulting from the requests.

2.1.3. Request layer

At the request layer the criteria are *self-identification* and request *inter-arrival times*. Some robots identify themselves by requesting the `robots.txt` file, which specifies the actions that may be performed by robots. This particular file request is a reliable identifier of robots since the file is hardly of any interest to a human. Unfortunately, not all robots check this file, though highly recommended by *net etiquette*. The request arrival process generated by human users typically exhibits an exponential distribution for inter-arrival times, while robots produce more periodic arrivals and, thus, quasi constant inter-arrival times.

2.2. The logs

The above criteria are applied to three actual logs. Obtaining HTTP logs from actual e-commerce sites can be a challenge since these logs may contain information that is quite revealing about the nature and degree of success of the business. We are grateful to an online bookstore which was kind enough to provide us with a sanitized version of their HTTP logs. Due to a non-disclosure agreement we are unable to name the company or to provide information on sale-related matters. The other two logs used in this paper are publicly available: logs from the UC Berkeley CS department Web server [11] and logs from the servers for the 1998 FIFA World Cup [10].

The characteristics from these logs are presented in Table 1. Notice that the number of functions issued by robots is largest for the bookstore. Because the site is a bookstore we found some ShopBots in the log, justifying the larger number of functions associated with robots. Notably, the logs of the bookstore and the World Cup servers contain more images than the Berkeley log due to the nature of the sites. Bookstores hope to improve sales by displaying images of book covers. The World Cup site used pictures of soccer players and games to attract visitors to the site. The Berkeley site, on the other hand, is an institutional site and does not exhibit a large amount of image files.

Table 1. Characteristics of the log files

	Source		
Interval:	Bookstore 01–15 Aug 1999	Berkeley 01–30 June 2000	WorldCup Site 23 May 1998
Number of requests	3,630,964	3,643,208	2,225,475
Percent of images	74%	44%	84%
Number of functions	955,818	2,038,249	340,719
% of robot's functions	33.51%	16.53%	6.46%
Number of sessions	130,314	371,242	33,995
Avg. robot's session length	2,409.60	1,324.93	1,398.16

Table 2. Criteria used for the identification of the ten most important robots in the bookstore log

Robot ID	Session Length	Function	Human-Likely Function	Embedded Files	Self Identification	IAT Distribution
2	•	S		•		
6	•	S		•		
8	•	S		•		
25	•	S		•		
104	•	S		•		
3784	•	C		•		•
0	•	C				•
45282	•	C		•	•	•
584	•	C		•	•	•
47277	•	C		•		•

Let us now discuss the application of the robot identification criteria to the three logs. Table 2 summarizes the results obtained for the bookstore log. Each column header labels a specific criterion and each line corresponds to a single robot. The id numbers are extracted from the logs and are used throughout this section to uniquely identify each robot. For each position in the table, except for column 2, a '•' sign indicates that the robot was identified by that specific criterion.

2.3. Applying the criteria

The criterion 'session length' (session layer) simply says that if a session has a length (in number of requests to functions) larger than a threshold, it is a robot with high probability. Fig. 2 plots the probability that a given session has more than x requests. Notice a sharp change in behavior at about 500 function-requests after which a heavy tail appears. We conjecture that this change is due to the increased fraction of robot sessions as the session length increases. Consequently, we used this value as the 'session length threshold': sessions longer than 500 requests to functions are considered to be originated by robots.

This criterion is very effective, and all the sessions we classified finally as robotic satisfy it. False positives, on the other hand, mainly mistake proxy servers for robots.

The criterion 'function' (session layer) regards the frequency of requests for each of the store's functions. The letters 'C' and 'S' in the table indicate a behavior that would

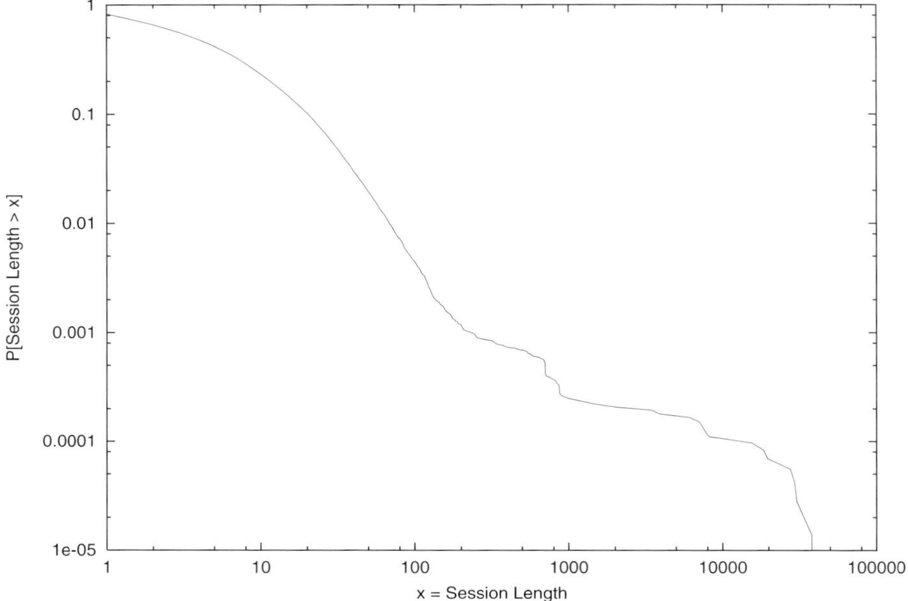

Fig. 2. Tail of the distribution of session lengths (1 - CDF) for all sessions in the bookstore log.

be expected for Crawlers (C) or for ShopBots (S). Some robots, previously identified as crawlers by manual inspection of their sessions had at least 65% of their functions corresponding to 'browse' or 'info' requests, while manually identified ShopBots exhibit 95% of 'search' requests. We used these numbers as criteria for automatically classifying other sessions. This procedure requires a semantic analysis of the frequency distribution of functions, and it cannot be used alone to determine the *type* of robot because these numbers may not always be valid, even though they showed to be effective in determining whether or not a session *is* robotic.

The 'human-likely function' criterion (function layer) says that a session is *not* associated with a robot if a function from a well-defined pool of typically human functions is present. For instance, in the case of the bookstore, a session with any request to the function 'pay' is considered non-robotic. It is important to note that this is a negative criterion: it does not imply that a given session exhibits human like behavior, but rather that it contains non-robotic functions. This criterion, unfortunately, did not classify any of the sessions in Table 2 as a robot.

The 'embedded files' criterion says that sessions with no or very few requests to embedded files are considered to be initiated by robots. This criterion may fail in the presence of some client or proxy cache configurations, because cached images might not be requested. Nevertheless, even cached images generally result in 'if modified since' requests, which appear in the log.

The 'self identification' criterion (request layer) assumes that only robots request the `robots.txt` file before accessing a site, since it describes the policies for robot access to the various site resources, such as which can be indexed and/or fetched.

The last criterion concerns the inter-arrival time distribution. Poisson processes generate exponentially distributed inter-arrival times (IAT). The request generation process for some automated robots is almost periodic with quasi-deterministic IAT. In fact, as we shall see, the IAT distribution for some robots was found to be very close to a log-normal distribution which concentrates around one value. This criterion is positive if the IAT distribution is not exponential, possibly indicating a request generation process not driven by humans.

The result of applying the above criteria to the sessions present in the log showed that no single criterion is always effective but a consensus among two or more of the presented criteria generally suffices for identifying a session as generated by a robot.

3. Robot workload characterization

In this section we identify and characterize robots from real logs applying our multi-layered approach (see Section 2). Thereby, we concentrate on the bookstore log because of its significant robot workload, but also because we identified a more diversified mix of robots than on the other logs.

The bookstore log shows requests that are not directly generated by browsers of human users. Through our analysis, we identified search engines' crawler agents, which are part of a broader class of agents that perform resource discovery and retrieval functions. In this class we can also find email address collectors, off-line browsers, site maintenance agents which probe the site at regular intervals to check whether it is alive, as well as database dumpers which, in the case of a bookstore, perform extensive ISBN searches for price comparison or retrieve information on books.

These agents are the actual robots, as they are entirely automated and have a request generation process that is not human-driven, but rather the consequence of a computer program. In this study we collectively call robots of this class *Crawlers*.

Another class of robots is that of agents associated with meta search engines and price comparison sites. We call them *ShopBots*. ShopBots are employed, e.g., by sites which search for prices of items in several e-tailers and present the findings summarized in a single page to the user. What is seen from the perspective of the bookstore is a long stream of requests coming from a single IP address, which can account for a significant portion of the store's load.

Proxy servers are a third source of requests that do not come directly from user browsers, but rather appear to the store as a long sequence of requests coming from a single IP address. By maintaining state information on the user, however, the store can identify the different user sessions present in the stream. We did not consider this type of request generating process, as it is essentially analogous to the direct human interaction.

3.1. Request layer characterization

We first analyze the distributions of the inter-arrival times (IAT) for each individual robot, and then show our results for the arrival rate sampled at multiple time scales.

3.1.1. Distribution of inter-arrival times

As mentioned, requests triggered by human interaction have a high potential to possess characteristics of a Poisson process, i.e., exponentially distributed IATs. In fact, over 1/2-

Table 3. Parameters for the fitted distribution of IAT's

ShopBots				Crawlers				
ID	λ	mean	σ	ID	M	S	mean	σ
2	0.0407	24.57	24.57	3784	0.448	1.3280	3.78	3.31
6	0.0188	53.19	53.19	0	0.230	0.9120	1.90	2.17
8	0.0280	35.71	35.71	45282	1.733	0.3750	6.06	2.35
25	0.0639	15.64	15.64	584	3.403	0.0031	30.05	0.09
104	0.0120	83.33	83.33	47277	1.057	0.1764	2.92	0.51

to 1-hour periods, session arrivals on Internet links have been shown to be consistent with a homogeneous Poisson process (e.g., see [6] for FTP and TELNET sessions, and [7] for Web sessions). Systematic crawlers, on the other hand, should be expected to show more regular, periodic behavior, i.e., IAT distributions which cluster heavily around an average value.

Fig. 3 displays the probability distribution function for the interarrival times (IAT) for Crawlers and ShopBots. The distribution for Crawlers exhibits a well defined peak, which varies from one robot to the other.

Crawlers, dumping a database or following links systematically and without human interaction will show a fairly periodic pacing of requests, i.e., a strong clustering of the IAT around their mean. Variability might be caused by network transfer delays – known to be sharply peaked log-normal [9] – and servicing delays. Indeed, we were able to successfully fit, by minimizing the sum of the squared residuals, sharply peaked log-normal distributions for the IAT of crawlers. The probability density function (pdf) for the log-normal distribution is given by $p(x) = 1/Sx\sqrt{2\pi}e^{-(\ln x - M)^2/(2S^2)}$, where M and S are the mean and standard deviation of $\ln(x)$, respectively. The parameters of the distribution, as well as the mean and variance thereof can be seen in Table 3.

Shopbots, on the other hand, show IAT distributions that are fairly well approximated by exponential distributions with pdf given by $p(x) = \lambda e^{-\lambda x}$ for $x > 0$, as can be seen on the plot at the bottom of Fig. 3. A slight mismatch can again be explained by accounting for the convolution with transfer delay (for an exponential, a convolution with a sharply peaked log-normal distribution has little effect). Again, the parameters for the fitted distributions for the Shopbots can be seen in the left half portion of Table 3.

3.1.2. Multi-scale time analysis

In this section we study the arrival rate of robot requests on different time scales, i.e., sampled in time intervals of varying length. Figs. 4 and 5 show the results for sampling intervals of 1 minute, 30 minutes, and 4 hours. A visual inspection of the plots reveals completely different behavior for Crawlers and Shopbots, at least on intermediate to large time scales.

Crawlers turn on sporadically, send requests at a high steady rate through the duration of their activity and produce clearly visible bursts of activity, not necessarily following any daily patterns. Human-triggered agents such as the Shopbots produce request arrivals that show characteristics similar to the overall requests (all clients). Here, trends emerge which show in terms of long sequences of increase or decrease of volume, particularly pointed at intermediate time scales of the order of minutes. This reflects the overall pattern of the human work-cycle.

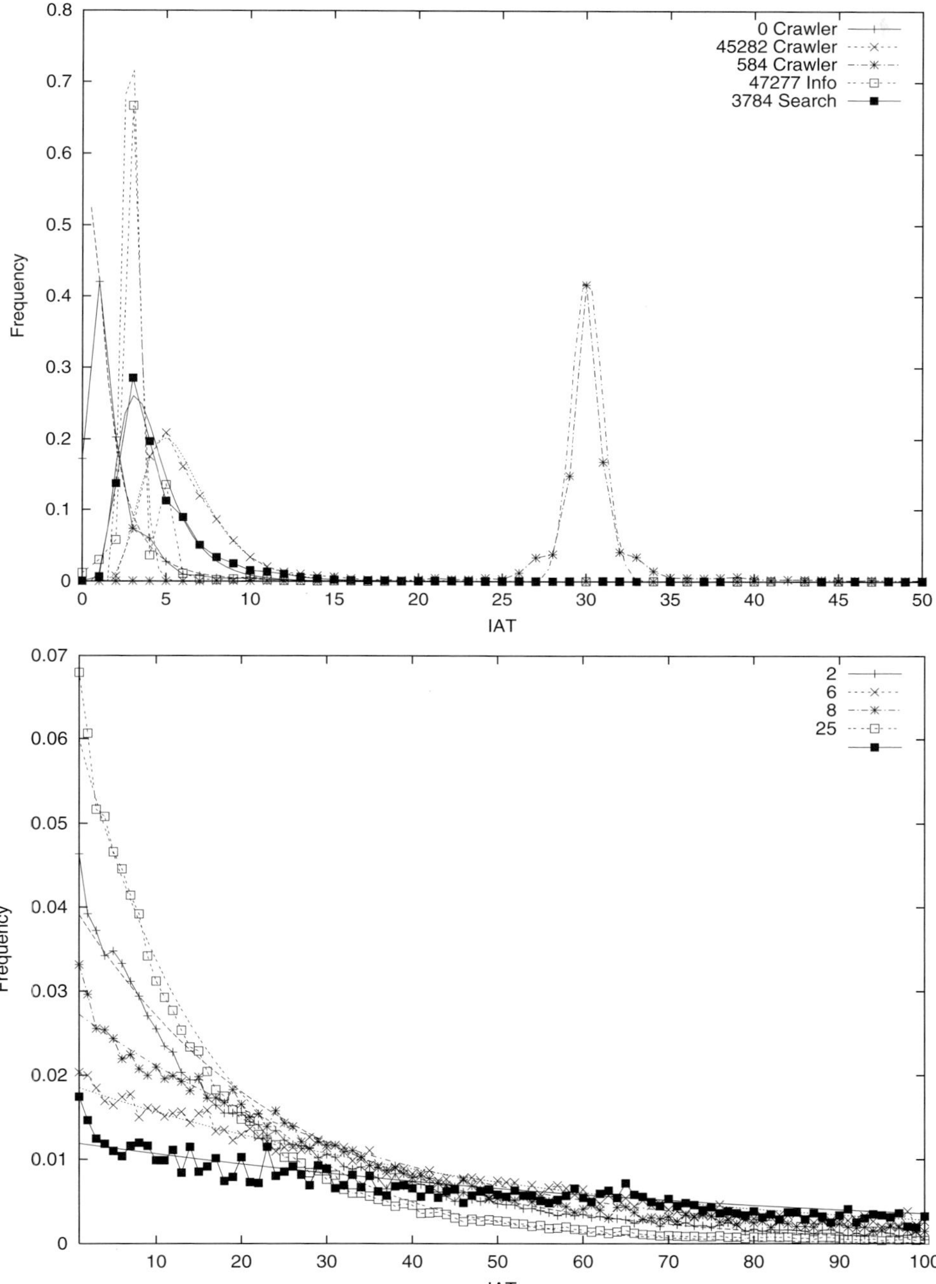

Fig. 3. Probability density functions of the IAT for Crawlers (top) and ShopBots (bottom). Plotted next to each curve is the fitted log-normal or exponential theoretical curve, which show underlying machine and human triggered request generation processes, respectively.

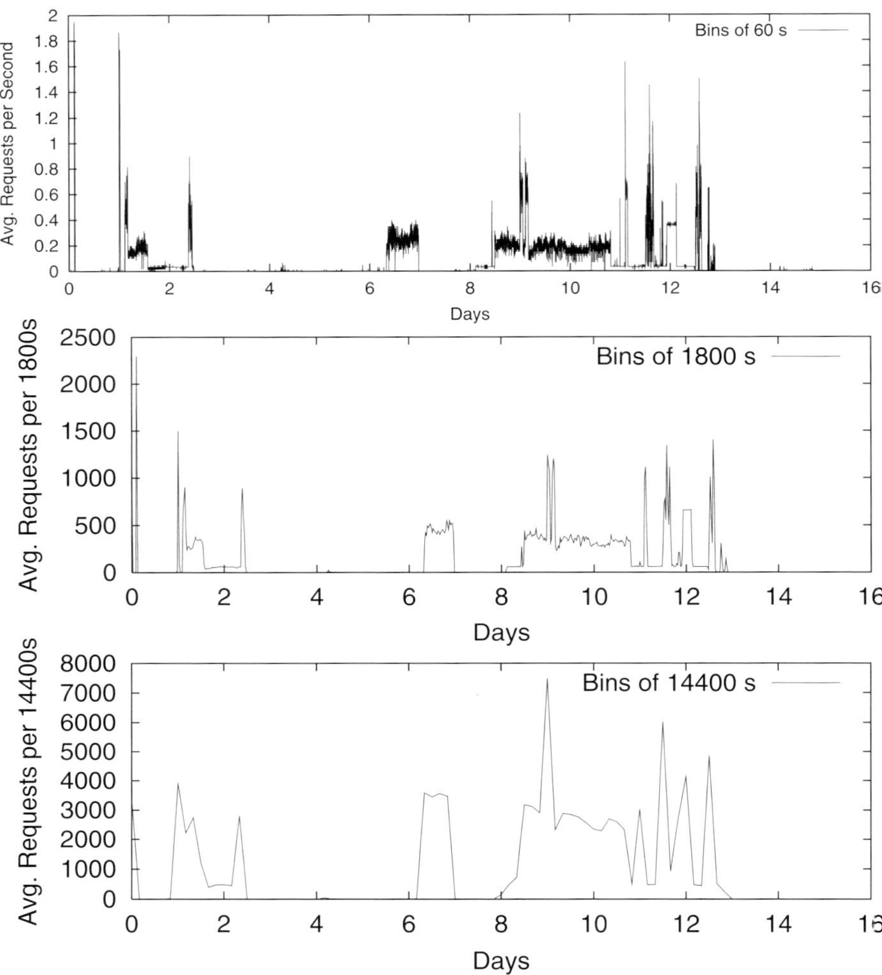

Fig. 4. Arrival process for the Crawlers combined, considering bins of 1 minute, 30 minutes, and 4 hours, showing well defined, short, and irregular bursts of requests.

It is also interesting to indicate the effectiveness of the multi-scale analysis to point out short bursts of activity, seen only on finer times scales. For example, in the case of Crawlers the arrival rate averaged over periods of 1 minute peaks at close to 2 requests per second (Fig. 4). These peaks are averaged out when larger sampling intervals are considered since they are of short duration. This can be invaluable when planning to handle bursts.

3.2. Function layer characterization

In this section we consider, at the function level, the pattern of object references of different robots. Here the term 'object' is employed in a broad sense, representing the

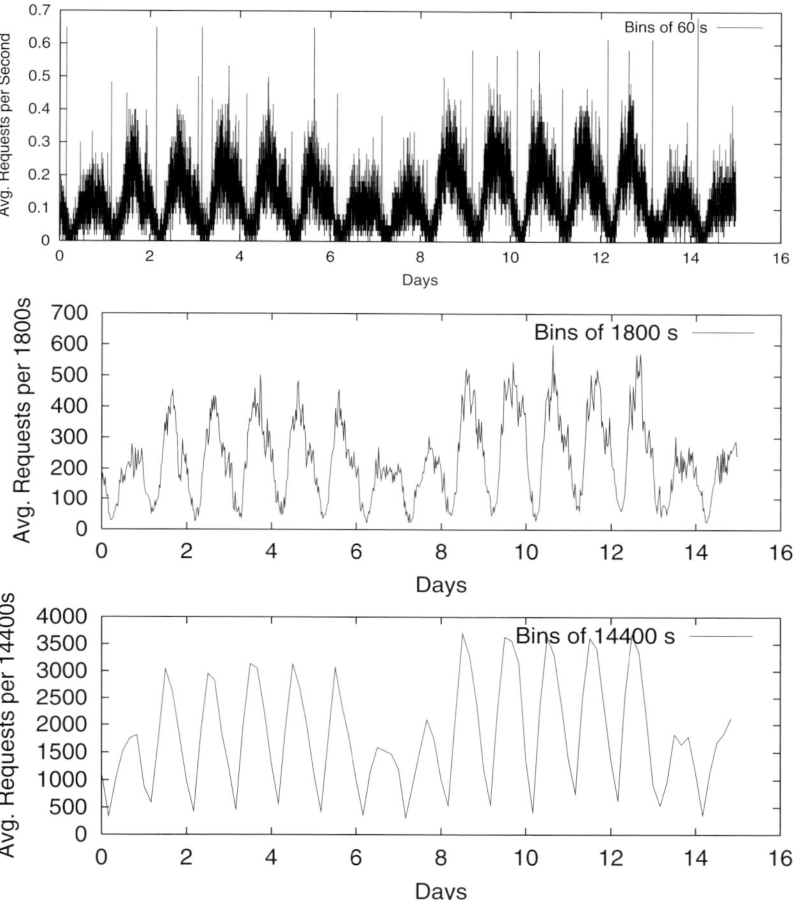

Fig. 5. Arrival process for the ShopBots combined, considering bins of 1 minute, 30 minutes, and 4 hours, showing a well defined pattern that follows the days of the week at the coarser scale, a very human pattern.

information targeted by a request, such as the query string for a search request, and the name of the category for a browsing request. For example, given a Search request, its parameter is the query string, and given a Book Info request, its parameter is the book itself. Intuitively, crawlers should request several items approximately the same number of times. Shopbots, on the other hand, should follow an object popularity similar to that of the human users that trigger the activation of the Shopbots, as discussed in more detail in what follows.

Consider a crawler that indexes a site or downloads the entire book database of an online bookstore. During its session, the crawler would typically visit each page once (or a constant number of times). Let the popularity of an object be defined as the number of times it is requested in a session, divided by the total number of requests in the session. For a crawler session, the popularity of all objects should be very similar.

The popularity of objects referenced by human beings, on the other hand, is far from constant. In fact, it has been shown in several domains that the distribution of the

Table 4. ShopBot CBMG

	Entry	Exit	Home	Search
Entry	0	0	0.118	99.882
Home	0	0	0	100
Search	0	0.003	0	99.997

popularity among objects of a referenced set is highly concentrated. If we rank the objects by the number of references, i.e., the most referenced objects first, Zipf's law states that the popularity is inversely proportional to the rank. Thus, in a doubly logarithmic plot of the popularity versus the rank Zipf's law appears as a straight line with negative slope given by a parameter α. The larger the absolute value of the slope, the more skewed the distribution is. This behavior should also determine the reference pattern of ShopBots, since they re-issue search requests that originate from humans.

Fig. 6 plots the rank versus the popularity for objects referenced by a typical Crawler and by a typical ShopBot, in a log–log scale, for the robots with identifications 0 and 25, respectively. We can see that they differ considerably. In the top plot, the Crawler exhibits very large quasi-horizontal regions, indicating near uniform referencing patterns for large groups of objects. In fact, for one of the crawlers we found that more than 90% of the objects were referenced only once. In the bottom plot, the ShopBot conforms very closely to a Zipf-like distribution. By using a linear least-squares fit we found a good fit for $\alpha = 0.49$. The popularity distribution for the objects referenced in the sessions which were classified as human-generated sessions exhibits a similar behavior, i.e., a Zipf-like distribution with $\alpha = 0.62$, indicating a more skewed distribution.

3.3. Session layer characterization

In this layer,we target the session lengths of the robots and the semantics derived from the access pattern to functions as represented by the Customer Behavior Model Graph (CBMG) [5]. This is a state transition graph used to describe the behavior of groups of customers who exhibit similar navigational patterns. The graph has one node for each possible state (e.g., home page, browse, search, select, add, and pay) and transitions between these states. A probability is assigned to each transition. Different types of users may be characterized by different CBMGs in terms of the transition probabilities. From the CBMG one can derive the session length and the average number of visits per session to each state, and the semantics of the access pattern.

We represent the CBMGs as square matrices, where an entry i, j represents the percent probability of going to state j from state i. We removed the states that had no visits.

Table 4 shows the averaged CBMG for the ShopBots. It shows a simple structure: the first state is almost always 'search', and the robot leaves the 'search' state with a very low probability. This is confirmed by Table 5, which shows the distribution of visits to each state per session, derived from the CBMG. The behavior indicates that the ShopBots perform (almost) exclusively searches, and that usually they have long sessions.

Table 6 shows the averaged CBMG for the various crawlers. The first observation is the much broader pool of states that are visited. This is only natural, since some of the crawlers tend to visit the whole site. This involves spanning various states, with the

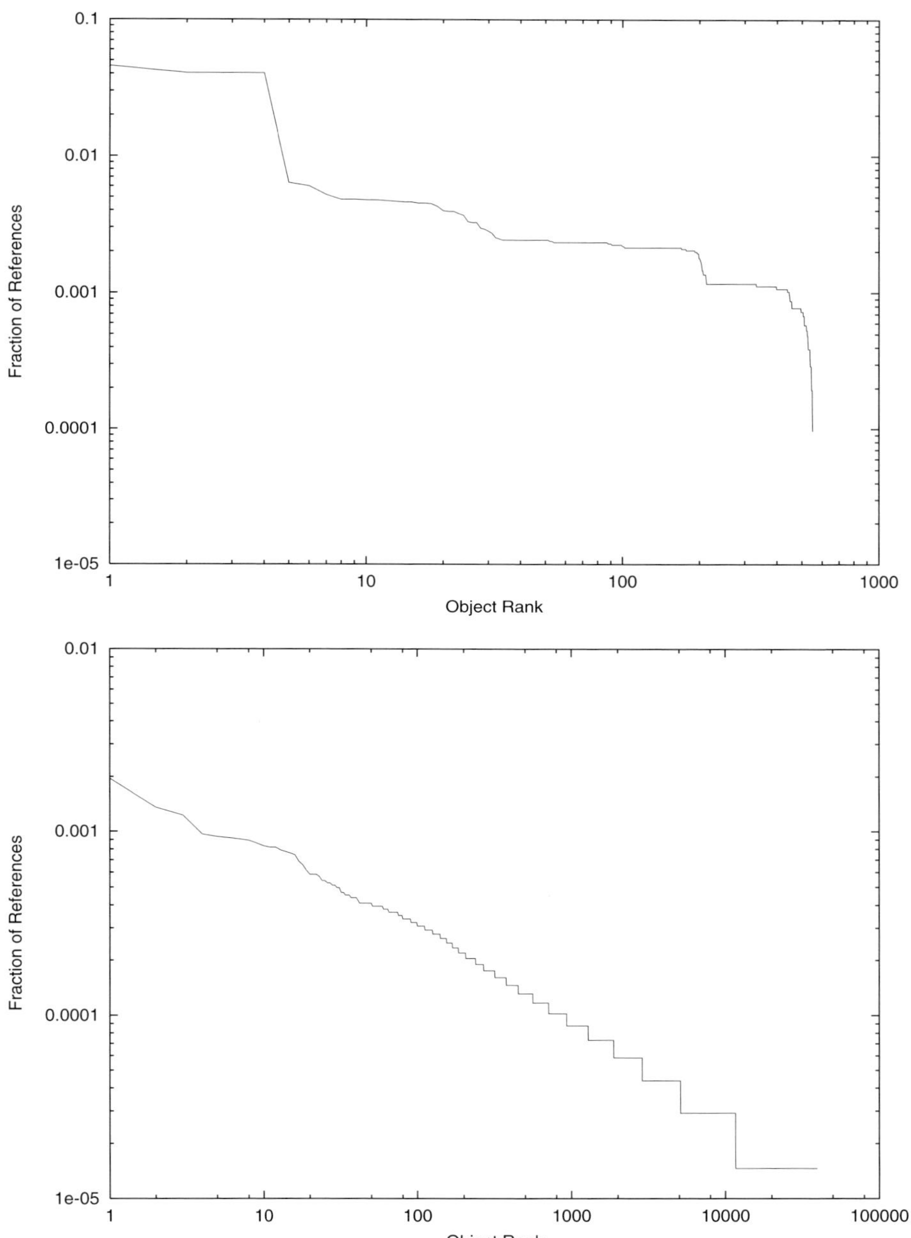

Fig. 6. Rank vs. popularity graph for a typical Crawler (top) and a typical ShopBot (bottom).

exception of the 'Humanoid Functions'. Most of the visits are to 'browse' and 'view' (information on specific items). Visits to the search state are rare, and they are usually associated with the initial search page that is reached by the crawler (see Table 7).

Table 5. ShopBots function distribution and number of visits

Function	Function distribution (%)	# of Visits
Home	0.12	36
Other	0.05	14
Search	99.83	30391

Table 6. Crawler CBMG

	Entry	Exit	Home	Browse	Search	View	Add	Acc	Robo	Aux
Entry	0	0	33.333	33.333	0	33.333	0	0	0	0
Home	0	0.0196	16.606	24.29	0.031	8.794	30.332	4.061	0.016	15.844
Browse	0	0.006	8.088	68.817	0.098	2.783	0.053	0.002	0.006	20.146
Search	0	0	1.426	54.028	16.125	25.716	0	0	0	2.705
View	0	0.0020	1.240	4.182	0.783	92.601	0.124	0.015	0	1.052
Add	0	0	6.979	0	0	0	11.419	81.119	0	0.483
Acc	0	0	2.292	0.040	0.040	0	3.023	13.485	0	81.121
Robo	0	0	50.000	0	0	0	0	0	0	50.000
Aux	0	0	1.832	26.017	32.916	13.273	0.060	0	0	25.903

Table 7. Crawler function distribution and visits

Function	Function distribution (%)	# of visits
View	38.34	6221
Browse	36.53	5926
Aux	13.61	2208
Home	4.41	716
Search	2.56	415
Acc	2.24	364
Add	2.09	339
Other	0.21	34
Robot	0.01	1

The CMBG is very effective in identifying the type of a robot, but it is worth noting that it should be used in conjunction with the other criteria, such as the arrival process characterization to correctly classify the robots. Indeed, we found a Crawler (actually a database dumper) that performed only searches.

4. Impact of robots on caches: a first cut

In this section we assess the impact that robots have on Web caching. Our discussion applies mostly to server-side caches or to other types of caches that are part of the server cluster.

We concentrate our analysis on the bookstore log. We start by partitioning the log using the criteria of Section 2 into three categories: crawlers, shopbots, and others (i.e., requests

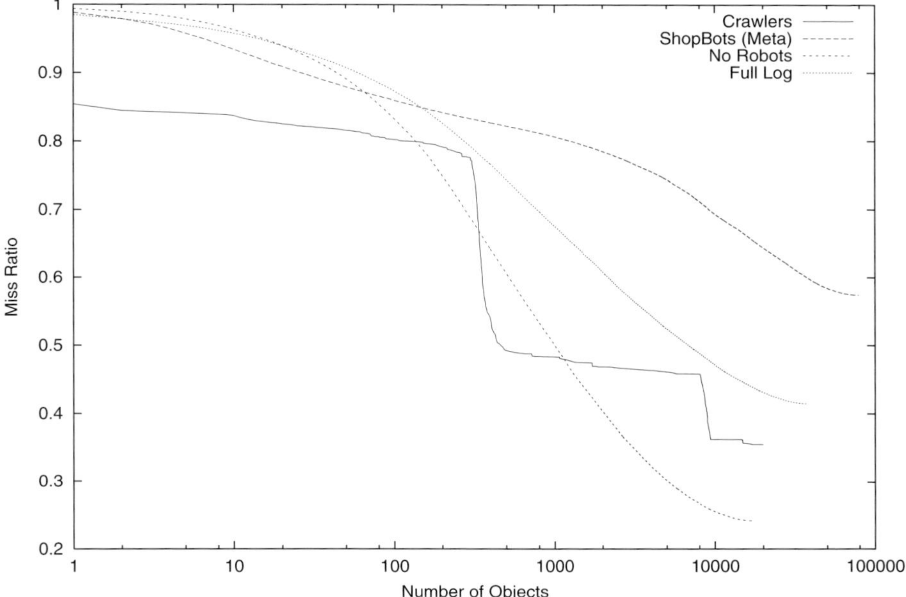

Fig. 7. Miss ratio as a function of cache size (in number of objects).

generated directly by human beings). This procedure yields three new logs, which we compare with the original complete log, leaving us with a total of four data sets. In order to compare the effectiveness of caching, we assume a server-side cache system which is able to cache results of dynamic requests, specifically search and info requests. From the four logs we derive the corresponding request streams that the cache would be subject to, by isolating the objects referenced in the requests to search and info functions.

Fig. 7 plots the expected miss ratio on a cache subject to the four streams discussed above, as a function of cache size, measured as the number of objects it can hold. We consider all objects to be equally sized. This model, albeit simplistic, can give us insight on the behavior of the cache for the different streams. We use the marginal distribution of Least Recently Used (LRU) stack distances to determine the cache miss ratio [12,14] under the LRU policy. If D is the random variable corresponding to the stack distances and F_D is the cumulative distribution function of D, then the miss ratio $m(x)$ for a cache of size x is given by

$$P[D > x] = 1 - F_D(x) = m(x).$$

We start by noting the significant difference in the asymptotical miss ratio of the four streams, i.e., if the cache had infinite size. The asymptotical miss ratio is due to the mandatory miss caused by the first reference to each object, and thus relates to the number of different objects in the reference stream. The 'No Robots' curve has the lowest miss ratio, lower than 25%, almost half that of the 'Full' log. It is also the one that decreases the most as we increase the cache size. The 'ShopBots' curve shows an asymptotical miss ratio close to 57%. The log we analyzed is from a specialized bookstore that has books from restricted domains. We conjecture that the human users that access the site know this and thus submit queries that are also restricted to a narrower domain. The ShopBots, on the other hand, submit queries to this and to other bookstores on behalf of users that are not aware of the domain of these backend bookstores. This behavior would tend to increase the number of different objects requested. The 'ShopBots' curve is also much less sensitive to increases in cache size. This is very much in tune with the observation that the inclination of the popularity versus rank curve is much lower for the Shopbots than it is for human users, indicating a less skewed distribution.

The 'Crawlers' curve is very different from the others, with very pronounced steps. It presents regions in which the miss ratio remains almost the same as the cache expands, to fall abruptly after threshold cache sizes. This is a consequence of the non-human request generating process, which can be also seen in Fig. 6 that shows the popularity distribution as a function of rank. The crawlers have a 'round-robin' like referencing pattern, requesting each object approximately the same number of times. Some crawlers have a list of items which they request sequentially, while others crawl the site in breadth-first order. In the database literature, it is well known that repeatedly reading a relation sequentially can render an LRU cache useless, unless the cache can hold the entire relation [13]. We interpret each step in the curve as the size of the set of pages requested by each different crawler, but this requires further investigation. Another interesting observation from the 'Crawler' curve is that with a cache of size 1 we can verify a hit ratio of almost 15%, while at the same size the other curves exhibit hit ratios close to 0%. We inspected the logs and found out that this is due to one particular crawler that always requests the same object twice within a very short interval. Even on a cache of size 1 the second references always generate a hit.

The main conclusion drawn from the above is that the presence of robots causes a significant increase in the miss ratio of a server side cache. Crawlers have a referencing pattern that completely disrupts locality assumptions, while ShopBots show a reference stream with less reference locality. Further, the arrival process of both Crawlers and ShopBots poses a significant additional load on the servers, which have to handle the costs associated with both a higher miss ratio and the requests submitted by robots. This suggests that robots should be treated differently than humans by the cache and by the server.

5. Conclusions

Robot activity may significantly impact the performance of a Web site. In fact, last year, a well-know auction site sued an auction aggregation site for sending crawlers to the auction site at rate of 100,000 times/day, accounting for 1.53% of the requests received by the auction site. This level of activity was sufficient to prompt the auction to take legal action to stop the flood of robot activity. Very few studies have been published regarding the behavior of robots on the Web and we are not aware of any studies that focus on the impact of robots on cache performance.

This paper used a hierarchical approach for workload characterization of requests generated by robots. Using several criteria, the paper shows the presence of different types of robots in logs from actual Web sites. The characterization was done at the session, function, and request levels. Statistical analyses of the robot request arrival process was carried out at different time scales. Using information derived from the log of a real online bookstore, the paper then discusses the impact of robots on the performance of Web caches. From the reference locality perspective, the presence of robots causes a significant increase in the miss ratio of a server side cache, resulting in higher costs for request responses, which affect already overloaded servers by the robot requests themselves. These results suggest the need for strategies of service differentiation between robots and human users, not only guaranteeing the response time of the later, but also the efficacy of cache mechanisms employed by the server.

References

[1] M. Diligenti, F. Coetzee, S. Lawrence, C. Giles and M. Gori, Focused Crawling Using Context Graphs, *Proc. 26th VLDB Conf.*, Egypt 2000.

[2] S. Chakrabarti, M. Berg, and B. Dom, Focused Crawling: a new approach to topic-specific Web resource discovery, Proc. 8th Int. World-Wide Web Conf., Canada, 1999.

[3] P. Tan and V. Kumar, Modeling of Web Robot Navigational Patterns, Proc. ACM WebKDD Workshop, 2000.

[4] D.A. Menascé, V. Almeida, R. Fonseca, R. Riedi, F. Ribeiro, and W. Meira Jr., In Search of Invariants for E-Business Workloads, *Proc. 2000 ACM Conf. in Electronic Commerce*, Minneapolis, 2000.

[5] V.A.F. Almeida, D.A. Menascé, R. Fonseca, and M. Mendes, Business-oriented Resource Management Policies for E-commerce Servers, *Performance Evaluation: An International Journal*, Vol. 42 (2000), pp. 223–239.

[6] V. Paxson and S. Floyd, Wide area traffic: The failure of Poisson modeling, *IEEE/ACM Transactions on Networking* 3, pp. 226–244, 1995.

[7] A. Feldmann, A.C. Gilbert. W. Willinger and T.G. Kurtz, The changing nature of network traffic: Scaling phenomena, *Computer Communication Review* 28, No. 2, pp. 5–29, April 1998.

[8] O. Heinomen, K. Hatonen, and M. Klemettinen, WWW Robots and search engines, Seminar on Mobile Code, Dept. of Computer Science, Helsinki University of Technology, Finland, 1996.

[9] W. Matthews and L. Cottrell, Internet End-to-End Performance Monitoring for the High-Energy Nuclear and Particle Physics Community, *Passive and Active Measurement Workshop (PAM 2000)*, Hamilton, 2000.

[10] Soccer World Cup Server log http://ita.ee.lbl.gov/html/traces.html.

[11] Berkeley CS Department Web Server log http://www.cs.berkeley.edu/logs/http.

[12] V. Almeida, A. Bestavros, M. Crovella, and A. de Oliveira. Characterizing reference locality in the www. In *Proc. 4th Int. Conf. on Parallel and Distributed Information Systems*, pages 92–103, December 1996.

[13] B.T. Jonsson, M.J. Franklin, and D. Srivastava. Interaction of query evaluation and buffer management for information retrieval. In *Proc. of the ACM SIGMOD Int. Conf. on Management of Data*, pages 118–129, June 1998.

[14] T. Kelly and D. Reeves. Optimal Web cache sizing: scalable methods for exact solutions. *Computer Communications*, Vol. 24, pages 163–173, February 2001.

Web Caching and Content Delivery
A. Bestavros and M. Rabinovich (Editors)

Using a Proxy to Measure Client-Side Web Performance

Richard Liston [1], Ellen Zegura [2]

College of Computing, Georgia Institute of Technology, 801 Atlantic Drive, Atlanta, GA 30332-0280, USA

Abstract

Accurately collecting measurements of client-side browsing behavior and performance is important for making decisions about the design and operation of protocols. In this paper, we present the design and implementation of a method for measuring various variables related to the client-side browsing of Web pages. For example, with this method we can measure the contribution of DNS lookups to the total latency for loading a Web page as experienced by the user. We provide a discussion of the criteria that such a method should meet. We then evaluate the effectiveness of our method and discuss its limitations with respect to our design criteria. We consider the scope of questions that can be answered using this method.

Keywords: World Wide Web; Performance measurement; HTTP; Proxy

1. Introduction

Accurately collecting measurements of client-side browsing behavior and performance is important for making decisions about the design and operation of Web-related protocols. Good measurements provide a reasonable foundation on which to base choices. They can also provide indications of where it is most fruitful to focus efforts on increasing Web performance.

Our eventual interest is in the role of DNS in the response time experienced by users. The advent of content distribution networks and more complex Web pages with content from multiple servers have potentially increased the importance of DNS in end-user performance. Because of this interest, we need measurements that capture the components of access response time, isolating DNS access times from object download times. We also need an accurate picture of the concurrency that results with parallel connections and the inherent overlaps in the various access times.

In addition, we are interested in measurements have the following characteristics:

- Taken from real user behavior. We want to collect measurements during standard user operation.

[1] E-mail: liston@cc.gatech.edu
[2] E-mail: ewz@cc.gatech.edu

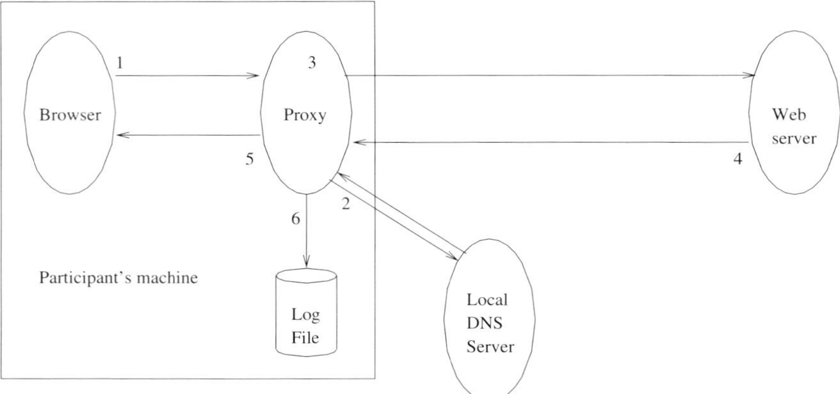

Fig. 1. Measurement architecture.

- Transparent to users. Since we will make measurements during operation, we want to minimize any performance degradation or other artifacts from measurement that might alter user behavior.
- Collected in a range of environments, broadly defined to include a variety of operating systems, browsers, access technologies, etc. This is to ensure that any local effects such as an atypically fast connection do not skew our conclusions. As a corollary, we require that the measurement technique require no special privileges (e.g., root access) on the part of the users participating in the study.

We describe related work in more detail later, but observe here that prior approaches to measuring user behavior have limitations in one or more of the dimensions listed above. Techniques that monitor using `tcpdump` require root access and therefore are limited to measurements in environments with privileged access. Modifying browser code to collect measurements has the potential to degrade performance; it also limits the measurement to users of browsers that we are able to instrument because source code is available.

To satisfy our objectives, we chose to implement data collection in a Web proxy with one proxy instance per browser instance, as illustrated in Fig. 1. It is not required that the proxy run on the same machine as the browser, but doing so minimizes the effects of other network traffic on the measurements. As illustrated, the proxy sits between the browser and any Web servers accesses; it also handles all calls for DNS resolution.

The proxy behaves as follows: (1) intercepts client requests, (2) performs the DNS resolution, (3) connects to the target server and passes the request to the server. The server then (4) responds to the proxy with a header and (typically) data for the requested object. As the proxy receives the responses, it (5) passes them to the client. As the proxy passes headers and data in both directions, information of interest is parsed from both the headers and the data and (6) gets logged to a log file. We post-process the log file to extract measurements of interest.

This paper presents the design and implementation of the proxy and post-processing. The next section describes more precisely the measurement information we want to capture via logging and post-processing. We describe in some detail what is logged by the proxy and how the post-processing is done. In Section 3 we discuss a number of issues affecting the design and implementation of the proxy.

2. Method overview

As described in the Introduction, our method consists of a proxy that operates between the client and the rest of the network. The proxy logs information to a log file, which is post-processed to extract information of interest. The design of the proxy must balance the goals of transparency to the user and ability to log the information necessary for recovery of measurement information.

From the standpoint of the proxy, the important characteristic of browser behavior is that the browser makes a request for a *base page*. The retrieved base page typically includes some number of *embedded objects* such as frames and images. HTML *tags* are character string tokens used by HTML to structure a Web page. The embedded objects are indicated by tags placed in the HTML code. As the server responds to this request, the proxy parses the response and logs information of interest. To keep the proxy as simple as possible so that its performance interferes minimally with the user's Web experience, the proxy only performs those functions related to the retrieval of objects and logging information of interest to the log files. Each line of the log file contains the following information:

- **ID:** An identifier which is unique to each object being requested by the proxy.
- **TYPE:** A string indicating the type of the line. The complete list of TYPES is given in Appendix A. The use of some of these TYPES is highlighted in Section 3 where we describe details of the proxy design.
- **ADDITIONAL INFO:** Each line type may cause additional information to be logged. For example, the actual IMG tag is logged on an IMG line type. Some line types, such as an **EOH** line, do not have additional info.

From the point of view of the proxy, each request is independent. The proxy maintains no explicit information specifying which objects are grouped together into pages. This function is performed by the browser as it determines how to display Web pages. Often, however, the variables we wish information about depend on how the objects are grouped together into pages. Therefore, one of the most important functions to be performed during post-processing is to reconstruct how the objects are grouped to form a complete Web page.

In Fig. 2 we illustrate a simple example of how we perform this grouping. Fig. 2A depicts the proxy's view of objects being transmitted over time. The horizontal axis is the time line, and the thick horizontal lines depict the time from the initial receipt of the request for the object at the proxy to the time the object has been completely transmitted to the browser. On the vertical axis the objects are numbered in the order in which they are requested. Not pictured is the fact that along with information about the timing of the objects, the logs also contain the URLs of the objects and any information about objects which may be requested as a result of receiving this object.

Fig. 2B depicts the post-processing, which occurs in two steps. First, for each object, we search the set of objects retrieved to date for a tag which caused this object to be retrieved. If one is found, we add an arrow extending from the retrieved object to the one that contains the tag.

When the complete log file has been processed, we have all the information necessary for grouping objects into pages. Fig. 2B also depicts this final stage in post-processing. Any object which does not have an arrow emanating from it is assumed to have been requested by the user. These are the base pages. We then group objects into a Web page by

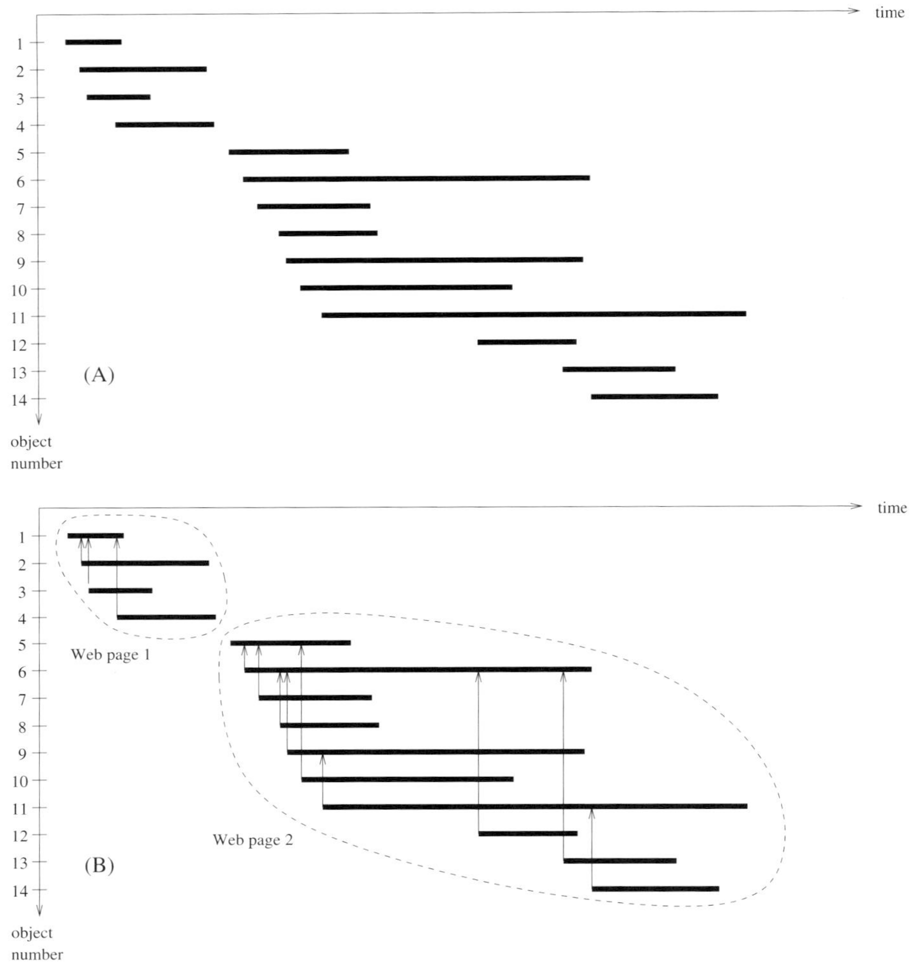

Fig. 2. Grouping objects into web pages during post-processing.

associating with each base page all objects which can reach the base page by following a path along the arrows and objects towards the base page. Two such groupings are depicted in the figure.

This discussion describes the simplest case of post-processing. Some issues which cause difficulties and the effects of these issues on our design are discussed in the next section.

3. Proxy design issues

In this section we discuss issues affecting the design and implementation of the proxy. These issues determine what information was actually chosen to be logged in the log files. In the following section we discuss some of the limitations of our method.

We group the issues affecting our design into three categories. First, we discuss the issues related directly to the HTTP protocol itself. These issues are involved with information in the HTTP headers of the request and the response. Next, we discuss the issues that relate to the actual content of the objects. Finally, we discuss issues that arise from interactions between the proxy and browser.

3.1. HTTP issues

3.1.1. Content-encoding

The HTTP protocol allows the data in a response to be encoded according to some encoding scheme. Requests may contain an 'Accept-Encoding' field in the request header that indicates to the server what encoding types the client is willing to handle. The server informs the browser via the 'Content-Encoding' header field how the data must be decoded. For example, the server can deliver a gzipped HTML page accompanied by the header field 'Content-Encoding: gzip'. This, however, causes all HTML in the transferred object to be unreadable by the proxy since the data will not be decompressed until it is received by the browser.

To alleviate this problem, the proxy intercepts the 'Accept-Encoding' field sent by the browser and changes it to 'Accept-Encoding: identity; q=1.0, ∗;q=0'. This causes the server to decode any encoded content, if possible, before sending. The proxy can then examine and parse the plain HTML. Doing so will cause a change in the timing of the rendering of the page. The degree to which this impacts proxy transparency warrants further study. However, during development of the proxy we noted few situations in which servers provided compressed HTML objects.

3.1.2. Location

The response header for an object may include a 'Location' field. This field indicates to the browser that the object being requested is found at an alternate URL, and provides the URL for the browser to automatically query. There may be more than one location indirection that must be followed before the request for the object is satisfied. The new URL may contain the same domain name as the initial query, a completely different domain name, or it may point to a different name within the same zone as the original query.

The proxy logs the 'Location' header field, and in post-processing, objects are linked to previous requests in which the response header had a matching 'Location' field.

3.1.3. Proxy-connection

Our proxy implements HTTP/1.0. It therefore does not handle Keep-Alive connections. Specifically, it does not handle more than one set of headers sent from the client to the server on a single connection. The proxy handles this by removing the 'Proxy-Connection: Keep-Alive' from headers sent to the server. This forces the server to close the connection after the requested object has been sent. It has the effect of requiring a separate process to be created for each requested object, each with a separate tcp handshake. Cohen et al. [6] suggest that the effect this has on our measurements is highly dependent on time of day. Their data shows that roughly 20% of the connection-establishment times to servers can take 400 msecs during busy hours, and 1% may take as long as 8 secs. We anticipate that we can modify the proxy to support Keep-Alive connections with minimal changes to the proxy.

3.1.4. Content-type

Objects with certain content-types will never generate subsequent requests from the browser. So in order to reduce the performance impact of the proxy, it examines the content-type of the object as it is received from the server. If it will not cause a request to be sent, the proxy passes the data directly to the browser without parsing it.

Also, if the content-type is application (e.g., application/x-javascript or application/ x-shockwave-flash), then we assume that another page caused it to be loaded. In this case, if no other heuristics have determined which base object this object should be linked to, we link it to the most recently identified base object.

3.2. Content-driven issues

3.2.1. JavaScript

JavaScript is a scripting language that allows for development of Web applications. Client-side JavaScript is dynamically interpreted by the browser and can cause the browser to retrieve remote objects. It is impossible for a proxy to predict with 100% accuracy what a request from a browser will look like when the page includes JavaScript and the browser has JavaScript turned on. A simple example of the problem is illustrated by the following JavaScript code:

```
<script lang="javascript">
NumR=Math.floor(Math.random()*10000000);
document.write('<IMG SRC="http://foo.bar/' + NumR + ' ">');
</script>
```

In the above case, the proxy and the browser will choose different random numbers and the resulting IMG tags will not match. The post-processor will be unable to match the incoming request with the page causing the request, so it will incorrectly interpret the new request as a base page. We handle this ambiguity by causing delimiters to be placed in the proxy's log when a section of JavaScript has been encountered (see START_JS and END_JS in Appendix A). During post-processing, any object that occurs between the delimiters is assumed to have been generated by the JavaScript section of the previous object.

As illustrated in Fig. 3 the delimiters cannot be logged while the stream is being received from the server since the timing of the proxy's parsing of the JavaScript tag and the subsequent browser requests are not synchronized. The figure shows two different timing diagrams of events seen by three entities: the browser, proxy and remote server. In Fig. 3A, the browser generates a request to the proxy which, at (1) is logged and forwarded to the server. The server responds with an object which contains HTML and JavaScript portions. At (2) the proxy logs START_JS to indicate the start of JavaScript code and at (3) it logs END_JS to indicate that the end of JavaScript code has been reached. However, the request generated by the JavaScript code is not seen by the proxy until (4), which occurs outside the delimiters.

The delimiters can be properly placed as shown in Fig. 3B. The idea is to cause the browser to send well-known requests to the proxy indicating when the JavaScript has begun and ended interpretation. The delimiters are logged when these requests are received by the proxy. Object requests resulting from the JavaScript interpretation will be more likely to fall between the two delimiters in this case. As before, the proxy logs and forwards the request at (1). At (2) the proxy receives an HTML tag

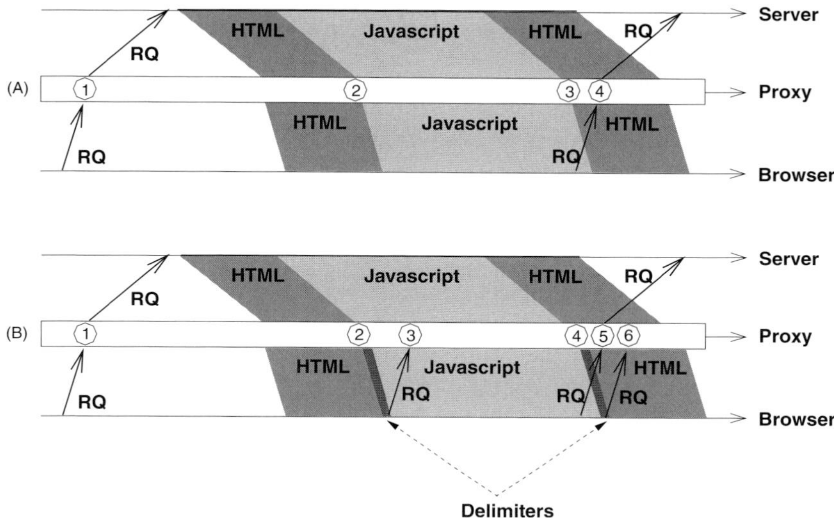

Fig. 3. Identifying requests generated by JavaScript.

of a form such as `<script language="javascript">` and the proxy embeds the tag `<script language="javascript" src="http://start.js">` into the page. This will cause a well-known request to be made from the browser to the proxy. The proxy intercepts this request at (3), places a START_JS delimiter in the log, and closes the connection to the browser. The browser continues parsing the subsequent HTML without making any changes to the rendering of the page. The request generated by the JavaScript code is seen by the proxy at (5), still inside the delimiters. When the `</script>` tag is encountered by the proxy at (4), it is passed to the browser followed immediately by an embedded tag similar to the above. The browser will make another well-known request to the proxy, which at (6) will place the END_JS delimiter in the log file, close the connection and continue sending the page to the browser.

3.2.2. Meta tags

Another form of redirection is performed when the HTML content of a page contains a tag such as `<meta http-equiv="refresh" CONTENT="5; url=foo.htm">`. This causes browsers to wait the number of seconds indicated by the CONTENT attribute before automatically generating a request to the URL indicated by the URL attribute. The proxy cannot distinguish between a user making this request and the automatic request made by the browser, so in this instance we consider both the original page and the page to which the browser is directed to be two separate user requests. In some instances this is appropriate since the amount of delay is forced by the CONTENT attribute. Counting this in the overall page loading would artificially inflate the amount of time we measured that it took to load a page. However, if the delay is specified as 0, the META tag will effect an immediate request, which should be treated as the 'Location' header field is treated. While we currently log META tags which may cause this form of redirection to take place, we do not currently count these redirections as belonging to the same request for a base page; the subsequent request is counted as a completely separate base page.

3.3. Proxy/browser interaction issues

3.3.1. Caching

The browser typically makes a request for a base page that includes some number of embedded objects such as frames and images. As the server responds to this request, the proxy parses the embedded objects and logs the information of interest. In post-processing, the objects are grouped together into Web pages.

Most browsers provide for caching of objects. Cached objects may be saved to memory and/or disk. When a browser detects that a request is being made for an object that it has in the cache, it may use the object immediately, or it may generate a request which contains an 'If-Modified-Since' header. The server determines whether the object has been modified, and responds either with the object, or with a 304 (not modified) Status Code, and no message body, causing the cached copy of the page to be used.

The case may arise where the cached copy of the base page is used without a request being generated, but a request is generated for an embedded object. This causes difficulty in determining how to group objects to form Web pages.

Our solution to this problem is to have the user flush the browser's disk and memory caches when the proxy is first turned on. Then for each retrieved object, we determine whether the same object was embedded in some previously requested Web page. If it was embedded in the immediately preceding page, it is assumed to belong to that page. If it was embedded in a page prior to the preceding page, it is assumed that page was re-requested and was retrieved from the cache. In this case we use the prior information to group the current objects that may appear to be unrelated.

Flushing caches will negatively affect browser performance during the period when the caches are being re-populated. After this transient period, the effect will become negligible.

3.3.2. Browser awareness of proxy existence

In order to use the proxy, the browser must be made aware of the existence and location of the proxy. This causes browsers to behave slightly differently. Two differences which have been identified are (1) instead of generating the header line 'Connection: Keep-Alive', the browser generates 'Proxy-Connection: Keep-Alive' and (2) without the proxy the browser normally generates a request line with a relative GET request such as 'GET/images/example.jpg', whereas with the proxy it generates a complete URL such as 'http://www.example.com/images/example.jpg'.

The header line generated by case (1) is removed as described in the section on 'Proxy-Connection' above, so the difference in behavior has no effect. With case (2), however, if this request line is passed without modification directly to the server, in rare cases the server does not return the requested object, but returns a 403 Forbidden error. We handle this case by removing the 'http://www.example.com' portion of the request. This worked without error for all servers we tested during development.

3.3.3. Streaming

When making a request for an object, the browser opens a TCP connection to the proxy and sends the request. The proxy performs the DNS resolution on the name of the server, opens a TCP connection to the server and forwards the request. The server responds with the header and data for the object.

The proxy reads the data sent by the server and parses it to determine whether one of the line types described in the previous section must be logged before sending the data to the browser. For example, the proxy may encounter an HTML tag such as `<IMG SRC="foo.jpg">`, which will cause an **IMG** line type to be logged.

Since TCP is a byte stream, however, a tag may occur across two consecutive data reads by the proxy. If no provisions are made for reconstructing tags that occur across consecutive data reads, many such tags will go undetected. Therefore, the proxy maintains a per-object working buffer in which partially received tags are stored. When complete tags have been received, they are parsed and the proxy determines whether the tag must be logged.

4. Limitations

The source code for the Internet Junkbuster Proxy™ [1] (IJP) was the starting point for implementing our proxy. IJP provided a framework for filtering request and response headers, and allowed for insertion of code to parse the content of responses. It is a relatively lightweight proxy, provides fine-grained manipulation of header fields and provides platform independence. It also allows us to relatively easily install the proxy on a per-user basis. The Windows version of our proxy, however, is still not sufficiently robust to deploy. Work continues to make our proxy available on this platform.

The ability to parse content on the fly instead of capturing a complete Web page before parsing the information we need to log appears to work extremely well. As qualitative evidence, we typically see browsers generate requests for objects while the base objects are being received, indicating that online parsing is working. While we believe the delay introduced in the received data stream by the proxy is relatively small, we have not yet evaluated the degree of this delay.

A limitation of the method is that it only measures network performance at the user's access point. It may be the case, however, that a page becomes useful to a user before all the data for the page has been received. Neither the proxy nor the post-processor can determine the point at which the page becomes useful to a user. There are several heuristics that can be applied to overcome this limitation. One is to consider each object being loaded to have a 'usability threshold'. This would consider a page to be usable when the percentage of the page that has been received exceeds this threshold. Another example is to consider a page as being usable when it has caused subsequent objects to be received. The heuristics could also be different for different object types.

Some of the above limitations are more serious than others. The types and degree of the limitations will determine which performance variables are sufficiently measured by our method, or whether other methods must be developed to measure them.

5. Evaluation

We evaluated our method using a single instance of browser and proxy, both running on a Sun Ultra 1, and logging to an NFS-mounted logfile. Anecdotally, we noted that highly popular Web pages tend to be the most complicated in terms of content and organization of embedded objects. Therefore, we used some of the most popular sites in several

Table 1. Results of testing

Site	# Additional Objects	# Correct / # Incorrect
www.real.com	68	68/0
www.napster.com	68	67/1
www.mp3.com	17	17/0
www.winamp.com	25	19/6
www.liquidaudio.com	51	49/2
www.peoplesound.com	95	74/21
www.audiofind.com	7	7/0
www.musicmatch.com	60	59/1
www.lyrics.com	4	3/1
www.launch.com	54	49/6
www.marsmusic.com	39	35/4
www.ubl.com	61	57/4
www.billboard.com	78	72/6
www.harmony-central.com	21	21/0
www.musiclyrics.net	45	43/2
www.music.com	68	64/4
www.mtv.com	59	54/5
www.discovery.com	54	49/5
www.abc.com	87	86/1
www.pbs.org	99	92/8
www.tvguide.com	35	32/3
www.gist.com	47	46/1
www.hollywood.com	75	72/3
www.ifilm.com	64	60/4
www.moviefone.com	62	60/2
www.movietickets.com	86	83/3
www.channel2000.com	79	76/3
www.thebostonchannel.com	91	85/6
www.imdb.com	49	49/0
www.movies.com	50	49/1
www.dragonballz.com	6	6/0
www.startrek.com	82	82/0
www.starwars.com	47	47/0
www.twistedhumor.com	18	17/1
www.funstun.com	45	45/0
www.windowsmedia.com	47	45/2
www.adobe.com	63	62/1
www.allposters.com	37	37/0
www.eonline.com	49	49/0
www.disney.com	37	35/2
www.ebay.com	62	57/5
Totals:	2191	2077/114

categories as ranked by Top9.com [2] to test our method. Note that this evaluation was performed prior to making the design change described in Section 3.3 under 'Caching'.

At this stage in development of our method, the most important task is to be able to properly group objects into Web pages during post-processing. We visited the selected sites, then post-processed the resulting logfile. The results are shown in Table 1. The table lists the 41 sites we used for stress testing. For each site, it shows the total number of objects in addition to the initial request that were retrieved to satisfy a request for a Web page. These additional objects include both embedded objects and Location indirections. 2232 objects in total were transferred to the browser for these 41 sites. 2191 of these were embedded objects or Location indirections. The third column shows the results of post-processing. The '# Correct' indicates the number of objects that were correctly identified as belonging to their base page. The '# Incorrect' indicates the number of objects where the method failed to identify the page to which they belonged. Objects that failed to be associated with the correct base page were identified as being base pages themselves. All the base pages were correctly identified as base pages.

114 of the 2232 embedded objects, or approximately 5%, were not correctly associated with base pages. The cause of the errors were primarily related in some fashion to the handling of JavaScript, although the specific reasons varied. For example, it is possible for a Web page to define, within the START_JS and END_JS delimiters, a JavaScript function which will retrieve an object, but to invoke the function outside of the delimiters. During logfile post-processing, without using other heuristics, we will not detect the subsequent object as being embedded in the page that invoked the function.

The objects that were identified as base pages included both those that were correctly and incorrectly identified as base pages. There are a total of $114 + 41 = 155$ such objects.

As noted in previous sections, we plan to evaluate the degree to which the proxy affects performance as experienced by the user. The major topics for this evaluation are (1) the impact of limiting the 'Accept-Encoding', (2) the impact of disallowing 'Keep-Alive' connections, and (3) the delay introduced by the proxy.

6. Related work

There are other tools and methods that have been developed to obtain Web performance data. They vary in their objectives and therefore, in their architectures.

Crovella, Cunha et al. [7,8] instrumented a browser to capture the URL, time of access and transfer time. As mentioned earlier, this method limits us to browsers for which source code is readily available.

A tool currently under development is called *Webtest* [9]. The objective of *Webtest* is closely related to ours. It is intended to measure various aspects of the performance of loading random Web pages. By default the Web pages it uses are drawn from a set of names from a large database of URLs obtained by a Web spider.

Choi et al. [5] developed a method for measuring user characteristics as an aid in modeling user behavior. While they achieve a high degree of accuracy with their measurements, their method requires access to privileged network information.

Some studies have used shared Web cache logs and domain proxy logs in order to measure various aspects of Web performance [3,4,6]. An advantage of this method is the ready availability of the logs. There are some drawbacks, however. First, the measurements are made on a machines which are not co-located with the user, and the effects of network characteristics between the user and the point of measurement are not available. Second, the domain proxy and Web cache do not capture all the information we are interested in. For example, DNS lookup time and how objects are grouped together to form a page are not logged. Finally, they reflect Web performance experienced in a limited number of settings.

7. Conclusions and future work

Our method provides us with the ability to relatively transparently measure Web performance as experienced by actual users. In the future we will be measuring the degree to which Web performance degradation will be perceived. The method can currently be applied on UNIX systems, and the proxy can be installed by users without special privilege. Work is continuing to make the proxy available on other platforms. In the following we discuss some of the variables we expect to be able to measure with our method.

DNS prefetching: Our primary interest in developing the tool was to investigate policies related to DNS prefetching. Prefetching is a general technique in which data that has a high probability of being required in the near future is retrieved and placed in a cache near the point where it will be used. It is most effective when the cache miss penalty is high. Prefetching has been applied at both the chip level (e.g., to prefetch instructions from memory) and the network level (e.g., to prefetch entire Web pages).
DNS prefetching is an application of the technique to DNS name resolution. Domain names which have a high probability of being resolved in the near future are resolved. Using this technique, some DNS cache misses can be avoided. When predictions are incorrect, however, resources are unnecessarily consumed. This has the potential, in fact, cause a decrease in performance. Some criteria for performing DNS prefetching are proposed in [6].
Using our method, we will investigate the contribution made by DNS lookups to user-perceived delays in loading Web pages, and consider the advantages and disadvantages of DNS prefetching in terms of speedup and consumption of resources: network bandwidth, nameserver load and memory usage.

Servers contacted: We will be able to model the number of servers contacted and the time that they are contacted during the loading of Web pages.

JavaScript performance: Since we are able to determine the point at which JavaScript code begins and ends execution, we will be able to estimate with a high degree of accuracy how long a specific section of JavaScript takes to execute on a variety of platforms.

Embedded objects: We intend to model the distribution by type of object embedded into Web pages. A simple extension to the proxy will allow us to log the size of each object by type. This is done by logging the 'Content-Length' header field of each received object.

Object Retrieval Depth: We define the *Object Retrieval Depth* (ORD) of a Web page to be the maximum number of links followed from any object retrieved for the Web page to the base page. As a (not farfetched) example, consider the following scenario: the response to an initial URL request contains a 'Location' header field; the object retrieved as a result contains three frames, one of which has JavaScript code; the JavaScript code causes a request for a URL which is an advertising banner; the response for the request for the advertising banner contains another 'Location' header indicating where the banner should be retrieved. In this example, the ORD is 4. We will be able to model the ORD of Web pages.

Acknowledgments

We wish to thank Matt Sanders for many stimulating discussions about this work and for general network support, and Hyoung-Kee Choi for providing the answers to many arcane questions about browser behavior, HTTP and HTML.

Appendix A. Log file line types

Line type	*Description*
ENTER	Provides a timestamp when the proxy first receives a request from the browser.
REQ	Logs the actual request line sent from the browser.
HOSTNAME	Name of the machine in the URL of the requested object, and the time it took for the name to be resolved.
EOH	Indicates that the proxy has received and parsed the complete header.
META	Indicates that the received object contained a META tag. META tags may contain a 'url' attribute causing another object to be requested.
BODY	Indicates that the received object contained a BODY tag. BODY tags may contain a 'background' attribute causing another object to be requested.
IMG	Indicates that the received object contained an IMG tag. IMG tags are required to contain a 'src' attribute which may cause another object to be requested.
INPUT	Indicates that the received object contained an INPUT tag. INPUT tags may contain a 'src' attribute causing another object to be requested.
TD	Indicates that the received object contained a TD tag. TD tags may contain a 'background' attribute causing another object to be requested.
TABLE	Indicates that the received object contained a TABLE tag. TABLE tags may contain a 'background' attribute causing another object to be requested.
EXIT	Provides a timestamp when the proxy has completed handling the request.
ELAPSED	Provides a calculation of how long the proxy took to load this object.
APP	Indicates that the received object is an application as specified by the **Content-Type** header field, and will not cause another object to be requested.
APPLET	Indicates that the received object contained an APPLET tag. APPLET tags may contain a 'src' attribute causing another object to be requested.
FRAME	Indicates that the received object contained a FRAME tag. FRAME tags may contain a 'src' attribute causing another object to be requested.
LOCATION	Indicates that the header for the requested object contained a **Location** header field. Upon receiving this header field, browsers immediately make a request to for the indicated object.
REFERER	Indicates that the header of the request contained a **Referer** header field. This field can indicate which object caused the immediate request for the object, or it can indicate the page that contained the link the user selected in order to retrieve the object.
START_JS	Provides an indication that the browser has begun interpreting a section of JavaScript. See Section 3.2.
END_JS	Provides an indication that the browser has completed interpreting of a section of JavaScript. See Section 3.2.

References

[1] Internet Junkbuster Proxy(TM). http://www.junkbuster.com/ijb.htmt.

[2] Top9.com. http://www.top9.com/.

[3] L. Breslau, P. Cao, L. Fan, G. Phillips, and S. Shenker. Web Caching and Zipf-like Distributions: Evidence and Implications. In *IEEE Infocom*, pages 126–134, March 1999.
[4] R. Caceres, F. Douglis, A. Feldmann, G. Glass, and M. Rabinovich. Web Proxy Caching; The Devil is in the Details. In *Proceedings of Workshop on Internet Server Performance*, Madison, Wisconsin, June 1998.
[5] H. Choi and J. Limb. A Behavioral Model of Web Traffic. In *Proceedings of International Conference on Network Protocols*, Sep 1999.
[6] E. Cohen and H. Kaplan. Prefetching the Means for Document Transfer: A New Approach for Reducing Web Latency. In *IEEE Infocom*, March 2000.
[7] M. Crovella and A. Bestavros. Self-Similarity in World Wide Web Traffic; Evidence and Possible Causes. In *IEEE/ACM Transactions on Networking*, volume 5(6), pages 835–846, December 1997.
[8] C. Cunha, A. Bestavros, and M. Crovella. Characteristics of WWW Client-based Traces. Technical report, TR-95-010, Boston University Computer Science Department, 1995.
[9] C. Huitema. Webtest – testing the internet quality of service. http://www.netsizer.com/webtest.html.

Web Caching and Content Delivery
A. Bestavros and M. Rabinovich (Editors)

The Medusa Proxy: A Tool for Exploring User-Perceived Web Performance

Mimika Koletsou [1], Geoffrey M. Voelker [2]

Department of Computer Science and Engineering, University of California, San Diego, 9500 Gilman Dr., MS 0114, La Jolla, CA 92093-0114 USA

Abstract

In this paper we describe the Medusa proxy, a tool for exploring user-perceived Web performance. The Medusa proxy is a non-caching forwarding proxy used in conjunction with a user's browser. The two key features that the Medusa proxy provides are (1) the ability to simultaneously mirror HTTP requests from the browser to different Web delivery systems and directly compare the results, and (2) the ability to transform requests, e.g., to transform Akamai URLs back into URLs to the customer's origin server. We show how the Medusa proxy can be used to explore user-perceived Web performance using two experiments that determine (1) to what extent using large-scale caching systems like the NLANR cache hierarchy improve user-perceived latency, and (2) to what extent content distribution networks like Akamai improve latency compared with using their customer's origin server. We found that the NLANR cache hierarchy served 63% of HTTP requests in our workload at least as fast as the origin servers, resulting in a decrease of average latency of 15%. By transforming and mirroring Akamai URLs to both Akamai edge servers and their customer's origin servers, we find that Akamai edge servers are able to serve HTTP requests an average of 5.7 times as fast as their customers. However, because requests to Akamai edge servers are only 6% of our workload, we find that using Akamai reduces overall mean latency by only 2% for our workload.

Keywords: User-perceived Web performance; Web proxy; Web caching; Content distribution networks

1. Introduction

In this paper, we describe the Medusa proxy, a tool for exploring user-perceived Web performance. There has been extensive work evaluating the macroscopic impact of Web infrastructure for improving overall Web performance, such as caching systems (e.g., [2,6,7,9,16,17,19,21,25,30,32,34]), prefetching systems (e.g., [4,11,15,18,27,29]), and to a limited extent content distribution networks (e.g., [20,22]). Surprisingly, however, there has been relatively little work characterizing the impact on Web performance *as perceived by the user* of various Web delivery systems. Although we have a relatively

[1] E-mail: koletsou@cs.ucsd.edu
[2] E-mail: voelker@cs.ucsd.edu

good understanding of how improvements in Web infrastructure impact overall latency, server load, and network utilization for large groups of users, we do not have a good understanding of how those improvements affect individual users at the desktop. In particular, there is no convenient mechanism by which users can determine the impact new developments in Web infrastructure, such as caching, content distribution, or prefetching, have on their Web browsing. For example, it is not uncommon for users to believe that Web caches impose noticeable overhead to browsing, or for content distribution network (CDN) companies such as Akamai [1] to make aggressive claims about improvements in download performance. Currently, though, there is no convenient way for users to validate those beliefs or claims.

Characterizing user-perceived Web performance is challenging because of the difficulty of generalizing conclusions about performance results across a wide range of user environments and network locations. Rather than try to generalize our conclusions across a diverse group of users, we have developed the Medusa proxy as a convenient tool with which individual users can explore their Web performance, and the impact of various Web delivery systems on that performance, from their desktop.

The Medusa proxy is a non-caching forwarding proxy used in conjunction with a user's browser. The Medusa proxy provides two key features for experimenting with user-perceived Web performance. The first feature is the ability to simultaneously mirror HTTP requests from the browser to different Web delivery systems and directly compare the results. For example, the Medusa proxy can mirror requests to a proxy cache and to the origin server to evaluate the effectiveness of the proxy cache on reducing latency. The second feature is the ability to transform HTTP requests. For example, users can install a filter that transforms an Akamai URL into the URL to the original object on the Akamai customer's origin server. By transforming and mirroring requests, the Medusa proxy can then simultaneously download the object from an Akamai edge server and the customer origin server and evaluate the effectiveness of having Akamai deliver that customer's content to the user.

In this paper we describe the features of the Medusa Web proxy and its uses for exploring Web performance, such as examining HTTP request headers, mirroring requests and monitoring performance, recording and replaying traces, transforming requests for privacy or experimentation, validating responses from experimental delivery systems, and accelerating performance; in this paper, we focus on user-perceived latency as the primary performance metric, although the Medusa proxy can be used to explore other performance metrics such as bandwidth, request rate, etc. We then use the Medusa proxy to answer the following performance and optimization questions:

- To what extent do large-scale cache systems like the NLANR cache hierarchy improve user-perceived latency?
- What is the potential of using the Medusa proxy as a Web accelerator, returning the fastest-of-n mirrored parallel requests?
- To what extent do content distribution networks like Akamai improve user-perceived latency over the performance of the customer's origin server?

The rest of this paper is organized as follows. Section 2 discusses related work. Section 3 describes the features and implementation of the Medusa proxy. Section 4 describes our experimental methodology and results for evaluating the NLANR, Akamai, and Squid Web delivery systems on user-perceived Web performance, and Section 5 concludes.

2. Related work

The work most closely related to the Medusa proxy is the Simultaneous Proxy Evaluation (SPE) system proposed by Davison [13]. The SPE system has a similar goal in that it proposes to use mirroring to compare the performance of Web delivery systems such as proxy caches from the perspective of clients. However, the goals of comparing a Web delivery system with the origin servers, or transforming requests, is not proposed (although it would seem straightforward to incorporate). SPE was not implemented when originally proposed, but Davison and Krishnan are currently implementing it as the Rutgers Online Proxy Evaluator (ROPE) [14].

There have been a number of studies investigating Web user behavior and client performance using passive monitoring. Cunha et al. collected an early client trace at Boston University by instrumenting the Mosaic browser used by people in their department, and derived statistical characteristics of the client workload such as object size and popularity [12]. Catledge and Pitkow also collected a trace of Mosaic events from users at Georgia Tech, and used it to study methods of user interaction with the browser as well as user navigation patterns [8]. Kelly has recently collected a very large anonymized client trace from WebTV, and has used it to explore browser cache performance, reference locality, and document aliasing [23]. All of these studies have used passive measurement to explore user behavior and client performance, whereas we use the Medusa proxy to compare the performance of various Web delivery systems using active measurement.

Krishnamurthy and Wills [26] studied end-to-end Web performance from a collection of client sites distributed around the world to over 700 popular Web servers. They used active measurements to study the performance tradeoffs of parallel, persistent, and pipelined HTTP connections, as well as the interactions of those connection schemes with caches and multi-server content distribution. Their study compared the user-perceived performance of various HTTP protocol mechanisms, whereas we compare the user-perceived performance of various Web delivery systems. They also transformed Akamai URLs to compare data rates of Akamai edge servers with Akamai customer origin servers, and characterized the prevalence of Akamai-served content in popular Web servers. We use the same transformation technique to compare response times between Akamai edge servers and customer origin servers, and characterize the prevalence of Akamai-served content in a small user workload.

Rajamony and Elnozahy recently presented a framework for measuring the user-perceived response time of clients accessing a particular Web service [31]. With this framework, the Web service provider can characterize client response times to the service to determine whether service performance needs to be improved. This framework measures user-perceived performance across all clients from the perspective of a single service, whereas the Medusa proxy measures user-perceived performance from a single user to all accessed services through a potential set of Web delivery systems.

There has been comparatively little work experimentally evaluating the performance of content distribution networks. In one recent study, Johnson et al. compare the performance of two CDNs, Akamai and Digital Island, in terms of their ability to select the servers with minimum latency to the client [22]. However, they do not evaluate the impact of the CDNs on user-perceived latency, only on the relative performance of server selection within the CDN.

There are tools that report user Web download performance, such as Net.Medic

[28], but they do not enable users to answer exploratory questions such as whether a proxy cache is degrading their performance, or how much added value CDNs are actually providing to them. Commercial systems such as the Lateral Line Network from Appliant.com [3] and various services from Keynote [24] report on the health and performance of customer Web sites from the perspective of many distributed users. However, as with the personal Web performance tools, these services do not compare alternative delivery systems and their impact on performance.

3. Medusa proxy

The Medusa proxy is a non-caching forwarding proxy that supports the Proxy Request form of HTTP requests. Since it was designed to explore user-perceived latency, it is typically configured as a personal proxy for the Web browser and it executes alongside the browser on the same machine. It can also serve as a proxy for multiple clients, but we have yet to explore its use in that way. For portability, we implemented the Medusa proxy in Java to support widespread use. Finally, our support for HTTP 1.1 persistent and pipelined connections is ongoing, and the Medusa proxy currently only supports HTTP 1.0.

The Medusa proxy has a number of features for exploring user-perceived Web performance:

Mirroring. The Medusa proxy can be configured to mirror HTTP requests from multiple incoming sources to multiple destinations. It can accept incoming connections sequentially to limit interference, or multiple simultaneous connections in parallel for performance. It can also mirror requests sequentially so that they do not interfere with each other, or in parallel to further accelerate performance. In both cases of parallelism, Medusa uses threads to implement the parallelism; because we expect the Medusa proxy to be primarily used by a single client, the number of simultaneous connections and destinations, and hence the number of threads, is reasonably low.

In the experiments in this paper, we mirror requests from an individual source (the browser or a trace) to at most two different destinations at any one time, in sequential mode, to limit interference when recording measurements. To further limit interference, the Medusa proxy could be executed on a machine other than the one running the browser, or one with multiple processors.

Note that mirroring requests is harmless when the request semantics are idempotent. However, some requests have potentially serious side effects, such as POST requests for making purchases at e-commerce sites, that would cause undesirable behavior if repeated more than once. The three POST requests in our trace log information to advertising servers, and so we did not filter them out. In general, though, we can provide a flag to conditionally filter POST requests.

Transformation. The Medusa proxy can install filters to transform HTTP requests as they are forwarded. In this paper we use this feature to transform Akamaized URLs to the original URLs that refer to customer origin servers. As an example of another use of transformation, a filter can be installed that strips or anonymizes user-specific HTTP header information, such as embedded user or login names.

Performance measurement. As it mirrors and transforms requests, the Medusa proxy can record performance information, such as request count and frequency, latency, and bandwidth consumed, in a performance log. In this paper, we focus on request count and latency.

Tracing and replay. As it receives requests, the Medusa proxy can record them in a trace for subsequent replay in non-interactive mirroring and transformation experiments. We replay traces to experiment with Akamai in Sections 4.3.

Validation. When building new infrastructure, such as a new proxy cache implementation, it is useful to be able to validate that the cache is responding with correct data. In conjunction with the mirroring feature, the Medusa proxy can be used to validate new implementations of delivery systems by directly comparing the response from the experimental cache with the response from the origin server. Comparing responses is not only useful for validating content data, but also for comparing metadata as well. Comparing responses from multiple delivery systems can also be used to explore the effects of metadata differences, such as the 'age penalty' from caches [10].

In the next section we use many of these features of the Medusa proxy to explore various aspects of user-perceived Web performance.

4. Experimental results

In this section, we use the Medusa proxy to explore the impact of using a large cache system (NLANR cache hierarchy) and a content distribution network (Akamai) on user-perceived download latency.

4.1. Methodology

To generate a workload for our experiments, we used the Medusa proxy for 8 days of everyday Web browsing as shown in Table 1. The browsing was relatively bursty, with most activity in the morning, around lunch, and in the evening. The total workload consists of 4743 HTTP requests, many of which are to generally popular Web sites like nytimes.com, espn.go.com, java.sun.com, etc., and some of which are to more domain-specific sites like nsf.gov. All requests are to Web servers outside of UCSD. We chose this workload because it is exactly the workload that we would like to understand and improve. Since it is impossible to generalize these results across all users, people can use the Medusa proxy to determine the extent to which the various Web delivery systems impact their own user-perceived Web performance.

Table 1. Trace periods (all days in 2001)

Period	Requests	Users
March 6	1548	2
March 31–June 1	540	1
June 4–June 8	2655	1

In all experiments, we executed the Medusa proxy on a 700 MHz Pentium III workstation with 256 MB of memory running Windows NT 4.0. We ran the Medusa proxy using Sun's Java 2 Runtime Environment (v1.3.0-C) with the same version of HotSpot. Because Medusa does not cache data, its memory requirements are low; it used 11 MB of memory during our experiments.

We used Internet Explorer 5 (IE) as the browser to generate our workloads. IE executed on the same machine as, and directly communicated with, the Medusa proxy. For the NLANR experiments in Section 4.2, we collected performance data and recorded the HTTP requests as we interactively browsed throughout the day to generate our workload. For the experiment in Sections 4.3, we replayed the collected traces directly using the Medusa proxy. The Medusa proxy can replay traces with variable delays between requests; we used 500 ms for the experiments in this paper as a tradeoff between reducing server load and being able to complete replays in a reasonable amount of time.

The Medusa proxy calculates download times from just before initiating a connection until it closes the connection. These times include the cost of the DNS lookup and the TCP connection setup and close. In our Java environment the Java timer has a granularity of 10 ms, limiting the accuracy of very fast downloads of small objects. Although we would prefer a much more accurate timer, we use the Java timer for the sake of portability.

4.2. NLANR cache hierarchy

In this section, we use the mirroring feature of the Medusa proxy to explore the extent to which a large-scale caching system, the NLANR cache hierarchy, improves user-perceived Web performance. Our goals are to characterize the effect of using the NLANR cache hierarchy on user-perceived performance, and to provide a mechanism by which users can determine whether using a cache system like the NLANR cache hierarchy improves their Web browsing performance. Because we use mirroring to explore cache hierarchy performance, we also determine the potential of using mirroring as a technique for implementing a (network-unfriendly) Web accelerator.

The NLANR cache system consists of a hierarchy of international Squid Web caches [33]. At the root of the hierarchy is a mesh of caches primarily located at the U.S. supercomputer centers. These caches are peers and query each other for cached content, and serve as parents to other Squid caches distributed throughout the world. The cache hierarchy reduces network utilization and server load, as well as user-perceived download latency. The cache hierarchy can improve performance when users request objects that have been previously requested by other users and cached in the hierarchy. However, the cache hierarchy can degrade performance, particularly for requests to objects that miss in the cache system, because of the overhead of additional hops between the user and the origin server and the latency for querying peers [32].

4.2.1. User-perceived latency

To explore the extent to which the NLANR cache hierarchy impacts user-perceived download latency, we used the Medusa proxy to mirror all HTTP requests from our Web browsers to both the NLANR hierarchy and the origin servers. The Medusa proxy first sends every request to the origin server, waits for the entire response to be downloaded, then sequentially mirrors the request to the `lj.us.ircache.net` cache, and records the download latency from each destination. The response from the server is discarded,

Table 2. NLANR results summary

All Requests (4743)	Mean	Median
Origin Server	253 ms	190 ms
NLANR Hierarchy	220 ms	111 ms
Server/NLANR	1.15	1.71
Accelerator	159 ms	100 ms
NLANR/Accelerator	1.38	1.11
Server/Accelerator	1.59	1.90

and the response from the cache is delivered to the browser. The mirroring is done online during interactive browsing so that requests to both destinations experience similar network behavior. The requests are sent sequentially to prevent contention within the Medusa proxy (the Medusa proxy can also mirror requests in parallel to accelerate browsing, as discussed below, but we do not use the parallel feature in any of the experiments in this paper).

Our results are slightly biased towards the NLANR cache hierarchy for a couple of reasons. First, the initial request to the server presumably preloads the object in the server cache, which could reduce the miss penalty for the cache hierarchy. An alternative approach would have been to randomly choose to send the initial request to either the cache or the origin server, but we preferred the known, deterministic algorithm of sending to the cache first. Second, we have excellent connectivity to the `lj.us` cache, which has a 1 ms ping round-trip time from the machine running the Medusa proxy. Although we do not expect this performance to be typical, this is what we experience and hence what we explore.

The top half of Table 2 summarizes our results comparing the performance of NLANR and the origin servers. The 'Origin Server' row shows the mean and median download latencies for downloading objects in our workload directly from the origin servers as determined by the URL in the request. The 'NLANR Hierarchy' row shows the corresponding latencies for downloading the objects through the cache hierarchy; the 'Server/NLANR' row shows the speedup NLANR provides relative to the origin server; and we discuss the remaining rows in Section 4.2.2 below. On average, NLANR noticeably improves download latency: the mean latency for NLANR is 15% faster than using the origin server, and the median latency for NLANR is 71% faster.

To display the effect of using the NLANR cache hierarchy on all requests in our workload, Fig. 1 shows the cumulative distributions of the relative performance of the NLANR cache hierarchy and the origin server across all requests. The x-axis shows relative speedup (on a log scale), and the y-axis shows the fraction of requests in the workload. Since the cache hierarchy is not necessarily faster, we separate the requests into two curves. The solid 'Server Faster' curve shows the speedup of those requests where downloading from the origin server was faster, and the dashed 'Cache Faster' curve shows the speedup of those requests where download from the cache hierarchy was faster. For example, looking at the solid 'Server Faster' curve, 31% of all requests were downloaded faster from the server and were downloaded with a speedup of 3 or less than from the cache hierarchy. Similarly, looking at the dashed 'Cache Faster' curve, 52% of all requests were downloaded faster from the cache hierarchy and were downloaded with a speedup of 4 or less than from the server.

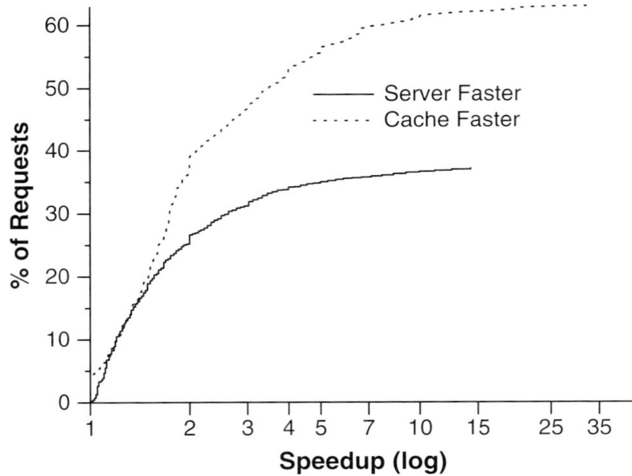

Fig. 1. Distribution of the relative download latency of the NLANR cache hierarchy and origin servers. Note the use of a log scale for the x-axis.

Although the NLANR cache hierarchy improves mean latency by 15%, Fig. 1 shows that for 63% of the requests the cache hierarchy returned responses faster or as fast as the origin server; for 37% of the requests, the origin server was faster; and for 4% of the requests they had equivalent download latencies (where the dashed 'Cache Faster' curve crosses the y-axis). Both the server and the cache hierarchy had large speedups relative to the other. These large speedups were for requests to small files (e.g., small images) where one system responded quickly (e.g., 10–20 ms) but the other experienced network delay or server load that caused significant relative latency (e.g., 100–500 ms).

4.2.2. *The medusa proxy as a Web accelerator*

Since the origin server is frequently faster than the cache hierarchy, it raises an interesting question of whether mirroring could be used as a technique to accelerate user-perceived Web performance. With the Medusa proxy, we can potentially mirror requests in parallel and return the fastest response to the browser, whether from the cache or origin server. Since mirroring consumes roughly twice the resources of normal Web browsing, it is a network-unfriendly technique and we do not condone its use in this way. However, we were intrigued to see what the potential was for such a technique.

To estimate the potential benefits of a mirroring accelerator, we selected the fastest response latency for each request in our workload and calculated the mean and median latencies across the requests. The results are shown in the bottom half of Table 2. The 'Accelerator' row shows the mean and median latencies of using the Medusa proxy as an accelerator; the 'NLANR/Accelerator' row shows the relative performance of the accelerator compared with just using the NLANR cache hierarchy; and the 'Server/Accelerator' row shows the relative performance of the accelerator compared with just using the origin servers. The results indicate that a mirroring accelerator has potential for improving performance: relative to the cache hierarchy, it improves mean latency by 38% and median latency by 11%. Furthermore, based upon median latency, at least half of the HTTP requests would be downloaded in under 100 ms.

4.2.3. Discussion

From these results, we conclude that using the NLANR cache hierarchy measurably improves the download latency for our workload. However, it is not clear what the user-perceived impact of this improvement is. If a page has only one object, then an average absolute improvement of 33 ms (NLANR) or 61 ms (accelerator) is below the human threshold for noticing the difference [5]. However, if a page has many embedded objects, then the cache system has the potential to make a large absolute improvement. The exact improvement, however, depends upon the number of objects and the overlap of multiple parallel connections, and remains an open question.

4.3. Akamai content distribution network

In this section, we use transformation to explore the user-perceived performance of Akamai, a large content distribution network [1]. Content distribution networks have the potential to significantly improve user-perceived Web performance because they bring content closer to users and are able to balance load across a large number of distributed servers. In contrast, most content providers have a single server site from which they deliver content, and this site is potentially far from many users and has to scale to handle all user load. In our experiments, we directly compare the performance of accessing Akamaized objects from Akamai edge servers with their customer's origin server, and estimate the overall impact of having content served from Akamai on our workload.

To perform our experiment, we transformed all HTTP requests to the Akamai network in our trace into requests to the Akamai customer's origin server (e.g., Krishnamurthy and Wills [26] and Cohen and Kaplan [10] employ the same technique). Akamai uses a well-formed scheme to 'Akamaize' customer content by prefixing an Akamai domain name and additional information to the original URL of the object on the customer's origin server. For example, a typical Akamai URL might be structured as follows:

```
http://a8.g.akamaitech.net/f/8/621/12h/www.customer.com/...
```

We can recover the original URL to the customer's origin server by removing the Akamai prefix:

```
http://www.customer.com/...
```

With both the Akamai URL and the customer server URL, we can then use the Medusa proxy to mirror requests to both the Akamai edge servers as well the customer origin servers and compare the resulting latencies.

As our workload, we used the traces recorded during the NLANR experiment in Section 4.2 and replayed them through the Medusa proxy, transforming Akamai URLs, mirroring requests, and recording the download latencies. We used the machine described in Section 4.1 to execute the Medusa proxy and replay the traces. We replayed our traces starting at noon PDT on Monday, June 11, 2001 to capture network congestion and server load, conditions which emphasize the positioning and distribution of Akamai edge servers.

To reduce variation, we replayed the traces five times and used the median download latency across the five runs for each object as its representative download time. Replaying the trace multiple times biases both the Akamai edge servers and the customer origin servers towards better performance since the replays warm their caches. When looking at the overall impact of Akamai, this makes our results conservative by giving the benefit of doubt to Akamai. Replaying also reduces the overhead of DNS lookups for Akamai; however, Akamai URLs in the trace only refer to 19 unique edge servers, so Akamai would significantly benefit from DNS caching even without multiple replays.

4.3.1. Direct impact

The top half of Table 3 summarizes our results for directly comparing the performance of downloading objects from the Akamai edge servers and the customer origin servers. These results take into account only those requests that were originally addressed to the Akamai network (in this case, 278 requests). The 'No Akamai' row shows the mean and median download latencies for objects downloaded from the customer origin server; the 'Akamai' row shows the corresponding download latencies for downloading those objects from the Akamai network; the 'No Akamai/Akamai' row shows the speedup Akamai provides relative to the customer server; and we discuss the remaining rows in Section 4.3.2 below.

As these results show, both the mean and median latencies for Akamai are quite low, on the order of 20–25 ms (the sample Akamai edge server we resolved has a ping round-trip time of 7 ms). Furthermore, Akamai delivers impressive speedups of 5.7 for the mean download latency and 6 for the median latency.

To display the performance across all Akamai requests, Fig. 2 shows the cumulative distribution of the relative performance of Akamai to the customer origin servers for all Akamai requests. The x-axis shows the speedup for sending the request to the Akamai network relative to the customer origin server, and the y-axis shows the fraction of Akamai requests in the workload. Each point on the curve corresponds to one request, and the requests are sorted in increasing order of speedup. As we can see from the graph, Akamai always delivers content faster than the customer origin server and, for nearly 20% of the requests, Akamai is at least 10 times as fast. The very large speedups are from requests to small images, where network conditions and customer origin server load add significant relative latency.

In terms of the content that Akamai delivers, the user-perceived performance of Akamai is excellent for our workload. However, this performance improvement is only for the portion of our workload that is served by Akamai. Since users are more interested in the performance impact on their overall workload, we explore this question next.

Table 3. Akamai results summary

	Mean	Median
Akamai Requests (278)		
No Akamai (Origin)	141 ms	120 ms
Akamai	24.7 ms	20.0 ms
No Akamai/Akamai	5.7	6.0
All Requests (4743)		
No Akamai (Origin)	259 ms	190 ms
Akamai	253 ms	190 ms
No Akamai/Akamai	1.02	1.00

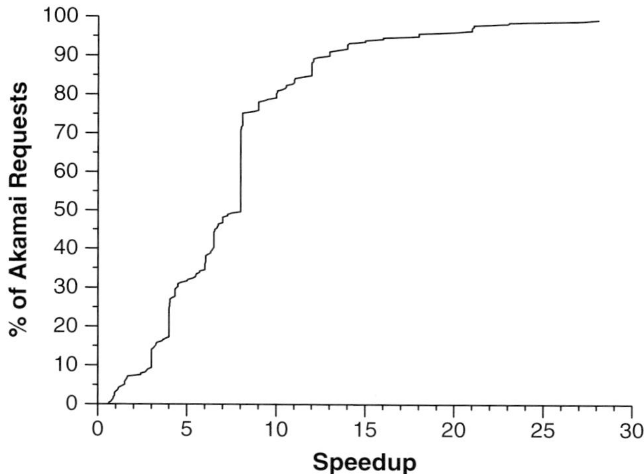

Fig. 2. Distribution of the relative download latency of Akamai and customer origin servers.

4.3.2. Overall impact

To estimate the overall performance impact of Akamai on our workload, we used the workload results from our Web browsing in Section 4.2 and replaced the fast download latencies of Akamai requests with the much larger latencies of downloading the same content from the customer origin servers obtained above. This replacement corresponds to a workload in which no content is served from Akamai and all content is served from origin servers. With the original workload that includes requests to Akamai and the modified workload that only has requests to origin servers, we can estimate the overall impact Akamai has on performance.

Our results are shown in the bottom half of Table 3. These results take into account all requests in the workload. The 'No Akamai' row corresponds to the workload where Akamai request latencies are replaced with the corresponding latencies for downloading from the customer origin server. The 'Akamai' row corresponds to the original workload that includes requests to the Akamai network. And the 'No Akamai/Akamai' row shows the relative performance of the two workloads. From the table, we see that the Akamai workload improves average download latency by only 2.4% over the workload that does not use Akamai. To put this result in perspective, recall that using the NLANR cache hierarchy improves average overall download latency for our workload by 15%. In other words, for our workload Akamai improves average user-perceived latency only slightly, and we would have experienced similar average performance if all of our content was from origin servers. Note that this result assumes that the absence of Akamai would not increase network congestion and customer origin server load considerably, but we cannot experimentally evaluate the effect of this assumption.

4.3.3. Discussion

The difference between the direct and overall impact of using Akamai is due to the fact that Akamai only serves 6% of all requests from our workload: 278 Akamai requests out of 4743 total requests. Although Akamai has excellent relative performance for the content it serves, it only captures a small fraction of our overall workload. These results are very much workload dependent, but, for rough comparison, Krishnamurthy and Wills found that 1.5% of base URLs to the home pages of 711 popular Web servers had embedded objects served by Akamai [26].

There are a number of conclusions one could make from these results, depending upon one's perspective. From Akamai's perspective, these results demonstrate that Akamai serves its content extremely well compared to their customer's servers. From an Akamai customer's perspective, these results show that Akamai improves the download latency for the content on Akamai's servers while offloading requests from the customer's servers. However, Web pages are compound documents. Since Akamai primarily serves images, the remaining content that comes from the customer's origin servers remain the bottleneck. Again, according to Krishnamurthy and Wills, 31–47% of objects and 56–67% of bytes on the home pages of a selection of popular Web servers that use Akamai still come from the customer's origin server [26, table 7]. Finally, from the user's perspective, Akamai has impact on those pages that include embedded objects served by Akamai, but only a minimal impact on the overall workload.

The overall conclusion that we make is that a content delivery network like Akamai is a very effective system for distributing content close to the user, and has great potential for making a significant impact on user-perceived latency. However, until CDNs like Akamai serve a larger fraction of the overall content requested in user Web workloads, the full potential that CDNs have to offer for improving user-perceived latency will remain unrealized.

5. Conclusion

In this paper, we describe the Medusa proxy, a tool for exploring user-perceived Web performance. We describe its use to determine (1) to what extent using large-scale caching systems like the NLANR cache hierarchy improve user-perceived latency, and (2) to what extent content distribution networks like Akamai improve latency compared with using their customer's origin servers.

For our personal workloads, we found that:

- When using the NLANR caches 63% of HTTP requests are served at least as fast from the NLANR caches as from the origin server, decreasing mean latency by 15%. However, in absolute time, this improvement is only 33 ms on average.
- Using the Medusa proxy as a Web accelerator, mirroring requests to both the NLANR caching system and the origin server in parallel and returning the fastest response, can improve mean latency by 38% compared with using the NLANR caching system alone.
- Akamai edge servers are able to serve HTTP requests an average of 5.7 times as fast as their customer's origin servers. However, because requests to Akamai edge servers are only 6% of our workload, we find that using Akamai reduces overall mean latency by only 2%.

Of course, these results depend upon the perspective of our workloads and our computing and network environment, and the results are surely different for other users. However, with the Medusa proxy, users can answer these questions relative to their own environments to determine the impact of Web delivery systems on their performance.

Acknowledgments

We would like to thank Terence Kelly and the anonymous reviewers for their helpful comments and suggestions. We would also like to thank Duane Wessels for giving us direct access to the `lj.us.ircache.net` NLANR cache. Equipment used in this research was supported in part by the UCSD Active Web Project, NSF Research Infrastructure Grant Number 9802219.

References

[1] Akamai. Akamai content delivery network. http://www.akamai.com.

[2] V. Almeida, A. Bestavros, M. Crovella, and A. deOliveira. Characterizing reference locality in the WWW. Technical Report 96-011, Boston University, June 1996.

[3] Appliant.com. Lateral line network. http://www.appliant.com/services/lln.htm.

[4] A. Bestavros. Using speculation to reduce server load and service time in the WWW. In *Proc. of the 4th ACM Intl. Conf. on Information and Knowledge Mgmt.*, November 1995.

[5] N. Bhatti, A. Bouch, and A. Kuchinsky. Integrating User-Perceived Quality into Web Server Design. In *Proc. Ninth Int. World Wide Web Conf.*, May 2000.

[6] L. Breslau, P. Cao, L. Fan, G. Phillips, and S. Shenker. Web caching and Zipf-like distributions: Evidence and implications. In *Proc. of IEEE INFOCOM '99*, pages 126–134, March 1999.

[7] R. Caceres, F. Douglis, A. Feldmann, G. Glass, and M. Rabinovich. Web proxy caching: The devil is in the details. In *Workshop on Internet Server Performance*, pages 111–118, June 1998.

[8] L.D. Catledge and J.E. Pitkow. Characterizing browser strategies in the World-Wide Web. *Computer Networks and ISDN Systems*, 26(6): 1065–1073, April 1995.

[9] A. Chankhunthod, P.B. Danzig, C. Neerdaels, M.F. Schwartz, and K.J. Worrell. A hierarchical Internet object cache. In *Proc. of the 1996 USENIX Technical Conf.*, pages 153–163, San Diego, CA, January 1996.

[10] E. Cohen and H. Kaplan. The age penalty and its effect on cache performance. In *Proc. of the 3rd USENIX Symp. on Internet Technologies and Systems*, pages 73–84, March 2001.

[11] M. Crovella and P. Barford. The network effects of prefetching. In *Proc. of Infocom '98*, April 1998.

[12] C.R. Cunha, A. Bestavros, and M.E. Crovella. Characteristics of WWW client-based traces. Technical Report BU-CS-95-010, Boston University, July 1995.

[13] B.D. Davison. Simultaneous Proxy Evaluation. In *Proc. of the 4th Int. Web Caching Workshop*, pages 67–77, March 1999.

[14] B.D. Davison and C. Krishnan. ROPE: The Rutgers Online Proxy Evaluator. In preparation, 2001.

[15] D. Duchamp. Prefetching hyperlinks. In *Proc. of the 2nd USENIX Symp. on Internet Technologies and Systems*, October 1999.

[16] B. Duska, D. Marwood, and M.J. Feeley. The measured access characteristics of World Wide Web client proxy caches. In *Proc. of the 1st USENIX Symp. on Internet Technologies and Systems*, pages 23–36, Dec. 1997.

[17] L. Fan, P. Cao, J. Almeida, and A.Z. Broder. Summary Cache: A scalable wide-area web cache sharing protocol. In *Proc. of ACM SIGCOMM '98*, Vancouver, BC, August 1998.

[18] L. Fan, P. Cao, and Q. Jacobson. Web prefetching between low-bandwidth clients and proxies: Potential and performance. In *Proc. of ACM SIGMETRICS '99*, May 1999.

[19] A. Feldmann, R. Caceres, F. Douglis, G. Glass, and M. Rabinovich. Performance of web proxy caching in heterogeneous bandwidth environments. In *Proc. of IEEE INFOCOM '99*, March 1999.

[20] S. Gadde, J. Chase, and M. Rabinovich. Web caching and content distribution: A view from the interior. In *Proc. of the 5th Int. Web Caching and Content Delivery Workshop*, May 2000.

[21] S.D. Gribble and E.A. Brewer. System design issues for Internet middleware services: Deductions from a large client trace. In *Proc. of the 1st USENIX Symp. on Internet Technologies and Systems*, pages 207–218, Montery, CA, December 1997.

[22] K.L. Johnson, J.F. Carr, M.S. Day, and M.F. Kaashoek. The measured performance of content distribution networks. In *Proc. of the 5th Int. Web Caching and Content Delivery Workshop*, May 2000.

[23] T. Kelly. Thin-Client Web Access Patterns: Measurements from a Cache-Busting Proxy. In *Proc. of the 6th Int. Web Caching and Content Delivery Workshop*, June 2001.

[24] Keynote. Keynote web performance services. http://www.keynote.com.

[25] B. Krishnamurthy and C.E. Wills. Study of piggyback cache validation for proxy caches in the World Wide Web. In *Proc. of the 1st USENIX Symp. on Internet Technologies and Systems*, Dec. 1997.

[26] B. Krishnamurthy and C.E. Wills. Analyzing Factors That Influence End-to-End Web Performance. In *Proc. Ninth Int. World Wide Web Conf.*, Amsterdam, May 2000.

[27] T.M. Kroeger, D.D.E. Long, and J.C. Mogul. Exploring the bounds of Web latency reduction from caching and prefetching. In *Proc. of the 1st USENIX Symp. on Internet Technologies and Systems*, pages 13–22, Dec. 1997.

[28] Lucent-NPS. Net.medic. http://www.ins.com/software/medic.

[29] V.N. Padmanabhan and J.C. Mogul. Using predictive prefetching to improve World Wide Web latency. *ACM Computer Communications Review*, 26(3), July 1996.

[30] M. Rabinovich, J. Chase, and S. Gadde. Not all hits are created equal: Cooperative proxy caching over a wide area network. In *Proc. of the 3rd Int. WWW Caching Workshop*, June 1998.

[31] R. Rajamony and M. Elnozahy. Measuring Client-Perceived Reponse Times on the WWW. In *Proc. of the 3rd USENIX Symp. on Internet Technologies and Systems*, pages 185–196, March 2001.

[32] R. Tewari, M. Dahlin, H. Vin, and J. Kay. Design considerations for distributed caching on the Internet. In *Proc. of ICDCS '99*, May 1999.

[33] D. Wessels and K. Claffy. ICP and the Squid Web Cache. *IEEE Journal on Selected Areas in Communication*, 16(3): 345–357, 1998.

[34] A. Wolman, G.M. Voelker, N. Sharma, N. Cardwell, A. Karlin, and H.M. Levy. On the scale and performance of cooperative Web proxy caching. In *Proc. of SOSP '99*, pages 16–31, December 1999.

Web Caching and Content Delivery
A. Bestavros and M. Rabinovich (Editors)

Comparative Measurements of Internet Traffic Using Cache-Triangle

Serge A. Krashakov [1], Lev N. Shchur [2]

Landau Institute for Theoretical Physics, 142432 Chernogolovka, Russia

Abstract

We discuss the possibility of comparative measurements of Web traffic. This paper is mainly focused on the traffic in the cache-mesh. We analyze the previous attempt based on the author's rewind-and-replay approach in detail. The new approach proposed uses a symmetric setup of cache-servers, a cache-triangle. We discuss the conditions under which such measurements could be done with a given accuracy.

Keywords: Cache hierarchy; Web network; Traffic measurement

1. Introduction

Optimization of the Web traffic is clearly one of the most practical problems in Internet. A number of approaches have been introduced in recent years, Web caching and content distribution [1]. The solution may depend on the purpose of the network. Commercial networks could be more efficient based on the content distribution network (CDN) concept, but the education networks could be preferably based on the cache-mesh architecture [2]. In this paper, we consider only the cache-mesh architecture for the simple reason that we work within the research and education network FREEnet.

In any case, for analyzing network efficiency, we need some traffic characteristics that can be measured reproducibly. In other words, we must define some quantities and the ideal experimental scheme in which these quantities could be measured. Clearly, these measurements should be reproducible, i.e., could be repeated by other groups and on other networks. This definition clearly reminds us of the measurement concept in physics.

Suppose that we must choose between two or more strategies for caching Web traffic. For example, we would like to choose the best path for getting information via a distributed cache-mesh. The following questions arise:

Q1: How can the strategies be compared to obtain the conditions under which some are preferable (are more efficient, minimize an average access time, or maximize channel efficiency, and so on)?

[1] E-mail: sakr@chg.ru
[2] E-mail: lev@landau.ac.ru

Q2: Are the measurements reproducible?

Q3: If so, what is the accuracy of the measurements?

Q4: Or, more simply, how long should the measurements be continued to attain an given accuracy, e.g., 5

In addition, we know some properties of Internet traffic that could lead to difficulties in measurement.

The first set of properties is connected with natural characteristics of human activity. In this connection, the daily working hours leads to a daily periodicity of the Web traffic, the work week leads to a weekly periodicity (weekends!), the annual calendar leads to an annual periodicity (winter and summer vacations!), and so on. Holidays and important events (political campaigns, etc.) can also affect the traffic.

The second set of the Web traffic properties is connected with the fact that the path from one point in the Web (e.g., user) and another point (e.g., server) is not stable. The path is often quite complicated and consists of a number of routers, channels, caches, etc., which changes with time because the network constantly develops. We thus have the problem that the Internet traffic is not constant in time. This reminds us of the ancient philosopher Heraclites, who asserted "You cannot step twice into the same river." We could say the same about the Internet river. It is perhaps early to discuss turbulence in the Internet, but we are really very close to formulating that concept.

The third set of properties further complicating the measurements discussed is connected with the dynamics of the Internet traffic for many autonomous systems (AS). This leads to random changes in the topology and therefore in the timing and loading characteristics. As a result, the Internet traffic route is sometimes very asymmetric (Fig. 1).

The last difficulty is connected with the resolution we use to examine the Internet. We could average the quantity of interest over the whole Internet; this could be the first approximation in which we answer any of the formulations of the question Q1 above. At first glance, the next approximation seems to be averaging on the scale of the top-level domains. But this is not the case at all, because many domains are inhomogeneous (i.e., have different outer-channel bandwidths and server response times for various reasons). Moreover, some are not compact. The best examples of noncompact top-level domains are *com* or *net*, which spread over the whole planet. Therefore, a special analysis is needed for understanding how this spreading or inhomogeneity could affect our measurement results. Probably, it is much better to choose ASs as the second level of coarse-graining we discuss. In practice, however, this needs more work and some modification of the existing software.

In fact, it is an independent and very interesting question to examine the data at the several scales of the global network. This interesting question will be the subject of independent research [3] for two reasons: first, we must define a clear and stable approach for the measurements and, second, this work requires considerable time.

One of the goals of the present work is to compare two different strategies for choosing the best way of getting information: directly from the original source, or indirectly from one of the parent cache servers in the cache hierarchy. The cache hierarchy allows forwarding requests to another cache server instead of the source server. This routing can be static by domains (e.g., one server is responsible for requests to the *.COM* domain, a second to the *.RU* domain, a third to the *.DE* domain, etc.) or by AS [4], or it can be dynamic as when the cache server can dynamically optimize the 'distance' from the

```
sakr@ netserv1> traceroute rtp.us.ircache.net
traceroute to rtp.us.ircache.net (128.109.131.47), 30 hops max, 40 byte packets
 1 Chernogolovka-ENS01.free.net (193.233.46.1) 0.726 ms 0.261 ms 0.239 ms
 2 Chernogolovka-BNS01.free.net (193.233.37.34) 5.205 ms 1.713 ms 2.596 ms
 3 Moscow-BNS045.free.net (147.45.20.53) 15.498 ms 5.949 ms 5.579 ms
 4 MirNet-gw.free.net (147.45.20.42) 18.530 ms 12.906 ms 15.077 ms
 5 MN-US.MIRNET.ORG (192.249.10.5) 304.520 ms 341.516 ms 319.086 ms
 6 st-mirnet.startap.net (206.220.240.181) 345.839 ms 295.835 ms 402.900 ms
 7 abilene-st.startap.net (206.220.240.206) 206.908 ms 302.631 ms 382.281 ms
 8 clev-ipls.abilene.ucaid.edu (198.32.8.26) 430.253 ms 350.469 ms 316.818 ms
 9 nycm-clev.abilene.ucaid.edu (198.32.8.30) 262.928 ms 392.853 ms 294.212 ms
10 wash-nycm.abilene.ucaid.edu (198.32.8.45) 352.848 ms 318.935 ms 326.812 ms
11 abilene-gw.ncni.net (198.86.17.61) 350.354 ms 341.399 ms 343.530 ms
12 rtp2-gw.ncren.net (128.109.52.6) 223.139 ms 230.230 ms 380.490 ms
13 rtp7-gw.ncren.net (128.109.199.2) 240.479 ms 215.965 ms 205.424 ms
14 webcache.ncren.net (128.109.131.47) 286.401 ms 279.812 ms 481.115 ms

sakr@netserv1> telnet rtp.us.ircache.net 3121
traceroute to 193.233.46.3 (193.233.46.3), 30 hops max, 40 byte packets
 1 rtp7-gw (128.109.131.245) 0.636 ms 0.417 ms 0.433 ms
 2 rtp2-gw (128.109.199.1) 0.377 ms 0.377 ms 0.469 ms
 3 rlgh1-gw (128.109.211.253) 1.870 ms 1.537 ms 1.039 ms
 4 dca-edge-02.qwest.net (63.148.128.121) 8.428 ms 8.613 ms 8.432 ms
 5 dca-core-03.inet.qwest.net (205.171.9.89) 8.747 ms 8.780 ms 8.565 ms
 6 ewr-core-01.inet.qwest.net (205.171.5.19) 12.793 ms 12.783 ms 17.086 ms
 7 ewr-cntr-01.inet.qwest.net (205.171.17.125) 12.874 ms 12.710 ms 13.176 ms
 8 jfk-core-02.inet.qwest.net (205.171.17.161) 12.935 ms 12.959 ms 13.009 ms
 9 jfk-brdr-01.inet.qwest.net (205.171.30.18) 13.014 ms 13.031 ms 13.170 ms
10 205.171.4.14 (205.171.4.14) 12.156 ms 12.489 ms 12.214 ms
11 acr2-loopback.Washingtondck.cw.net (206.24.226.62) 13.445 ms 14.955 ms 14.377 ms
12 bcr2-so-0-2-0.Frankfurt.cw.net (166.63.193.201) 125.484 ms 125.641 ms 125.598 ms
13 iar1.Frankfurt.cw.net (166.63.194.6) 125.970 ms 125.625 ms 125.684 ms
14 cable-and-wireless-internal-isp.Frankfurt.cw.net (166.63.198.2) 183.811 ms 180.665 ms 180.661 ms
15 demos-cwrussia.MSK-CORE.cwrussia.ru (213.152.129.14) 182.483 ms 192.737 ms 183.724 ms
16 m9-1-FA6-0-100M.Demos.net (194.87.0.65) 208.117 ms 191.722 ms 191.399 ms
17 RFBR-Demos-512K.Moscow.LL.Demos.net (195.133.61.173) 582.537 ms 204.710 ms 196.148 ms
18 Chernogolovka-gw.free.net (147.45.20.54) 240.766 ms 232.821 ms 315.786 ms
19 Chernogolovka-ENS01.free.net (193.233.37.33) 582.929 ms 366.017 ms 234.937 ms
20 netserv1.chg.ru (193.233.46.3) 264.191 ms 497.566 ms 451.724 ms
```

Fig. 1. One of the snapshots of the asymmetry in the traffic routing.

information source to its consumer. The distance can be measured by number of hops and round-trip time (RTT) for test packets. This possibility (ICMP-pinging and netprobe database) is realized, for example, in Squid starting Version 1.1.9 [5,6]. We are not aware of any publications on the NLANR cache-mesh dynamic routing performance.

2. Rewind-and-replay

In this section, we describe our first approach toward the understanding the problem of comparative measurements. This approach is based on the rewind-and-replay idea. Running squid we accumulated an archive of log files. Their records contain the queries with the timestamp, destination URL and so on (we emphasize only the information we need). These records could be used to repeat queries to the same destination at the same time of day and day of week. It seems that we could thus avoid the first problem mentioned in the previous section, i.e., the influence of the daily and weekly periodicity.

To be definite, suppose we are interested in the latency time t_l experienced by a user surfing Web-space [7]. We assume that this time is a function of the position x_u

of the user computer in Internet and of the position x_d of the destination server, i.e., $t_l(x_u, x_d)$. We can neglect the difference between the user-computer position x_u and the our experimental-setup position x_e because the transaction time t_i inside the campus network is typically much shorter then the latency time t_l. Finally, we use the notation $t_l(x_d)$ omitting the first variable: all measurements are performed from the same point, the experimental set placed in the NOC of AS 9113.

The position of the destination x_d could be regarded as the same for all servers within the given domain. This is a very rough assumption that is good for some extremes, like the domain *jp* or *tw*. For these domains, the main influence on the latency time is due to the overseas links. But such an assumption seems unsuitable for other extremes, like communication with the domains *com*, *org* and *net*, which are geographically noncompact. In this case, we can expect that the distribution function of the latency time for the destination servers in these domains might be multimodal.

We expect that in the limit of an infinite number of user requests R_D to the given domain D, the mean value $T_l(D)$ of latency times $t_l(D)$ exists:

$$\frac{1}{R_D}\sum_{r=1}^{R_D} t_l(D) \longrightarrow T_l(D).$$

We should not expect the distribution of the latency times to be Gaussian. Moreover, it could be multimodal in the case where the domain D is divided in some parts with essentially different throughputs of the external connections [8] (due to different link bandwidths and/or router performance). Therefore, the distribution could typically contain several characteristic times. Changing some external parameter, we could make one maximum larger than other and vice versa; therefore, a parameter value parameter should exist at which the two maximums are equal, demonstrating a phenomenon similar to the first-order phase transition in statistical mechanics. The simple and clear model of that phenomena will be analyzed elsewhere [8].

In the case where the distribution is unimodal, it seems to have a log-normal body with a power-law long tail [9,10]. Many authors usually use the median value $T_l^{(m)}(D)$ as the adequate measure for the latency time [10]. It is clear that the number of requests R_D over which we sum in the above equation should correspond to a time period T much larger than the inverse of the dominant frequency ω of traffic 'oscillations,' $T \gg 1/\omega$, in order to smooth their influence. This means that the average will have a reasonable value when taken over at least some number of days.

How could the latency times for two strategies of Internet traffic management be compared analytically?

We use the rewind-and replay procedure to compare measurements of the latency time T_l as follows. We take the log files for several periods and use them to imitate user requests. We send the imitation requests at the same time of the same weekday as the original ones, and we send them twice to the cache-servers with different strategies. We then compare the values of the averaged quantities. We can thus diminish the influence of the day-of-week and hour-of-day influences. The ratio $\mathcal{R} = T_l^I / T_l^{II}$ of the mean values of the latency times t_l^I and t_l^{II} for two different strategies I and II can be expected to be measured with reasonable accuracy.

As an example of the rewind-and-replay approach, we used two test machines imitating user activity. These machines used a number of log files grouped into set-1, set-2, set-3, and set-4, taken from the cache server www-cache.chg.ru – proxy server of the Scientific Center of the Russian Academy of Sciences at Chernogolovka. These sets are log files for the 24 hours accumulated on different weekdays (Monday, Tuesday, Wednesday and Thursday) in January and February 2000.

The same queries were simultaneously sent to two different cache servers. Both servers used identical hardware with 256MB RAM and 9GB-disk space under the FreeBSD operation system running the cache software squid-2.3.Stable2. The second server, setup #2, was configured for direct access, and the first one, setup #1, was configured to be able to use five main NLANR [2] cache servers (uc.cache.nlanr.net, bo.cache.nlanr.net, pb.cache.nlanr.net, sd.cache.nlanr.net, sv.cache.nlanr.net) as parents with the closest-only option. This option means that our setup #1 sent requests to the parent only when this way was expected to be the shortest one (in sense of RTT).

Setup #2 with direct access used default routing via several external channels: the 512 kbps sub-channel demos.net (Moscow) – cw.net (New York) rented from Demos Ltd, the channel RBnet (Moscow) – TeleGlobe (New York) for access to some Canadian European networks (for example, NorduNet), and 6 Mbps MIRnet channel to StarTap (Chicago) for access to some American universities, members of vBNS/Internet2. According to the agreement between FREEnet and NLANR, setup #1 was able to use the 6 Mbps MIRnet channel for access to all the NLANR cache servers.

The resulting log files were analyzed using the calamaris-2.29 package [12], which calculates the average speed of the data transfer $v = S/t_l$ as the ratio of the document size S to the latency time t_l and the ratio $R = T_l^I / T_l^{II}$. Here, $T_l^I /$ and T_l^{II} are the mean values of latency times measured by the respective servers setup #1 and setup #2.

Fig. 2 shows the mean efficiency parameter R averaged additionally over all four sets (actually, the most heavy weakly traffic), measured for different top-level domains. This figure clearly shows the advantages of using cache mesh. The value of the efficiency parameter R averaged for all requests (all domains) is about 2. Only some domains (*edu*, *ca*, *se*, and *de*) have values of R close to 1. This is probably because direct access to those domains use alternative channels (MIRnet or RBnet) which are the same (MIRnet in the

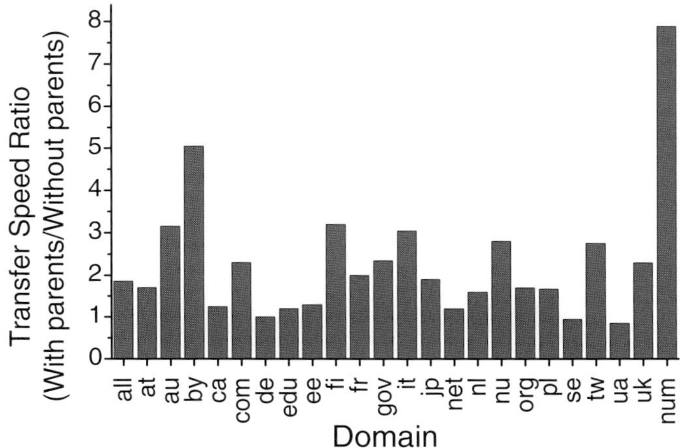

Fig. 2. The ratio of mean speed of the document retrieving from the Web for some top-level domains with and without cache mesh.

case of edu) or relatively underloaded (RBnet in the case of *ca*, *se*, and *de*) as with setup #1 using MIRnet.

Although this method seems to be a good candidate in the arsenal of measurements it has a drawback. This method practically doubles Internet traffic and could therefore change the conditions under which the measurement is performed (reminiscent of the observer problem in quantum mechanics). However, we could not estimate the value of these changes.

Analysis of the results shows that this procedure, unfortunately, does not give stable results for the latency times as expected [7] and the latency times seem to be random. At first, we believed that this was due to insufficient statistics. But, in fact, the greatest effect comes from the change of the network itself. We will discuss this in another publication.

3. Cache-triangle

We introduce the cache-triangle experimental setup of servers in order to minimize the influence of the network properties discussed above on the results of the comparative study of Internet traffic. It is constructed from three cache servers as show on Fig. 3. The first one, the Master, only sends queries to two slaves, the Left-slave and the Right-slave. Both slaves can communicate with the rest of the world. The Master sends queries to slaves alternatingly, for example, odd queries to the Left-slave and even queries to the Right-slave. It is obvious that for a sufficiently large number of queries, we could not distinguish between right and left. Therefore, our configuration is fully symmetric in the limit of an infinite number of queries. It is very important that this symmetry holds for any configuration of slaves. As a consequence, we could compare statistics of the Left- and

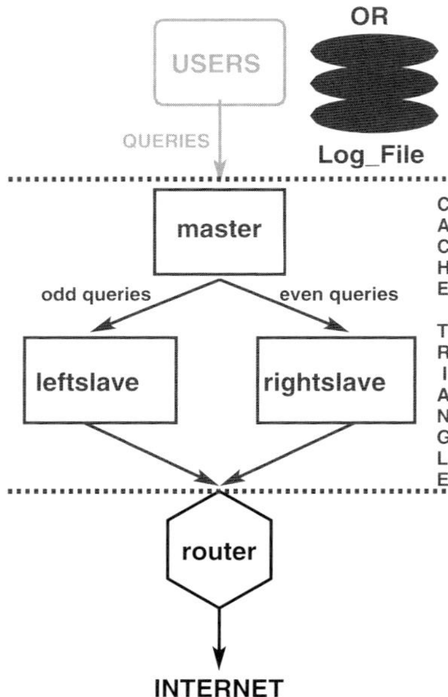

Fig. 3. The symmetric configuration of servers for the measurements — cache-triangle.

Right-slaves being sure they are not subject to daily or weekly periodicity, or the fact that sysadm Smith at the University of the Middle of Nowhere has changed the routing of his domain. He is not able to destroy the symmetry of our cache-triangle.

Moreover, we occasionally check the sensitivity of our experimental device. We found asymmetry in the first measurements, and this was due to a wrong configuration of the two cache-servers on the next level of the hierarchy. These servers were wrongly communicating with one of the slaves as with a parent.

The first configuration used was built with Master-cache (P-II/300, 192MB RAM, 8GB disk cache), which was configured to send all odd queries to the Left-slave cache (P-II/400, 192MB RAM, 8GB disk cache) and all even queries to the Right-slave cache (Celeron/433, 192MB RAM, 8GB disk cache). All cache servers were running the same version of the software Squid-2.2.Stable. The Master served real user requests (acted as a real proxy.chg.ru server) and was configured with the options 'parent no-query round-robin htcp no-netdb'. Both slaves were configured identically with the options 'parent closest-only' to use NLANR cache servers [8], and with the options 'parent closest-only htcp' to communicate with ikia.ru.ircache.net and dau.ru.ircache.net servers, and with the option 'sibling' with webcache1.free.net. This setup produced log files on the Master running three weeks in the period from 13 December 2000 to 4 January 2001.

The resulting log files were processed with the seafood-1.13 software [13] (version dated 09.06.2000) and only real non-HIT queries from the master to both slave caches were taken into account. The traffic speed was calculated in Kbit/sec as the ratio of $\sum$ Kbit/ $\sum$ sec.

3.1. Measurement results over three weeks of the symmetric configuration

First, we determined how symmetric are (1) the total number of queries, (2) the total traffic, and (3) the average speed of the traffic.

(1) We plot the number of queries for different top-level domains in double log scale in Fig. 4. Data is ordered in descending order for the Left-slave (solid stars), and

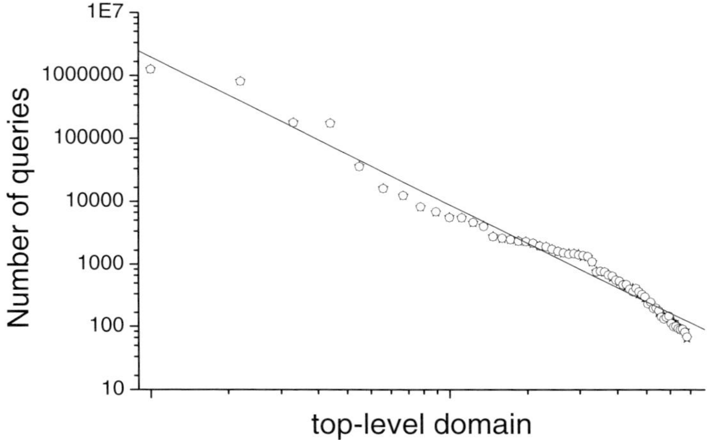

Fig. 4. Total number of queries during the three weeks of work of the cache-triangle in symmetric configuration. See text for the details.

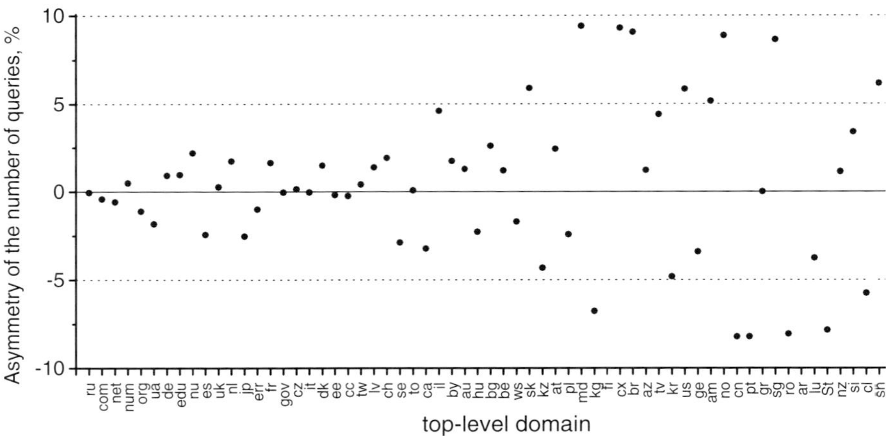

Fig. 5. Relative difference in the number of queries served by the Left-slave and by the Right-slave.

the corresponding number of queries for the Right-slave are marked by open circles. Clearly, the picture demonstrates that the number of queries coincides in the log–log scale. It is interesting that the number of queries decreases with the domain number by an approximate power law $n^{-2.34(5)}$ shown by the solid line, although this law is not perfect and there are some oscillations of the number of queries. Here and throughout paper, n denotes the rank of a given domain in the ordered sequence. The one-sigma uncertainty in the last digit is shown in parentheses. We call the effect of the power-law decay in the number of queries the *power-law decay of domain popularity*. This is very similar to Zipf's law distributions of Web objects [10,11].

To check asymmetry in the number of queries, we plot the relative difference in the number of queries, measured in percent, $\frac{N_r - N_l}{N_l}100\%$, where N_l (N_r) is the number of queries served by Left-slave (Right-slave), in Fig. 5. The respective labels *num* and *err* denote unresolved domain names and requests with errors in URL. The two horizontal lines show the 5% acceptance interval chosen as the good accuracy for the measurements. All events are within this accuracy for the domains with more than 700 queries. The fluctuations are larger than 5%, but still less than 10% in the tail of the decay in domain popularity.

(2) In the Fig. 6, we plot the total traffic in Megabytes as a function of domain-name rank. Domains are ordered as described in 1. The open circles (closed stars) represent the total traffic for the Right-slave (Left-slave). Both curves almost coincide. The decay of the traffic is described by the power law $n^{-2.25(16)}$, which is the same as for the number of queries within a two sigma error.

Nevertheless, there is a visible asymmetry for some domains. We examine this in more detail.

In Fig. 7 in double log scale, we plot the relative difference of the total traffic coming through the Left- and Right-slaves $100(t_l - t_r)/t_l$, where t_l (t_r) is total traffic for Left-slave (Right-slave). We exclude all domains with less than 250 queries because of the very large fluctuations. The horizontal solid lines show the 10% acceptance interval we choose for the accuracy of the symmetry of the total traffic. There is a large asymmetry for some domains.

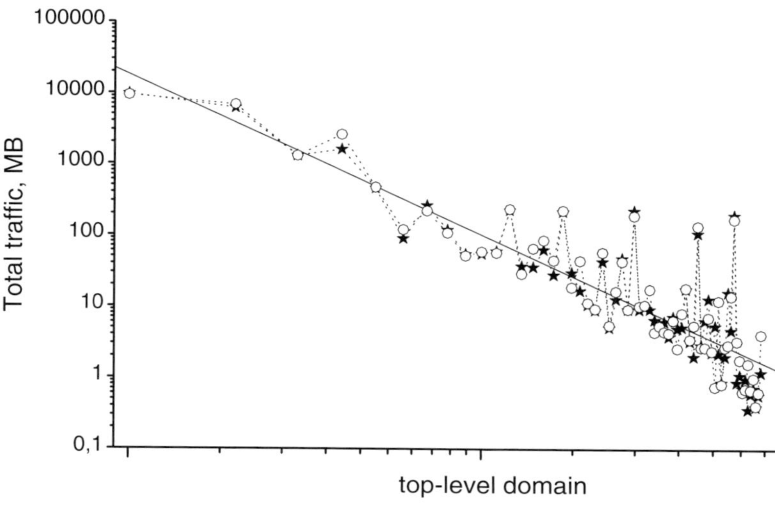

Fig. 6. The total traffic served by the Left-slave (closed stars) and by the Right-slave (open circles) in double-logarithmic scale. Solid line is the linear fit to the data.

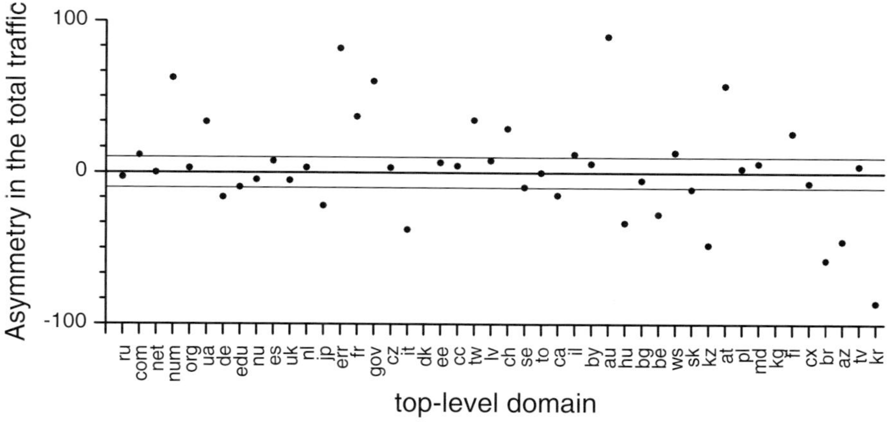

Fig. 7. Relative asymmetry of the total traffic shown on Fig. 6. Solid lines is the 10% interval.

The large deviation for the domain with more than 1000 queries is for the artificial domains *num* and *err*, which could be dropped from the analyses, and for the domains *ua* (33), *jp* (−22), *fr* (37), *gov* (60), *it* (−38), *dk* (163), *tw* (34), *ch* (28.7), and *au* (90). What is the origin of these deviations? We examine the average document size m for a given top-level domain. It could be calculated as the ratio of the total traffic to the total number of queries. The average document size for the Left-slave is 8.3 KB and for the Right-slave is 8.9 KB. The asymmetry in the average package size is about 7% and is rather large. Although asymmetry in the number of queries is 0.1%, it is 6.6% in the total traffic. This explains our choice for the acceptance interval for deviations from symmetry.

The largest document sizes are 1347KB (Left) and 1287KB (Right) for the domain *pt*, 256KB and 370KB for the domain *fi*, 152KB and 133KB for the domain *ca*, and

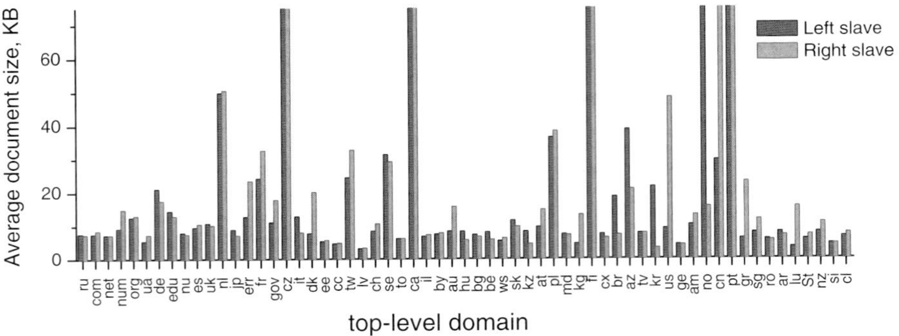

Fig. 8. Average document size for the symmetric configuration.

93KB and 95KB for the domain *cz*. Size of the packages for the domain *fi* have a very simple explanation. In Russia, the most popular Finnish network source is the ftp server ftp.funet.fi. It is clear that in the case of a large average file size for a given domain, we will have large fluctuations in the averages.

The typical document size distribution is known to be log-normal [9,10]. The rare requests for very large files could lead to enormous fluctuations in the averages. Analysis of the data supports this idea: the largest deviations occur for such domains where the average sizes of documents are far from the average value for all domains. This is especially well demonstrated with the domains *no* (average package sizes are 95KB and 16KB) and *cn* (30KB and 97KB).

In Fig. 8, we show average document sizes for the top-level domains. We exclude data for the above-mentioned domains to make the figure more readable. Generally, the average size is less than 10KB, and totally this picture clearly supports the influence of the rare and large packages on the distribution of the average package size.

In fact, the most interesting quantity is the average latency time, which is connected to the speed with which we receive packages.

(3) In Fig. 9, we show values of the average speed for the domains ordered in the same way as before.

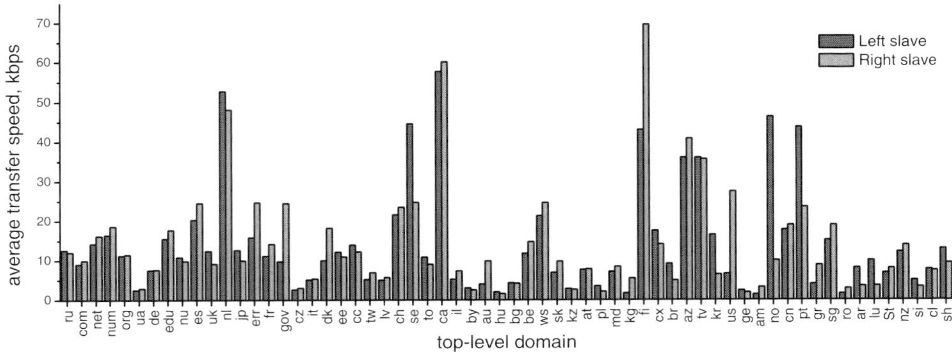

Fig. 9. Average documents transfer speed in Kbit/sec, which served by symmetric cache-triangle configuration.

Clearly, there is some correlation of the document transfer speed served by the Left- and Right-slaves, although fluctuations are quite large. The origin of these fluctuations is clearly connected to the above-mentioned long-tail distribution of the package sizes: the maximum speed and the difference in speed are for *fi*, *ca*, *pt*, *no*, etc. However, this is not the case, for example, for the domain *cz*. This quantity is probably also very sensitive to the nonuniformity of some domains and/or to the geographical spreading of some domains.

We have discussed the results of analyzing three weeks of measurement. We also analysed the data for each of the three weeks separately in the same manner as for the summary of three weeks. We did not find any essential difference. This means that averaging over three weeks gives some stable results, which give us confidence that the effects we discussed are not something cached from the random flow of Internet traffic rivers.

3.2. Measurement results over three weeks of an asymmetric configuration

For the next series of experiments, we increased the symmetry and power of the cache-triangle and introduced an asymmetry in the slave strategies. The Master (proxy.chg.ru) was based on the CPU AMD Athlon/850 with 512 Mb RAM and 30 Gb disk cache. Both slaves, the Left (ath2.chg.ru) and the Right (ath3.chg.ru), were absolutely identical and based on the CPU AMD Athlon/850 with 384 MB RAM and 20 GB disk cache. All three servers were running Squid-2.3.Stable4 under FreeBSD-4.2.

Master related to both slaves as 'parent no-query round-robin no-netdb'. The Left-slave (ath2) communicated with the NLANR-servers (*uc, pb, sd, bo, sv* as 'parent closest-only' and with ikia.ru.ircache.net, dau.ru.ircache.net and webcache1.free.net as 'parent closest-only htcp'. The Right slave was configured to obtain information only directly from the origin.

The Master served real user requests, and the log files accumulated in the period from 10 February 2001 to 3 March 2001 was processed with the seafood-1.13 software [13] (version dated 09.06.2000) and only real non-HIT queries from master to both slave caches were taken into account.

The total number of queries decayed with the same exponent as in the previous experiment. Moreover, the data coincide quite well. This is additional support that statistics over about three weeks are stable. Analysis shows that the same statement is also valid for the total traffic.

The average document size served by the Left-slave configured to use cache-mesh and through the Right-slave with direct access to the origin is shown in Fig. 10. Comparison of Fig. 10 with Fig. 8 immediately shows the difference. Namely, the average package sizes are larger in the case of cache-mesh usage.

We note that the following domains are excluded from the picture: *pt* (average document size is 2923.3KB(!) with 90 Left requests and 32.7KB with 102 Right requests), *kr* (211KB and 275KB), and *it* (231KB and 218KB).

In Fig. 11, we show the average document transfer speed. We note that there are no visible differences between the two strategies for many domains, but the preference of using cache-mesh is clear for many others (*com*, *net*, *org*, *ua*, *tw*, *fr*, *ca*, *pl*). Probably, we must find some another parameter in this case. This reminds us of one more statement of Heraclites. We do not hesitate to place it here as the ending message of our analyses: 'The hidden harmony is better than the open'. We are going to hunt it!

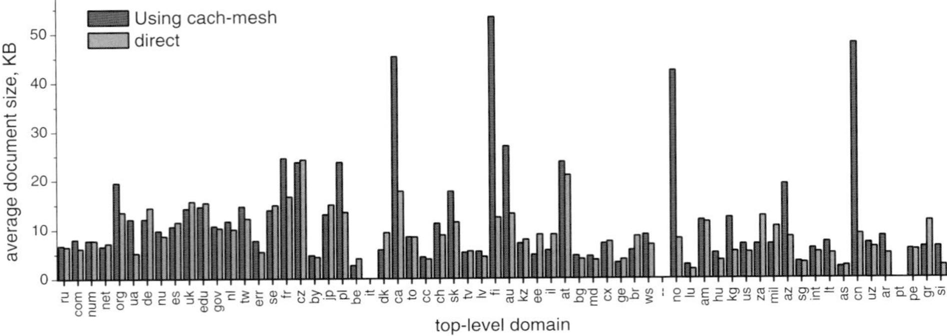

Fig. 10. Average size of the documents served by the Left-slave server using cache-mesh and by the Right-slave server with the direct connection to the origins.

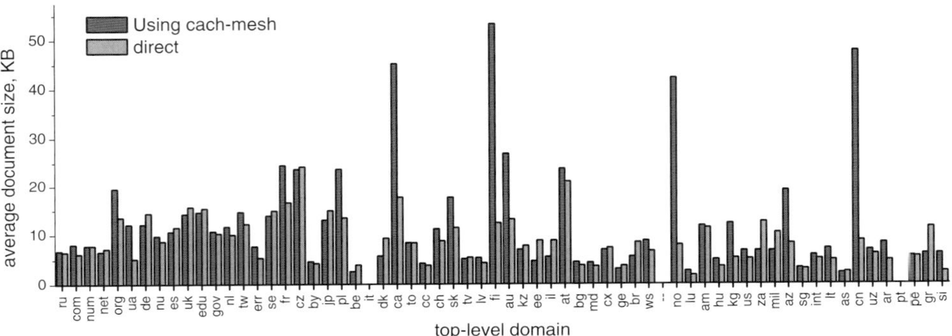

Fig. 11. The average documents speed in Kbit/sec. See caption to Fig. 10.

4. Conclusion and proposals

The analyses presented here show that the cache-triangle could be used for comparative measurements of Internet traffic. We have started a new set of measurements in which we combine both our ideas. Namely, we use the rewind-and-replay strategy with the cache-triangle. The preliminary results look very stable. We hope to extract more detailed information on the structure of Internet flow from this set of experiments.

Acknowledgments

This work was supported in part by the RFBR (Grant Nos. 99-07-90084 and 01-07-90119). One of the authors (LNS) acknowledges the CARIPLO fellowship and the Landau Network–Centro Volta for the financial support and University Milano-Bicocca for the kind hospitality during the final stage of this work.

References

[1] S. Gadde, J. Chase, M. Rabinovich, Web caching and content distribution: A view from an interior, *Computer Communs.*, 24, 222–231 (2001).

[2] Duane Wessels, The NLANR Cache System, http://www.ircache.net/Cache/

[3] L.N. Shchur and S.A. Krashakov, Coarse-graining of network and Internet traffic, in progress.

[4] C. Grimm, J.-S. Vockler, H. Pralle, Request routing in cache meshes, *Computer Networks and ISDN Systems*, 30, 2269–2278 (1998).

[5] D. Wessels, K. Claffy, ICP and Squid Web cache, *IEEE J. Selected Areas in Communs.*, 16, 345–357 (1998).

[6] D. Wessels, Squid Web proxy cache, http://www.squid-cache.org

[7] S.A. Krashakov, L.N. Shchur, Active measurements (experiments) of the Interne traffic using cache-mesh, *International Journal of Modern Physics C (Physics and Computers)*, 2001, to be published.

[8] L.N. Shchur, and S.A. Krashakov, First order phase transition in the Internet traffic, in progress.

[9] D. Helbing, B.A. Huberman, S.M. Maurer, Optimizing traffic in virtual and real space, In: *Traffic and Granular Flow'99*, Ed. D. Helbing, H.J. Hermann, M. Schreckenberg, D.E. Wolf, Springer: Berlin, 2000.

[10] P. Barford, A. Bestavros, A. Bradley, M. Crovella, Changes in Web client access patterns. Characteristics and caching implications, *World Wide Web J., Spec. Issue on Characterization and Performance Evaluation*, 2, 15–28 (1999).

[11] L. Breslau, P. Cao, L. Fan, G. Phillips, S. Shenker, Web caching and Zipf-like distributions: Evidence and implications, *Proc. IEEE INFOCOM'99*, 126–134 (1999).

[12] Cord Beerman, Calamaris, http://Cord.de/tools/squid/calamaris/

[13] J.-S. Vockler, Seafood: Extended cache statistics, http://www.cache.dfn.de/DFN-Cache/Development/seafood.html

Web Caching and Content Delivery
A. Bestavros and M. Rabinovich (Editors)

An Interactive Video Delivery and Caching System Using Video Summarization

Sung-Ju Lee [a,1], Wei-Ying Ma [b,2], Bo Shen [a,3]

[a] *Hewlett-Packard Laboratories, 1501 Page Mill Road, Palo Alto, CA 94304-1126, USA*
[b] *Microsoft Research China, China*

Abstract

With the advance of high-speed network technologies, the availability and popularity of streaming media content over the Internet has grown rapidly in recent years. The delivery and caching of streaming media must be handled in a different fashion than that of traditional non-streaming objects such as HTML or image files, because of its distinct characteristics and user viewing patterns. We propose a novel scheme that provides users with the video summary (a number of key-frame images) before they download the file, and options for them to select the starting playback position. We introduce the content analysis service to achieve these functionalities. The video content analysis performs shot boundary detection, key-frame selection, and face detection and tracking. The results of the processing are a segmented video sequence and an XML-based meta-data describing the video content. We also design a caching system that utilizes our video abstraction and summarization technique. Our integrated video delivery and caching system combines content-aware segmentation, prefix caching, prefetching, and cooperative caching. We describe how our scheme can be applied in three proposed caching architectures.

Keywords: Streaming media delivery; Web caching; Content distribution networks

1. Introduction

With the popularity growth of the Internet and the wide availability of high-speed network access, an increasing number of streaming media objects are being distributed over the Internet. Compared with just a few years ago, larger files are found on the Web today because of improved video resolution and longer video length. Class lectures, news reports, sports highlights, movie trailers, commercial ads, and personal home videos are just a few examples of videos on the Web.

Conventional video streaming systems use a linear playback scheme that forces users to download from the beginning of a video. Users often need to download and view at least a portion of the video to decide if the content is what they expected. Even during the

[1] E-mail: sjlee@hpl.hp.com
[2] E-mail: wyma@microsoft.com
[3] E-mail: boshen@hpl.hp.com

playback, users may wish to skip some of the parts and jump directly to a specific scene to save time or network bandwidth. Although fast-forward and rewind functionalities are provided by some streaming media servers, long delays and processing are experienced. Moreover, without the knowledge of what is contained in the video and the precise position of a video shot boundary, users usually fail to promptly locate the desired scenes they wish to watch. These problems and limitations have considerably affected user viewing experience and wasted network resources. A recent study [2] reports that almost half of the video requests stopped during near the beginning of the playback. This result indicates that an improved video delivery scheme needs to be developed to manage the user video browsing behavior.

Web caching has been used to accelerate the delivery of Web objects such as HTML files and images. Streaming video objects differ from these Web objects in several ways. First, the size of video files is usually larger than non-streaming files by orders of magnitude. Storing the entire video file in a single proxy cache is therefore inefficient or even impossible. Second, video objects are mostly static contents with the WORM (Write Once Read Many) property. Hence, the cache consistency and coherency are not important issues in video caching. Moreover, user video access behavior and streaming media workload show different characteristics than those of non-streaming objects, as reported in [2] and [6]. Because of the special characteristic of streaming videos, a more suitable caching system that is different from traditional proxy caching systems must be developed.

We propose an integrated interactive video delivery and caching system that provides users with a better viewing environment. The main goal of our work is to design a video system that supports and utilizes the automatic video analysis and summarization technique. The video analysis performed in our system includes shot boundary detection and key-frame selection. When a client requests a video, our system first shows the key-frames that summarize the video to the user, instead of streaming the video from the beginning. Users can quickly browse through the summary images to decide if they want to download any portion of the video. This key-frame provision helps the users avoid wasting time and network bandwidth on the video they are not interested in. Our system also enables users to easily select and jump to a scene. When a user decides to download the video after viewing the summary, the user can choose the starting playback position by selecting a key-frame. The clients can watch the video immediately from the segment they select. This feature is similar to chapters and 'jump to a scene' features of a DVD player. The key difference is that on DVD this information is created by content providers. In today's Internet, the content providers rarely offer this information, and hence we designed a system that makes video analysis and interactive video delivery a value-added service to content providers and end users.

A video caching system is designed to take advantage of the high-level information extracted from the video analysis. We utilize several well known caching techniques such as prefix caching, prefetching, and cooperative caching with the assumption that the video is segmented and spread across multiple proxies for cache sharing and cooperative caching. Segmentation facilitates the distribution and balance of server load, and allows the usage of a fine grain replacement algorithm. Prefix caching [23] is a scheme that stores only the beginning of the video to minimize storage. We apply this technique for each video segment to reduce the start-up latency. Prefetching [15] is performed at the client cache of our system to also reduce the delay. We propose three cooperative proxy architectures and illustrate the operation of video delivery and caching in each of the architectures.

The remainder of this paper is organized as follows. Section 2 provides the overview of our system architecture. The video analysis technique is presented in Section 3, followed by video delivery and caching description in Section 4. We report the current status in Section 5, and conclude the paper in Section 6.

2. System architecture overview

Fig. 1 depicts the overview of our proposed video delivery and caching system. Video is analyzed by an application proxy server, which can be installed by content providers as a gateway in front of their content servers or deployed by a third-party service provider that has the authorization to process the video on behalf of the content providers. In either approach, we assume a trust relationship between the application proxy server and the origin server, so the video is processed and value-added before it is distributed on the Internet.

This architecture matches well with the business model of content distribution networks, with the video summarization and interactive delivery being provided as a value-added service to their customers, i.e., content providers. Note that this service is an off-line procedure performed before the video is replicated and distributed to the caching proxies at the edges of networks.

Ma et al. [11] proposed another new layer of Internet infrastructure, called a content services network, that is built around content distribution networks. This layer consists of

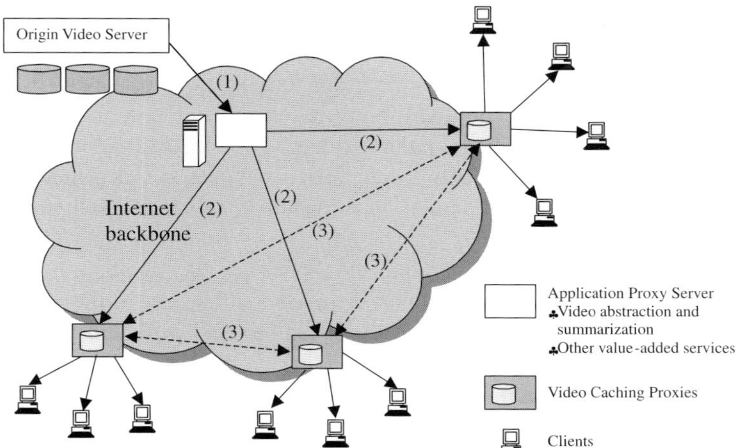

(1)	Video is transferred fr om the origin server to the application proxy server that analyzes video content and performs value -added services. This application proxy server may be installed (and owned) by content providers as a gateway, or provided by a third -party content services provider that has the authorization to process the content on behalf of content providers.
(2)	The segmented video and the associated meta-data resulted from the services of application proxy server are distributed to video caching proxies at the edge of the Internet. This may be a service provided by content distribution networks.
(3)	Video is served from a caching proxy close to the client. In case of a local cache miss, it may communicate with other cooperative caches for a possible cache hit.

Fig. 1. The system overview. The application proxy server is located near the origin server and performs content service on behalf of a content provider.

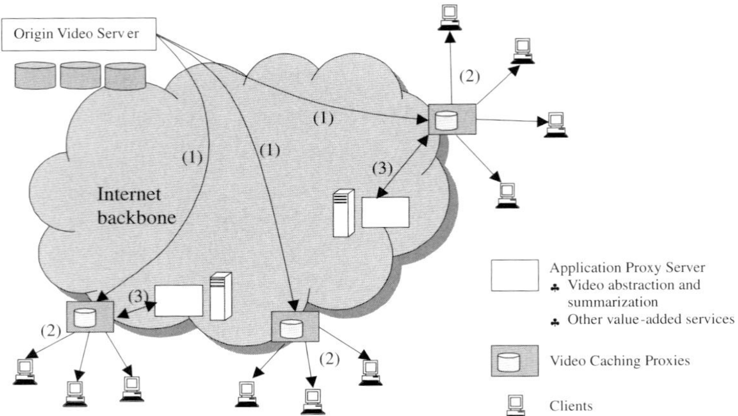

(1)	Assuming the video is served from the origin server, the caching proxies, installed within local area networks by ISPs or corporations, will cache the video after it has been requested by a local client.
(2)	Because of the processing delay, the first client requesting the video does not receive the value -added video delivery services.
(3)	While the video is being cached, the caching proxies can send it to a cooperative app lication proxy server for video summarization and other value-added services. The subsequent client requests for the same video will receive the benefit of the services.

Fig. 2. The system overview. The application proxy servers are located near the clients and perform content service on behalf of end users.

a network of cooperating application proxy servers that provide computational resources and value-added services to content providers or end users. The system interaction described in Fig. 1 corresponds to the pre-distribution service performed by a content services network on behalf of content providers as described in [11].

Fig. 2 shows the overview of another possible deployment scenario, where the application proxy server performs the video summarization on behalf of the clients. The application proxy server only processes the video that has been requested by a local user. After the video is downloaded, the caching proxy sends it to the application proxy server for video summarization and other content services. The video summarization could also be conducted while the video is being downloaded since our video analysis algorithm does not require the video to be fully downloaded in advance. Note that to perform summarization of the whole video, the caching proxy must continue to download the entire video even if the first user that requested the video object halts in the middle of the session. The limitation of this deployment scenario is that because of the processing delay, the first user is not able to receive the value-added services provided by the application proxy server, and the video is served in the form the origin server provides. This problem is similar to that of proxy caching where the client that first requests an object does not receive the benefic of caching.

The system interaction described in Fig. 2 corresponds to the post-distribution service performed by a content services network on behalf of end users as described in [11].

3. Content analysis services

The video content analysis performs shot boundary detection, key-frame selection, and face detection and tracking. The results of the processing are a segmented video sequence and an XML-based meta-data describing the video content. In this section, we discuss the video parsing techniques used in our application proxy server. In our study, we assume the streaming video files are of MPEG-1 or MPEG-2 format. Since the principle encoding schemes for RealNetworks Media, Microsoft Windows Media, and Apple QuickTime are proprietary information and not released to the public, our algorithm has not been applied to those media formats. For a more detailed description of our video parsing technique, readers are referred to [12].

3.1. Shot boundary detection and key-frame selection

In order to partition a long video sequence into smaller and meaningful components, we apply shot boundary detection to identify the discontinuities between different shots. Each shot corresponds to a sequence of frames recorded contiguously and represents a continuous action in time and space. We have developed a very efficient and robust shot boundary detection scheme that operates directly on MPEG compressed data at real-time processing speed [12]. The scheme first looks for a potential shot boundary within a group-of-pictures (GOP) by comparing the difference between two consecutive I-frames based on their DCT (Discrete Cosine Transform) information. A typical MPEG video sequence may have a structure of $IBBPBBPBB$ (first GOP) $IBBPBBPBB$ (second GOP), ... When a potential shot boundary is detected, a further examination is applied to all the B- and P-frames in-between to identify the exact location of a shot boundary. This examination only requires partial decompression of the video to retrieve the macro-block modes. Note that P-frame uses its preceding I- or P-frame as a reference to perform motion compensation, and B-frame uses both preceding and succeeding I- or P-frames as a reference. By checking the degree of such references from their macro-block modes, we can locate the precise shot boundary.

The video is summarized through the selection of key-frames that represent the content of each video shot. In our system, key-frame selection is performed along with the video segmentation process. The algorithm selects the first frame in each shot that passes the image blur test as a key-frame. It finds a new key-frame by continuously searching for the next I-frame that is sufficiently different from the previous key-frame. The I-frames are compared with one another using the color information extracted from the frames. The required degree of difference for key-frame selection can be adjusted in the algorithm to control the approximate number of key-frames generated. Note that to be selected as a key-frame, each key-frame must satisfy a certain requirement to ensure it is not blurred [13]. Key-frames from each shot are clustered to form a hierarchical representation that provides multiple levels of granulations for video browsing and navigation [30]. Fig. 3 shows the results of video content analysis.

3.2. Face detection and tracking

People are often the most important objects in a video. Hence, the knowledge of who is in the video and in which part of the video they appear can make video delivery and client navigation more effective and efficient. We have incorporated face detection [22] and tracking techniques into our video parser. Face detection is applied on every I-frame and the location of detected faces is matched with the face locations currently under tracking. If a match is identified, the new location of a tracked face is updated and the

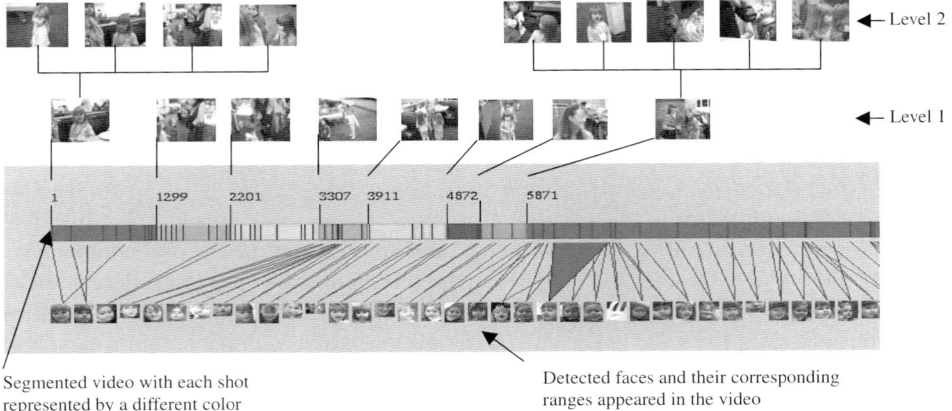

Fig. 3. The results of video content analysis. The video is segmented into shots that can be managed separately. The key-frames from each shot are selected and clustered to form a hierarchical representation that is used to assist video delivery and caching.

detected face is labeled as the same person as the tracked one. Whenever there is an uncertainty for identifying a newly detected face or there is no match for a current tracked face, the face tracking is applied. The face tracking uses the motion information contained in the macro-blocks of P- and B-frames to predict face locations from the previous I-frame to the next I-frame. Because face detection algorithm only detects frontal faces in scattered I-frames, face tracking is essential to identify the correspondence between these detected faces and associate them to the same person within a continuous video shot. The tracking stops when the projected face region leaves a scene or a shot boundary is detected.

Face detection is also used to assist the selection of key-frames. When a new face is detected, the corresponding frame is selected as a key-frame. In addition, for a set of similar frames, face information is used to help select the best key-frame. That is, a frame that contains larger and better-positioned frontal faces with more people appearing inside will replace the previously selected key-frame if their contents are similar.

3.3. Meta-data for video content description

The results of video content analysis are stored in a meta-data whose format is shown in Fig. 4. This meta-data uses XML-based language to describe the temporary structure and summarization of video. In this example, the video has been segmented into 13 shots, with each shot represented by a key-frame URL in the first-level cluster denoted by `<kf_cluster level="1">`. The range of each video shot is represented by *begin* and *end* tags. The seventh video shot, represented by kf-0000685.jpg, has more than a key-frame because it contains rapid scene changes. Those key-frames are put into the second-level cluster denoted by `<kf_cluster, level="1.7">` for further detailed browsing if necessary. The meta-data also contains the information about the coordinates

```
<video structure>
   <kf_cluster level="1">
      <img src="kf -0000132.jpg" begin="132" end="227"/>
      <img src="kf -0000228.jpg" begin="228" end="336"/>
      <img src="kf -0000354.jpg">
         <face coords="179,69,37,41">
            <playback begin  ="337" end="385"/>
         </face>
         <playback begin="337" end="385"/>
      </img>
      <img src="kf -0000386.jpg" begin="386" end="458"/>
      <img src="kf -0000459.jpg" begin="459" end="576"/>
      <img src="kf -0000577.jpg" begin="577" end="684"/>
      <img src="kf -0000685.jpg" begin="685" end="764"/>
      <img src="kf -0000765.jpg" begin="765" end="800"/>
      <img src="kf -0000801.jpg" begin="801" end="852"/>
      <img src="kf -0000885.jpg" begin="853" end="894"/>
      <img src="kf -0000912.jpg" begin="895" end="950"/>
      <img src="kf -0000951.jpg" begin="951" end="992"/>
      <img src="kf -0000993.jpg" begin="993" end="1008"/>
   </kf_cluster>

   <kf_cluster level="1.7">
      <img src="kf -0000717.jpg" begin="717" end="764"/>
      <img sr c="kf-0000762.jpg" begin="762" end="764"/>
   </kf_cluster>

   <video src="rtsp://www.hpl.hp.com/test.mpg"/>
   <logo src="hp -logo.jpg" coords="6,6"/>
<video structure/>
```

Fig. 4. An XML-based meta-data describing the information about the video.

of detected faces and their corresponding ranges in the video. The URLs for the video and a possible logo to be inserted are also included in the representation.

This meta-data serves two purposes. First, upon the client's request, the server sends this meta-data along with key-frame images to the client. The media player uses this information to render the video so that the user can browse the summary in advance of downloading the video file. In most scenarios, the summary contains enough information for the user to decide whether to download. If users find the summary (key-frames) uninteresting or do not see the expected content, they can decide not to download the file. In the case of using other existing applications, users must initiate the streaming session in order to view the content. When users do not appreciate the content and decide to stop in the middle of a session, bandwidth and power are wasted just to decide whether users want to access the video file. A study in [2] showed that nearly 45% of video file requests stopped the session during the first 5% of the video playback period. Based on this user access behavior, we believe providing users with the video summary can conserve network resources. Second, using the information provided in the meta-data, the client could communicate with the server to control how the video is streamed to the client. When the clients browse the summary (key-frames), they can select any particular frame that interests most. By clicking the specific key-frame, the client can view the video starting from the segment represented by the selected key-frame. Therefore, users can watch the interesting parts of the video without having to stream it from the beginning of the entire video. Note that each key-frame (or face) in the meta-data represents a video segment that can be played back independently and immediately. This requires a special handling on the server to ensure that the beginning of each video segment corresponds to a breakable point in the compressed video data. For MPEG-1 and MPEG-2 videos, this point is the beginning of an *I*-frame, as it does not depend on any previous frames to decode it.

4. Video delivery and caching

4.1. Goals and design overview

Streaming media have different characteristics than non-streaming objects. Video files are much larger and their contents do not change. User access behavior and workload of video files and streaming media are shown to be different from those of non-streaming objects [2,6]. Based on these characteristics of streaming video files, we take an approach that is different from traditional proxy caching systems. The main goal of our work is to design an integrated video delivery and caching system that supports and utilizes the content analysis and summarization technique introduced in Section 3. The key technical components of our system, which we discuss below, are segmentation, prefix caching, prefetching, and cooperative caching.

4.1.1. Content-aware segmentation

A video segmentation module divides the video into segments based on the result of shot boundary detection. Each segment corresponds to a continuously recorded sequence of frames and we can manage each segment separately. The segments of a video are spread across multiple proxies for cache sharing and cooperative caching. Note that in contrast with the simple equal-sized segmentation technique used in [1] and [10], the size of segments may vary in our system. It is desirable however, to have constraints on segment lengths, as having too many or too few segments may cause difficulties in object management.

Segmenting the streaming media files has several advantages. By placing segments on several proxy caches, we can better distribute the load. In addition, spreading the video into several caches allows us to perform intelligent caching. Instead of taking an 'all or nothing' approach where either the video file is stored in its entirety or not cached at all, we cache the streaming objects by segments, i.e., the cache replacement granularity is the segment. Therefore, at some instances, only popular parts of the video may be present at the caches of the network edges. We discuss the caching algorithm we use in Section 4.5.

4.1.2. Prefix caching

Storing the entire video file into proxies may be inefficient as video files can be very large. This is particularly true if the cached streaming media object is not popular. Prefix caching [23] stores only the first few frames of the popular video files. When a client requests a video stream and the prefix is cached, the proxy delivers the prefix to the client while it requests the remainder of the video to the origin server. By caching the (large enough) prefix, the start-up latency perceived by the user can be reduced. The challenge could be in determining the optimal prefix size. Items such as roundtrip delay, server-to-proxy latency, video specific parameters (e.g., size, bit rate, etc.), and retransmission rate of lost packets must be considered in calculating the appropriate prefix length [23].

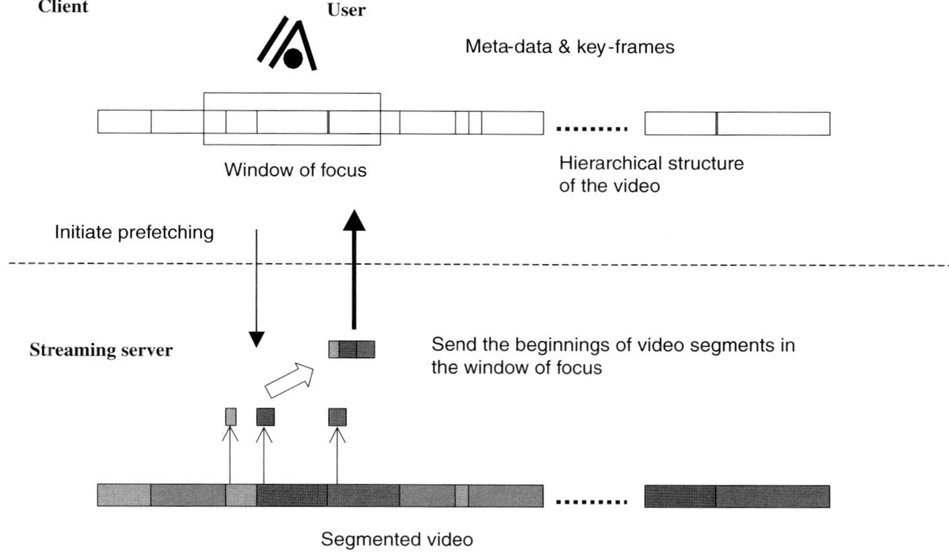

Fig. 5. The video prefetching scheme.

As our system has multiple segments for a video object, we adopt prefix caching for each cached segments. When users click one of the summary frames provided by our content analysis and summarization technique, our system delivers the specific segment immediately to the client (and not from the beginning of the video file, unless the user requested the first segment). Hence, we store the prefix of each segment to benefit from prefix caching in our system.

4.1.3. Prefetching

Prefetching [4,15,31] is another scheme to reduce the user perceived latency. Prefetching can increase the caching efficiency by predicting the client request pattern and caching the objects in advance of user requests. The sacrifice however, is the increase in traffic. Studies report other potential costs of prefetching. [26] shows that prefetching is beneficial only when traffic is lightly loaded and the prediction algorithm is very effective. [7] reports that prefetching affects the queueing behavior and increases network burstiness. Prefetching should be performed with extra cautions in streaming media delivery systems as they are dealing with much larger objects.

We use prefetching at the client cache instead of the proxy cache. Prefetching scheme on the client side further reduces the startup latency. Since the user is browsing the video based on the meta-data already downloaded, this interaction provides a window of opportunity for the client device to initiate a prefetching based on the availability of the resources such as bandwidth and storage in the client cache. The user's browsing behavior provides more clues to help the prediction algorithm to be more effective. We propose the following prefetching algorithm that decides when and which portion of the video is downloaded while browsing. As shown in Fig. 5, if the focus window of the user's browser stays at certain section for more than t seconds, the first n bytes of each video segment within the window are prefetched.

The duration t is proportional to the number of key-frames showing in the browser window. In addition, the parameter pair (t, n) is designed to satisfy certain constraints posed by the resources limitation. For example, if the connection between the client and proxy is congested, the algorithm can choose to increase t and decrease n in order to reduce the prefetching frequency and payload, respectively.

4.1.4. Cooperative caching

Cooperative caching [17,27,29] is widely studied and deployed in many content delivery systems, starting from Harvest [5] and Squid [24]. A number of proxies cooperate and share the cache with one another to improve the cache hit rate. When a proxy receives a request to an object that is missing from its cache, it checks whether the object is cached on other proxies within the cooperative network. The most well known schemes are broadcast probing [5,24,28], directory service based [8,9,21], and hash-partitioned namespace approach [25].

As our system divides the streaming media object into segments, it is natural that our system spreads them across several proxies and uses a Web cache sharing technique. Our cooperative caching scheme needs an agent that determines and has the knowledge of which segment is cached on which proxy. The segment assignment policy is important as each segment has different sizes. Note that there are no duplicate segments cached on different proxies within our cooperative caching network.

Our video delivery system can be implemented in various cache sharing architectures. They are centralized, distributed, and hybrid cooperative caching, and none uses a hierarchical cache structure. Each proposed scheme is examined in the following three sections.

4.2. Video delivery with centralized cooperative caching

In the centralized cooperative caching scheme, a *master cache* coordinates the interactions between the client and the cache array. For each video object, the master cache stores the key-frame and the prefix of each segment. In addition, the master cache assigns and knows the location of each segment, i.e., the information regarding which cache keeps which segment. The request from the client is redirected to the master cache. Upon a request, the master cache provides the key-frames to the client. When the client selects a certain segment, the master cache transmits the proper prefix to the client (and hence reduce the startup delay) while instructing the appropriate proxy, which cached the requested segment, to deliver the segment. The video stream is always delivered to the user through the master cache.

For the illustration of this scheme, we use the following example that is also used in the description of the other two schemes. As shown in Fig. 6, the video object is segmented into three sections and each segment is represented by a key-frame. The first segment is cached in the proxy cache C1, the second in C2, and the third in C3. The key-frames and prefixes are stored in the master cache along with the location information of each segment.

Consider a client requests a video and browses through the key-frames. Subsequently, the client requests to watch from the second segment, and continuously views through the third segment towards the end of the video.

The interactions involved in the above scenario are explained as follows:

(1) The client requests a video.

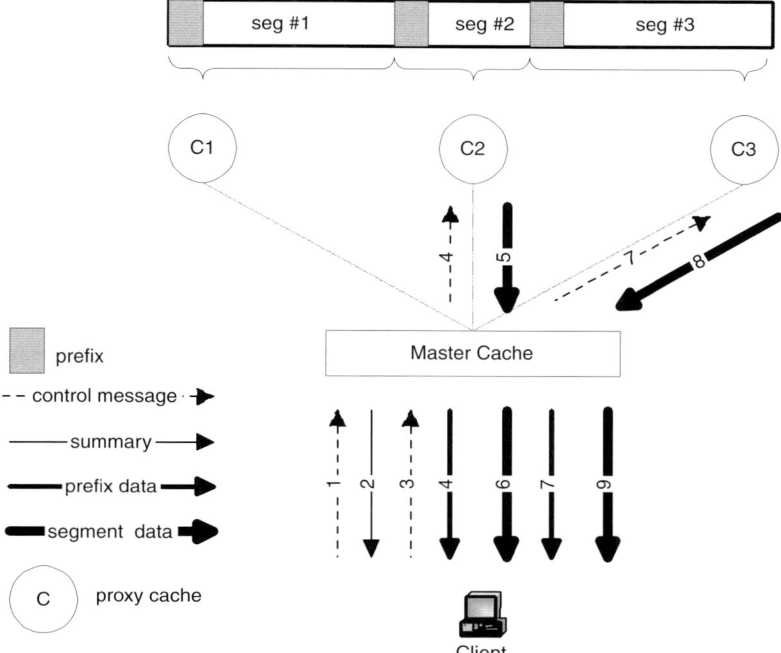

Fig. 6. A video delivery example in centralized cooperative caching.

(2) If the requested video is not in a cache, the master cache sends a request to the origin server. The video object is segmented and summarized in key-frames by the content analysis service (this process is performed by the application proxy server, as described in Section 2). The master cache hosts the key-frames and prefixes and distributes the segments to appropriate proxy caches. It then sends the video summary to the client. Note that if the requested video is already in the cache, the master cache simply provides the video summary to the client.
(3) After browsing the summary, the client selects the segment #2 as the starting playback position.
(4) The master cache sends the prefix of segment #2 to the client and requests the rest of the segment from C2.
(5) C2 sends segment #2 to the master cache.
(6) The master cache forwards segment #2 to the client.
(7) Right after the completion of delivering segment #2, the master cache sends the prefix of segment #3 to the client and requests the rest of the segment from C3, similar to step 4.
(8) C3 sends the segment #3 to the master cache.
(9) The master cache forwards the segment #3 to the client.

Note that the length of prefix stored by the master cache must be large enough to ensure the client does not experience delays between viewing the prefix and the rest of the segment. The segment assignment and distribution must be handled with care by the master cache. If the number of segmented portions is smaller than the number of proxies, segment distribution to overloaded caches should be avoided. On the other hand, if there are more video segments than the caches, intelligent assignment must be performed. For example, consider there are four segments to be spread across three proxy caches, and the second cache is the least loaded. Instead of assigning the segment #1 to cache #1, segment #2 to cache #2, segment #3 to cache #3, and segment #4 to cache #2, we can distribute the segment #1 to cache #1, segments #2 and #3 to cache #2, and segment #4 to cache #3. As users that watch segment #2 are likely to access segment #3 next as they are continuous, this assignment policy can reduce coordination processing and the control traffic between the master cache and proxies.

The centralized cooperative cache scheme is simple and easy to implement and manage. No communication is needed between proxy caches as the master cache holds all necessary information. Since every object and stream goes through the master cache, however, it can easily be overloaded and congested. In addition, the master cache creates the single point of failure problem.

4.3. Video delivery with distributed cooperative caching

A master cache does not exist in the distributed architecture. Instead, each proxy cache has a control unit that has the functionality of the master cache. In this architecture, the summary key-frames and the prefix of each segment are replicated and cached in each proxy. Each cache also holds the location information of all the segments. The proxies must communicate with each other to exchange this information. Schemes such as summary cache [8] or cache digest [21] can be used for this purpose.

As shown in Fig. 7, the client's initial request is redirected to the *entry point*. The entry point serves as a gateway to the client and it could be as simple as a forwarder. The basic function of the entry point is to select a proxy that coordinates the caching and delivery of a video object for each request. The election algorithm can be a round robin mechanism, for example. When this proxy receives a request to the segment that it does not hold, it sends the prefix of the requested segment to the client and forwards or redirects the request to the appropriate proxy.

Let us study the systematic process of this architecture using the same scenario as in Section 4.2.

(1) The client requests a video.
(2) The entry point receives the request and forwards it to the selected proxy (C2 in this example).
(3) If the C2 does not have the requested video, it sends a request to the origin server. The video object is segmented and summarized in key-frames by the content analysis service. C2 distributes the segments to appropriate proxy caches and sends the key-frames and prefixes of the video to all the proxies. It then delivers the video summary to the client. Note that if the requested video is already in the cache, C2 simply provides the video summary to the client.
(4) After browsing the summary, the client selects segment #2 as the starting playback position.
(5) As C2 has cached segment #2, it delivers the entire segment to the client.
(6) Right after the completion of delivering segment #2, C2 sends the prefix of segment #3 to the client and sends a request to C3 to deliver the rest of the segment to the client.

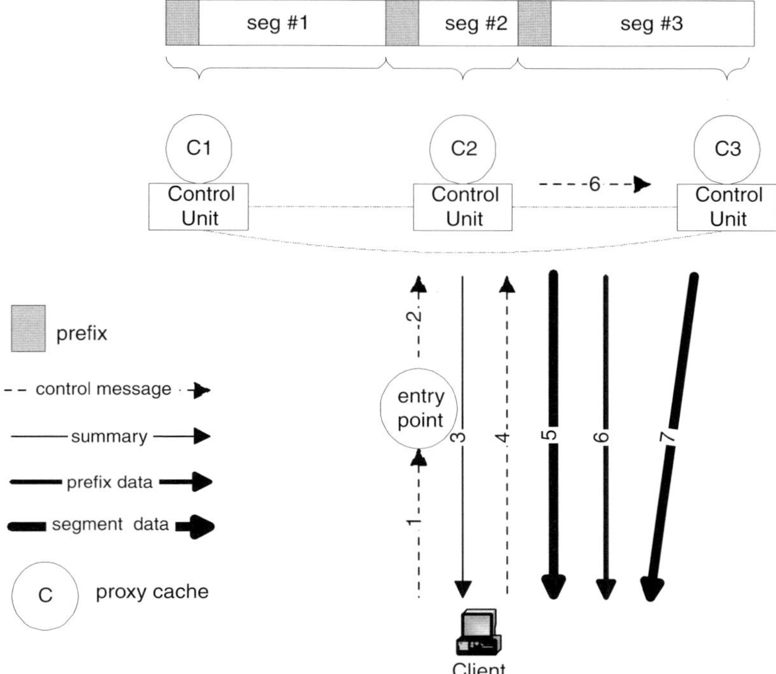

Fig. 7. A video delivery example in distributed cooperative caching.

(7) C3 sends segment #3 directly to the client.

In this architecture, all possible problems of having a master cache are eliminated. The cost is the added complexity for each proxy. Streaming server must be implemented in each control unit, as each proxy streams the video content to the client. Each proxy cache cannot hold as many video segments as in the centralized architecture since the storage is also used for caching the prefixes and key-frames. In addition, session handoff scheme must be implemented among the proxy caches. A simple entry point is also needed to handle the initial request from the client.

4.4. Video delivery with hybrid cooperative caching

In the centralized cooperative caching, the bulk of the video content is delivered through the master cache. This easily overloads the master cache. In the distributed scheme, each proxy needs added capability and coordination can be complex. In this section, we propose a hybrid architecture where a master cache is used, but its role is reduced to only controlling the interactions and delivering the key-frames and prefixes. The delivery of the video segments to the client is done directly by the proxy caches.

Fig. 8 shows the interactions using the example scenario.

(1) The client requests a video.

(2) If the requested video is not in a cache, the master cache sends a request to the origin server. The video object is segmented and summarized in key-frames by the content analysis service. The master cache hosts the key-frames and prefixes

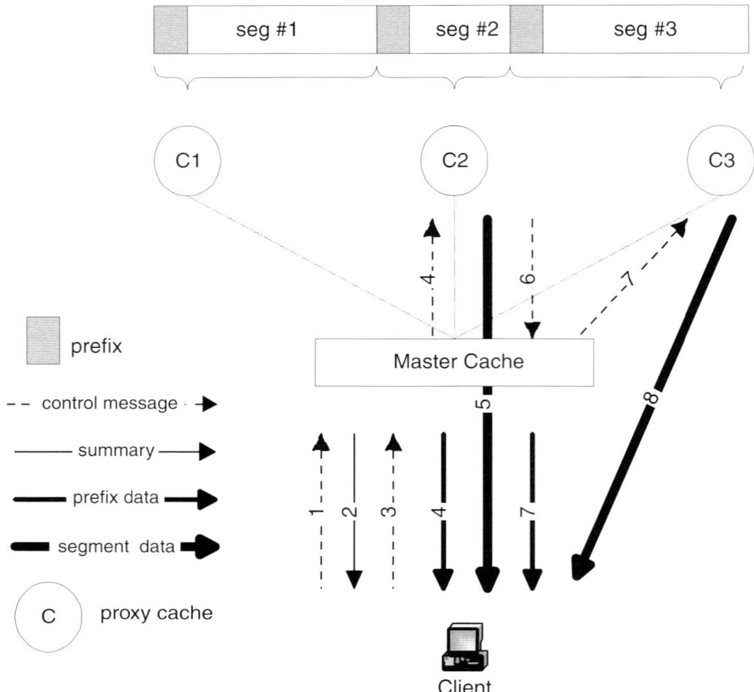

Fig. 8. A video delivery example in hybrid cooperative caching.

and distributes the segments to appropriate proxy caches. It then sends the video summary to the client. Note that if the requested video is already in the cache, the master cache simply provides the video summary to the client.

(3) After browsing the summary, the client selects segment #2 as the starting playback position.

(4) The master cache sends the prefix of segment #2 to the client and sends a request to C2 to deliver the rest of the segment to the client.

(5) C2 sends segment #2 directly to the client.

(6) Towards the end of sending of segment #2, C2 informs the master cache with the status.

(7) The master cache sends the prefix of segment #3 to the client and sends a request to C3 to deliver the rest of the segment to the client, similar to step 4.

(8) C3 sends segment #3 directly to the client.

Since the bulk of the video is delivered directly from the proxy caches to the client, the master cache is less prone to overload, congestion, and failure. The master cache is mainly in charge of the control message exchanges. The connection handoff however, must be resolved as the clients request is sent to the master cache but the data delivery is from the proxy caches. Depending on the communication protocol used in the video access, the master cache should be able to hand the data delivery duty to the proxy caches. For example, if the communication is UDP based, the master cache can forward the client address with the request (e.g., in steps 4 and 7). On the other hand, if the client is involved in a TCP session, we must resolve TCP handoff between the master cache and the proxy caches.

4.5. Cache replacement granularity and policy

As segments of a video are spread across multiple proxies, granularity of our cache replacement scheme is segments. If certain segments of a video are popular, only popular segments are cached. This partial video caching differs from the 'all or nothing' approach where the object is either cached in its entirety or not cached at all. A 'cache hit' is measured in segments. Using the example scenario from Sections 4.2 to 4.4, when the client selects the segment #2 as the starting playback position and continues to view through segment #3, cache hits are recorded for both segments #2 and #3.

Recent studies [2,6] indicate that client requests to video files show strong temporal locality. A cache replacement algorithm such as LRU-k [14] can exploit temporal locality [1]. When the cache is full and a new item must be inserted, LRU-k replaces an object whose kth previous request is the least recent. Hence, the LRU scheme is LRU-k with $k = 1$. Each proxy cache of our system runs this LRU-k scheme as the cache replacement algorithm.

The cache replacement takes place at two locations in our system: the master cache (or control units) and proxy caches. When a video segment is replaced by a proxy cache, the prefix of that segment remains in the master cache (in the centralized or hybrid architectures) or all the control units of proxy caches (in the distributed architecture). If there is a request to the replaced segment, the prefix can be sent to the client while the rest of the segment is requested to the origin server. When all the segments of a video are removed from caches, the key-frames and prefixes can also be deleted. Note that the prefix should not be removed before the actual segment is replaced. When the prefix of the segment does not exist, our system considers that the segment is not cached and hence it will not be accessed.

There are also three levels of replacement: key-frame level, prefix level and segment level. A prefix is always physically stored along with a key-frame. On the other hand, a prefix is logically associated with a segment since it is the initial part of the segment. Since key-frames and prefixes consume less resource, we assign higher priorities to them. In the caching replacement algorithm, object of higher priority is less likely to be replaced. Therefore, a weighted LRU-k scheme can be applied considering the different priorities we assign to each level.

5. Current status

We implemented a prototype system based on the RealNetworks software development kit (SDK) [18]. Several RealSystem plug-ins are implemented to give the end users the control on the playback of a video stream. On the server side, a file-format plug-in is implemented to provide the RealServer the ability to interactively deliver a MPEG video. On the client side, a rendering plug-in is implemented to enable the RealPlayer to render a MPEG video interactively. The file-format and rendering plug-ins use the XML-based meta-data to communicate with each other in the video streaming process. This system allows users to quickly browse through the entire video content by viewing key-frames

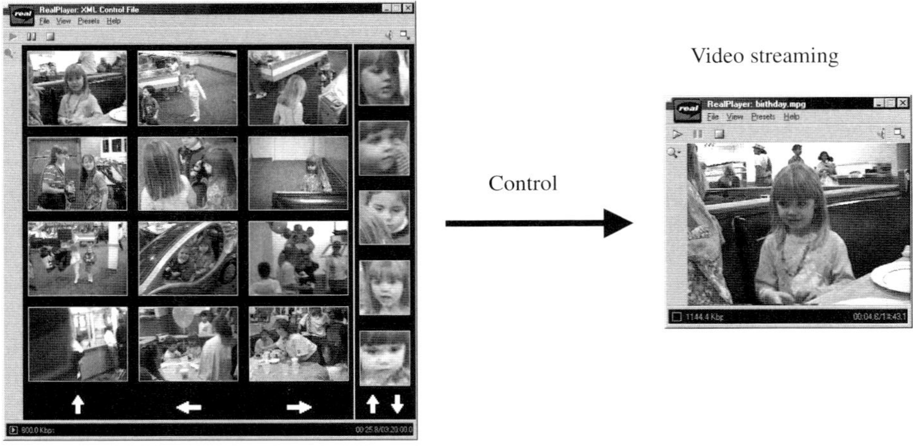

(a) Interactive video delivery to a desktop PC.

(b) Interactive video delivery to a handheld computer.

Fig. 9. A prototype system is implemented on (a) the SDK provided by RealNetworks System and (b) MFC on Windows CE platform.

and faces. Each key-frame and face represents a video segment that can be played back individually according to the user interests. Fig. 9a shows the snapshot of this system on a desktop PC. Note that two RealPlayer windows launch when the user clicks on a video that is processed and value-added by our application proxy server: one window shows the hierarchical video summary and the other window plays the video.

To apply our technique to video streaming on a handheld computer with a small form factor, we implemented a video player using the Microsoft Foundation Class (MFC) [16] on the Windows CE platform. The player connects to the video server that is extended from the Apache Web server. The player sends an HTTP request to the server with a special header specifying the starting point of the requested video. The server performs *fseek* or switches between different video segment files before packetizing the data. The server has the information about the byte location associated with the beginning of each video segment or where the individual segment is stored. Fig. 9b shows a picture of the interactive video delivery to a handheld computer (HP Jornada 720) with a wireless LAN connection. Because the screen is small, only two key-frames are shown each instance. When the user clicks on a particular key-frame, the left window is used to play the video and the right window continues to be used to browse the summary.

6. Conclusions

We presented an integrated interactive video delivery and caching system that utilizes the content analysis services to provide better user interfaces and conserve network resources. The content analysis service performs shot boundary detection, key-frame selection, and face detection and tracking. When a client requests a streaming video file, our system initially provides the video summary to the user. The user quickly browses these summary images to decide whether to download the video. If the user selects to download, the user can also choose which part of the video to download. We believe our summary provision offers better video viewing environment to the users, and we expect user access behaviors to change.

Our video system uses content-aware video segmentation, prefix caching, prefetching, and cooperative caching techniques to enable users to view any part of the cached video without long delays. By segmenting the video, we are able to use a fine grain cache replacement algorithm that exploits temporal locality and multi-level caching. We described the operation of video delivery and caching mechanism on three proposed cooperative caching architectures: centralized, distributed, and hybrid. Our system is designed to utilize the content analysis service that is currently applied to videos of format MPEG-1 and MPEG-2. We believe that our system can also be used for other streaming formats. We can still perform segmentation, prefix caching, and cooperative caching to those video formats, even though we cannot apply content analysis and provide video summary to the users because of proprietary issues.

We currently have a content analysis service prototype implementation on the SDK provided by RealNetworks and MFC on the Windows CE environment. It operates on our desktop PCs and wireless mobile handheld computers. We are continuing our work in several ways. Simulation is in progress to evaluate the performance of three system architectures, various replacement algorithms, and the optimal k size in LRU-k. Based on the lessons we learn from simulation, we plan to implement our integrated video delivery and caching system on a real test-bed.

References

[1] S. Acharya and B. Smith, MiddleMan: A Video Caching Proxy Server, *Proceedings of the NOSSDAV 2000*, Chapel Hill, NC, June 2000.

[2] S. Acharya, B. Smith, and P. Parnes, Characterizing User Access To Videos On the World Wide Web, *Proceedings of the SPIE/ACM MMCN 2000*, San Jose, CA, January 2000, pp. 130–141.

[3] E. Bommaiah, K. Guo, M. Hofmann, and S. Paul, Design and Implementation of a Caching System for Streaming Media over the Internet, *Proceedings of the IEEE RTAS 2000*, Washington, DC, June 2000, pp. 111–121.

[4] P. Cao, E.W. Felten, A.R. Karlin, and K. Li, A Study of Integrated Prefetching and Caching Strategies, *Proceedings of the ACM SIGMETRICS'95*, Ottawa, Canada, May 1995, pp. 188–197.

[5] A. Chankhunthod, P.B. Danzig, C. Neerdaels, M.F. Schwartz, and K.J. Worrell, A Hierarchical Internet Object Cache, *Proceedings of the 1996 USENIX Technical Conference*, San Diego, CA, January 1996, pp. 153–163.
[6] M. Chesire, A. Wolman, G.M. Voelker, and H.M. Levy, Measurement and Analysis of a Streaming-Media Workload, *Proceedings of the USITS'01*, San Francisco, CA, March 2001.
[7] M. Crovella and P. Barford, The Network Effects of Prefetching, *Proceedings of the IEEE INFOCOM'98*, San Francisco, CA, March 1998, pp. 1232–1239.
[8] L. Fan, P. Cao, J. Almeida, and A.Z. Broder, Summary Cache: A Scalable Wide-Area Web Cache Sharing Protocol, *Proceedings of the ACM SIGCOMM'98*, Vancouver, Canada, September 1998, pp. 254–265.
[9] S. Gadde, M. Rabinovich, and J. Chase, Reduce, Reuse, Recycle: An Approach to Building Large Internet Caches, *Proceedings of the IEEE HotOS-VI*, Cape Cod, MA, May 1997, pp. 93–98.
[10] M. Hofmann, T.S.E. Ng, K. Guo, S. Paul, and H. Zhang, Caching Techniques for Streaming Multimedia over the Internet, *Bell Laboratories Technical Report*, BL011345-990409-04TM, April 1999.
[11] W.Y. Ma, B. Shen, and J.T. Brassil, Content Services Networks: The Architecture and Protocol, *Proceedings of the WCW'01*, Boston, MA, June 2001.
[12] W.Y. Ma and H.J. Zhang, An Indexing and Browsing System for Home Video, *Proceedings of the EUSIPCO 2000*, Tampere, Finland, September 2000, pp. 131–134.
[13] X. Marichal, W.Y. Ma and H.J. Zhang, Blur Determination in the Compressed Domain Using DCT Information, *Proceedings of the IEEE ICIP'99*, Kobe, Japan, October 1999, pp. 386–390.
[14] E. O'Neil, P. O'Neil, and G. Weikum, The LRU-K Page Replacement Algorithm for Database Disk Buffering, *Proceedings of the ACM SIGMOD'93*, Washington, DC, May 1993, pp. 297–306.
[15] V.N. Padmanabhan and J.C. Mogul, Using Predictive Prefetching to Improve World Wide Web Latency, *ACM SIGCOMM Computer Communication Review*, vol. 26, no. 3, July 1996, pp. 22–36.
[16] J. Prosise, *Programming Windows with MFC*, 2nd edition, Microsoft Press, May 1999.
[17] M. Rabinovich, J. Chase, and S. Gadde, Not All Hits are Created Equal: Cooperative Proxy Caching over a Wide-area Network, *Computer Networks and ISDN Systems*, vol. 30, no. 22–23, November 1998, pp. 2253–2259.
[18] RealNetworks Software Development Kit, http://www.realnetworks.com/devzone/tools/.
[19] R. Rejaie, M. Handley, H. Yu, and D. Estrin, Proxy Caching Mechanism for Multimedia Playback Streams in the Internet, *Proceedings of the WCW'99*, San Diego, CA, April 1999.
[20] R. Rejaie, H. Yu, M. Handley, and D. Estrin, Multimedia Proxy Caching Mechanism for Quality Adaptive Streaming Applications in the Internet, *Proceedings of the IEEE INFOCOM 2000*, Tel Aviv, Israel, March 2000, pp. 980–989.
[21] A. Rousskov and D. Wessels, Cache Digest, *Proceedings of the WCW'98*, Manchester, England, June 1998.
[22] H.A. Rowley, S. Baluja and T. Kanade, Neural Network-based Face Detection, *IEEE Transactions on Pattern Analysis and Machine Intelligence*, vol. 20, no. 1, January 1998, pp. 23–38.
[23] S. Sen, J. Rexford, and D. Towsley, Proxy Prefix Caching for Multimedia Streams, *Proceedings of the IEEE INFOCOM'99*, New York, NY, March 1999, pp. 1310–1319.
[24] Squid Internet Object Cache, http://squid.nlanr.net.
[25] V. Valloppillil and K.W. Ross, Cache Array Routing Protocol v1.0, *IETF Internet Draft*, draft-vinod-carp-v1-03.txt, February 1998.
[26] Z. Wang and J. Crowcroft, Prefetching in World Wide Web, *Proceedings of the IEEE Global Internet'96*, London, UK, November 1996, pp. 28–32.
[27] Z. Wang and J. Crowcroft, Cachemesh: A Distributed Cache System for World Wide Web, *Proceedings of the WCW'97*, Boulder, Colorado, June 1997.
[28] D. Wessels and K. Claffy, Internet Cache Protocol (ICP) version 2, *IETF Request For Comments 2186*, September 1997.
[29] A. Wolman, G.M. Voelker, N. Sharma, N. Cardwell, A. Karlin, and H.M. Levy, On the Scale and Performance of Cooperative Web Proxy Caching, *Proceedings of the ACM SOSP'99*, Charleston, SC, December 1999, pp. 16–31.
[30] H.J. Zhang and W.Y. Ma, Structured and Content-based Video Browsing, *Proceedings of the 32nd IEEE Asilomar Conference on Signals, Systems, and Computers*, Pacific Grove, CA, November 1998.
[31] Z.-L. Zhang, Y. Wang, D.H.C. Du, and D. Su, Video Staging: A Proxy-Server-Based Approach to End-to-End Video Delivery over Wide-Area Networks, *IEEE/ACM Transactions on Networking*, vol. 8, no. 4, August 2000, pp. 429–442.

Web Caching and Content Delivery
A. Bestavros and M. Rabinovich (Editors)

Joint Server Scheduling and Proxy Caching for Video Delivery

Olivier Verscheure [1], Chitra Venkatramani, Pascal Frossard, Lisa Amini

IBM T.J. Watson Research Center, Hawthorne, NY 10532, USA

Abstract

We consider the delivery of video assets over a best-effort network, possibly through a caching proxy located close to the clients generating the requests. We are interested in the joint server scheduling and prefix/partial caching strategy that minimizes the aggregate transmission rate over the backbone network (i.e., average output server rate) under a cache of given capacity. We present multiple schemes to address various service levels and client resources by enabling bandwidth and cache space tradeoffs. We also propose an optimization algorithm selecting the working set of asset prefixes. We detail algorithms for practical implementation of our schemes. Simulation results show our scheme dramatically outperforms the full caching technique.

Keywords: Content distribution networks; Streaming media; Server scheduling; Partial caching; Batch patching; SLA

1. Introduction

Streaming media represents a unique opportunity for Service Providers – unlike other Web objects which are enhanced by edge delivery, quality video actually requires edge of network services to attain reasonable user experience. As access providers roll out faster last-mile connections, upstream congestion in the provider's backbone, peering links and best-effort Internet will limit their ability to meet customer expectations for these premium links. While streaming media brings additional complexities (very large objects, isochronous delivery, and interactivity), there are clearly many advantages of edge delivery. Attributes making it especially well-suited for edge delivery include its static nature, high value to Content Providers, distribution and delivery revenue potential to Content Delivery Service Providers, and the potential for content services (transcoding, ad insertion, digital rights management) best offered through decentralized techniques.

Techniques to address the lack of end-to-end bandwidth to support streaming media include (i) multicasting to groups of clients, and (ii) caching at streaming proxies located closer in the network to the end user.

Multicast scheduling strategies, such as *Periodic Broascasting* and *Batching*, have been proposed to simulate on-demand access. Although multicast significantly reduces network bandwidth, it is often considered impractical due to its reliance on a fully multicast-

[1] E-mail: ov1@us.ibm.com

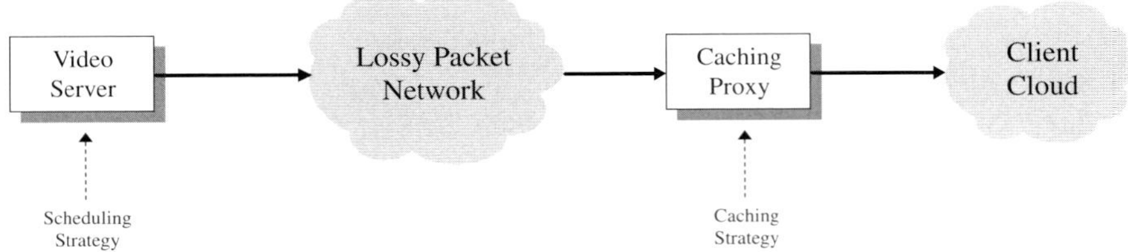

Fig. 1. Illustration of our joint scheduling and proxy caching strategy.

enabled network. Additional drawbacks of multicast scheduling strategies include client requirements for receiving multiple streams, large client buffers, and lack of flexibility in providing user-level QoS. Because video distribution and delivery incurs high storage and transmission costs, and requires specialized servers at the edge, Service Providers will target valued content, for which QoS guarantees are a must and best-effort service is unacceptable.

Caching audio/video objects in streaming proxies at the network edge is another attractive solution. Besides providing improved performance to the end-user, caches save on network bandwidth between the access provider network and the origin server. Caching strategies for video objects range from caching of full video objects to caching partial video objects by segmenting the video in the temporal and/or spatial domain(s). There are at least two issues with the caching of whole videos. First, the time and bandwidth required to bring an entire video into the cache associates a very high penalty with erroneous caching decisions. Second, ongoing streams may prevent deletion at cache replacement time causing the cache to be less reactive and to drift away from the optimal operating point.

Therefore, our objective is to create a content distribution system for streaming media, as opposed to a best-effort video caching system. We achieve this by placing a streaming proxy in the path between the server and the clients. We develop a scheme which combines stream scheduling at the origin server and caching at the proxy to minimize the aggregate transmission rate over the network while maintaining configured user-level quality of service (QoS) constraints (Fig. 1). The QoS constraints are expressed in terms of maximum playback delay and application-level packet loss ratio (PLR). Object prefixes reflecting either popularity or contracted service levels are positioned at proxies to reduce startup latencies and enable on-demand access.

The paper is organized as follows. In Section 2 we present relevant research in the multicast and streaming media caching areas. In Section 3, we present our scheme for video stream delivery along with simulation results highlighting the bandwidth savings and cache space usage tradeoffs under different scenarios. Section 4 describes a practical algorithm that is being implemented in our prototype and discusses practical issues. Finally we present our conclusions and future work in Section 5.

2. Related work

Streaming video over multicast consumes less network bandwidth and imposes less of a load on the sender than does streaming video over multiple unicast channels. Among schemes that attempt to capitalize on the benefits of multicast for VOD are those based on the Periodic Broadcast idea [1–4] The video is divided into many portions which are continuously broadcast over multiple channels and are as such bandwidth efficient only when the request arrival rate is high. Another technique is the simple batching scheme where the server accumulates requests over a batching interval and starts a new multicast stream at the end of each interval if there were any requests in the batch. A more bandwidth efficient scheme is that of Patching ([5,6]). In this scheme, each batch is served over one or two channels – either a regular channel alone or the combination of a regular channel and a patching channel. A regular channel delivers the full video from start to finish while a patching channel delivers only the missing part of the video from the start until the point at which the clients join the regular channel. The client receives both the patch and the ongoing stream and buffers the latter while playing back the former. Once the patch is exhausted, the client switches to the buffered regular multicast. [5] compared the performance of patching with simple batching and found that patching was able to support true VOD at much higher request rates for a typical server configuration. Further research in this area can be found in [7] where the authors present the Optimized patching scheme which defines a Patching Window beyond which it is more efficient to start a new regular multicast rather than generate patches. Finally, [8] extends the above technique to allow for client-controlled latency/cost trade-off to provide classes of service by varying the batching interval.

The other relevant body of research is that of video caching. Techniques range from caching whole videos (applying conventional memory caching techniques with modifications to account for the size) to partial objects segmented in the temporal and/or spatial domain(s). Segmentation in the temporal domain is achieved by splitting the video into constant time length (CTL) segments and segmentation in the spatial domain is achieved by encoding videos at multiple resolutions.

Full-caching strategies for video in a cluster of caches is considered in [9]. Key conclusions are that in streaming proxies, replication or striping of objects based on explicit tracking of request frequencies achieves higher hit rates rather than doing LFU or LRU on a per-request basis. They found that the cache replacement policy (LRU or LFU) did not make any difference because most videos had ongoing streams and could not be chosen for replacement. For this reason and the fact that bringing a large video file to a cache is very expensive, partial caching (including prefix caching) were proposed.

In [10], the authors present a caching scheme for adaptive, layered video (segmented in the temporal and spatial domains) such that the *quality* of the cached stream is proportional to its popularity. They also combine it with a fine-grained cache replacement strategy that tracks statistics per layer of video and eliminates the least popular segments of the video. The scheme has been designed with the goal of being adaptive to the network but not with the explicit goal to minimize the bandwidth streamed out of the origin server. Secondly, although this method results in caching the most popular parts of a video, the quality of video playback can be variable among different viewers of the same video, which might be undesirable. Finally, the adaptive scheme works well with layered encoding of videos, which is not employed in most popular formats. Another work that considers partial caching is *MiddleMan* [11]. This scheme works over a cluster of proxies on a LAN and the combined space is managed by a central *MiddleMan* who does the cache replacement decisions. The caches store only as much of the object as is played back by the client. Other video caching schemes include Resource-based Caching

RBC [12] which focuses on the management of resources in the cache. RBC determines which objects (partial or whole) to cache such that the space and bandwidth of the cache are uniformly utilized. Prefix caching is proposed in [13] and [14]). Although caching the prefix can hide the startup latency and jitter in the network, this scheme does not reduce the aggregate transmission from the origin server.

In this paper, we build on some of the ideas in the multicast research area to minimize the aggregate bandwidth streamed out of the origin server and also present a practical scheme in which videos are cached in a proxy such that the space used by the video can be proportional to its popularity and the available bandwidth to the server.

3. Partial caching and batch patching

In this section, we develop a scheme which combines efficient stream scheduling at the server, and both prefix and partial caching in a proxy located close to the clients generating the requests.

Our main objective may be formulated as follows: given a set of video assets and their respective characteristics, minimize the average rate streamed out of the origin server under a cache of fixed capacity $\mathcal{X}$. We assume that the network is ideal (i.e., jitter-and error-free environment) and that the clients wish to be served instantaneously (i.e., null playback delay). Section 4 explains why these apparently strong assumptions do not lead to any loss of generality.

The motivation behind this problem formulation results from the following observation: minimizing the average backbone rate is equivalent to maximizing the average byte hit ratio (BHR) at the proxy under a given server scheduling strategy. The problem formulation is refined in Section 3.5 after the complete description of our joint strategy. The study is first performed on a single video asset. Then we consider a heterogeneous set of video assets and related request patterns. We now describe the server scheduling strategy we build our scheme on.

3.1. Optimized batch patching

White and Crowcroft have recently introduced the concept of optimized batch patching [8], which aims at minimizing the average server output rate (i.e., backbone rate). Basically, client requests are batched together on an interval basis before requesting either a patch or a regular multicast (RM) from the server. The interval is fixed and noted b. Following the reasoning from [7], there is an optimal *Patching Window*, noted W, after which it is more bandwidth efficient to start a new regular multicast rather than send patches.

They refer to an RM-epoch as one in which a regular multicast was started and a non-RM epoch as one in which a regular multicast did not begin. The average backbone rate, R, is calculated in terms of the mean of the aggregate number of bytes contained in all patches commencing between two adjacent RM epochs chosen at random and the mean interval between RM epochs:

$$R = \frac{(1-P_b)rW^2 + (1-P_b)brW + 2rbT}{2bW + \dfrac{2b^2}{1-P_b}}, \tag{1}$$

where $P_b = P_b(0)$ denotes the probability of gathering zero request in a batch of duration b (empty batch), T is the duration of the video and, r denotes the streaming rate of the video asset. The optimal patching window W is derived by differentiating R and setting the result equal to 0. This yields:

$$W = \frac{-b + \sqrt{P_b b^2 + 2(1 - P_b)bT}}{b(1 - P_b)} \tag{2}$$

This scheme outperforms other multicast-based techniques in terms of average backbone rate over a large range of request rates. Fig. 2 compares the normalized backbone rate (that is, R/r) required by this scheme versus the optimal patching algorithm [7] for different Poisson request rates (that is, $P_b = e^{-b\lambda}$) and a batching interval b set to 1 minute. Optimized batch patching clearly outperforms optimal patching, albeit at the expense of higher latency (playback delay). Actually, the higher the interval b over which requests are batched, the better the performance. Therefore the authors integrated the concept of classes of service (CoS) in their scheme. Also these multicast-based techniques rely on multicast-enabled routers. In the remainder, we propose an extension to this scheme which alleviates the above problems and even adds some flexibility.

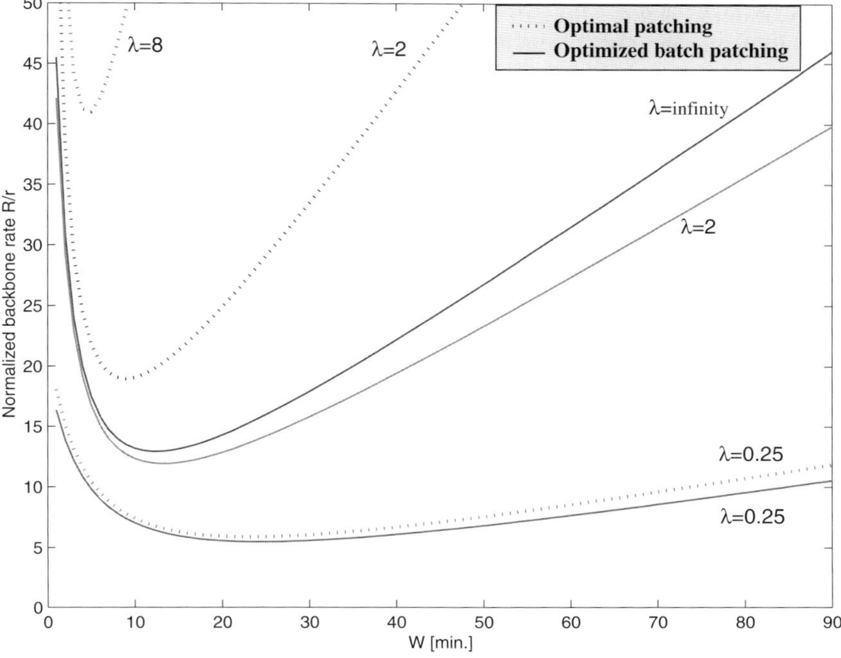

Fig. 2. Optimized batch patching versus optimal patching. This graph shows how the normalized backbone rate evolves with the size of the patching window W for different average inter-arrival rates following a Poisson distribution λ. The duration of the video asset T is 90 minutes. The batching interval b is set to 1 minute.

3.2. Partial caching applied to batch patching

We build on the optimized batch patching idea by introducing a proxy cache in the path from the origin server to the clients cloud. We adopt the intuitive approach consisting of storing the first b units of time in the proxy cache (i.e., batching period). That is, the proxy *permanently* caches a *prefix* of b units of time. Moreover we impose the proxy cache to play the role of a client for the origin server. That is, all the patches and regular multicasts streamed out of the server are requested by the proxy and are thereby streamed through it. This design approach has several advantages among which, (i) it eliminates the need for network-level multicast, (ii) it allows for client-based stream adaptation (heterogeneous client capabilities), and (iii) it has the potential to decrease the number of streams concurrently streamed to a given client. The former leads to a change of terminology. In the remainder, we use *regular channel* and *patch channel* instead of regular and patch multicasts.

Our scenario is illustrated by Fig. 3. The proxy divides the time axis into intervals $[t_{i-1}, t_i]$ of duration b units of time. Assume a request arrives at the proxy at time $t_1 \in [t_{k-1}, t_k)$. The proxy immediately starts streaming the requested asset to the client. Assume the most recent regular channel (RC) was started at time t_s, with $t_s < t_1$ is an integral number of b units of time. *If* t_k is such that $t_k < t_s + W$, the proxy joins the RC at time t_k and streams it through to the client, which buffers the stream while playing back the prefix. Also at time t_k, the proxy requests a patch of duration $t_k - t_s$ and passes it on to the client. However *if* $t_k \geq t_s + W$, a new regular channel of the asset of duration $T - b$ (the prefix of duration b is sitting in the proxy) is requested from the server at time t_k. In practice the streams requested from the server are unicast to the proxy, which implements multicast at the application level to provide the services mentioned above.

The average backbone rate is computed from Equations (1) and (2) by replacing T with $T - b$. Fig. 4 compares the optimized batch patching technique with and without prefix caching in terms of the required normalized backbone rate versus the duration of the prefix b in minutes. We again assume a Poisson arrival process such that $P_b = e^{-b\lambda}$. The two techniques provide approximately the same normalized backbone rate for small values of b. The difference becomes noticeable for $b > 10$ minutes. Also each technique provides the same performance independent of the request rate for batching intervals $b \geq 15$

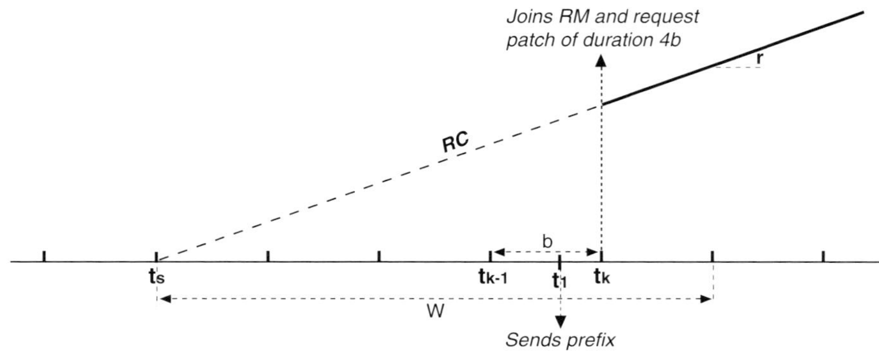

Fig. 3. Optimized batch patching with prefix caching. A Regular Channel of duration $T - b$ starts at time t_s. A client requests an asset at time $t_1 \in [t_{k-1}, t_k)$. The interval limit t_k is such that $t_k < t_s + W$.

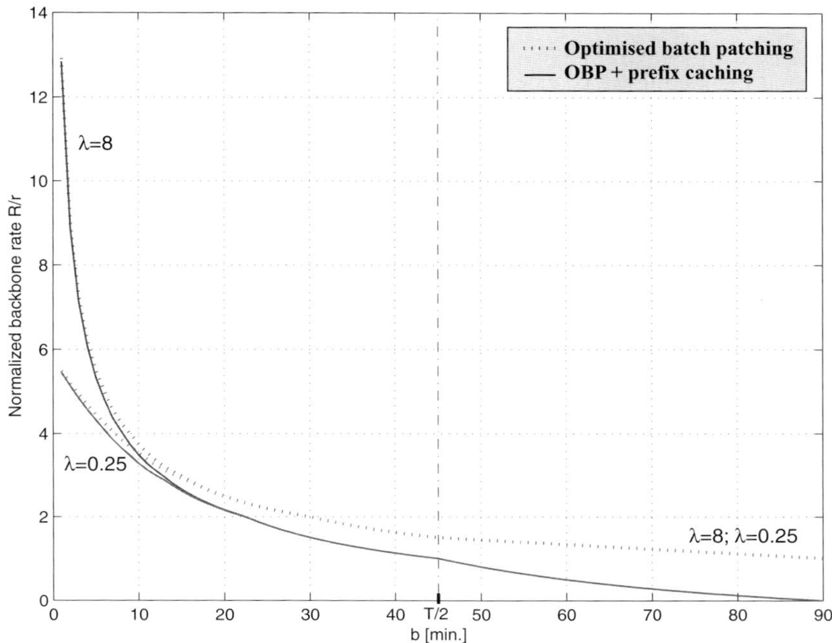

Fig. 4. Optimized batch patching with and without prefix caching. This graph shows how the normalized backbone rate evolves with the duration of the batching interval b (duration of the prefix) for different average inter-arrival rates λ following a Poisson distribution. The duration of the video asset is 90 minutes. The patching window is computed from Equation (2) with T being replaced by $T - b$ when a prefix of b is cached.

minutes. Note that increasing b is equivalent to increasing either the client playback delay (without prefix) or the cache occupancy (with prefix). Note also that for $b \geq \frac{T}{2}$, the optimal patching window is zero ($W^{\text{opt}} = 0$) when a prefix is cached. Therefore R/r reduces to:

$$\frac{R}{r} = \frac{(T-b)(1-P_b)}{b} \leq (1-P_b).$$

The drawbacks of this straightforward extension are twofold. *First*, the link connecting the requesting client to the proxy must accommodate up to three concurrent streams. Indeed the first client of a batching period will have already triggered the streaming of the regular channel and of the patch which will be needed by the late arrivals in the same batching period, which are still playing back the prefix. *Second*, the client buffer must accommodate up to $W + b$ units of time at the streaming rate r. Indeed the client must buffer the on-going regular channel while receiving the patch of maximum size W. Also the last client of the batching interval must store up to b extra units of time. Thus, $B = (W + b)r$, which may not be practical.

Therefore we extend this first approach by considering the *temporary* partial caching of either (i) the patch only or (ii) the patch and the regular channel. In the first case, the proxy eliminates the need to stream the patch to the clients by temporarily caching the *right* portions of it (the client manages only up to two concurrent streams). In the second case, the proxy caches whatever it takes to allow for sequential streaming of the asset from beginning to end to the clients (the client manages only a single stream).

We now examine these two extensions separately and derive the equations leading to the estimation of the average backbone rate R, the average cache occupancy X and the client buffering requirements B. The derivations of all the equations are not presented here due to space constraints and can be found in [15].

3.3. Partial caching of patch only

The proxy eliminates the second stream to the client by caching the patch. Let $[t_{k-1}, t_k)$ denote a batch which requires a patch of k buffers in the interval b to kb. At t_k, the proxy determines which patch intervals are not cached[2] and starts fetching the first required interval and completes it at t_{k+1}. At this time, it is aware of whether or not there are requests in $[t_k, t_{k+1})$. If there are requests, it does not free the buffer when all the requests in $[t_{k-1}, t_k)$ are serviced but retains it to service requests in $[t_k, t_{k+1})$ and subsequent non-zero batches. Every time there is a batch with zero requests, the buffer is released once it has been streamed to all the clients in the previous batch.

By caching the patch, we clearly save on bandwidth from the server compared to the previous approach. The number of patch buffers streamed from the server, in units of time, is given by μ (refer to [15] for details):

$$\mu = b \sum_{i=1}^{\lfloor \frac{W}{b} \rfloor} \left[i(1 - P_b) P_b^{\lfloor \frac{i}{2} \rfloor} + \sum_{j=1}^{\lfloor \frac{i}{2} \rfloor} (2j - 1)(1 - P_b)^2 P_b^{j-1} \right] \tag{3}$$

The normalized average backbone rate R/r is thus obtained from:

$$\frac{R}{r} = \frac{\mu r + (T - b)r}{b(1 + n)},$$

where n is the mean number of batches between two regular channels and is derived in [8] as:

$$n = \frac{W}{b} + P_b(1 - P_b)$$

Note that the reason why we average over $(n + 1)$ intervals instead of over the entire duration of the stream is that the patch buffers obtained for one period of $n + 1$ cannot be used in the next $n+1$ interval. This is because of the one intervening batching interval that triggers a regular channel. Requests in this batching interval do not require any patch and will consequently release the buffer $[b, 2b]$, which will be needed by the next batching interval. This triggers a new cycle of patch byte requests to the server as described earlier.

The cache buffer occupancy, which includes the prefix of duration b, is given by Equation (4) below [15].

$$X = b + b\left[\left(\left\lfloor \frac{W}{b} \right\rfloor - 1\right)(1 - P) + \sum_{i=1}^{\lfloor \frac{W}{b} \rfloor} (1 - P)^i P^{\lfloor \frac{W}{b} \rfloor - i}\right] \tag{4}$$

The client still needs to buffer the on-going regular channel while playing back the patch. Late clients in a batching period buffer an additional b units of time. Thus, $B = (W + b)r$.

[2] It needs to fetch at least one patch interval which is between $(k - 1)b$ to kb.

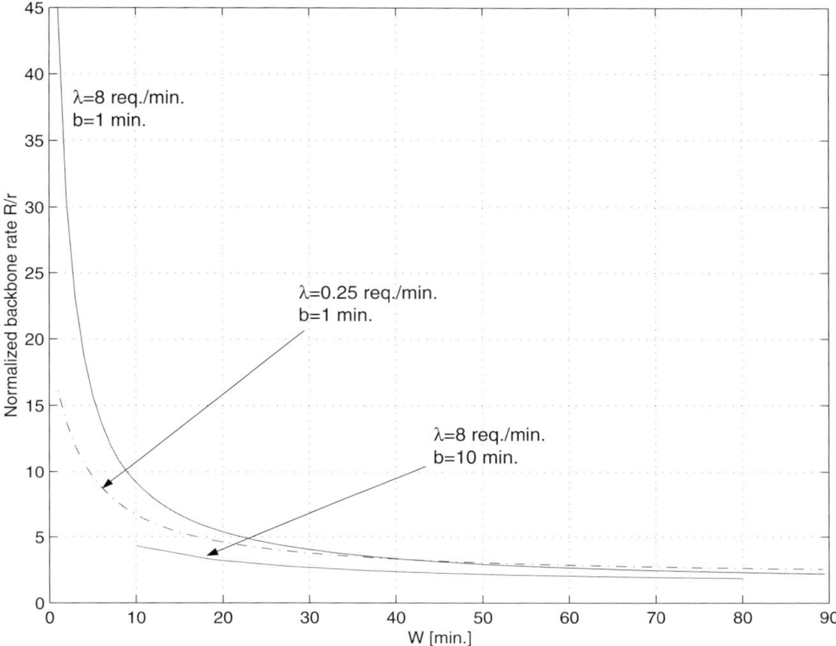

Fig. 5. Optimal batch patching with prefix and patch caching. This graph shows how the normalized backbone rate evolves with the duration of the patching window W for different average inter-arrival rates $\lambda = \{8, 0.25\}$ req./min. following a Poisson distribution, and prefix durations $b = \{1, 10\}$ min.

Fig. 5 shows the evolution of the normalized backbone rate R/r versus the duration of the patching window W under different average inter-arrival request times λ following a Poisson distribution and batching intervals b. Clearly the longer the patching window, the lower the backbone rate. That is, the backbone rate may no longer exhibit a minimum value for a patching window duration within $[0, T - b]$. Indeed the longer the duration W, the higher the temporary patch buffer size required at the proxy.

Fig. 6 highlights this remark. Note that for $\lambda = 8$, P_b tends to zero and therefore, $W = T - b$ leads to $X = T$ (b permanently stored and $T - b$ units of time temporarily buffered). The tradeoff between permanent (prefix) and temporary buffers is also shown. Increasing the prefix duration leads to a gain in normalized rate (see Fig. 5) at the expense of higher buffer occupancy (see Fig. 6). The set of equations clearly indicates that the optimal solution to our optimization problem is full asset caching if the proxy cache can accommodate for it. We elaborate on this in Sec. III-E. Finally note that the slope of these straight lines is dictated by the factor $b\lambda$.

3.4. Partial caching of patch and regular channel

In this scheme the client receives a single unicast stream from the proxy. The proxy caches data from the regular channel and forwards it to the clients. The client buffer requirement is zero in this case. Since the proxy serves all the requests in an interval of $W + b$ from a single regular channel, it has to maintain a circular buffer of up to

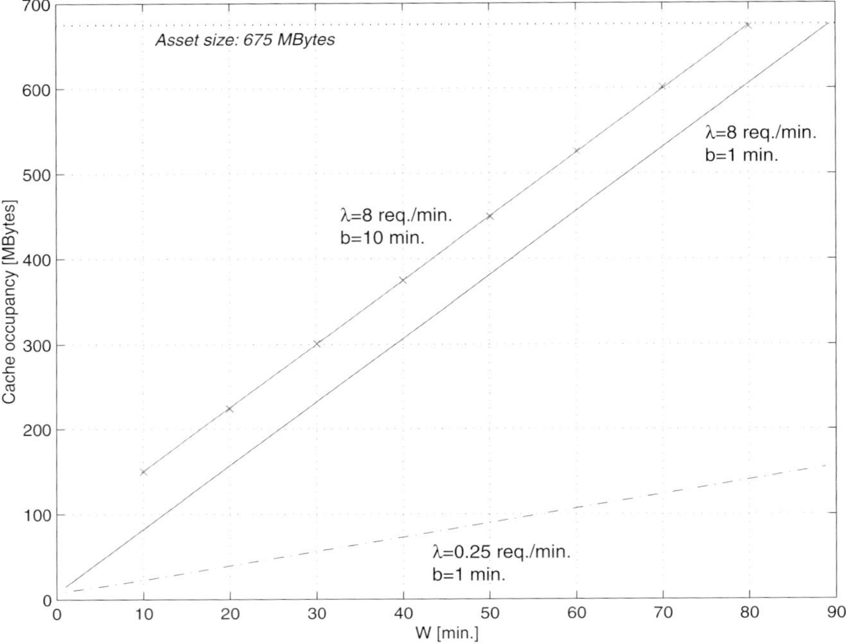

Fig. 6. Optimal batch patching with prefix and patch caching. This graph shows the cache occupancy versus the duration of the patching window W for different average inter-arrival rates $\lambda = \{8, 0.25\}$ req./min. following a Poisson distribution, and prefix durations $b = \{1, 10\}$ min.

$(W + b)$ units, continuously saving data from the regular channel, for the entire duration of the video. This buffer is required for each instance of the regular channel which is triggered every $(n + 1)$ intervals. The size of this buffer for each regular channel depends on the batching intervals that have non-zero requests. If there are requests in an interval $[t_{k-1}, t_k)$ that require a patch of $(k - 1)$ buffers, then kb needs to be buffered from the ongoing stream while these requests are playing back the patch and/or the prefix. This is irrespective of whether or not the previous batching interval had any requests.

The scheme is better explained with an example. Suppose there are five batching intervals $([t_{i-1} - t_i), i = 1, 5)$ in $W + b$, that is, $W = 4b$. The interval $[t_0, t_1)$ triggers the regular channel at t_1. The proxy buffers b from the regular channel to accommodate late requests in this interval that are playing back the prefix. Suppose $[t_1 - t_2)$ had requests, then at t_2 the proxy adds another buffer to circular buffer and does not request the server for any patch bytes. Suppose the next two intervals do not have any requests and the fifth interval $[t_4 - t_5)$ has a request. At t_5 the $2b$-long circular buffer allocated by the first two intervals would have advanced with the regular channel and will contain the interval $[3b - 5b]$. The fifth interval requires the buffer to be $5b$ long and so it adds three more buffers of size br to the circular buffer. The proxy then fetches the missing patch bytes in the intervals $[b - 2b]$ and $[2b - 3b]$ from the server while storing the interval $[5b - 6b]$ from the regular channel.

Here again, we reuse buffers that are allocated by each interval of W for subsequent intervals. Each regular channel results in the caching of the stream equivalent to the circular buffer (X) allocated to it, thereby reducing the length of the stream to be transmitted by the server by X. Taking this into account, the average backbone rate R/r over the total asset duration is given by [15]:

$$\frac{R}{r} = \sum_{i=1}^{\frac{T-b}{n+1}} \left(\mu + (T-b) - (i-1)X^*\right)$$

where μ is obtained from:

$$\mu = b(1-P)P \sum_{i=1}^{\lfloor \frac{W}{b} \rfloor} \sum_{j=1}^{i} j P^{j-1}$$

and the cache occupancy X^* computed over $(n+1)$ batching intervals is:

$$X^* = b \sum_{i=1}^{\lfloor \frac{W}{b} \rfloor} i(1-P)P^{\lfloor \frac{W}{b} \rfloor - i},$$

To obtain the cache occupancy X over the total asset duration, we simply multiply X^* by $\frac{T-b}{n+1}$ to account for the multiple regular channels that are active simultaneously, each of which uses a storage of X^*. Therefore if we have a request in every single interval of b (i.e., $P_b = 0$), we end up caching the whole stream in average.

The same conclusions about R/r versus W for different λs and bs as in the previous scheme hold in this scheme as well. However, this scheme clearly uses more temporary buffer at the proxy (higher likelihood to fully cache the assets), while decreasing the backbone rate significantly. Moreover this scheme results in a single stream to the clients and requires no storage from the client device (i.e., $B = 0$), which makes this approach well suited to streaming multimedia assets to handheld devices. This scheme is very similar to Interval Caching [16] where $W + b$ is the length of an interval. The difference is that this interval is cached in the proxy and is stored for use by future intervals.

3.5. Multiple assets

The multiple assets problem may be formulated as follows: *Given* a cache of capacity $\mathcal{X}$, and a set of N videos assets characterized by their streaming rate r_i, duration T_i and interval-based request probability P_{b_i}, *find* the tuple $\{b_i, W_i\} \forall 1 \leq i \leq N$ that *minimizes* the aggregate backbone rate $R = \sum_{i=1}^{N} R_i$, *under* the constraint $\sum_{i}^{N} X_i \leq \mathcal{X}$.

Clearly this problem can be solved via standard optimization techniques. However its multi-dimensional nature makes it computationally expensive. Therefore we propose a simplification which relies on the previous observation that both an increase of the prefix duration b_i or the patching window W_i for asset i always result in a lower backbone rate R_i and a corresponding increase of the temporary buffer X_i. Also, we have shown that W_i must be null for $b_i \geq T_i/2$. These observations lead to the following simplification: we impose $W_i = b_i$ for all $b_i < T_i/2$. This simplification slightly degrades the performance of our system but dramatically decreases the complexity.

We now briefly describe the algorithm based on the above simplification: First, we impose a video unit (e.g., a group-of-pictures) by which the prefixes b_i will either be decreased or increased. Then we calculate, for every asset, the product of its popularity by its respective size (similar to the SLRU technique). Assume all the b_i are first set to T_i. We eliminate a number of video units from the prefix duration b_i. This number is inversely proportional to the product value for asset i. Finally we iterate until the sum $\sum_i^N X_i \leq \mathcal{X}$.

We compared the full caching technique with the optimal batch patching with prefix and patch caching scenario. We assumed a Poisson distribution of the request inter-arrival times, a Zipf distribution of the asset popularity with various parameters (from which the λ_i are derived), a set of 100 videos with constant streaming rates and durations uniformly distributed in, respectively [56, 1500] kbps and [15, 90] minutes, and a cache size $\mathcal{X}$ three times smaller than the sum of all the asset sizes. Preliminary results show that the gain in backbone rate is tremendous (from approximately 4 to 8 times lower depending on the parameter of the Zipf distribution). Moreover our scheme rapidly adapts to changes in request statistics, while this is a known drawback of a full caching scenario.

In the remainder, we detail algorithms for practical implementations of the schemes proposed in this section.

4. Practical issues

In all of the scenarios, the proxy receives the client requests, immediately starts streaming the prefix and also batches them, on a per asset basis. At the end of each batch the proxy determines if a regular channel needs to be started or a patch needs to be requested from the origin server, based on the value of W computed using the expression in Section 3.

The proxy also runs the optimization algorithm described in Section 3.5 periodically to determine the prefixes that need to be stored in the cache. Initially, the cache starts out with Constant Time Length (CTL) prefixes of the most popular videos. The optimization algorithm may be triggered either periodically, when the network utilization at the proxy falls below a certain threshold or when the access probabilities of assets change significantly. In all cases, the algorithm requires an estimate of P_b for each of the assets, to determine the length of the prefix to cache and thereby maximize the byte hit ratio (BHR). Note that the value of P_b changes with the value of b. The bigger the chosen b, the smaller is the probability of having zero requests in the batch. Various methods can again be adopted to determine the value of P_b. As a simple approach, we could assume the inter-arrival request rate follows a Poisson distribution and track the inter-arrival time of requests over a certain time window. A more accurate but complex method would be to track the inter-arrival times, fit it to a well-known distribution and use the characteristics of the distribution to estimate P_b.

The optimization algorithm determines the value of the prefix b for each asset, given the access probabilities. The proxy then updates the cache to the new state computed by the algorithm. With the prefixes stored in the cache, it streams videos to clients using one of the three scenarios. The following subsections describe the algorithm in the proxy for the three different schemes described in Section 3.

4.1. Cache prefix only

The proxy only stores prefixes of videos. When a request is received, the proxy may send up to three concurrent streams to the client – the prefix, the patch stream and the regular channel. In our scheme, an application level multicast is used to stream the latter two. The client listens on three ports for streams from the proxy – the prefix, the patch and the regular multicast. While playing back the prefix, if data is received from the patch stream, it is cached and so is the data from the ongoing multicast. The buffer used by the client is at most $(W + b)r$.

4.2. Cache prefix and patch

In this scenario, the proxy caches data from the patch, besides the prefix, and streams these to the client thus reducing the number of streams to the client to two. For each asset that has ongoing streams, the proxy maintains an interval table, which holds information about which intervals of the video are currently cached. Each interval buffer is b time units long and is retained as long as there are requests being served from it. Since a patch can be at most W time units, we have $\frac{W}{b}$ intervals in the interval table. The pseudocode for the proxy is presented in Fig. 7.

Each time a request is received by the proxy, it increments the request count against each of the patch intervals that this request needs. And, at the end of each batch, the proxy checks to see if the batch triggers a regular channel or a patch. If it triggers a regular channel, the proxy requests a unicast stream from the origin server and application-level multicasts it to all the clients in the batch. If not, it determines which of the required patch intervals are locally cached and fetches the remaining intervals from the server over a unicast patch channel. The patches are not multicast, but are streamed to the client individually since they may be at different points in the playback of the prefix. The proxy also joins all the requests in this batch to the ongoing regular channel.

The client receives two streams in this case – the patch and the regular channel. It buffers the regular channel while playing back the patch. The client may buffer a maximum interval of $W + b$ from the regular channel while it is playing back the prefix and the patch.

4.3. Cache prefix, patch and regular channel

In the third scenario, we save significantly in the required client storage and also in the number of simultaneous streams to the client. The client needs to buffer nothing and receives only one unicast stream from the proxy. The proxy stores data from the regular channel and serves patches from this buffer instead of requesting it from the origin server. Although this reduces the bandwidth streamed from the server, it requires a larger buffer in the cache on average. For a discussion in the bandwidth/buffer tradeoff, see Section 3.

The difference between this scenario and the previous one is that, in the previous case, in addition to the prefix, only patch buffers were being allocated at the proxy. At any time, there can be a maximum of $\frac{W}{b}$ buffers active. However, when data is stored from the ongoing stream, the cache has to hold on to the buffer allocated in each window of $W + b$, for the duration of the video, continuously caching ahead from the ongoing stream. The algorithm presented below is applied by proxy separately for each regular channel (Fig. 8).

At the end of each batch, the proxy determines how large the interval cache is.It would consist of as many intervals as was required by the last non-zero batch in this patching window. It then increases the circular buffer to be as big as the patch required for this batch plus the extra b. This can be better explained with an example. For ease

```
ProcessRequest(r)
{
  CreateThread(StartStreamToClient(r));
  // add this request to the current batch
  addRequestToCurrBatch(r);
  // Incr. the rqst count in each relevant
  // interval
  for (i=1; i<=currBatch.numPatchIntervals; i++)
    IntervalTable[i].RequestCount++;
}

StartStreamToClient(r)
{
  StreamPrefix();
  //b time units have elapsed and the
  //next reqd. patch has been fetched
  for (i=1; i≤currBatch.numPatchIntervals; i++)
    StreamInterval(IntervalTable[i].buffer);
}

// This runs on a separate thread.
CloseCurrentBatch()
{
  for(;;;) {
    Sleep(b) // wait for batch to end
    currBatch = startNewBatch();
    currBatch.startTime = now;
    currBatch.endTime =
      currBatch.startTime + b;
  If (newRCReqd())
    currRC = StartNewRC();
  // Add clients to regular channel
  currRC.AddBatchedClients();
  for (i=1;i<=currBatch.numPatchIntervals;i++) {
    if (IntervalTable[i].RequestCount == 0)
      // If there are no requests, free it
      // This happens if currBatch has zero
      // requests
      free(IntervalTable[i].buffer);
    else if (IntervalTable[i].buffer == NULL) {
      // get patch in new segment buffer
      IntervalTable[i].buffer = newBuffer();
      //Fetch patch interval so that it is
      //available when needed by
      // StartStreamToClient
      FetchFromOriginServer((i-1)*b, i*b);
      // once the segment is fully obtained,
      // update the table and get next segment
    }
  }
}
```

Fig. 7. Algorithm at the proxy for scenario 2.

of explanation, batch b_i refers to a batch which requires a patch of $b * i$ segments. For instance, if we are at the end of batch b_4 at $t_5 b$ and the last non-zero batch was b_2, then the interval cache for this regular channel would be $2 * b + b$ long and since it is caching the ongoing stream, the buffer would contain intervals $2b - 3b$, $3b - 4b$ and $4b - 5b$. Batch

```
CloseCurrentBatch()
{
   for(;;;) {
    Sleep(b) // wait for batch to end
    currBatch = startNewBatch();
    currBatch.startTime = now;
    currBatch.endTime =
      currBatch.startTime + b;
    If (newRCReqd()) {
      currRC = StartNewRC();
      CircularBuffer = new CircBuffer(b);
    }
    if (currBatch.numRequests > 0) {
       n = currBatch.numPatchIntervals+1 -
         numAllocatedIntervals;
      CircularBuffer.Grow(n*b);
      numAllocatedIntervals++;
    }
    CreateThread (
    FetchMissingPatchIntervals())
    BufferRegularChannel()
  }
}
```

Fig. 8. Algorithm at the proxy for scenario 3.

b_4 needs $b - 2b$ as a patch and buffer $5b - 6b$ from the regular channel. So, it allocates two buffers, and starts storing the ongoing stream in one while simultaneously filling the other with the patch $b - 2b$ from the origin server, while the clients are playing back the prefix. Once the requests complete the prefix, the interval $b - 2b$ is available in the buffer and they continue to play back the stream and continue through the circular buffer until the end of the stream. Note that in this scheme, each client gets an individual stream and true application-level multicast is not done.

The number of active intervals in each $W + b$ is as large as the number of non-zero batches. Intuitively, if all batches during the duration of the stream have non-zero requests, this video is really popular and we much cache the entire video and not have to request the origin server. This is the result that the optimization algorithm yields. If it determines that the space used by the prefix and the interval cache is as large as the entire video, it instructs the proxy to do a full-caching of the video.

4.4. Discussion

When discussing streaming video using batching and multicasting, it is important to address issues such as network delays, jitter and random seeking (VCR functions), that most multicasting schemes do not address. The fact that our design uses application level multicasting addresses the network delay and jitter issues.

First, since all the data flows through the proxy and the proxy is aware of the network bandwidth to the server and to all the clients, it can perform QoS-related adaptations to the stream. Our implementation considers network adaptation on two planes. The optimization algorithm determines the prefix to cache for each asset depending not only on the popularity of the asset, but also on the bandwidth available to the server. The prefix cached is enough to mask the network latency and jitter to stream from the server. Also, when the proxy determines that it has to request a stream from the server (patch or regular channel), it determines the available bandwidth on the link and requests the stream from the server a δt time earlier. The time estimate could also be influenced by contracted service levels for given objects. Additionally, the proxy has the ability to also perform stream adaptation services to cater to heterogeneous clients.

As part of ongoing work, we are investigating schemes to support VCR functions in our framework. Various schemes for supporting VCR functions in a multicast-based VOD system are presented in [17–19].

5. Conclusions

In this paper, we present a joint server scheduling and proxy caching scheme aimed at minimizing the bandwidth streamed from the origin server. The scheme combines the bandwidth-saving merits of multicast streaming with QoS and content adaptation service capabilities of a proxy. We present multiple schemes with different bandwidth and cache-space tradeoffs that are applicable in different scenarios with different service requirements. Our schemes enable the honoring of service levels (SLAs) at the network-edge streaming proxies by adopting different tradeoffs for assets with different SLAs. From our simulations it is evident that our scheme far outperforms full-caching schemes where an asset is cached fully or not at all. We are working on various aspects of this scheme currently, one of which is the support for VCR functions. We are also in the process of implementing a prototype version of this technique in IBM's VideoCharger Server [20].

References

[1] C.C. Aggarwal, J.L. Wolf and P.S. Yu, A permutation based pyramid broadcasting scheme for Metropolitan VOD systems, *Proc. of the IEEE International Conference on Multimedia Systems*, June 1996.

[2] A. Dan, D. Sitaram and P. Shahabuddin, Scheduling Policies for an On-Demand Video Server with Batching, *Proceedings of ACM Multimedia*, Oct. 1994.

[3] K.A. Hua and S. Sheu, Skyscraper Broadcasting: A new Broadcasting Scheme for Metropolitan VOD systems, *Proceedings of the ACM SIGCOMM*, 1997.

[4] S. Viswanathan and T. Imielinski, Metropolitan Area Video-on-Demand Service using Pyramid Broadcasting, *Multimedia Systems*, vol. 4, August 1996.

[5] K.A. Hua, Y. Cai and S. Sheu, Patching: A multicast technique for True On-Demand Services, *Proceedings of ACM Multimedia*, Sept. 1998.

[6] S. Sen, L. Gao, J. Rexford and D. Towsley, Optimal patching scheme for efficient multimedia streaming, *Proc. of IEEE International Conference on Multimedia Computing and Systems*, June 1996.

[7] Y. Cai, K. Hua and K. Vu, Optimizing Patching Performance, *Proceedings of ACM/SPIE Multimedia Computing and Networking*, Jan 1999.

[8] Paul P. White and Jon Crowcroft, Optimized Batch Patching with Classes of Service, *ACM Communications Review*, October 2000.

[9] Martin Reisslein, Felix Hartanto and Keith Ross, Interactive Video Streaming with Proxy Servers, *IEEE Infocomm*, 2000.

[10] Reza Rejaie, Mark Handley, Haobo Yu and Deborah Estrin, Proxy Caching Mechanism for Multimedia Playback streams in the Internet, *Proceedings of the 4th International Web Caching Workshop*, March 1999.

[11] Soam Acharya and Brian Smith, MiddleMan: A Video Caching Proxy Server, *Proceedings of NOSS-DAV*, June 2000.

[12] Renu Tewari, Harrick Vin, Asit Dan and Dinkar Sitaram, Resource-based Caching for Web servers, *In Proceedings of MMCN*, 1998.

[13] S. Sen, J. Rexford and D. Towsley, Proxy prefix caching for multimedia streams, *IEEE Infocomm*, 1999.

[14] Y. Wang, Z-L. Zhang, D. Du, and D. Su, A network conscious approach to end-to-end video delivery over wide area networks using proxy servers, *IEEE Infocomm*, April 1998.

[15] O. Verscheure, C. Venkatramani, P. Frossard and L. Amini, Joint Server Scheduling and Proxy Caching for Video Delivery, *IBM Technical Report Number RC21981*, 2001.

[16] A. Dan and D. Sitaram, A generalized interval caching policy for mixed interactive and long video environments, *SPIE Multimedia Computing and Networking Conference*, January 1996.

[17] E.L. Abram-Profeta and K.G. Shin, Providing Unrestricted VCR Functions in Multicast Video-on-Demand Servers, *IEEE International Conference on Multimedia Computing and Systems*, June 1998.

[18] K. Almeroth and M. Ammar, On the Use of Multicast Delivery to Provide a Scalable and Interactive Video-on-Demand Service, *Journal on Selected Areas of Communication*, August 1996.

[19] Fei, Z., Kamal, I., Mukherjee, S. and Ammar, M., Providing Interactive Functions for Staggered Multicast Near Video-on-Demand Systems (Extended Abstract), *Proceedings of the IEEE International Conference on Multimedia Computing and Systems (Poster paper)*, June 1999.

[20] IBM, The IBM VideoCharger Server, details available at http://www.ibm.com/software/data/videocharger/.

Author Index

Acharya, A., 165
Almeida, V., 249
Amini, L., 169, 327
Ardaiz, O., 125
Arlitt, M., 87

Beck, A., 109
Beck, M., 217
Bestavros, A., 147
Biliris, A., 19
Brassil, J., 89
Buford, J., 235
Byers, J., 147

Cain, B., 169
Cao, P., 87
Chase, J.S., 1
Coffman Jr., E.G., 171
Cranor, C., 19

Dahlin, M., 185
Davison, B.D., 203
Day, M., 169
Douglass, F., 169
Douglis, F., 19
Doyle, R.P., 1

Estrin, D., 55

Farber, D., 169
Fei, Z., 71
Fonseca, R., 249
Freedman, A., 169
Freeh, V.W., 131
Freitag, F., 125
Frossard, P., 327

Gadde, S., 1
Govindan, R., 55

Hofmann, M., 109, 217
Hughes, A.S., 129

Jelenković, P., 171

Kangasharju, J., 39
Kelly, T., 219
Kokku, R., 185
Koletsou, M., 281
Krashakov, S.A., 295

Lee, J., 235
Lee, S.-J., 309
Li, M., 235
Liston, R., 267

Ma, W.-Y., 89, 217, 309
Meira Jr., W., 249
Menascé, D., 249
Miniscalco, W., 235
Mogul, J., 87
Momčilović, P., 171

Navarro, L., 125
Nottingham, M., 35, 217

Panteleenko, V.V., 131
Peligrinelli, F., 249

Rabinovich, M., 19
Radoslavov, P., 55
Riedi, R., 249
Roberts, J., 39
Ross, K.W., 39
Rost, S., 147
Rousskov, A., 87
Rzewski, P., 169

Shaikh, A., 165
Shambroom, W.D., 235
Sharif, S., 185
Shchur, L.N., 295
Shen, B., 89, 309
Sibal, S., 19

Spatscheck, O., 19
Sturm, W., 19

Tewari, R., 165
Touch, J.D., 129

Vahdat, A.M., 1
Venkataramani, A., 185
Venkatramani, C., 327
Verma, D., 165
Verscheure, O., 327
Voelker, G.M., 281

Williamson, C., 87

Yalagandula, P., 185

Zegura, E., 267

Keyword Index

Average-case analysis, 171

Batch patching, 327
Bootstrap, 235
Browser trace, 219

Cache hierarchy, 295
Cache simulation, 219
Caching, 71
Client trace, 219
Concurrency, 147
Consistency, 71
Content delivery and distribution, 109
Content delivery network, 89
Content distribution, 185
Content distribution network, 19, 39, 55, 71, 281, 309, 327
Content-oriented services, 109
Cooperation, 39

Digital fountain, 147
Domain name system, 19
Duplicate suppression, 219

e-Commerce, 249

FEC, 147

Hit rates, 219
HTTP, 203, 267

iCAP, 109
Instrumentation, 219
Intelligence at the network edge, 109
Internet Content Adaptation Protocol, 89
Internet proxy services, 89
Internet service delivery, 89
Invalidation, 71

Load balancing, 1, 131
Lognormal models, 219
LRU stack distance, 219

Optimal replication strategies, 39

Partial caching, 327
Peer-to-peer networks, 39
Performance analysis, 249
Performance measurement, 267
Popularity, 147
Prefetching, 185, 203
Propogation, 71
Proxy, 267
Proxy cache, 235

QOS, 203

Remote callout, 109
Replica placement algorithms, 55
Request distribution, 1
Robots, 249
Router fanout, 55
Rule engine, 109

Server scheduling, 327
Service execution environment, 109
Service invocation rules, 109
SLA, 327
Stream merging, 171
Streaming media, 327
Streaming media delivery, 309
Success function, 219

TCP, 147
Tornado codes, 147
Traffic measurement, 295

URL hashing, 1
User-perceived Web performance, 281

Video-on-demand, 171

Web booster, 131
Web cache, 249

Web caching, 19, 109, 185, 203, 235, 281, 309
Web network, 295
Web performance, 19
Web proxy, 281
Web proxy cache, 1
Web server, 131
Web workloads, 235
Webserver, 147
WebTV, 219
Workload characterization, 219, 249
World Wide Web, 219, 267

Zipf, 1